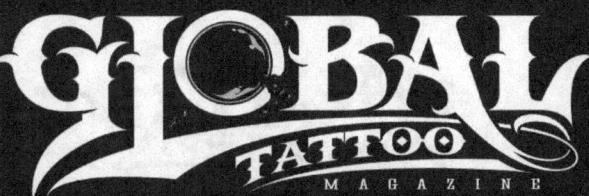

GLOBAL
TATTOO
MAGAZINE

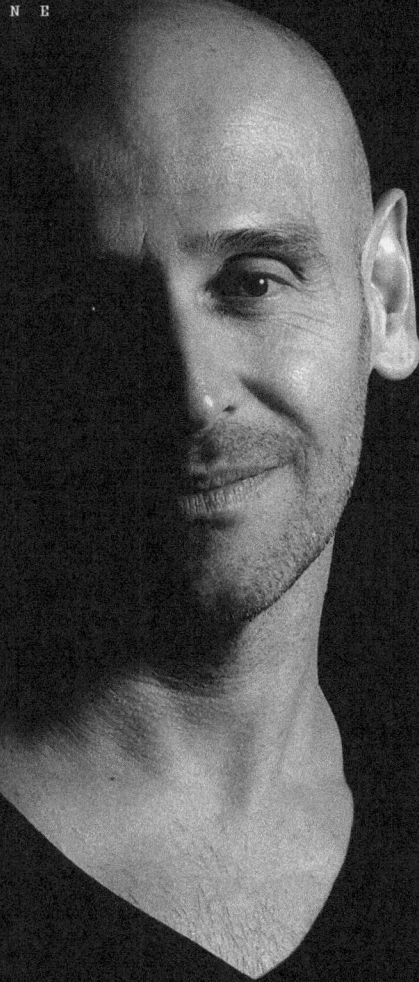

Boris
chapter III
Interview

CASTINO LUCILLA-NELSON SACRAMENTO
GREGORY PAZDNIAKOU-JUBS
SUDE ERDEM INK

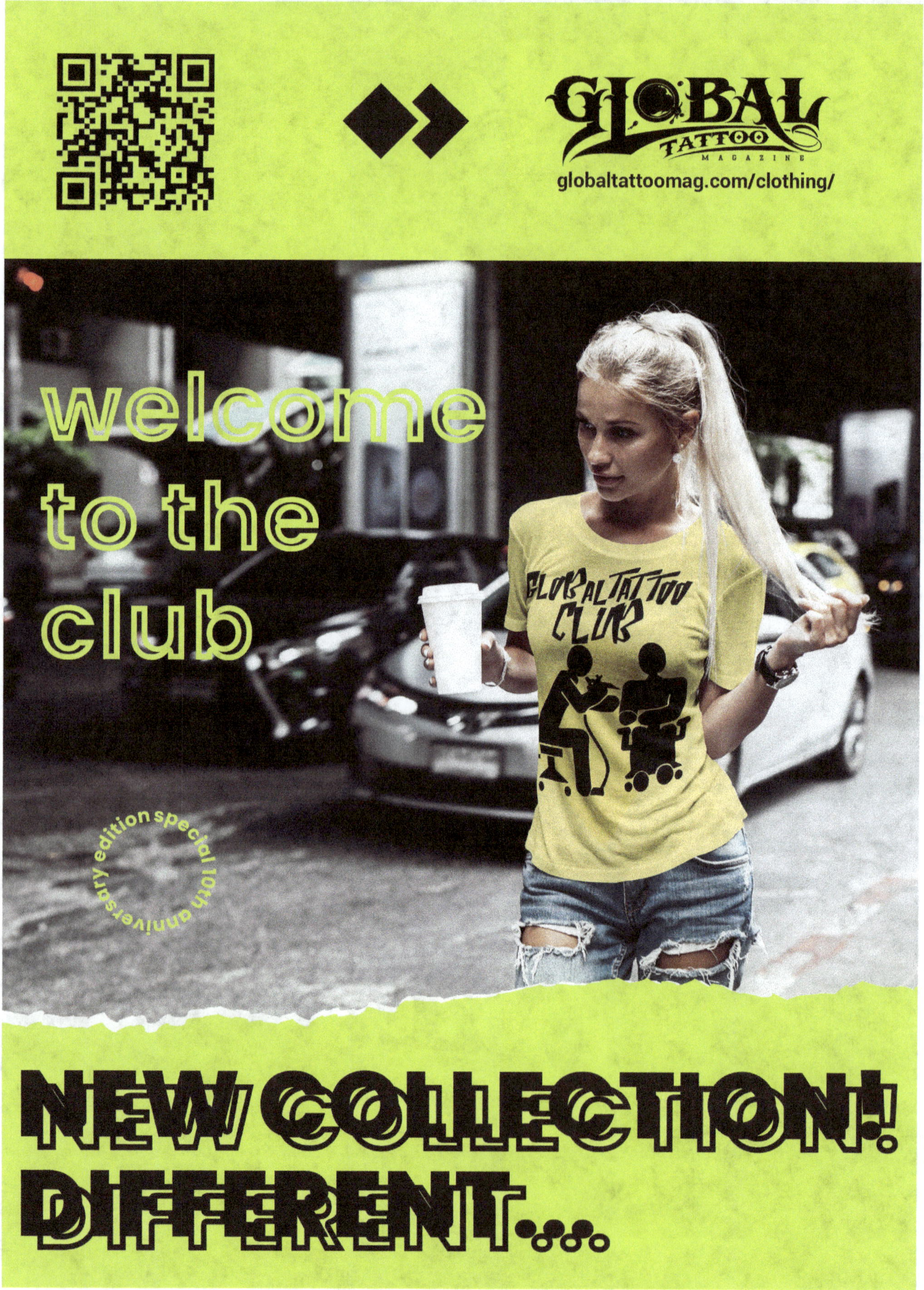

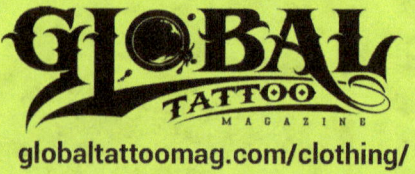

globaltattoomag.com/clothing/

welcome
to the
club

special 10th anniversary edition

NEW COLLECTION!
DIFFERENT...

CONTENTS

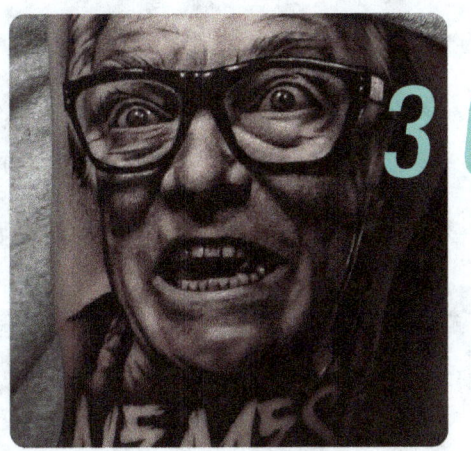

30

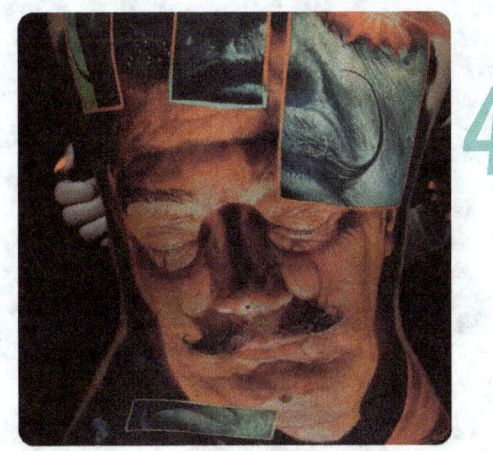

4

Cover | **Boris**

Logo by GTM | **Zisto**

Follow us

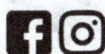

www.globaltattoomag.com

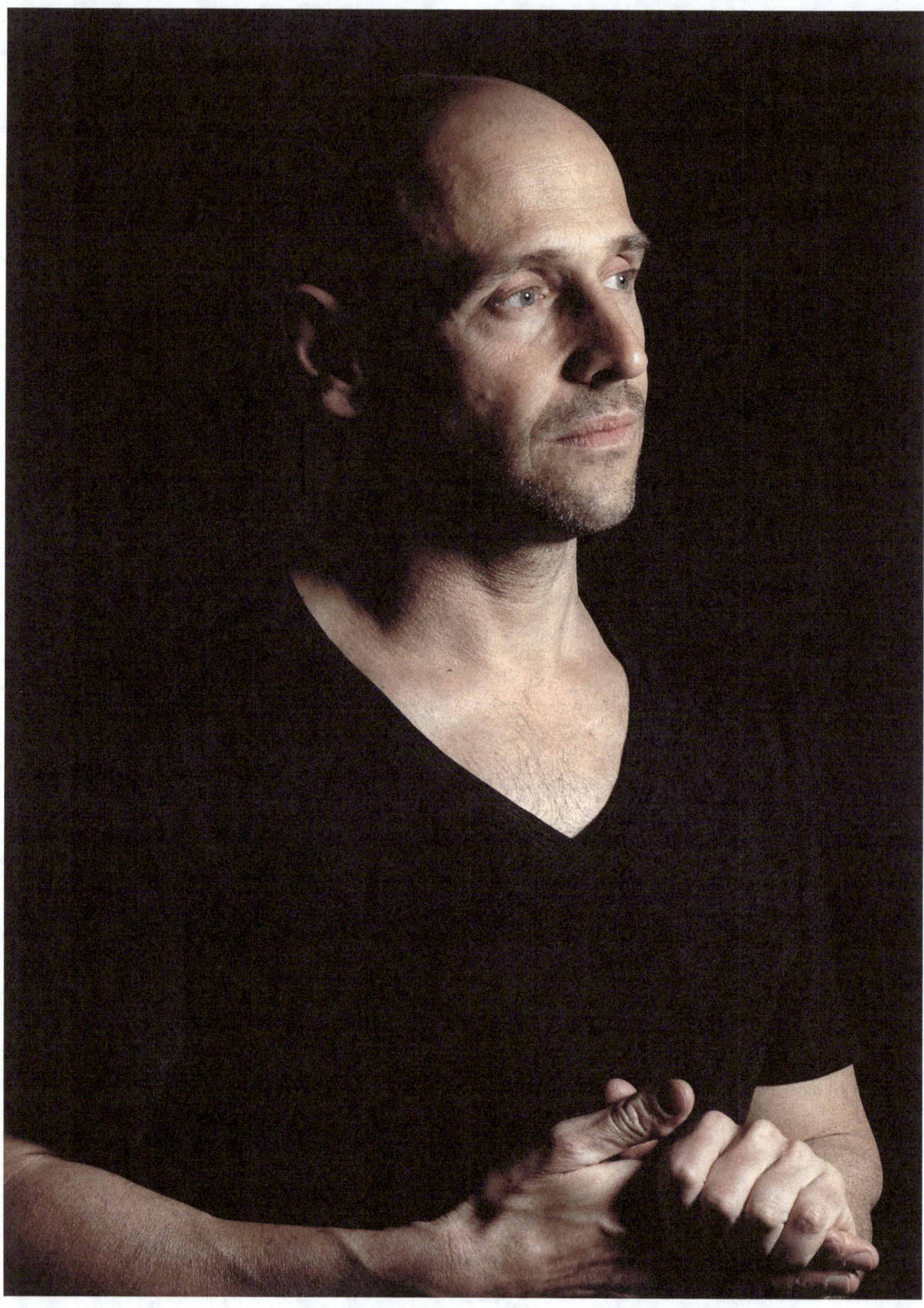

BORIS

MASTER OF FANTASY AND REALISM

First of all, let me introduce myself. My name is Boris, a nickname I got from my friends when I was a kid, and it's stuck with me ever since.

How did you get your start in the tattoo world? How did you learn the skills?

I'm Hungarian by origin, but my work has been in Austria for 10 years. I started tattooing in 1992 in Hungary, where at that time there was no history of professional tattoo artists and there was no such thing as a tattoo world. I am a first-generation tattoo artist from post-communist Eastern Europe. Since there were no masters of tattooing before, we acquired our knowledge by practicing techniques we had learned from the ranks of the audience at tattoo conventions in Eastern Europe. It was quite a hard road, full of uncertainty and mistakes, but it was the road that changed and reformed professional tattooing as it was known at the time. Since our generation had no masters or teachers to show us the way, we trod new paths. Back then, realism - whether black and white or color-was taboo. Older tattooers thought it was not durable enough and would not stand the test of

BORIS TATTOO

Chapter III

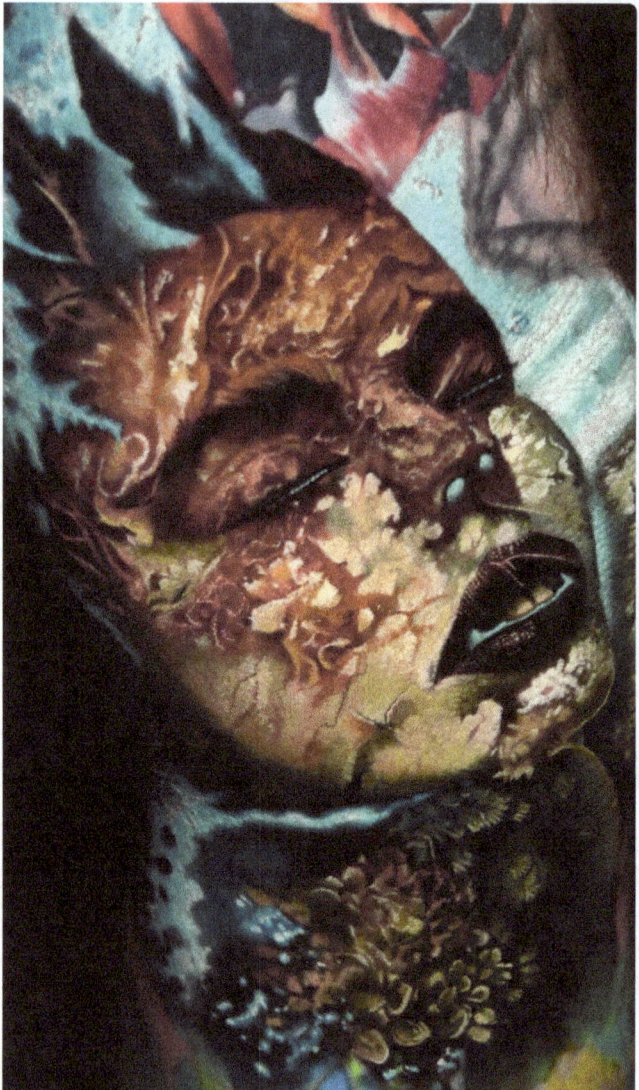
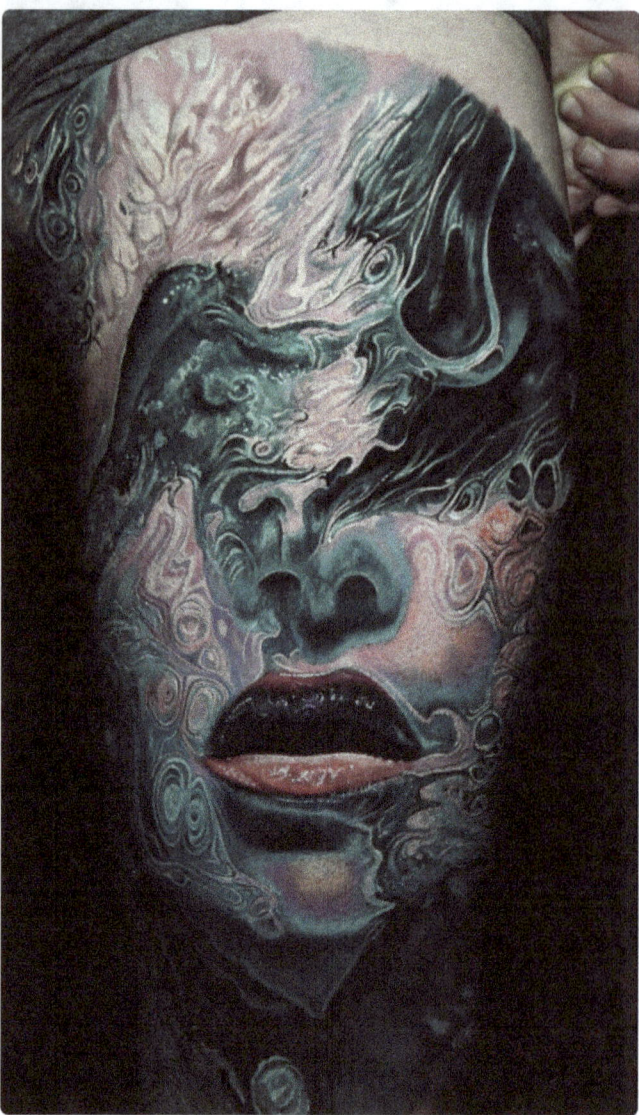

time. Since we didn't know that, we did it. So now this and related styles have become fully accepted. And so, 30 years on, I can say that they will stand the test of time if done properly!

How do you move from your initial ideas to the final product? Tell me how you make things.

The initial idea always comes from the client. I am the kind of tattoo artist for whom tattooing is not about artistic expression, but more about the client. I like to say that for me, the client is always my muse. Usually, when I accept a request, I ask for reference photos in which I can visualize the guest's vision, and then adding my own imagination and knowledge, using realistic reference photos, I create the design using photoshop. I use all available sources. Often my own photos, which are selected from my own collection, or I create the pattern myself. But if I don't have the opportunity to use my own photos (because it is very rare to take a photo of a snow leopard or Salvador Dali in person), I naturally use google. But in all cases, I make sure to use the reference images as a reference. Transform them, reshape them, and make them part of the new design, not copy them as I find them. It is rarely the case that my guests do not accept the design. After that, tattooing is a piece of cake.

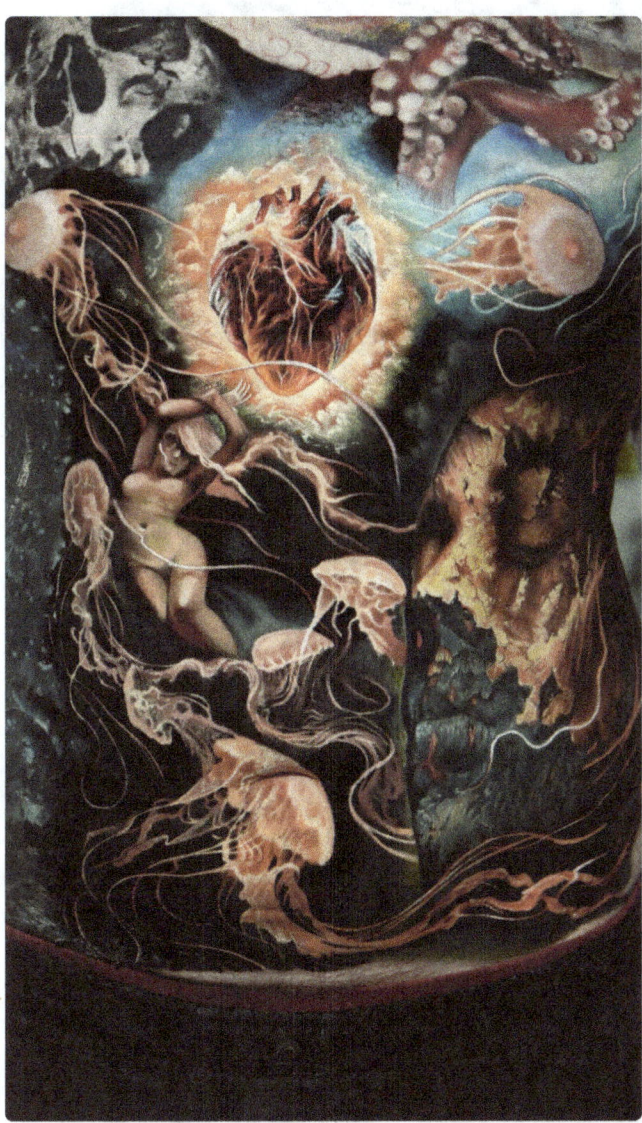
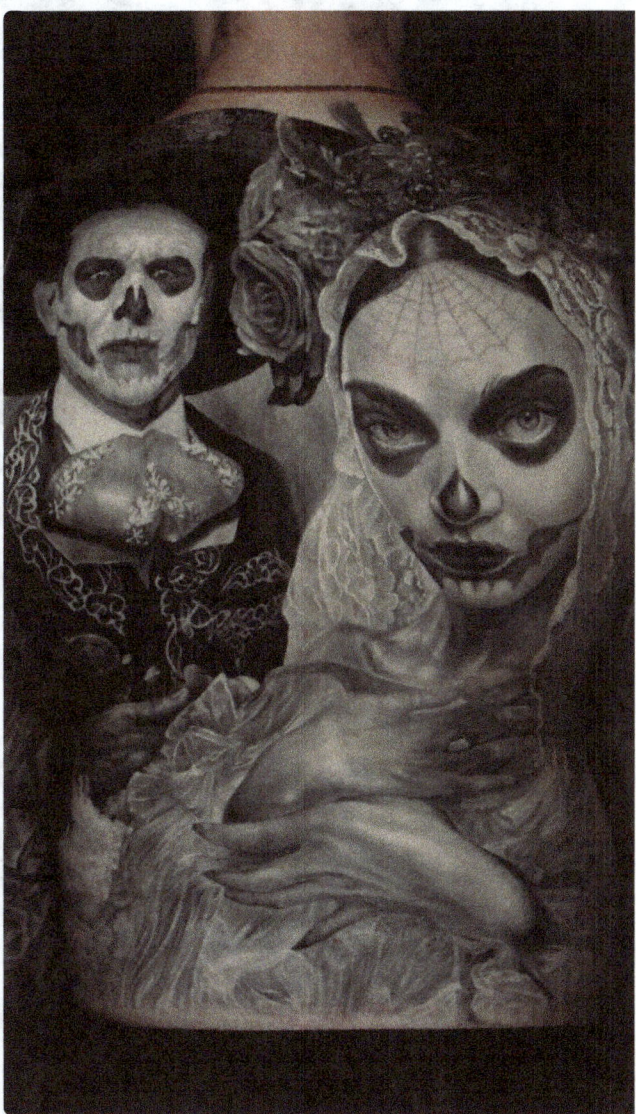

How do you envision the tattoo world in ten years?

I don't even try. It's all so big and has so many players now that I don't think anyone can predict what it will be in 10 years. We all have plans and ideas that we're trying to make happen, and as those energies add up, the tattoo world itself is already growing almost organically. When I look back at the past, I see that some trends are becoming more popular while others take a back seat. Then forgotten trends reappear and become more popular again. While the more upbeat ones are pushed back for a while. For my side, I only want to make good tattoos 10 years from now!

Tell us what you recommend to advance in the world of tattooing. Improve artistic quality and increase popularity.

In the first case: by recognizing the characteristics of artistic styles and integrating them into our art, and by constantly practicing to improve our techniques. There is a lot that could be written about this, which I'm sure there is neither space nor

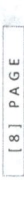

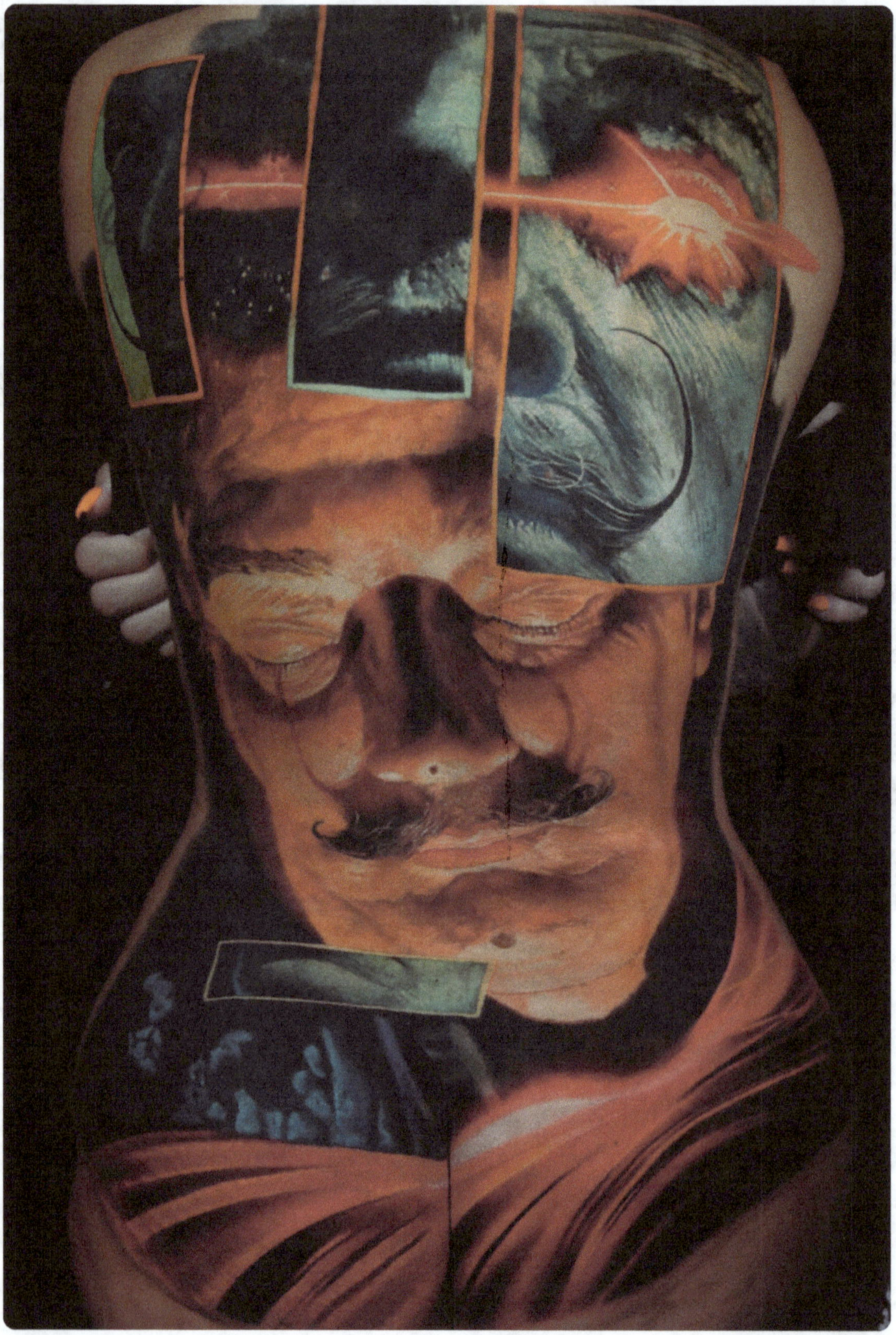

Every small step is a small success on the road to the big dream, just as every stumble is a small success. If we can learn from our stumbles, get up and move on - keep going - then we are already successful. "

time for here, but if anyone is interested in my thoughts on this, please visit my website tattooingatoz.com. There I deal with it very extensively in the "motive" section.

If we are talking about increasing popularity: Then basically every tattoo artist just has to do his best work according to his skill and knowledge. This is moving the success of tattooing forward. From now on, the presentation of these good works to a wider audience is also an extensive topic, which I cover in the "communication" and "additional works" sections of my site
.   But I think that even in this technological world, perhaps the most important thing is good relations with clients.

What comes to mind when you hear the word success?

Success means different things to different people. Success means achieving a dream, a goal, for everyone. These goals can be small or big, but never forget that the path to achieving big goals is a series of small steps. Every small step is a small success on the road to the big dream, just as every stumble is a small success. If we can learn from our stumbles, get up and move on - keep going - then we are already successful.

What are the most common tattoo misconceptions and errors?

The reason I can't say anything about that is that I have been working with a clientele for 20 years, with colleagues who have experience, and who have been through what is and is not allowed. So everyone understands and knows what is allowed and what is not. I don't encounter such mistakes and misunderstandings in my environment. I may have encountered such things 25 years ago, but that was a long time ago different times. Today we can get so much information that we don't have to face making mistakes.

Thanks for the good questions. Good luck with your work, readers have fun with tattoos.

{ **IG | @boristattoo**
https://tattooingatoz.com

CASTINO LUCILLA

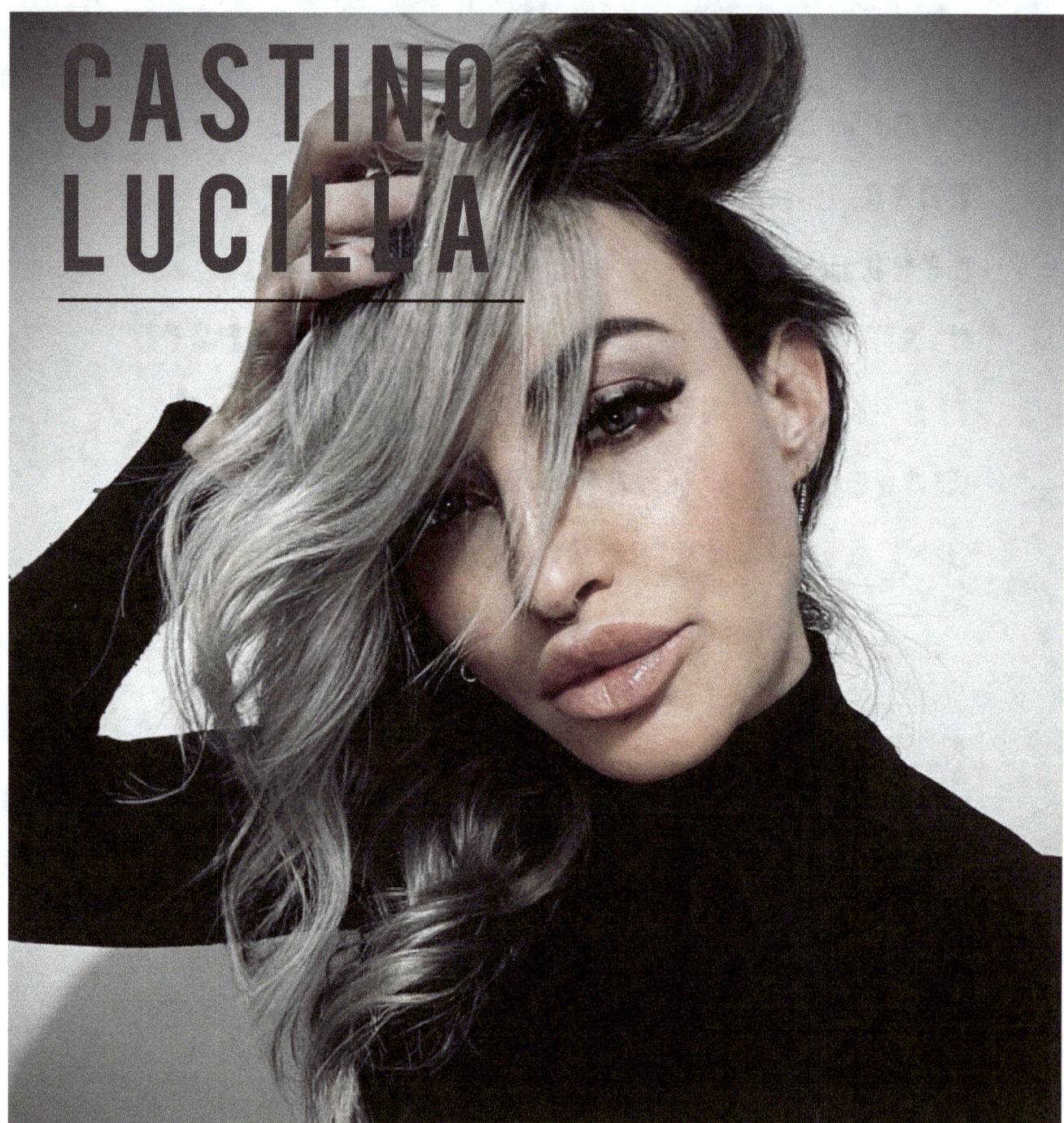

When and why did you start tattooing?
I began tattooing five years ago because I wanted to display my work in public rather than confine it to an art gallery.

How would you define your style?
My approach is undoubtedly realistic, but yet quite artistic.

What do you do besides tattoos?
Tattoing takes up the majority of my time, but I also enjoy painting and drawing.
They continue to be my first love.

What is the best source of inspiration for your work?
I attempt to narrate tales about the skin.
My inspiration is a combination of life experiences and my pursuit of powerful and memorable images.
I look to emotions and art for inspiration and try to infuse my creations with soul.

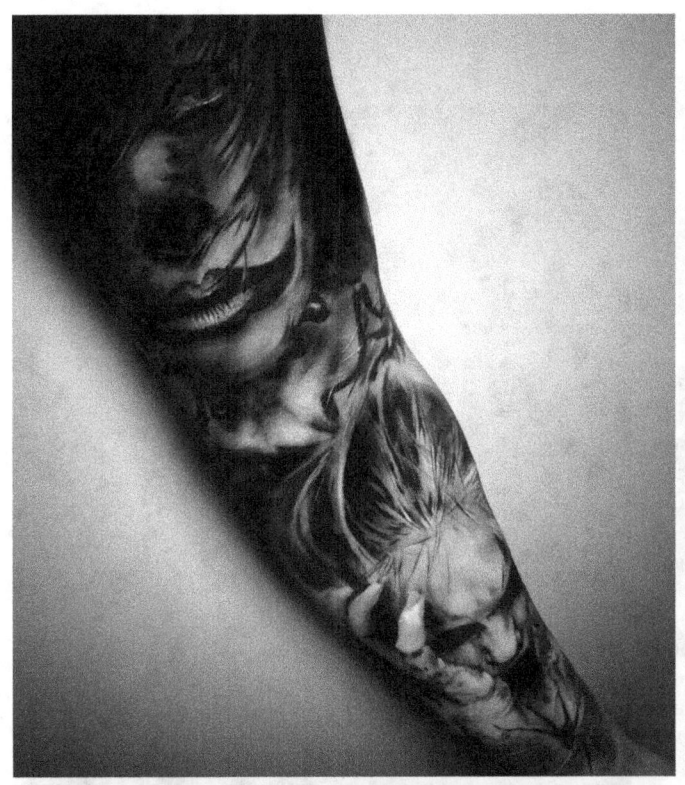
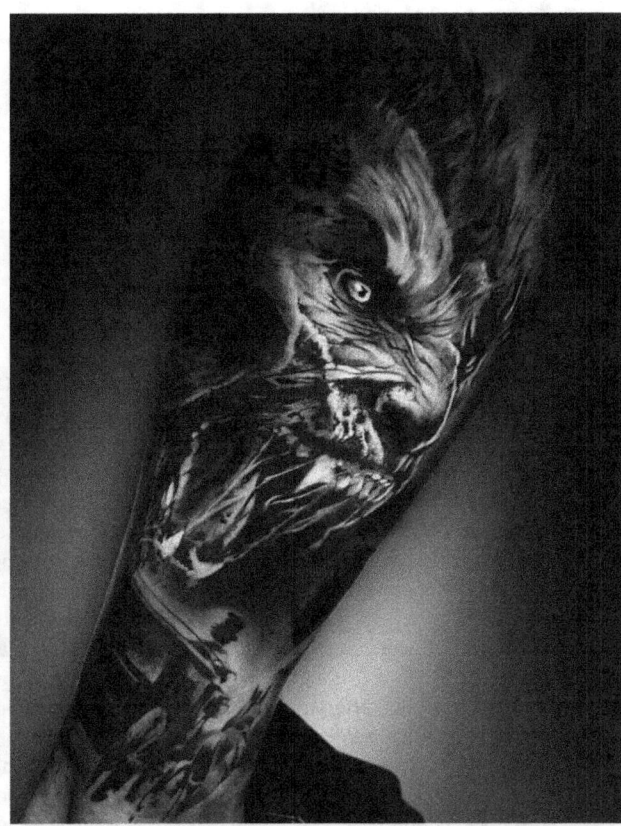
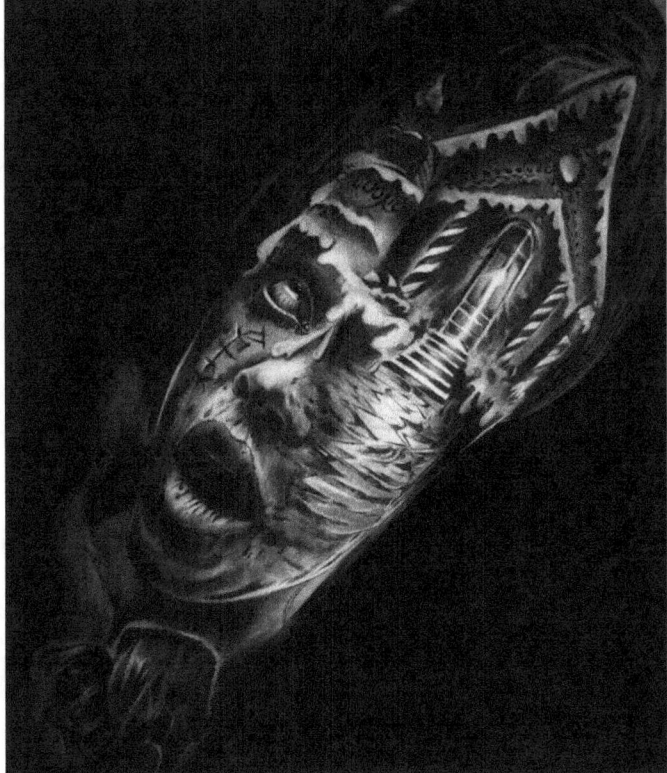
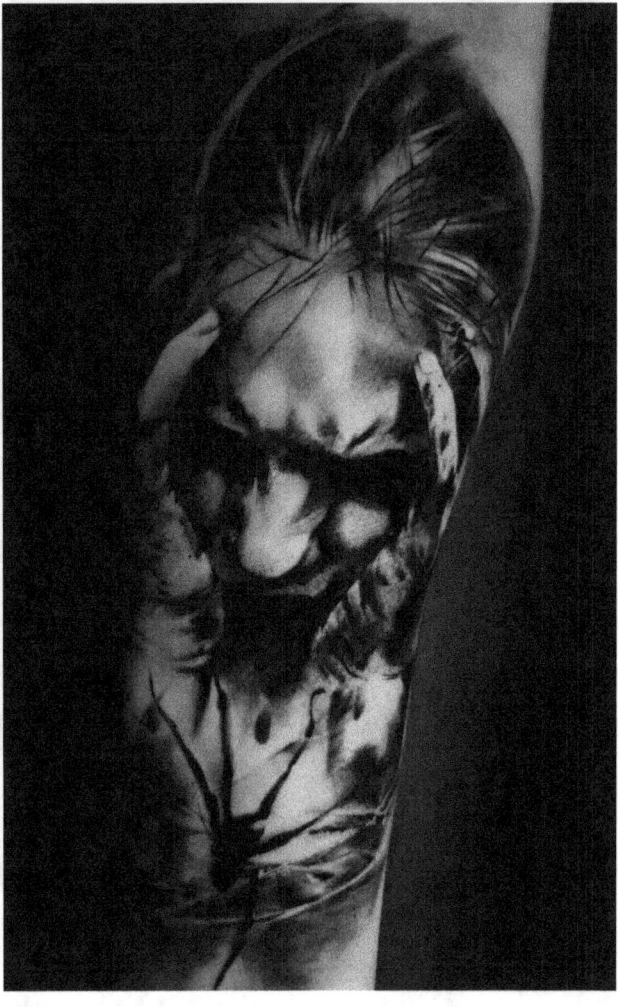

@lucillacastinotattoo

81's Black Sheep Tattoo Studio

Torino, Italy

Gregory
Pazdniakou

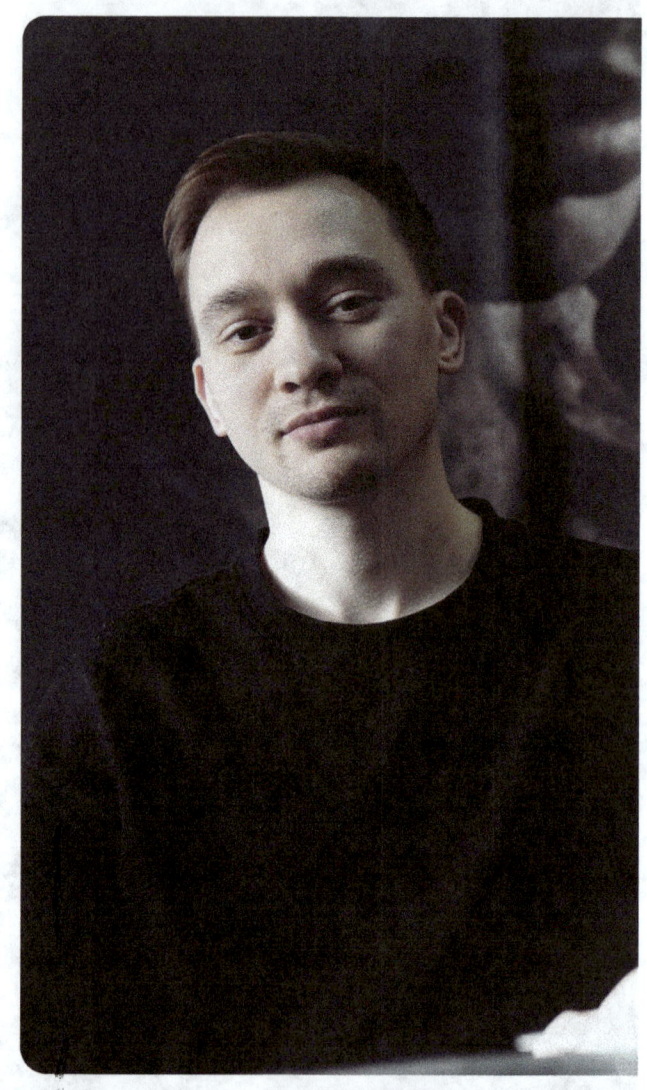

My name is Grigory, I am 32 years old. I was born and raised in Belarus, where I began to engage in tattooing in 2009. Now I live and work in Germany. I also visit other studios for guest-spot in other countries within Europe. I have liked tattoos since the age of 14. I was desperate to get one but I could not because of being underage. At that time, you could only get a tattoo in a tattoo salon at the age of 18 and we didn't know any other options were available until once we met a new friend who had a tattoo on his leg and he was only 15 years old. It turned out he got one done by somebody who worked as a 'tattoo master' in his apartment in incomprehensible conditions. The quality of that tattoo left much to be desired, but at that time, we didn't care. We were obsessed and we wanted one too. Soon we all went together to visit this master and got our tattoos. Drawing has been my hobby since school time and after my encounter with this tattoo master, I was inspired and decided to make tattoos myself. As soon as my friends found out that, I am getting tattoo equipment they started to ask me to make them some tattoos so I didn't have to look for my first clients. I have been making tattoos ever since.

Over the years, I tried different styles, but most of all I liked realism both color and black and white. I do not have many works in color in my portfolio, almost none. The reason is that I simply could not find customers that would like to get a color tattoo in the style I would like to make it. I've only made a couple in neotraditional and old school. However, with black-and-white

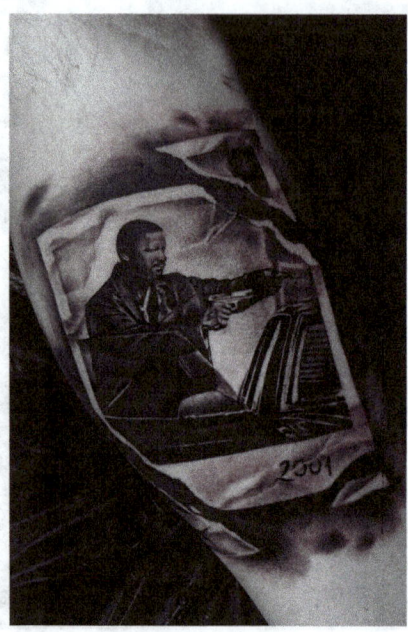

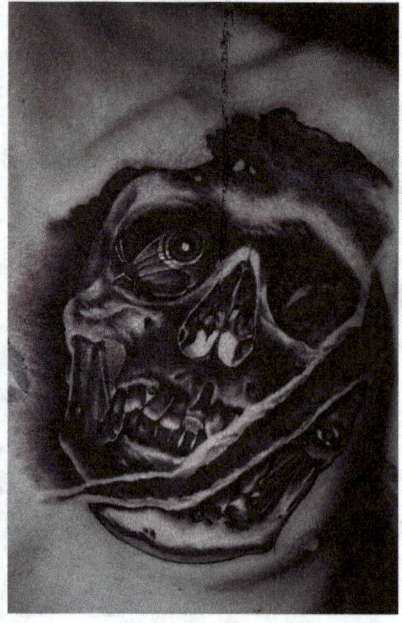

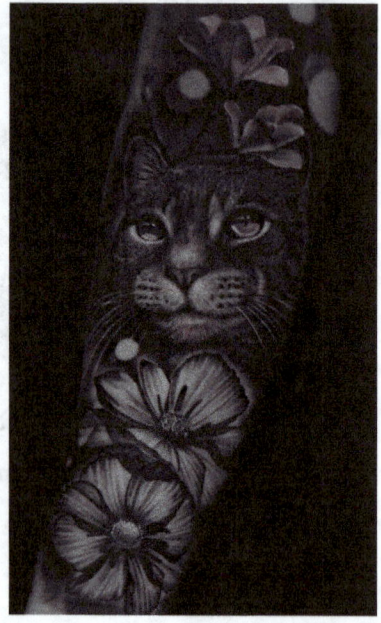

realism, things were much better and after a while, I decided to completely abandon the color and stay only in black-and-white tattoos. I now use color only for canvases. I have always liked black-and-white realism, and when looking at the works of other tattoo masters, I wanted to see more details. So this is exactly what I am focusing on in my works

In addition to tattooing, I do sports. Sports is what lifts me out of bed and makes me productive. In summer, it is wakeboarding and surfing, in winter it is snowboarding, as well as a gym and tennis of course. Shortly, I want to try kitesurfing. I also try to make time for drawing.

The best source of inspiration for me is architecture and street art. I travel a lot and always try to walk around the cities I visit and look for unusual objects of architecture, whether it is an old small building or a whole set of modern constructions. I also try to find traces of street artists among these buildings. Since childhood I was fond of graffiti, it is always very interesting to observe how this direction develops and how the modern style changes through time, and how new styles are born in the background of contemporary cities and street art.

@gregory_gptattoo

Germany

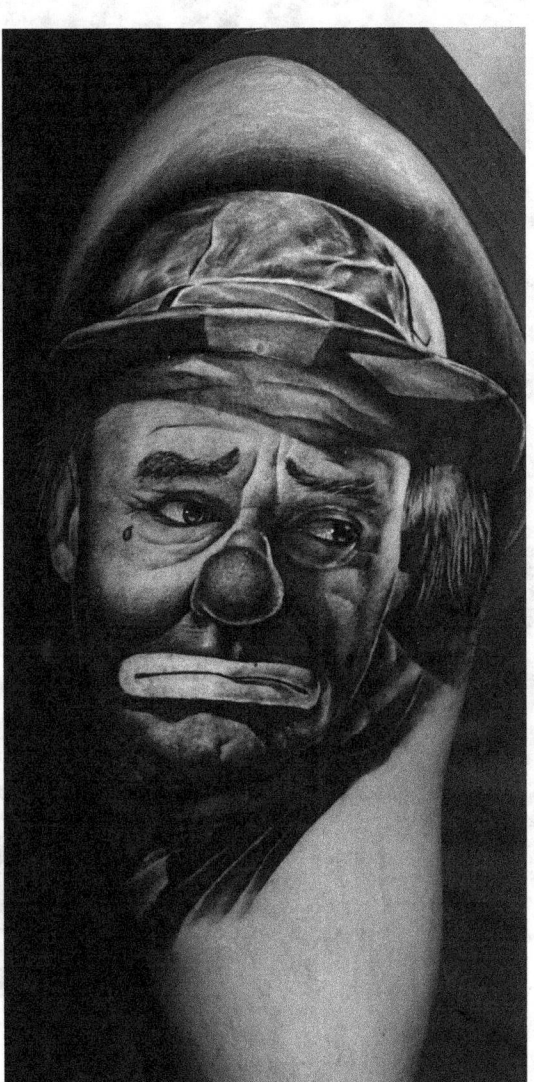

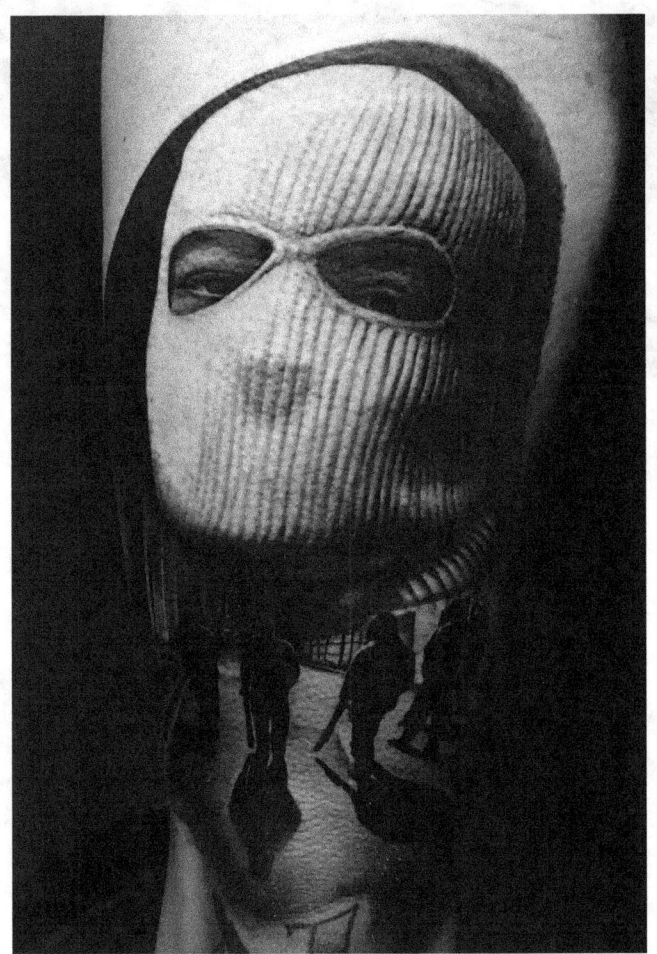

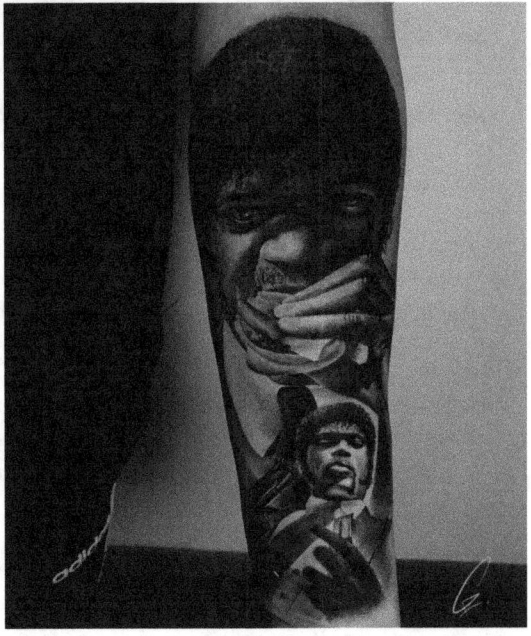

JUBS
Fatal Furink

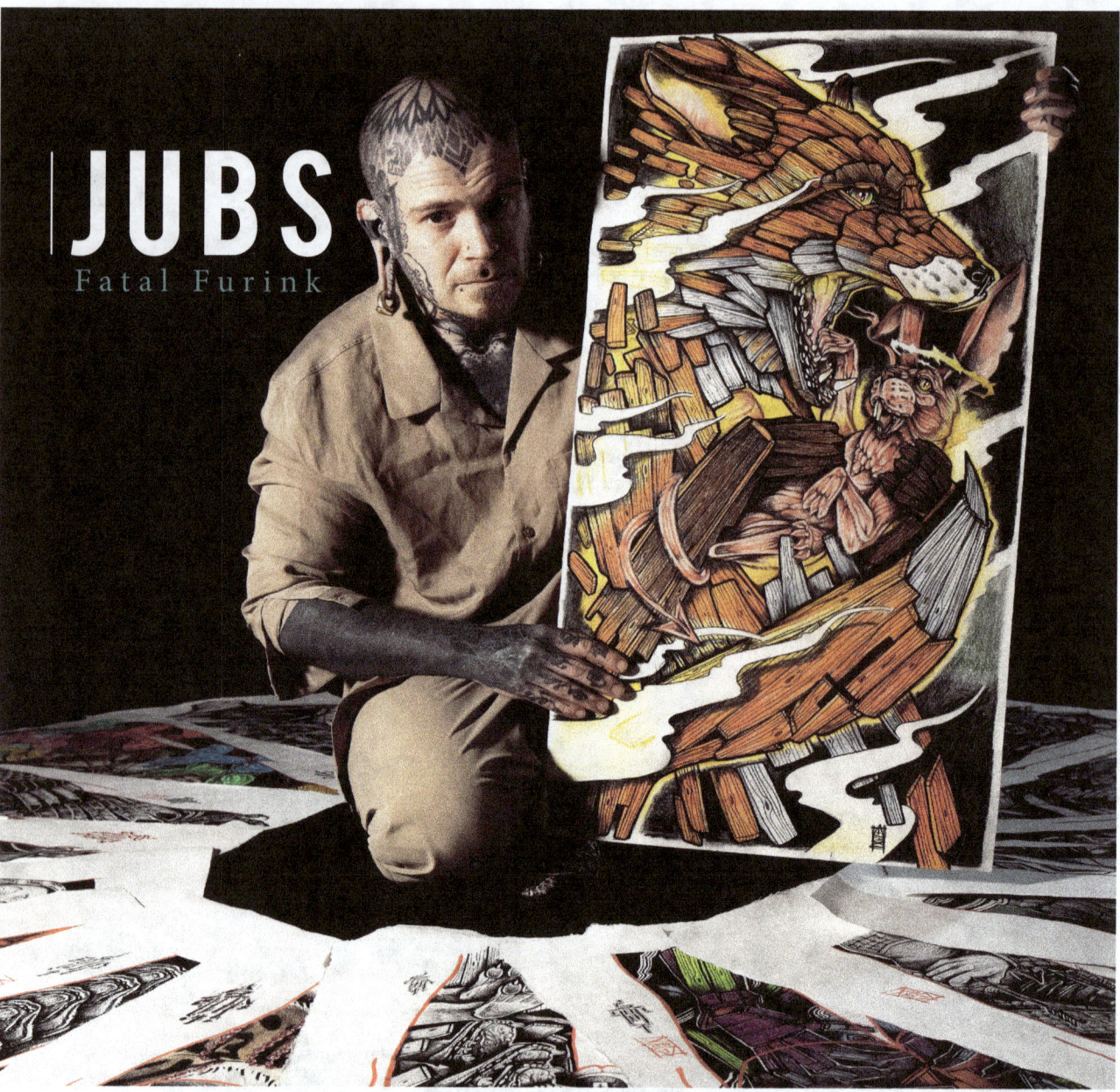

WHEN AND WHY YOU BEGAN TO TATTOO?

I started tattooing 15 years ago. I was a piercing apprentice on side of my literature study, and one day I borough a tattoo machine for one of my colleagues to try to tattooing myself on my tight, and I fall in love with it. I learned myself, and I opened my shop Contraseptik right after one year of practice. After 3 years I started to do guest spot all around Europe and make convention to improve my technic. After 5 years of traveling, improving my tattoo again, winning awards, and make grow social media I finally extend my guest to Asia (Taiwan, Hongkong, Seoul, Japan). This experience in Asia gave me the envy to push myself to be in-

terested in a really big project like a half-body suit and body suit cause asian tattooists are the masters of that. I finally left my shop Contraseptik to create Fatalfurink a private tattoo atelier with Clement Sombre Jours and Pierre reb.

At this time I push myself to extend again my career to the USA, I apply for a work visa and now I work between HIDDENHANDTATTOO (Seattle USA), FATALFU-RINK (Strasbourg France), and CONNEXION23TATTOO (Huningue France) the atelier of my girlfriend loo.ttt, we do a lot of collabs together on a big and medium project.

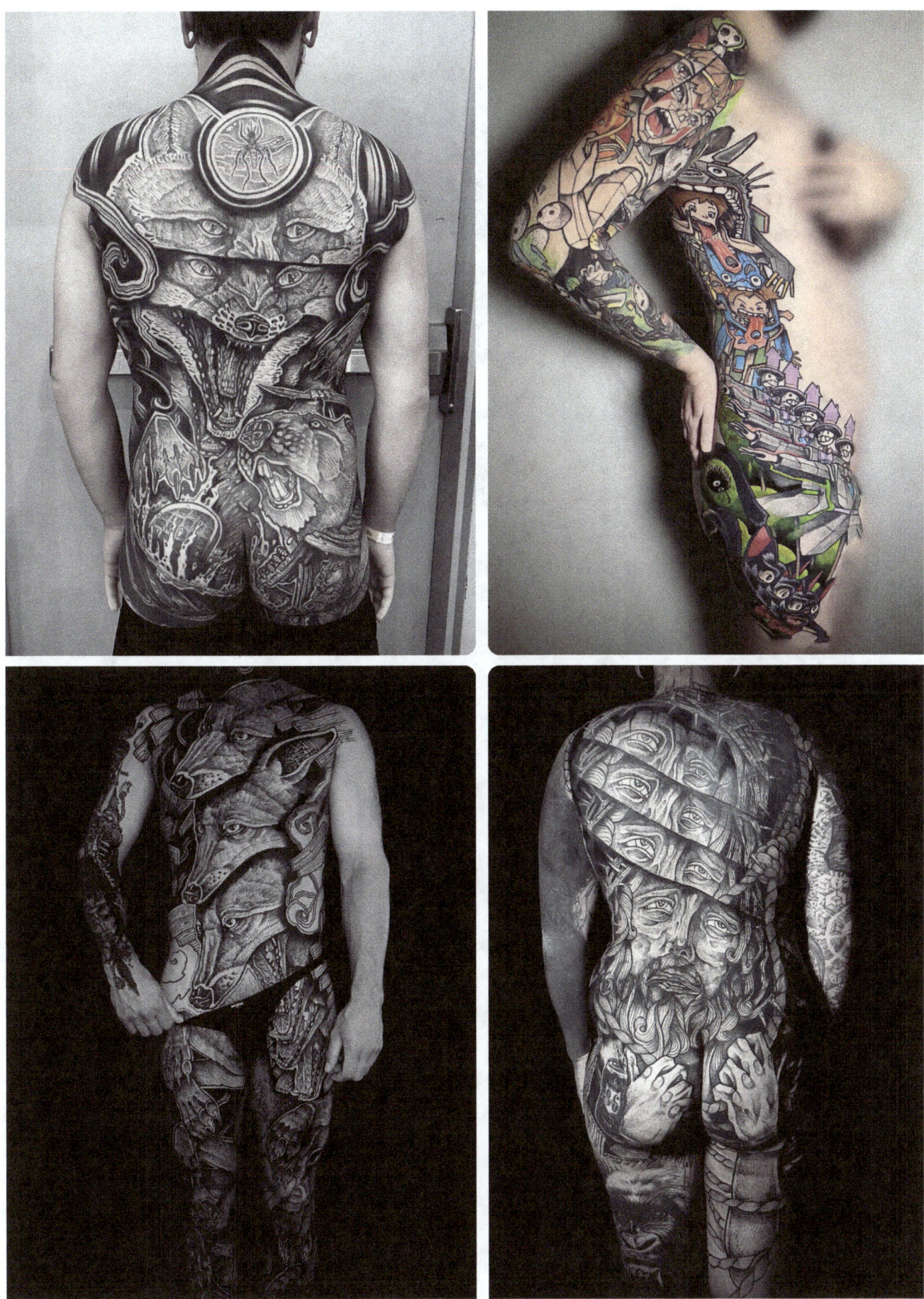

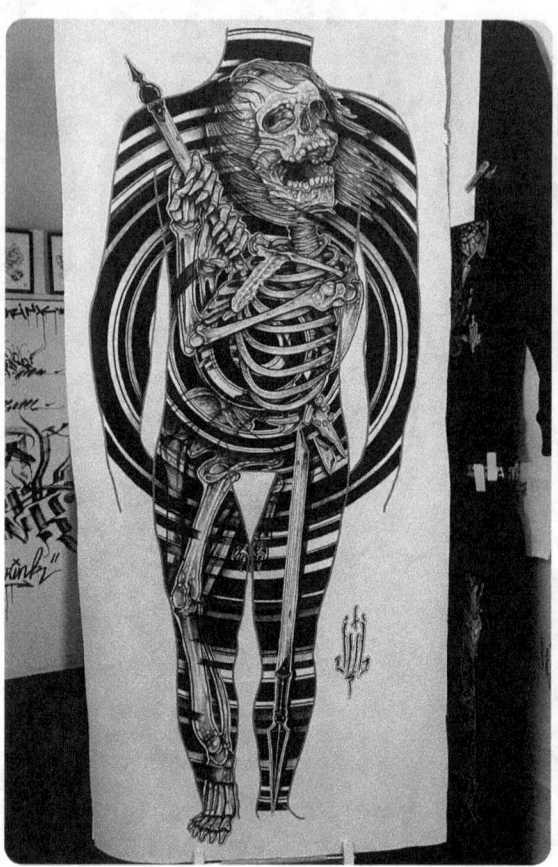
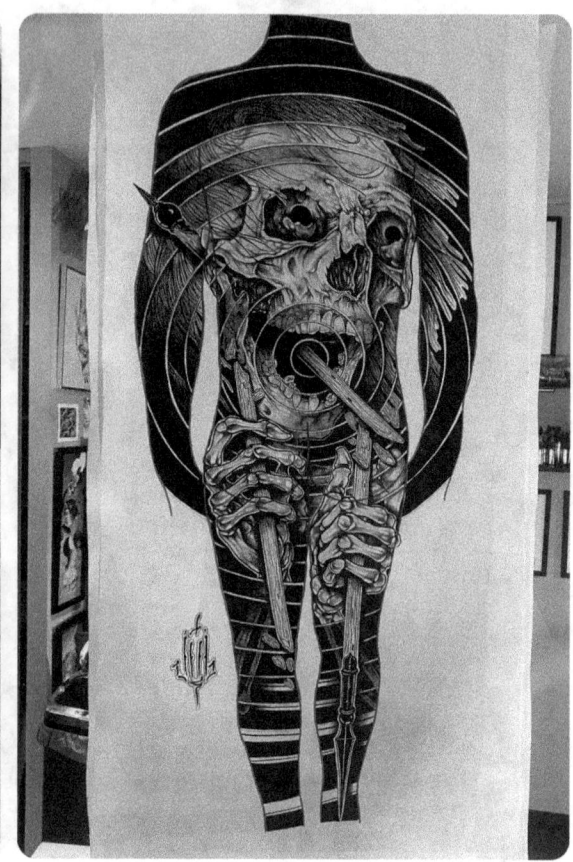

HOW WOULD YOU DEFINE YOUR STYLE?

It's really difficult to answer myself. Most people tell me I have a crazy style, and it s difficult to describe. I would say psychedelic illustrative but honestly, I think pictures will talk by themselves hahahahaha. But for sure I love working in color but for a couple of years, I also love to do black n gray. I love to use repeat sections or wood plates effect or chimera with food etc

WHAT DO YOU DO BESIDES TATTOOING?

I screamed in a grindcore PV band called CHIENS for almost 10 years but after that everything is connected to art. I do painting, and sculpture, and since the covid appear I made a lot of bodysuit designs humanly size. Today I have almost 40 pieces of these bodysuit designs, and I started to make a huge exhibition touring around the world at tattoo conventions or galleries. This exhibition is the most important project I got besides tattoos even if it s connected, cause if I have free time now you can be sure I will draw a new bodysuit, I love it, working to design an entire body is kind of very excited and the medium of the body is the most inter-

esting in my opinion. In the next months, you could catch the exhibition at the International Inkfactory convention in LYON (France)and the Wildtattoo expo in NAMUR (Belgique)

WHAT IS THE BEST SOURCE OF INSPIRATION FOR YOUR WORK?

At first, I was really in interested the graphic vein of tattoo artists from Germany, and the east of Europe Meistergrim and Peter Bobek were the artist who gave me the envy of tattoos. But now I need to say my inspiration come from WEED mostly hahahaha, Japanese tattoo, fashion creator for composition, all form of art, street art, food, family, friends, travel, etc.Honestly, I love life and tattoo, it means i think all the shit I do or look or ear during the day could inspire me

@jubsyking

jubsyking@gmail.com

France, Strasbourg

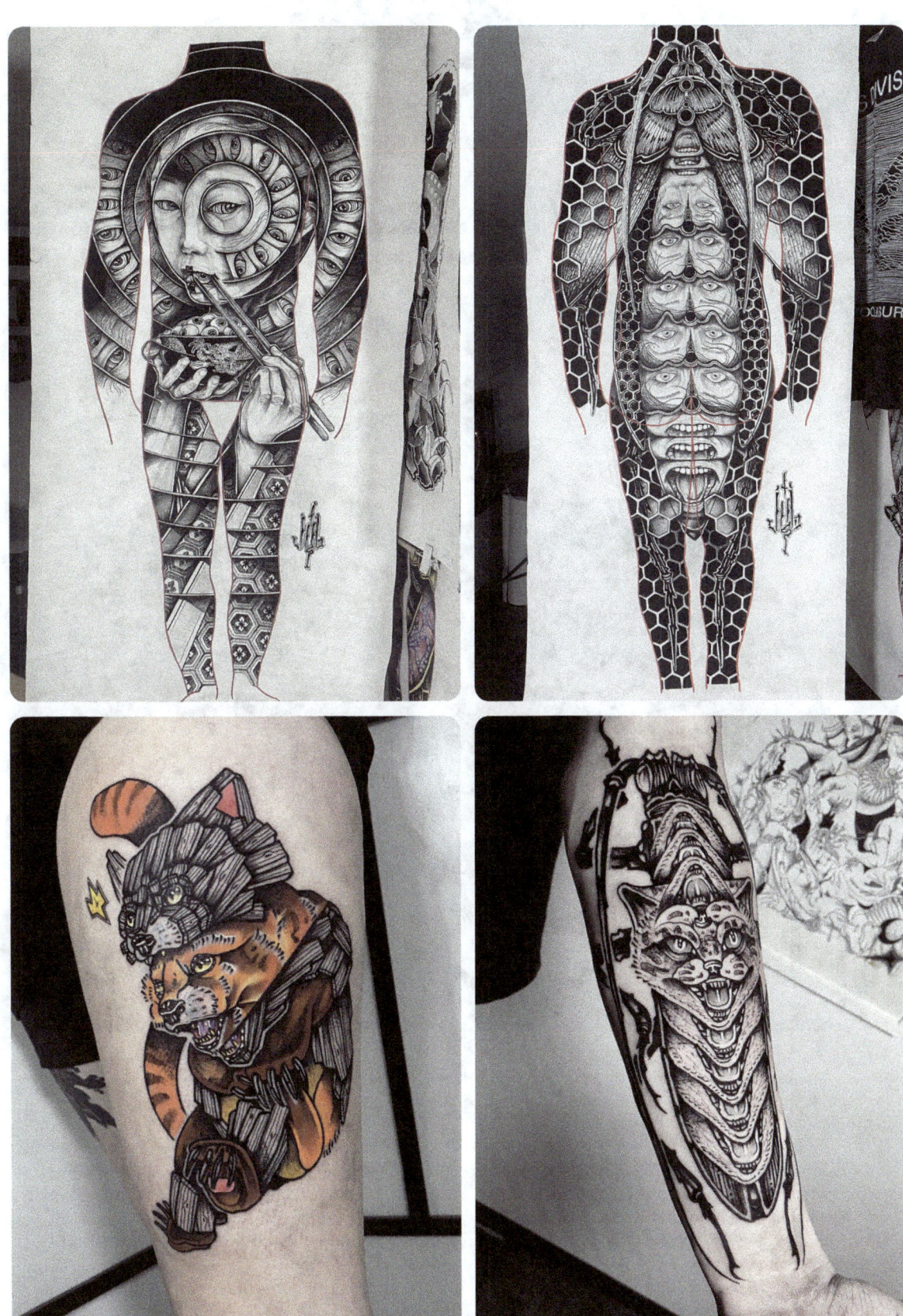

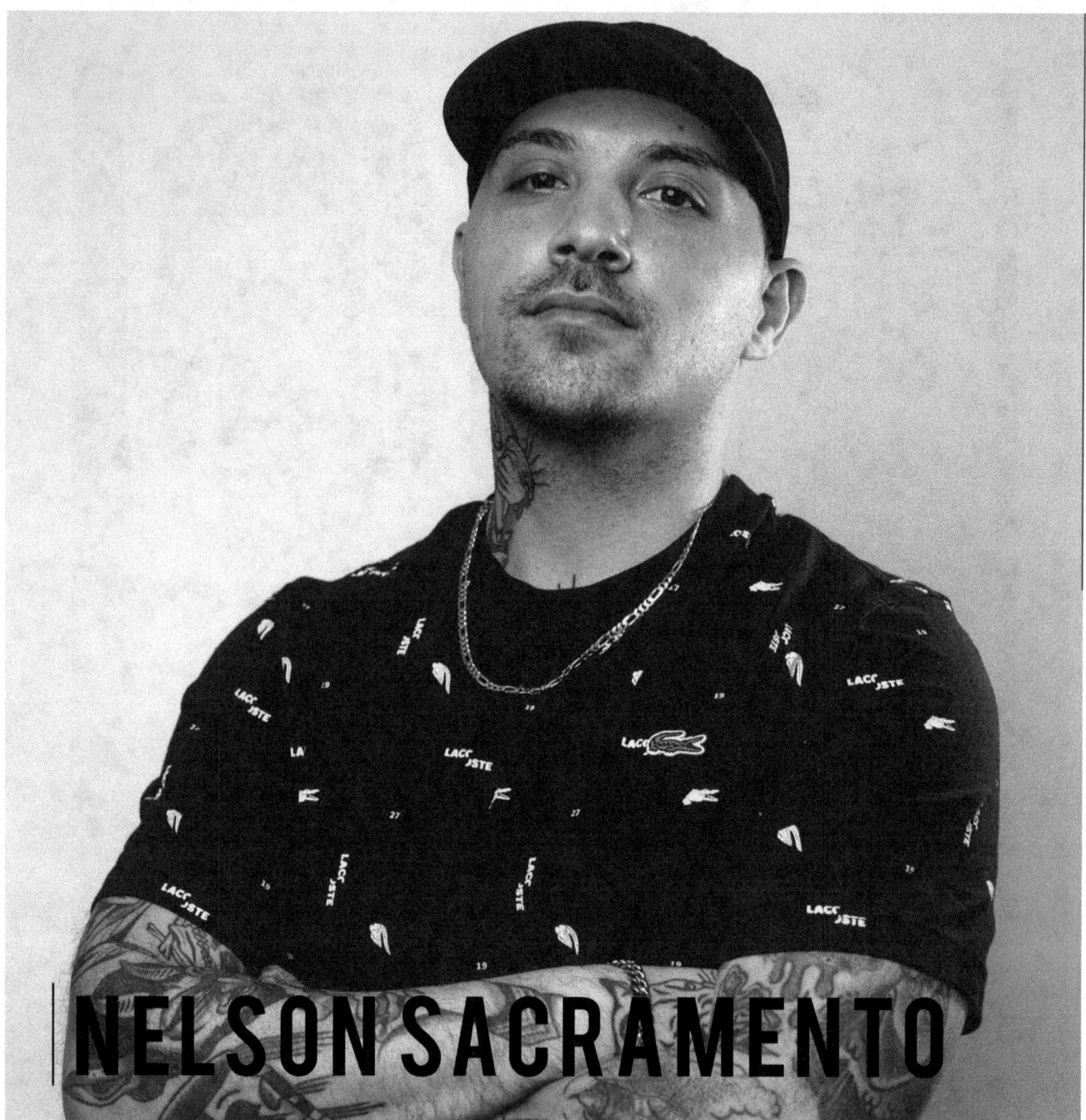

NELSON SACRAMENTO

Nelson Sacramento is a tattoo artist from Lisbon, Portugal is well known for being specialized in two distinguished styles like realistic black and grey and Neo-traditional colors as many as many trophies in international tattoo conventions. Born on 6 march 1986 in the Amadora suburbs of Lisbon the first contact related to art was graffiti, studied art in school and graphic design years later. Always connected with some form of art and did some custom paintings, fashion, and events photography. Their first contact related to tattooing was in 2011 after being tattooed by a friend he pursued the dream and started an apprenticeship In 2014 he opened his first studio Lighthouse Tattoo that today is a reference in the market, nowadays have two more in the Historical Center of Lisbon and Cascais.

In 2015 he made his first travel outside the country his first guest spot was in Switzerland it was the first of many. The profession permitted them to travel around showing their art, connect with other artists and share some knowledge with them making them grow in the techniques that he uses while working. He was invited to countries like Switzerland, Germany, Luxembourg, United Kingdom, Netherlands, etc...

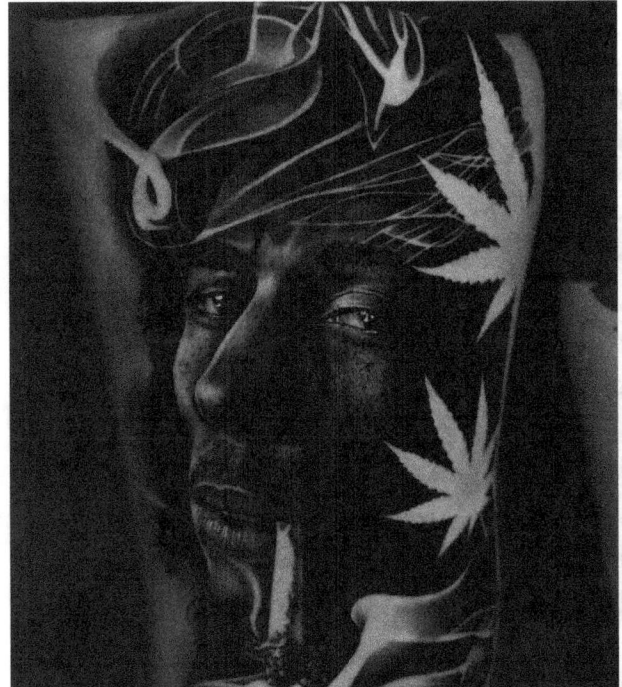

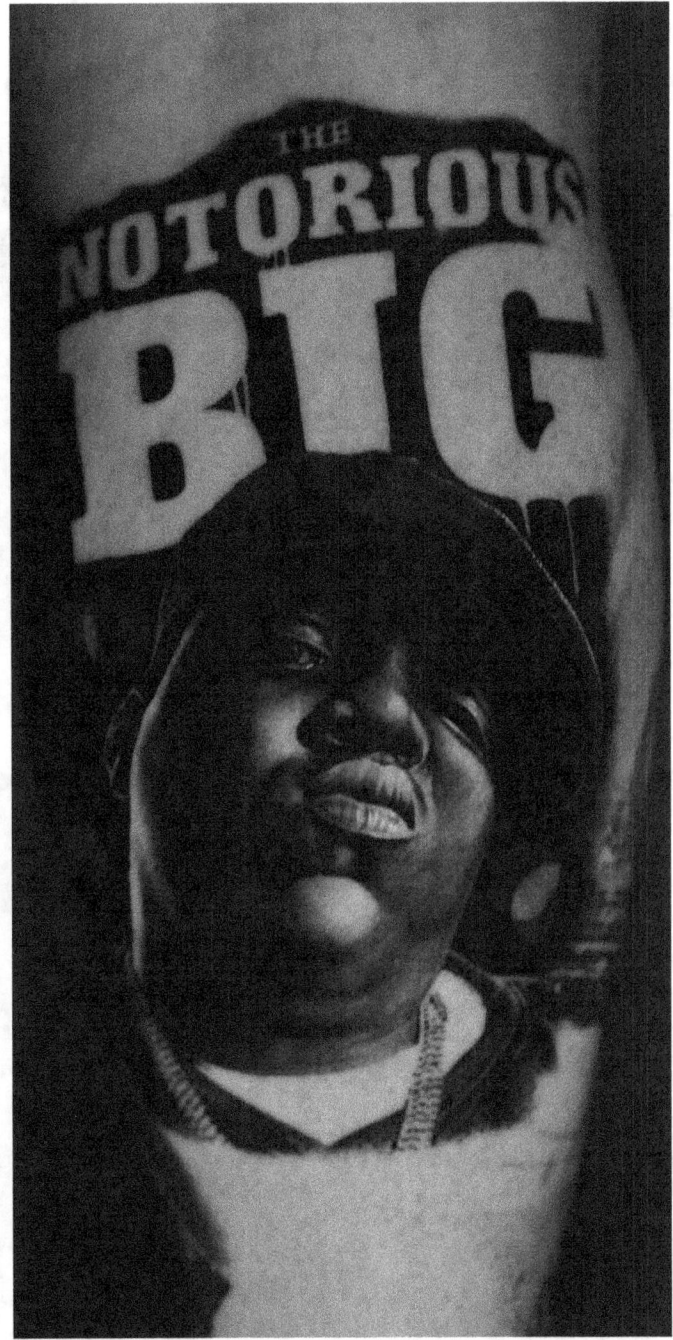

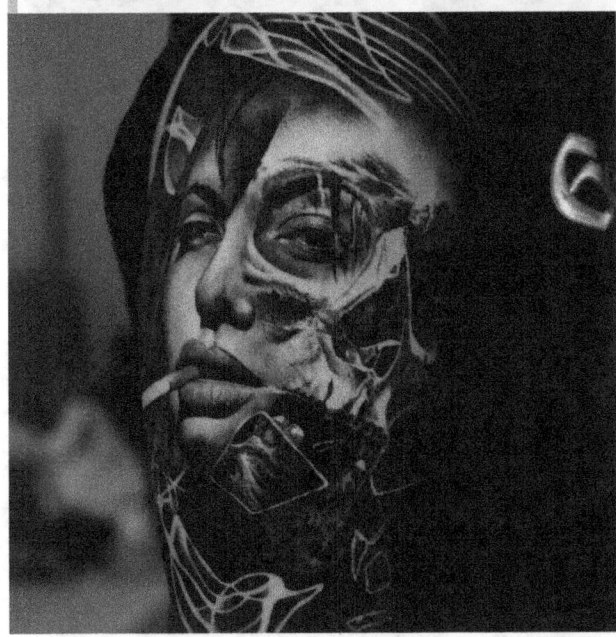

Nelson got 11 years of experience and 45 Tattoo Awards in International Tattoo Conventions and is the founder of 3 Tattoo Studios in the Lisbon Metropolitan Area and is sponsored by the best brands in the tattoo industry.

In Realistic tattoos, he specialized in mix o techniques between textures and soft shadings known by doing themes like landscapes, animals, and portraits. Neo-Traditional tattoos his style is fantasy themes, classic shapes, and balance between muted tones and bright colors. Some of the themes are witches, warriors, jewelry, and florals. If you ask for something Nelson creates custom designs for you either the style. Due to the demand of people asking for formation in the area, he started public and private tattoo workshops and share some tips on social media. Nelson was a judge in Preston and Setubal tattoo show

@*nelsonsacramento***
FB/kamytattoos

Portugal, Lisbon

AL KINSELLA
Cubism Tattoo Artist

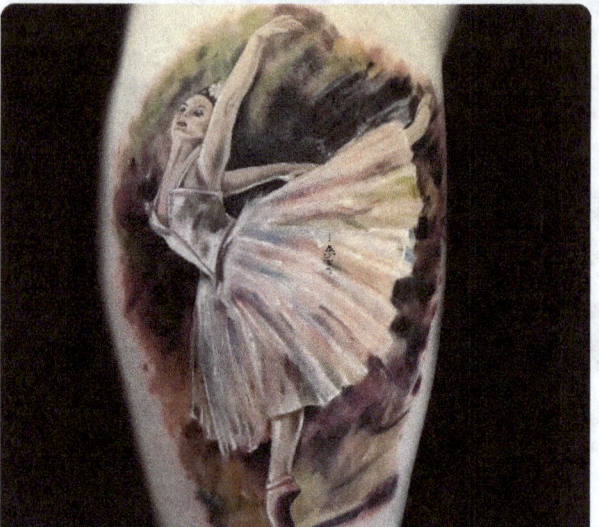

My journey seems so long it's hard to remember when I started tattooing.

My wife Jen and I were traveling the world and experiencing life, I was just working crappy jobs and playing music to get by. Living life from a backpack and guitar case. I used to keep my underwear inside my guitar to save space when traveling. We had a great time and opened our minds to the world.

At some point, we came back home to Ireland and I lost my brother who was my best friend. I was devastated. Realizing that life is way too short to waste in pointless jobs, I decided to focus on my passions, music, and art.

So music helped keep the bills paid while I learned to tattoo. I was always a sketch artist and painter but struggled to transform that into the technical skin art form of tattooing. Chunky heavy loud coil machines were a little different from a paintbrush. Luckily I stuck with it but almost gave up a thousand times.

I used to say I was self-taught but I now realize that I had many mentors over the years, I stood on the shoulders of giants and soaked up information from all around me. The journey was tough, but that's how you learn. It's still tough, life continues to throw crazy days at me, but now I realize it's just something I need to overcome to move on to the next level.

As I transitioned through my career I've gone through all kinds of styles, techniques, forms, equipment, and methodology. And I will most likely continue to do so. But I've always been a misfit, and I think my work reflects that a little. I like to tattoo outside the box, step out of my comfort zone and create from within.

Right now I focus a little more on cubism and lose painterly styles, but still explore Neo-traditional, Art Nouveau, and Art Deco.

With my 16 years of tattoo experience, I've realized that the old saying, "bold will hold", is very true. So even though my work may look loose and artsy I'm still hiding a solid structure within each piece. Another element of tattooing that I enjoy is human interaction, I believe you attract what

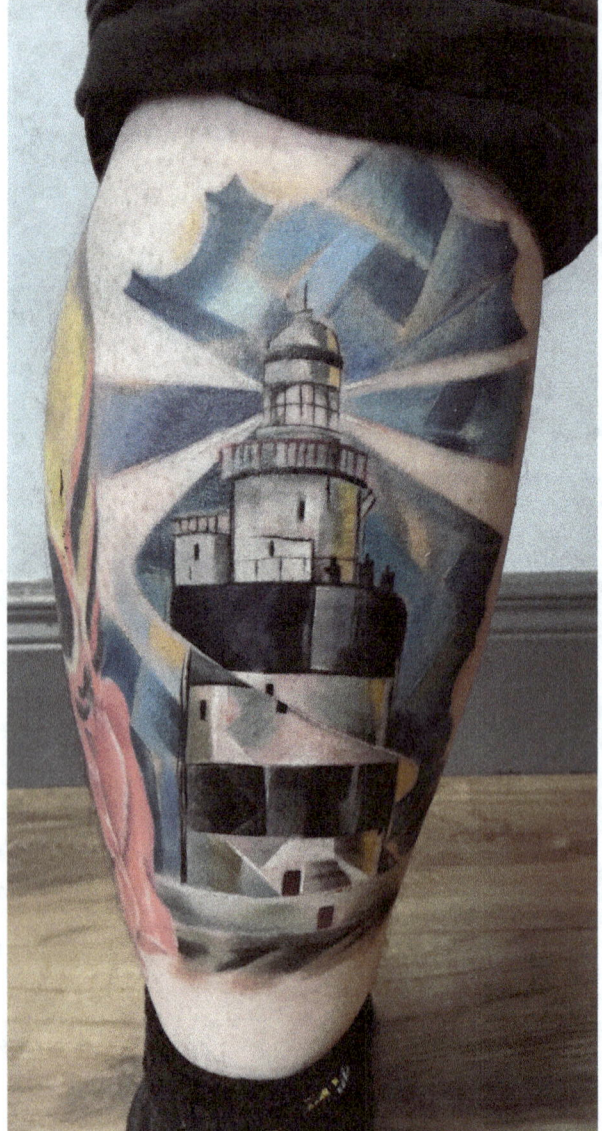

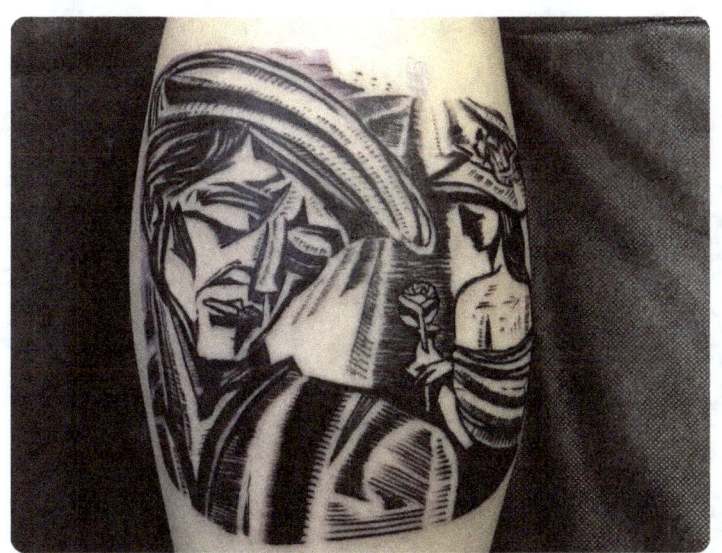

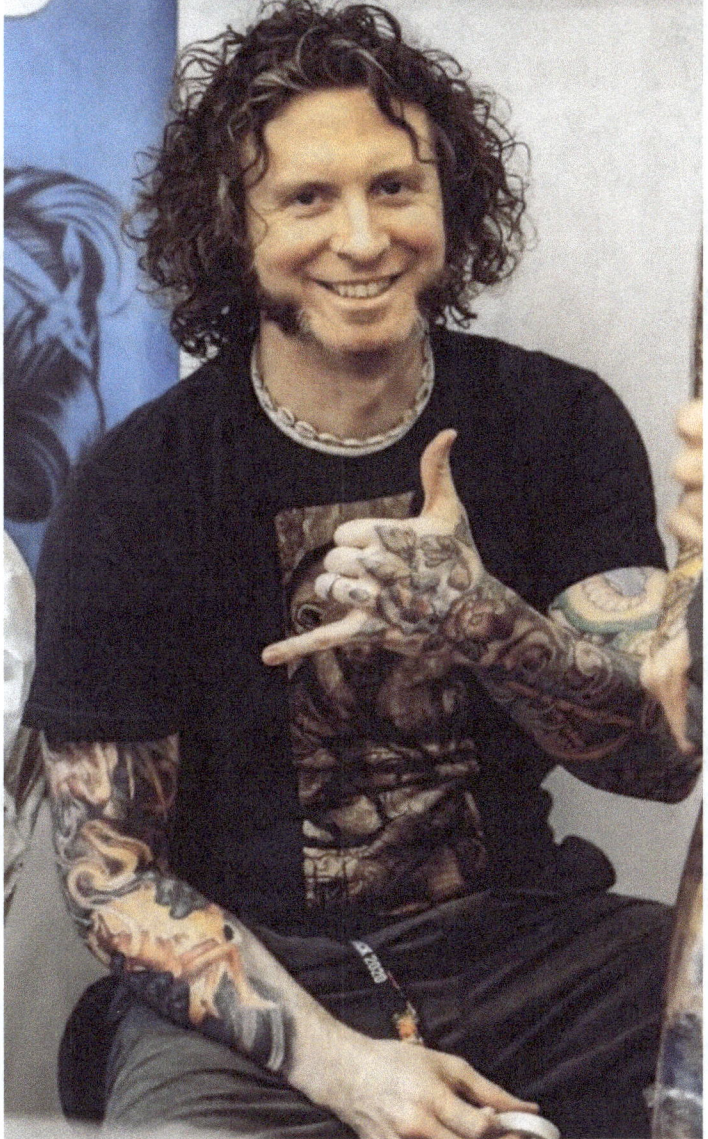

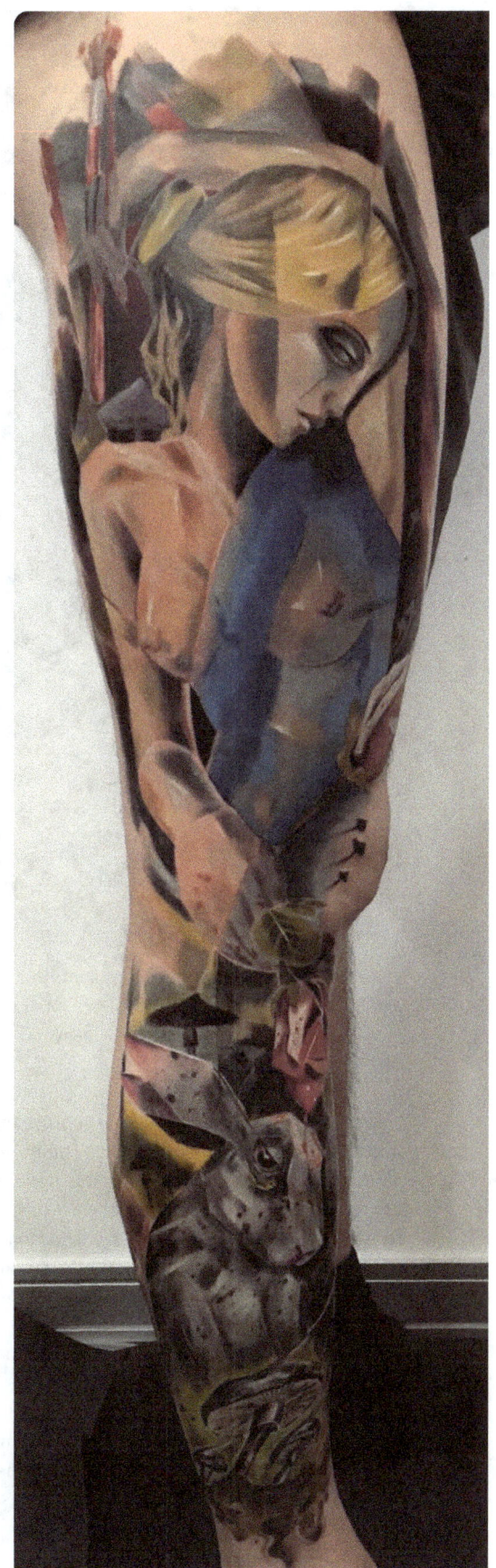

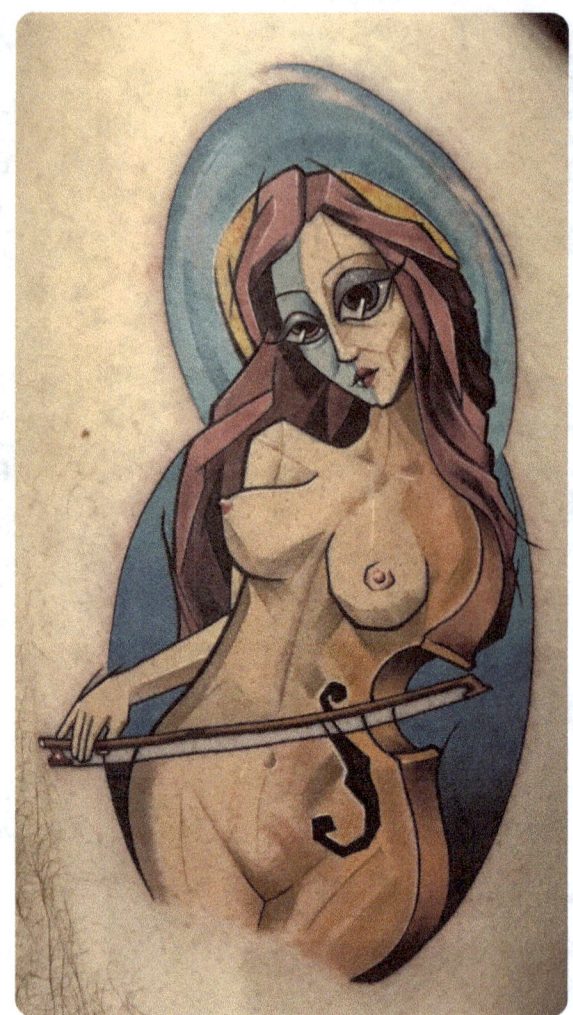

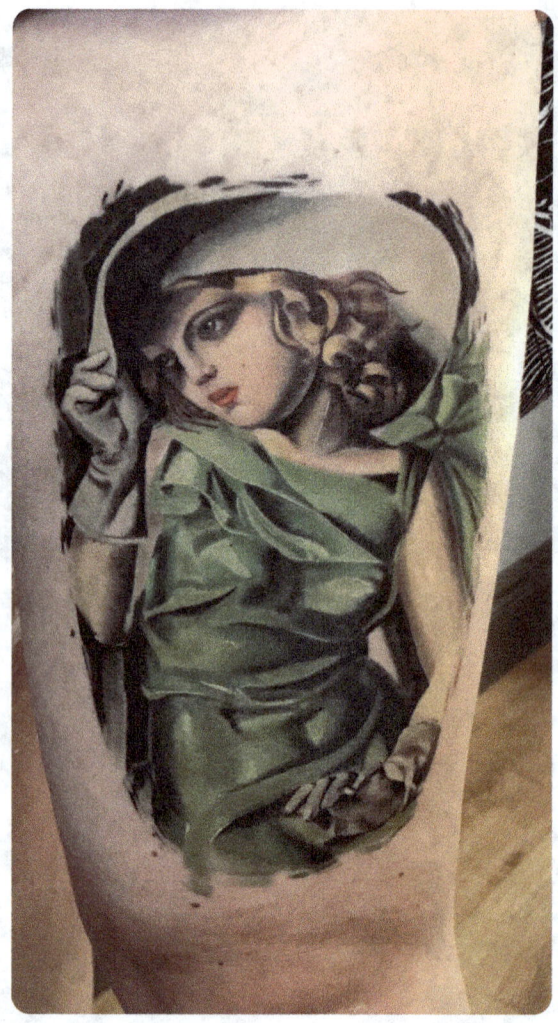

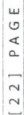

you align with, and I have amazing clients that I vibe with and have great conversations with. As a lot of my work is on a large scale we sometimes have many days and can dive into some crazy topics.

I'm very driven and love to grow and improve throughout my career. I've burned myself out many times, working 13-hour days and tattooing into the wee hours of the morning at conventions. So to counteract this, I love to travel and relax. Surfing is my favorite pastime. I've surfed many places around the world, it rivals my passion for art. I love to do large-scale oil paintings.

I meditate quite often and delve into my spiritual side and the mysteries of existence.
I also love to ride custom motorcycles, skate, play music, and of course spend time with my beautiful family. They keep me grounded and happy. Without them, I'd

be a crazy wilderness man, living on a remote beach, tattooing with sharpened fish bones for surfing tips.

I get inspiration from my surroundings for my artwork. Nature and spirituality are always an inspiration, and whatever shape morphs into my mind, be it psychedelic, esoteric, or whichever way my mind is meandering, it can influence my art quite a bit.
I've loved studying the master oil painters and incorporating some of that style into my work.

In the very near future", I am going to uproot and travel again, bringing my art to the world. Experience new life and places and people. Life is a journey, I'm gonna take it all in along the way.

@alkinsellatattoos
www.alkinsellatattoos.com
Wexford, Ireland

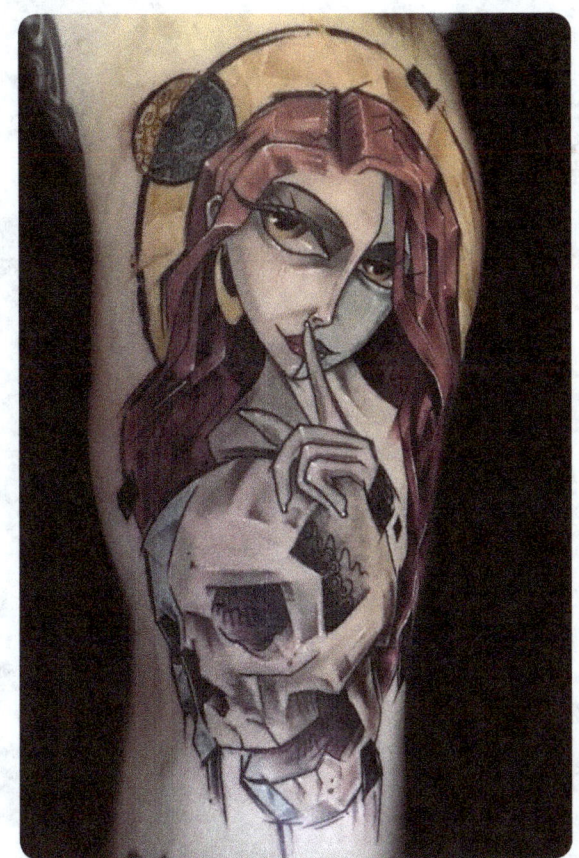

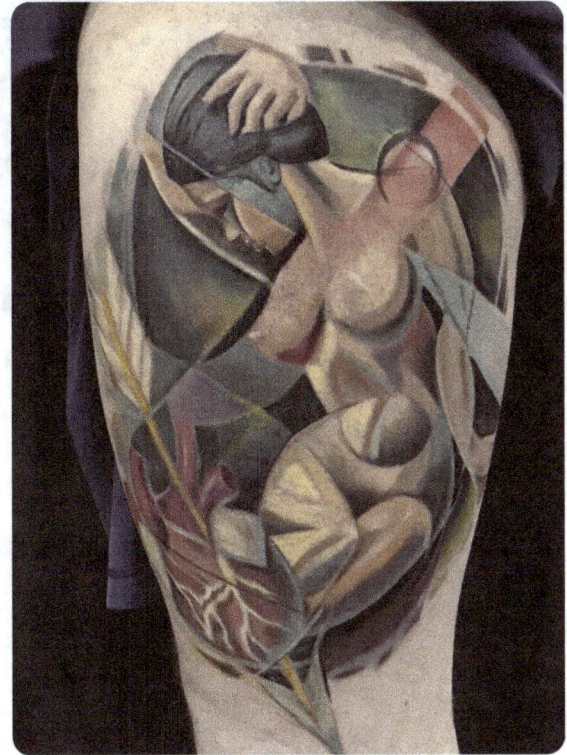

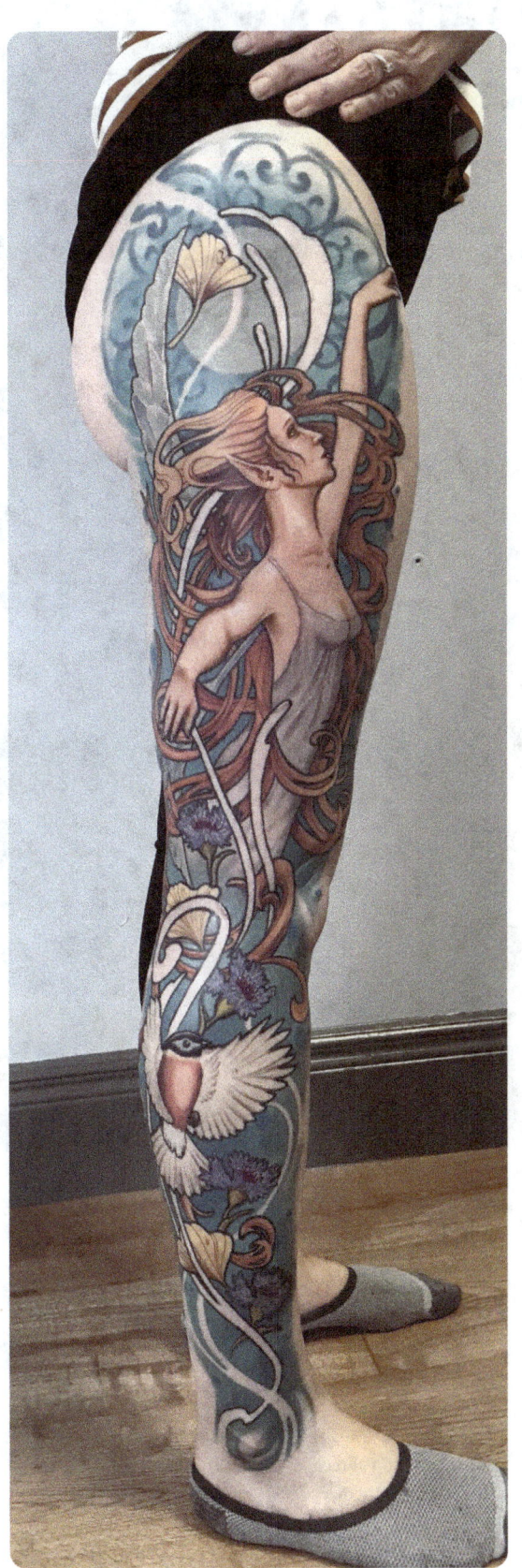

Chapter III

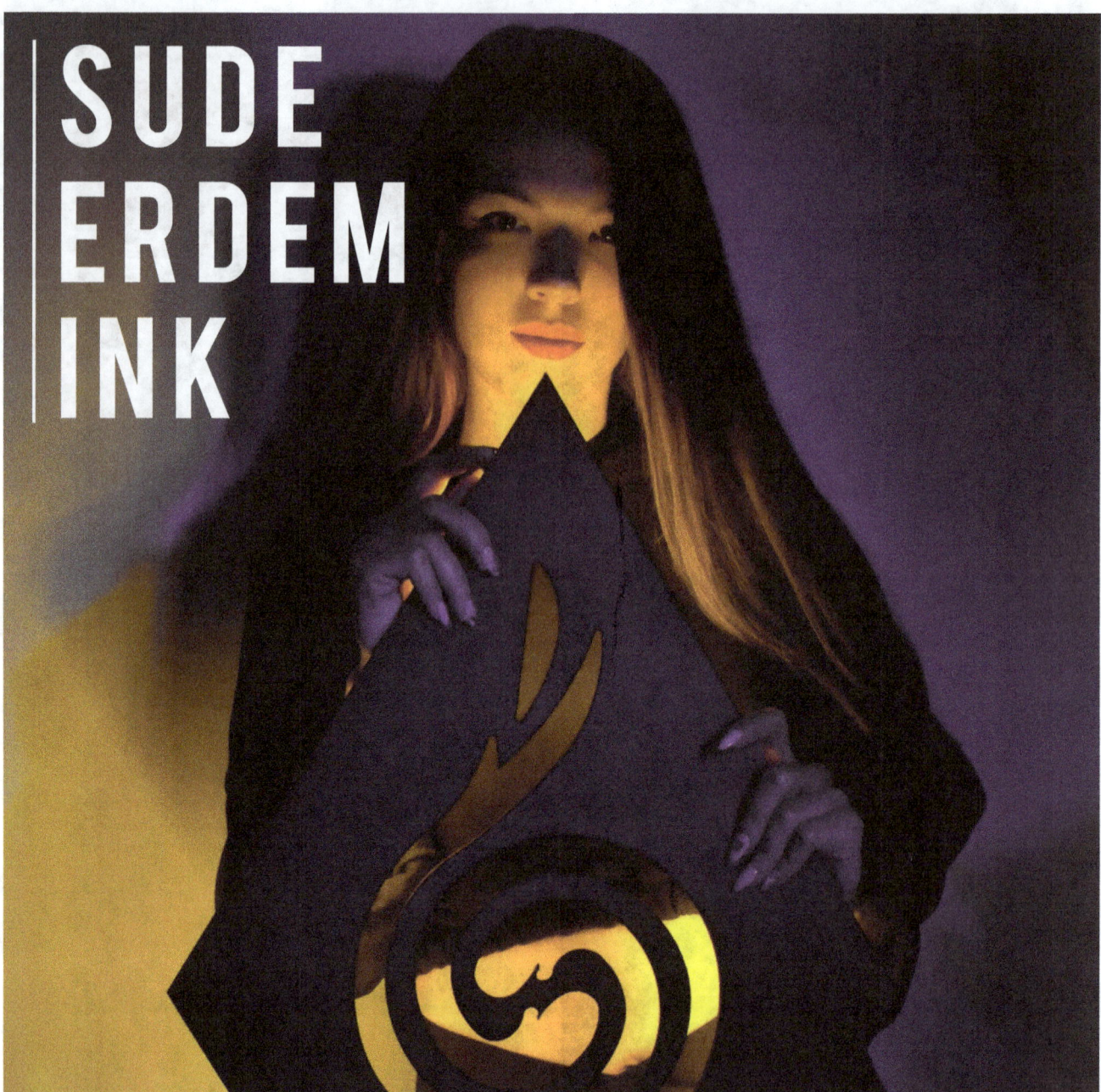

SUDE ERDEM INK

Hi! Tell us about you

Hi! I am Sude from Turkey. I was engaged in art from a very young age. I studied art in high school and majored in art at university. After I get my degree I taught drawing and did freelance illustration for a short time before starting tattooing. I am a self-taught tattoo artist and never worked for someone else's studio. it has been two and a half years now since I start tattooing and own my private studio which I and my husband run together

When and why did you start tattooing?

I use to teach drawing in some courses but I had to move to my now husband's place from my family's place because of some prived issues. My country is kinda conservative toward women so my moving to my then boyfriend's place without wedlock pissed my bosses. They fired me because I don't share the same lifestyle as them. After that I looked for a job where I feel free, I met a person who encourage me to try tattoos and let me try on him my first tattoo. I fell in love with tattooing and make it my full-time job. I am free since I start tattooing.

How would you define your style?

My style is mostly black&gray realism. I like doing por-

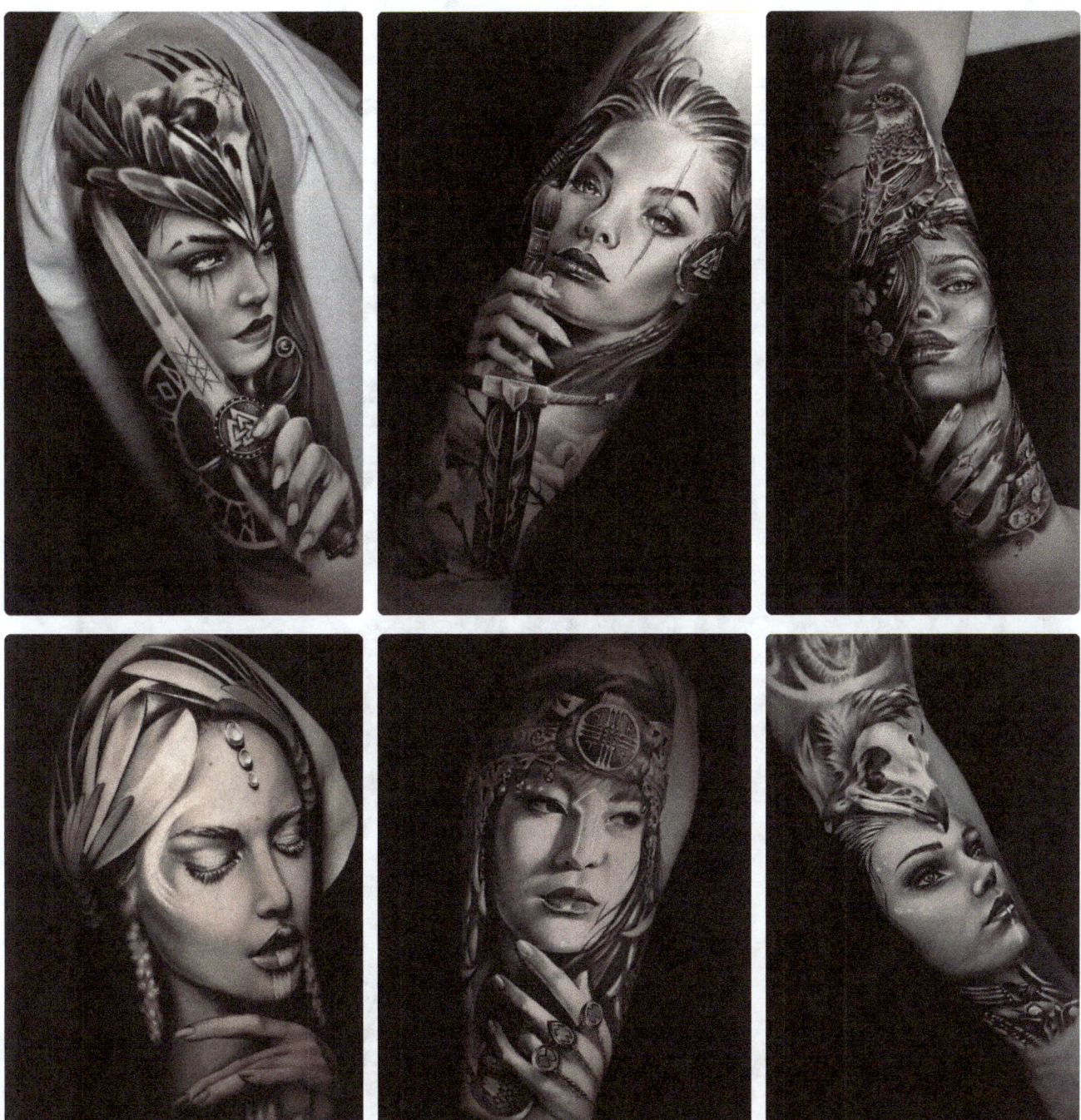

traits of warrior women. I generally work on big pieces like a sleeve. But I enjoy doing colored pieces every once in a while.

What do you do besides tattoos?

I used to dance salsa and bachata but stopped when the pandemic happen. These days my whole life is surrounded by tattooing. I tattoo the whole day and do design while I rest. On my and my husband's free day, we criticize our business's situation and set a goal or do yearly plans. I would like to start dancing again but I am so focused on my business right now. I will slow down and start again when I reach my goals.

@sudeerdemink

https://sudeerdemink.com/

Eskisehir, Turkey

ABBIE UNDERWOOD

FAT FUGU | @ABBIEUNDERWOODTATTOO | UK, NORTHAMPTON

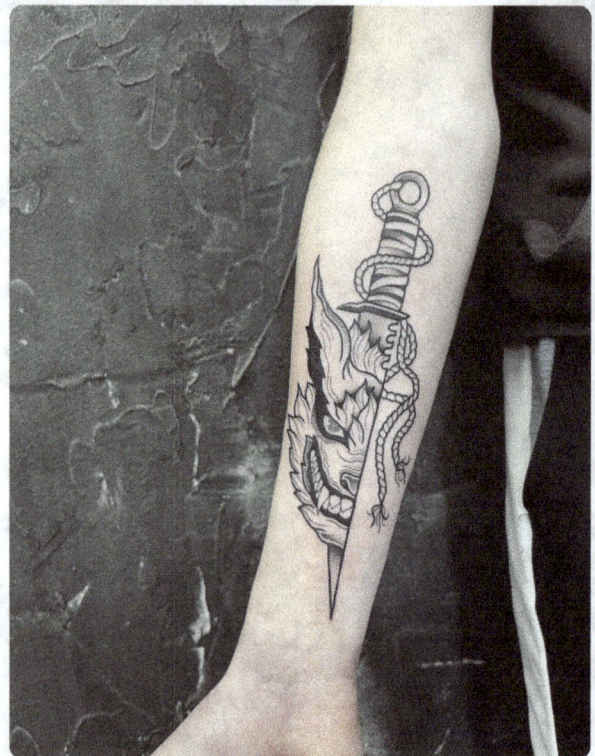
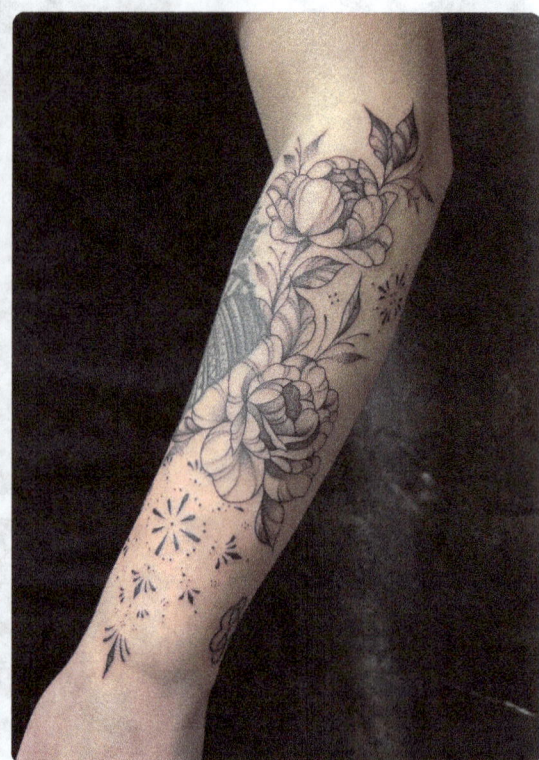
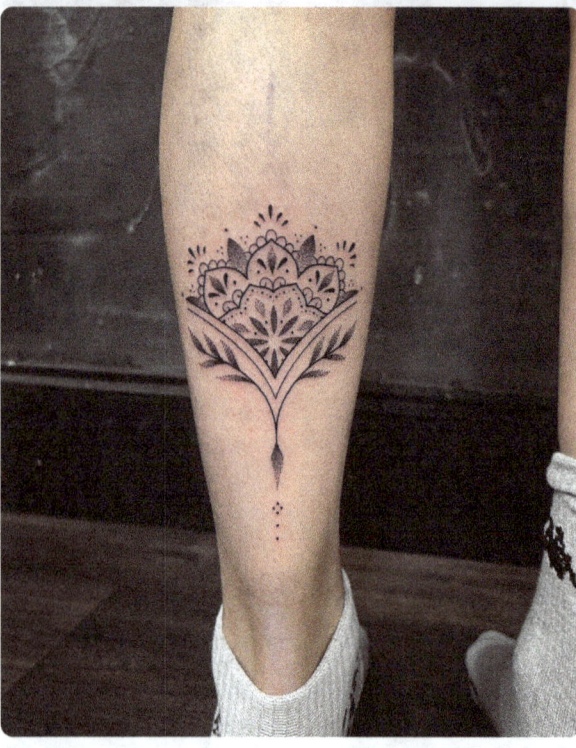
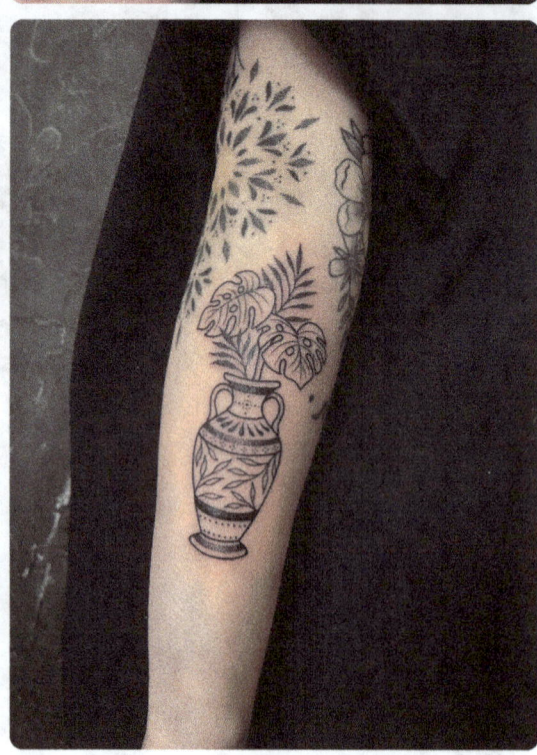

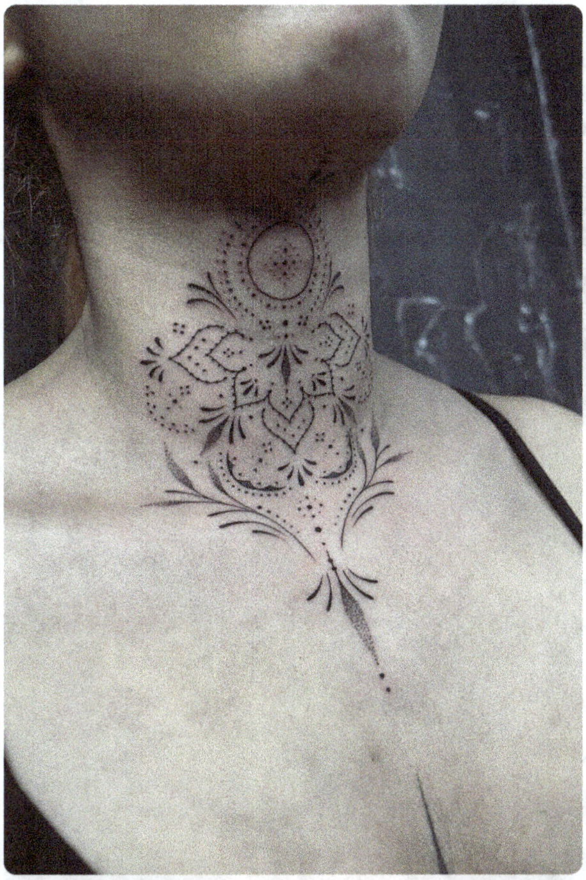

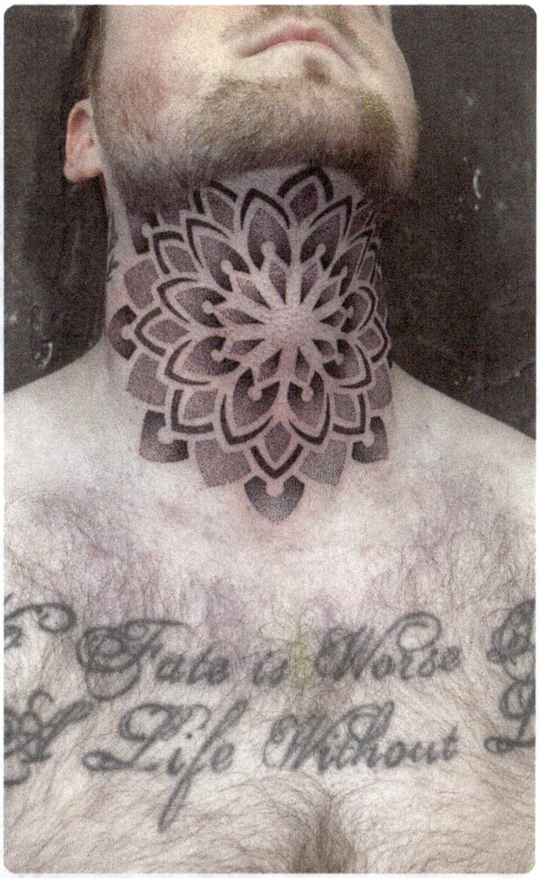

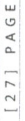

Chapter III

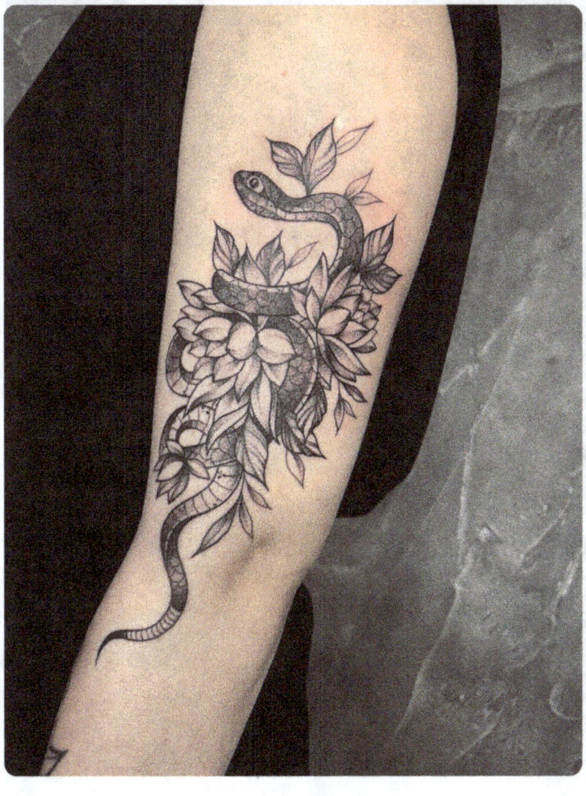

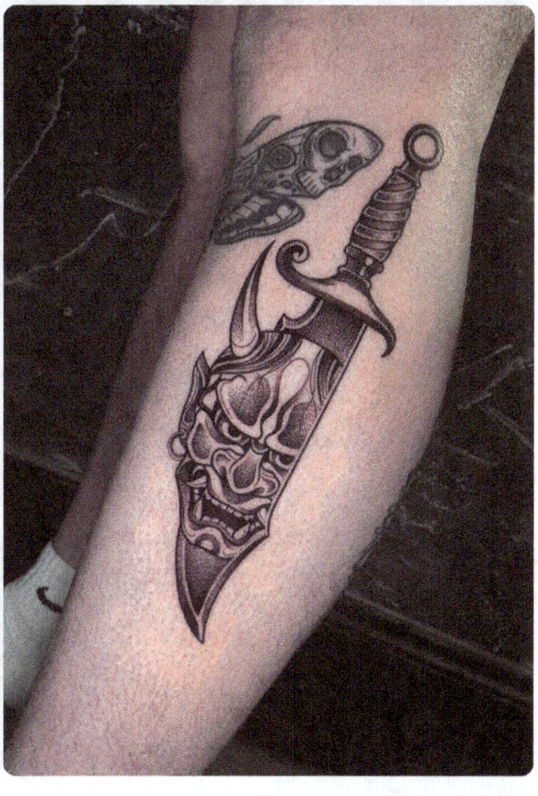

ALENA ZOZULENKO

DOT CREATIVE GROUP | FB: ALENA.BLACKART | @ZOZUTATTOO | USA, NEW YORK

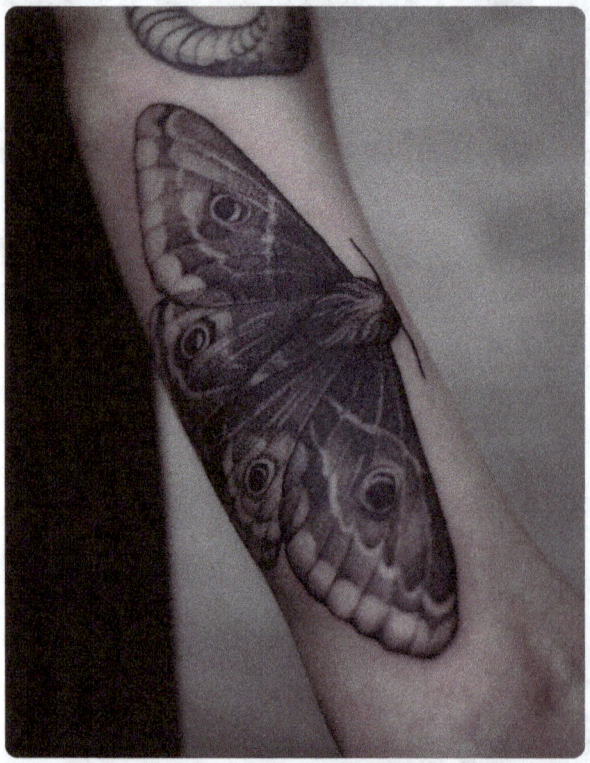

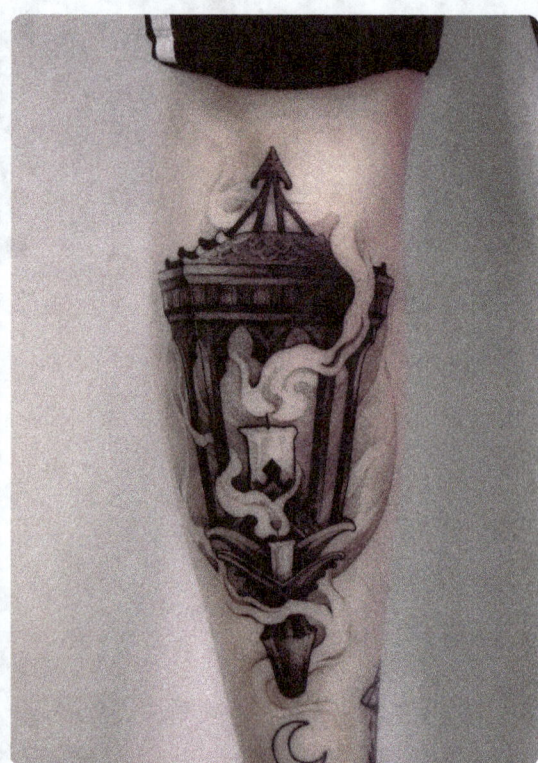

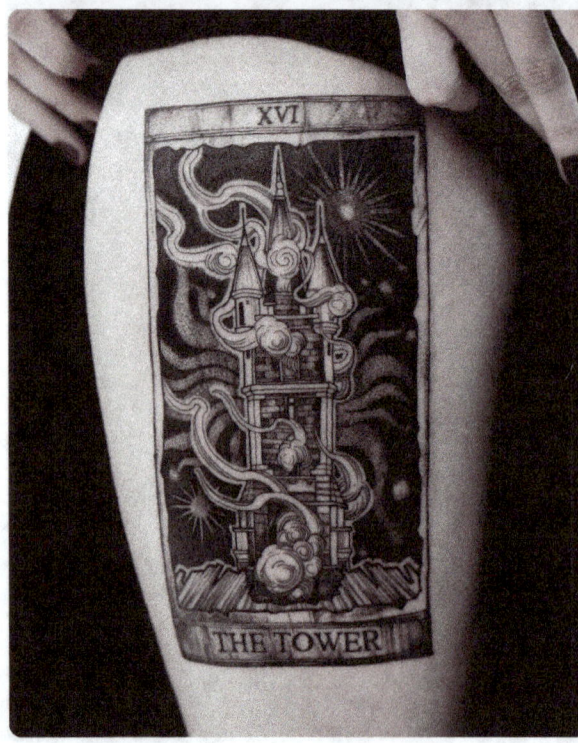

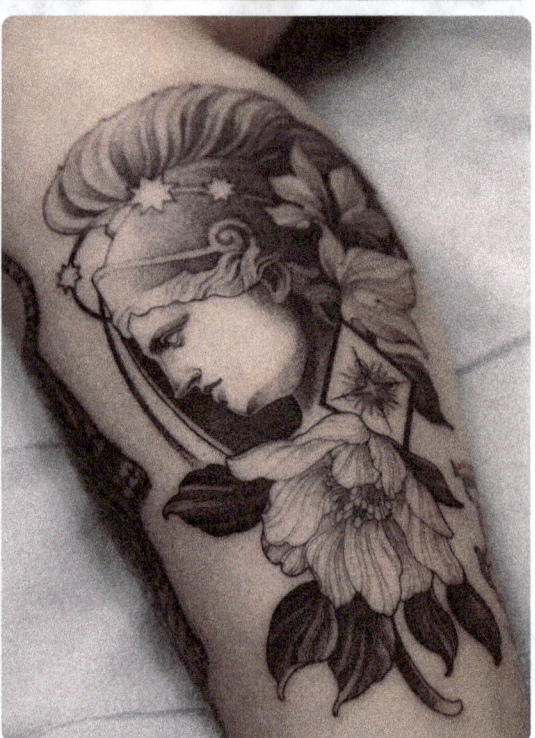

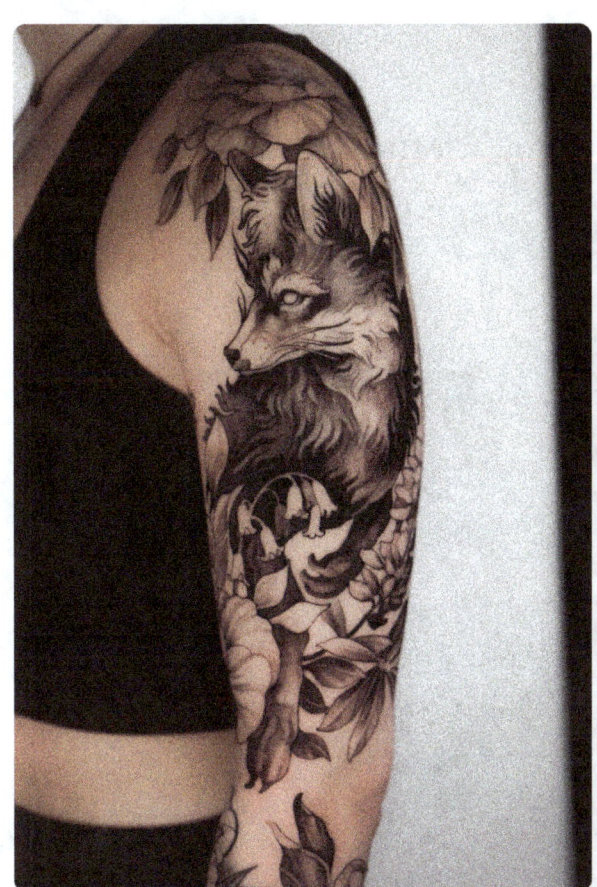

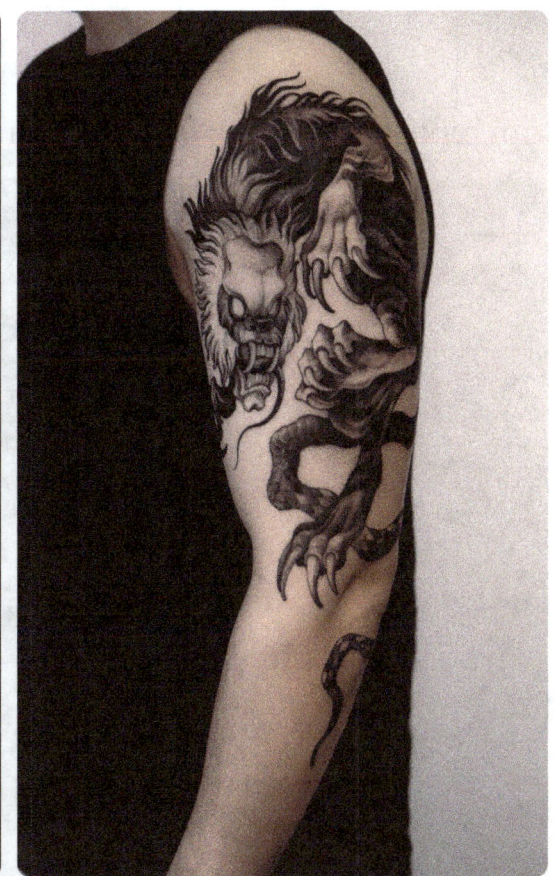

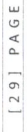

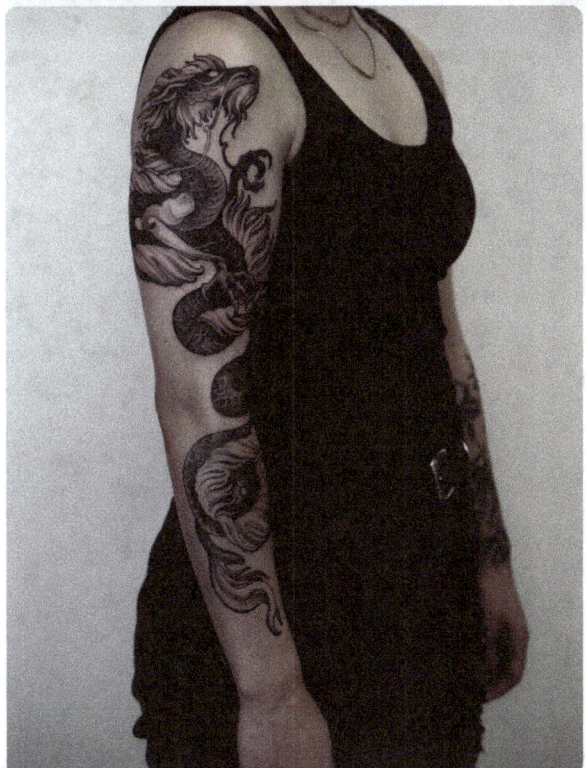

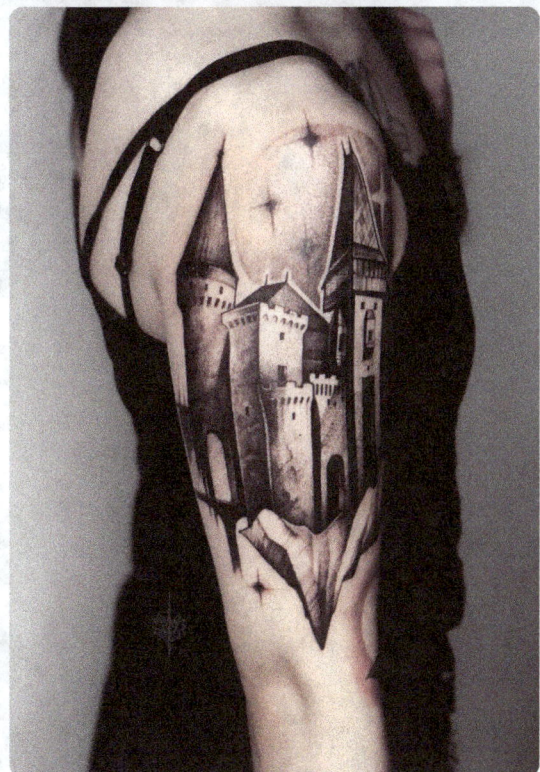

Chapter III

A L E X   P A N

GOLDEN CAT TATTOO | @ALEXPAN_TATTOO | SPAIN, BARCELONA

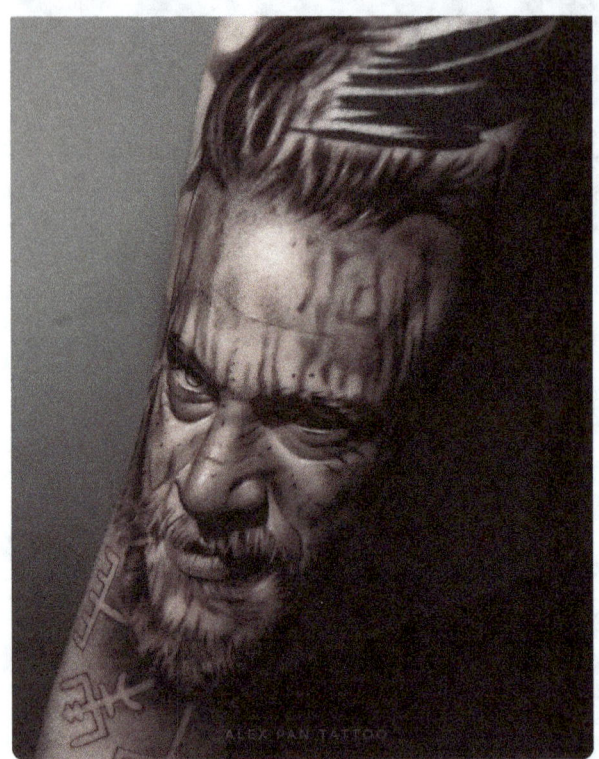
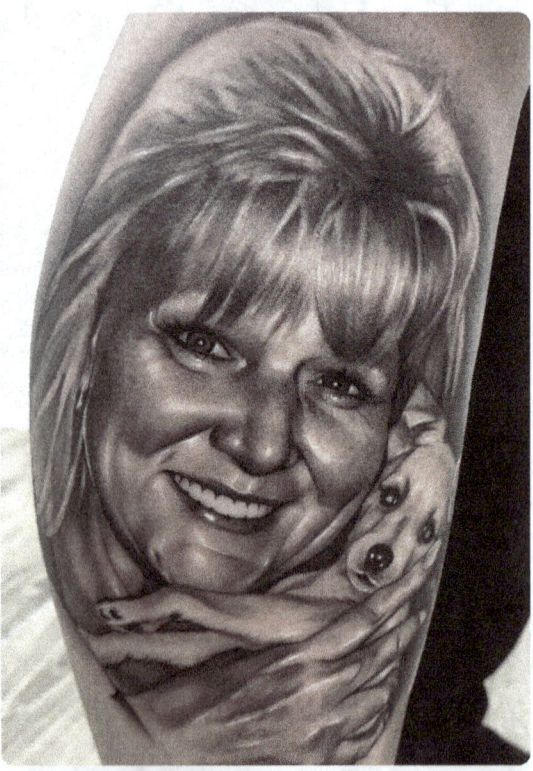
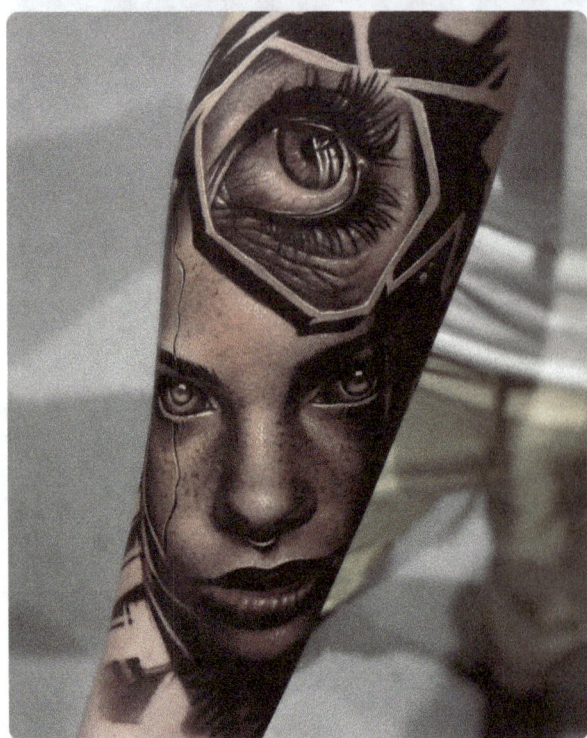
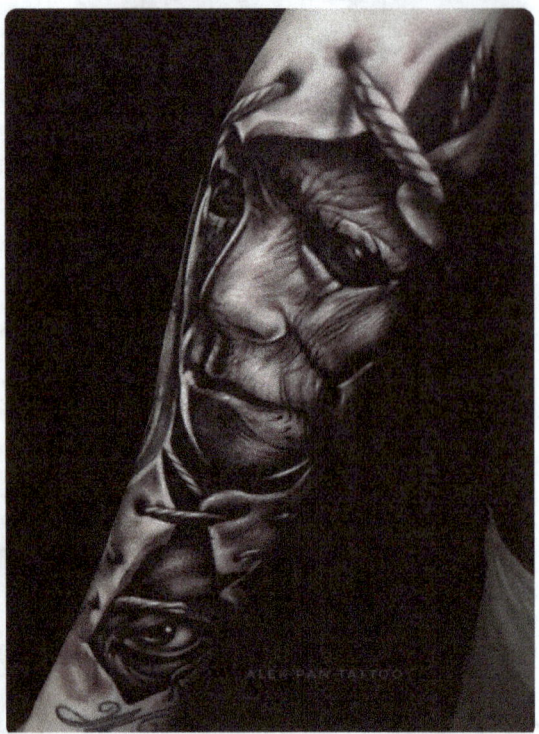

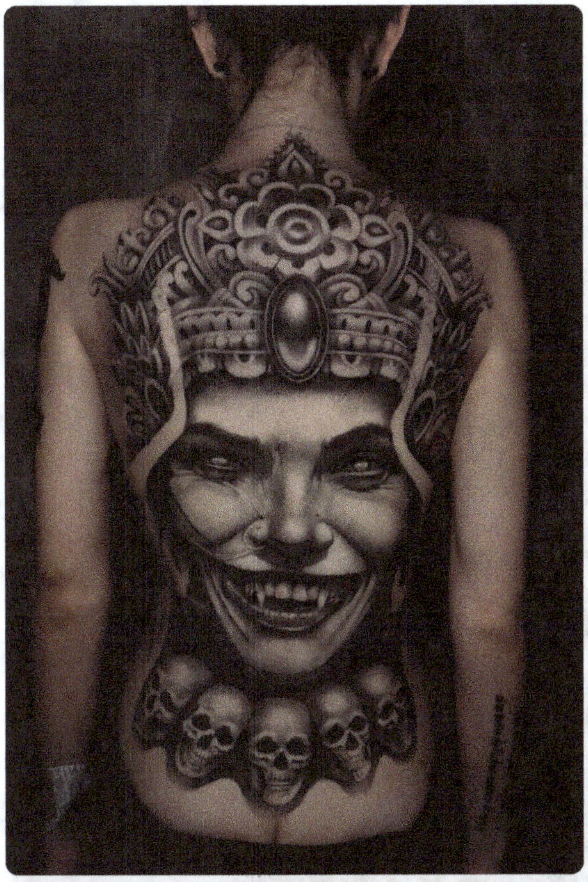

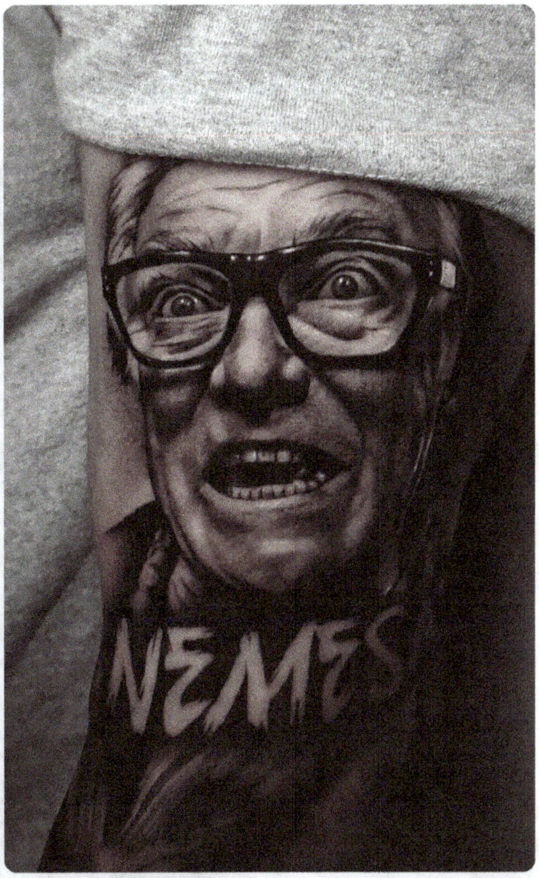

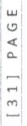

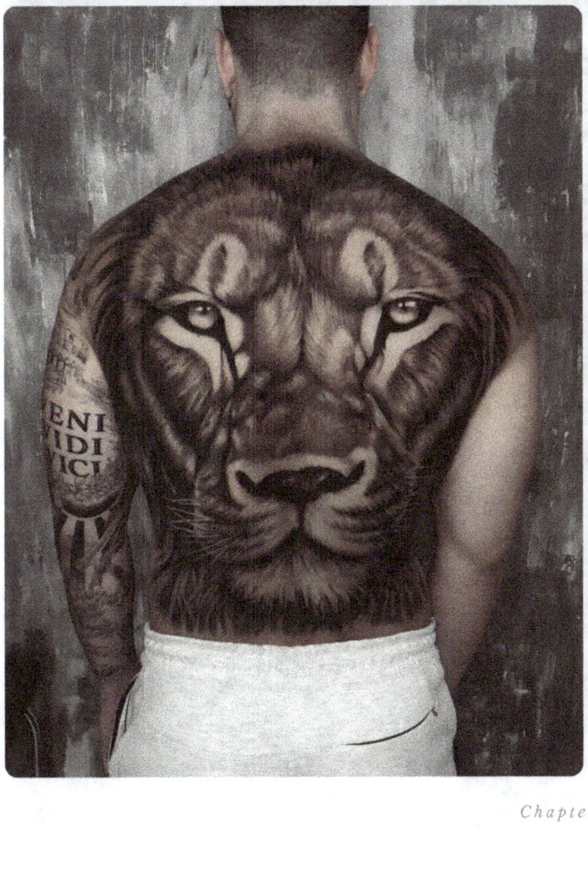

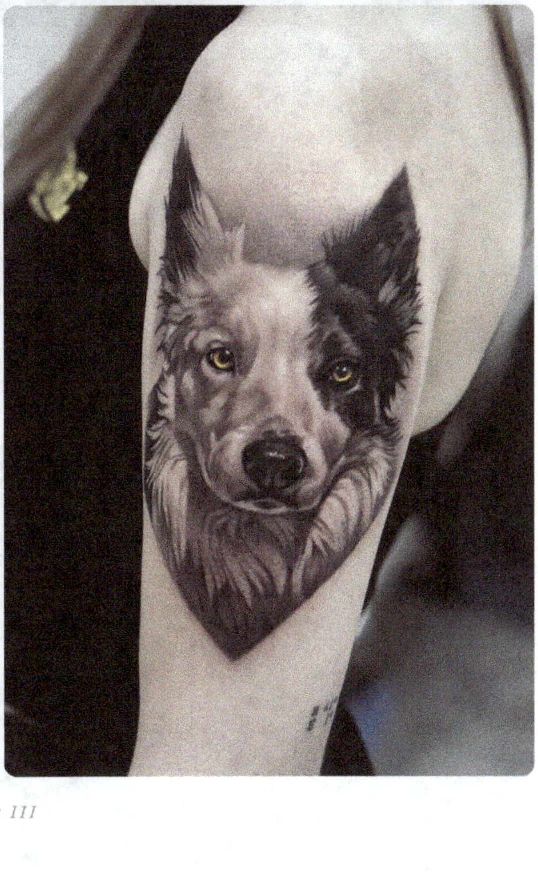

Global Tattoo Magazine

ALEXANDER BELENKOV

MELNIK PRIVET | @ART.ALEXWHITE | FB: ALEX WHITE | THE NETHERLANDS

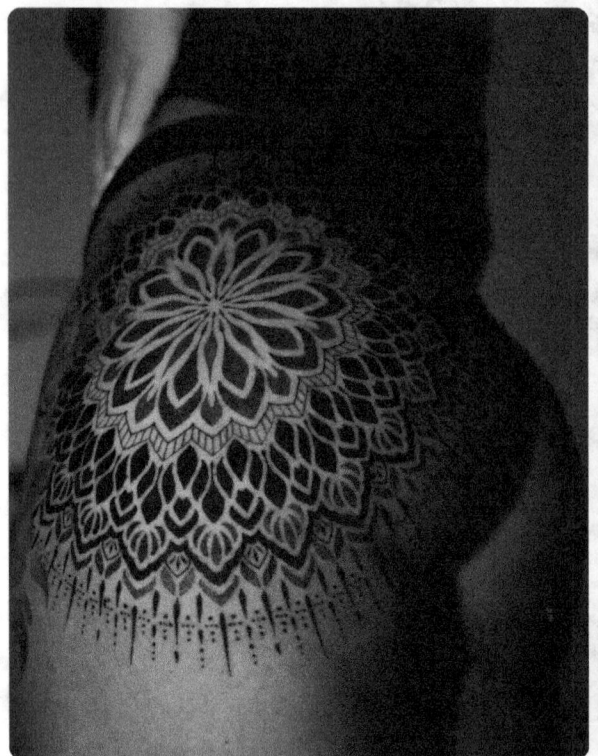
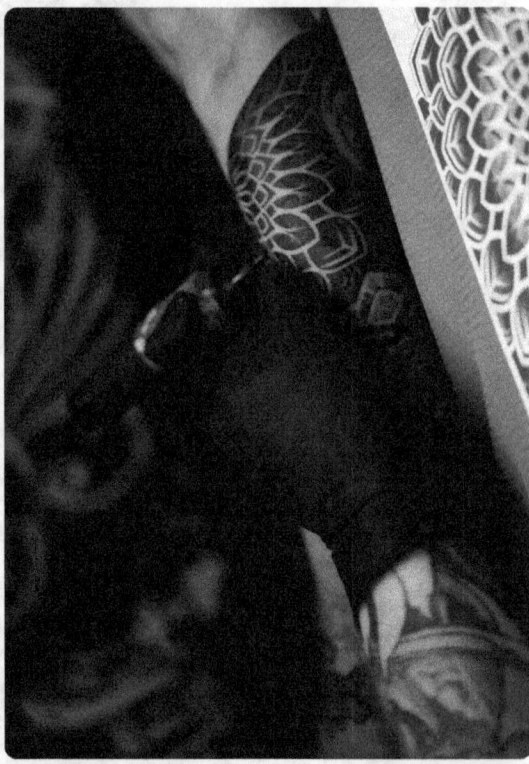
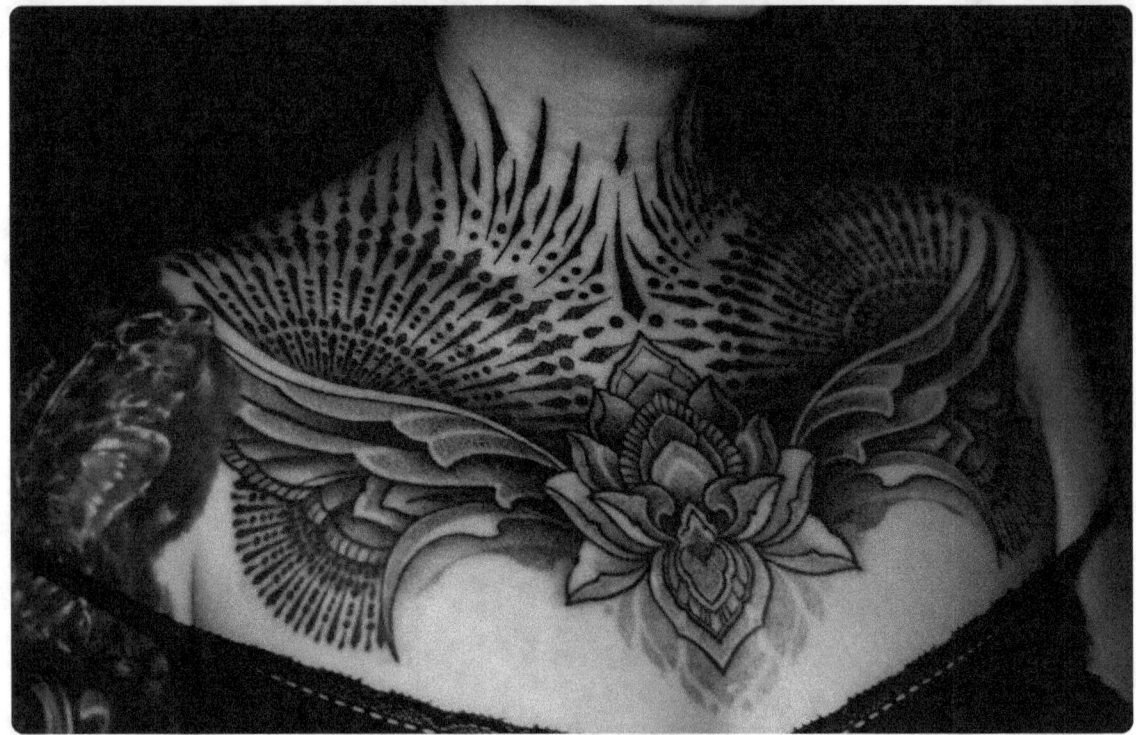

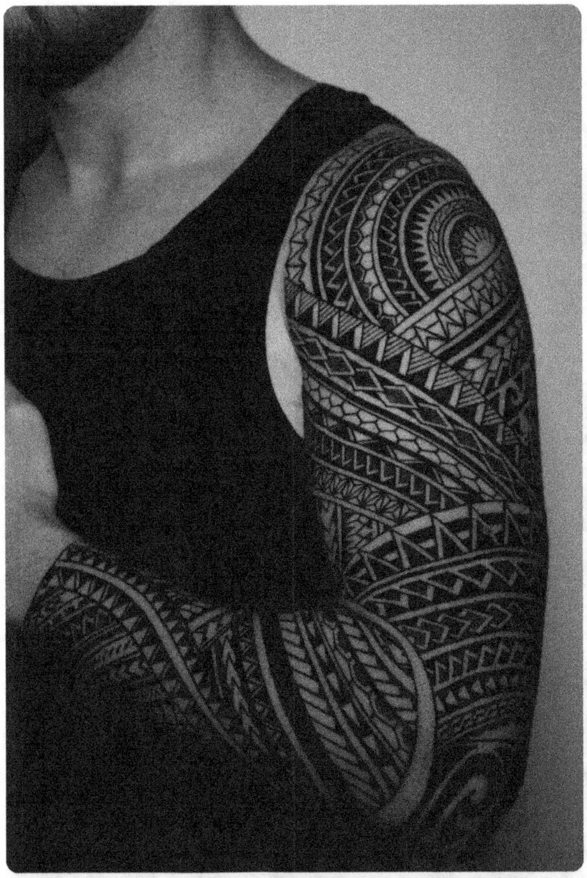

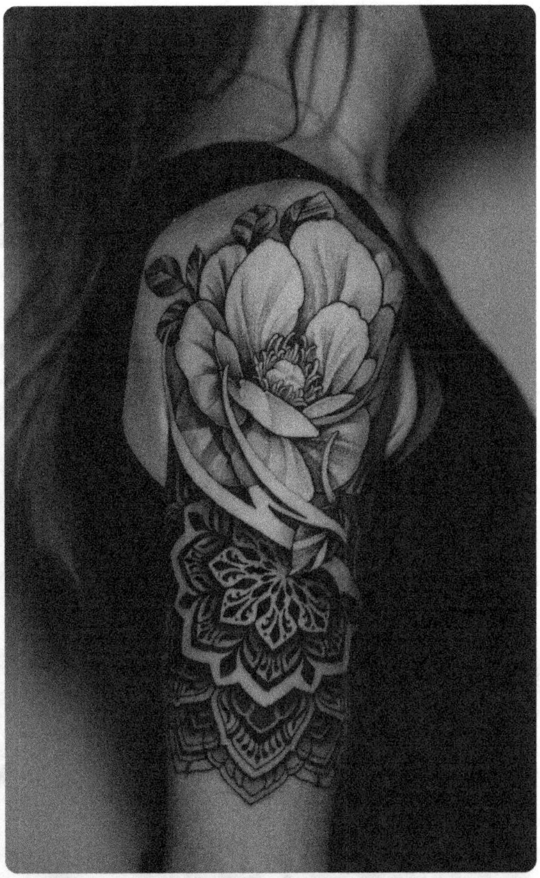

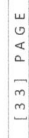

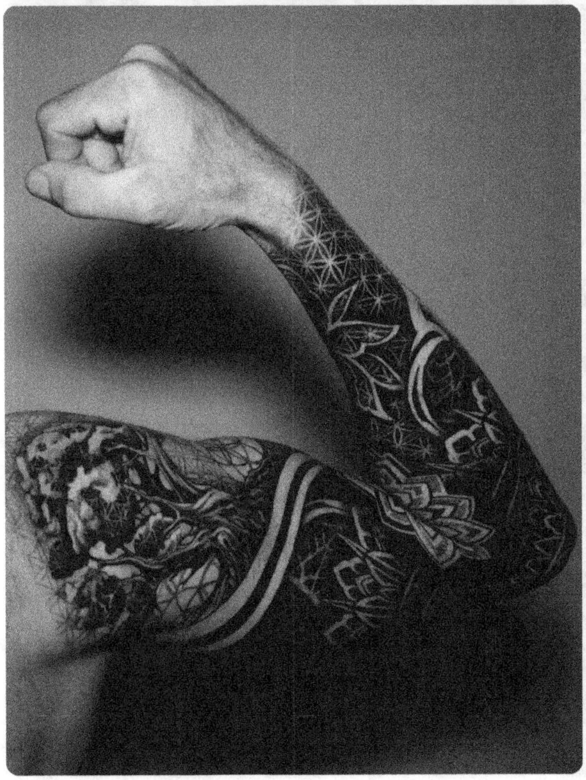

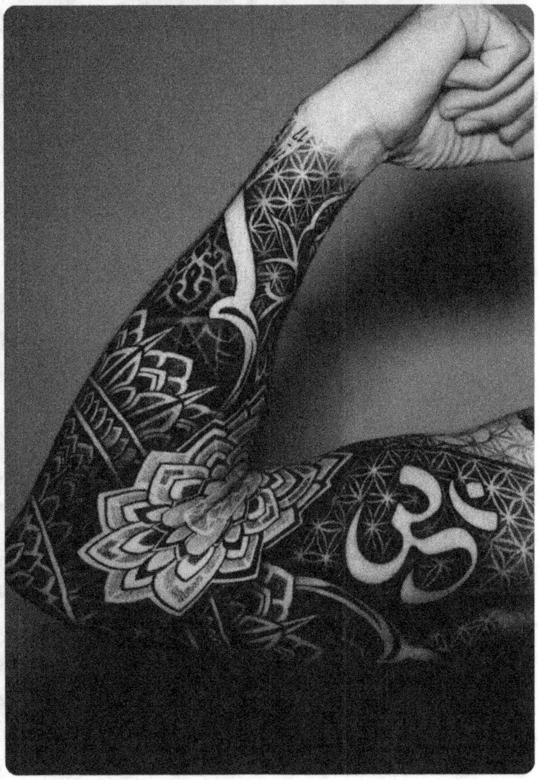

Chapter III

ALICE RIGAL

BLEU DRAGON TATTOO | @ALICETATTOOER | FRANCE, LE HAVRE

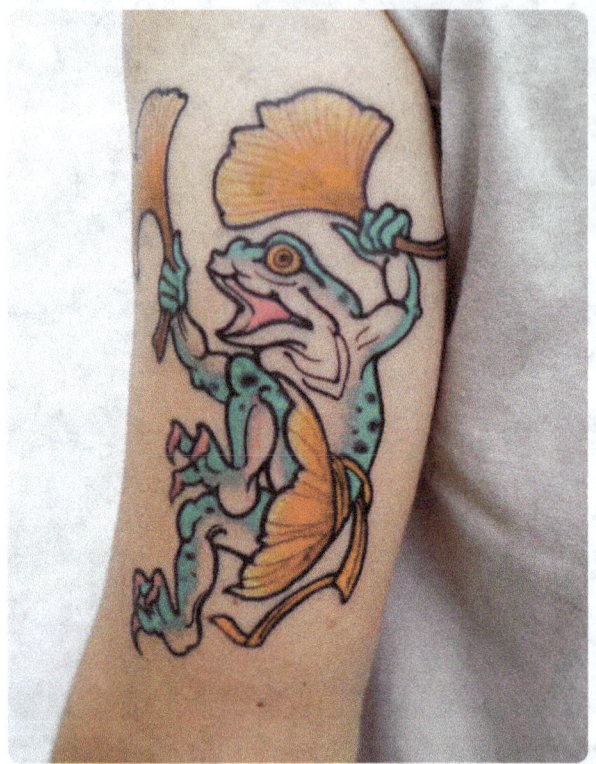
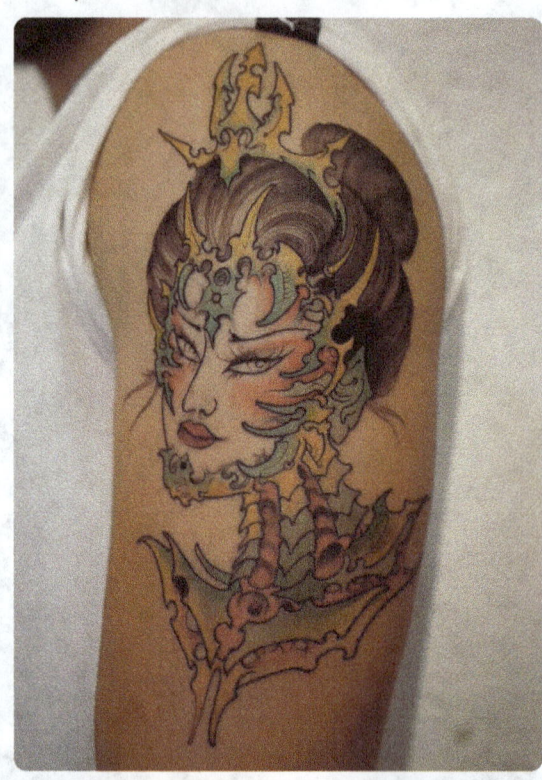
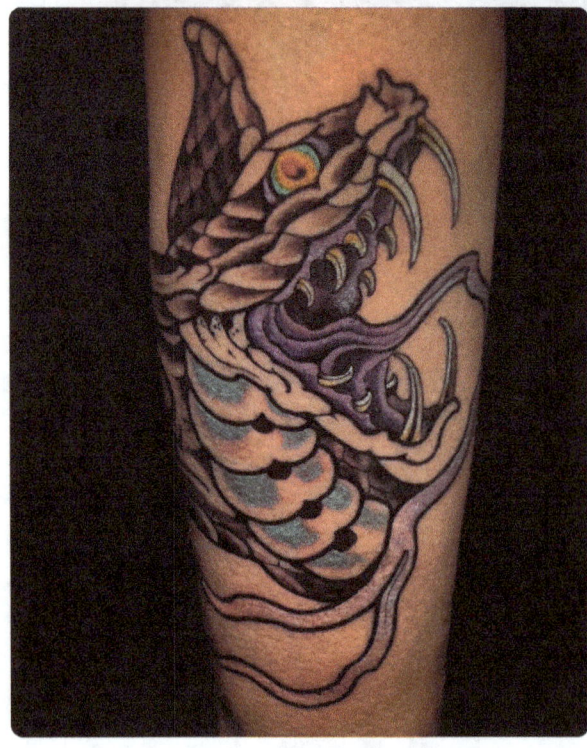
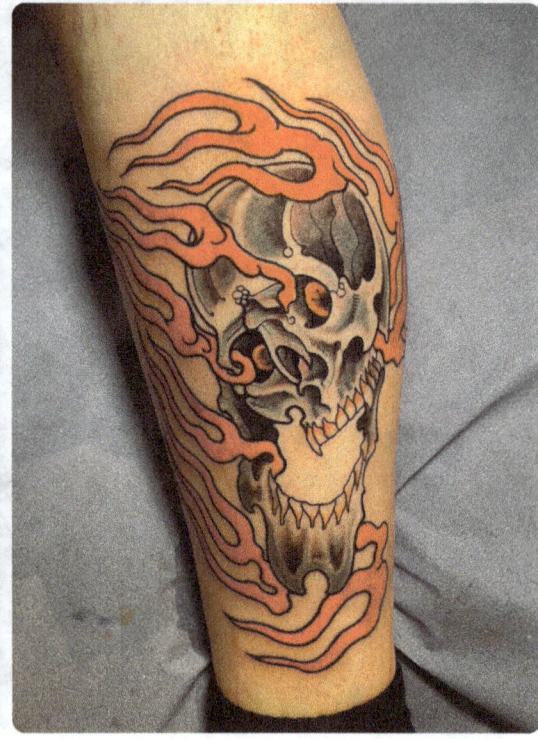

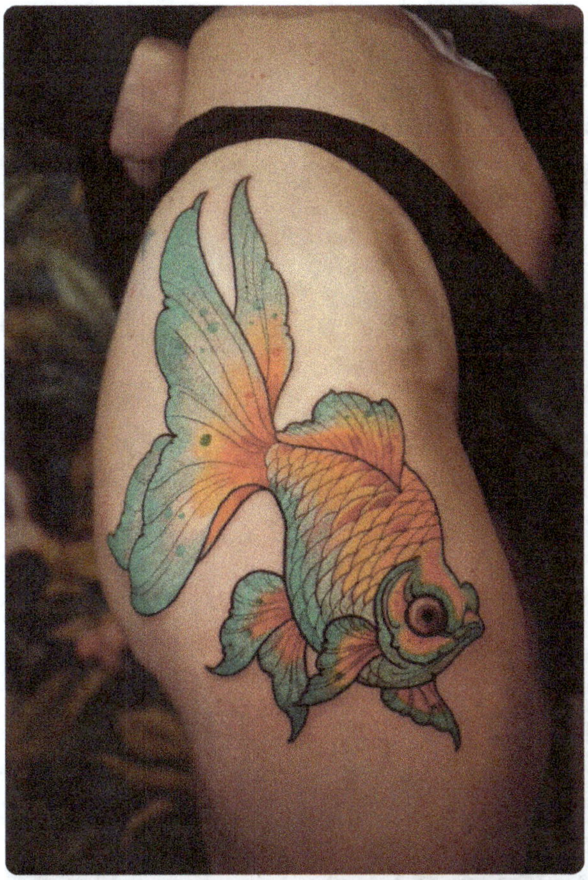

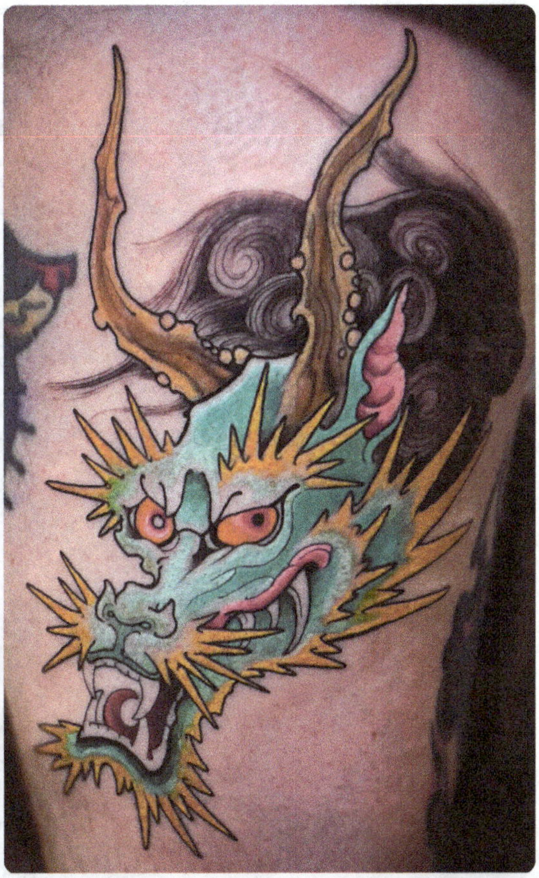

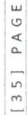

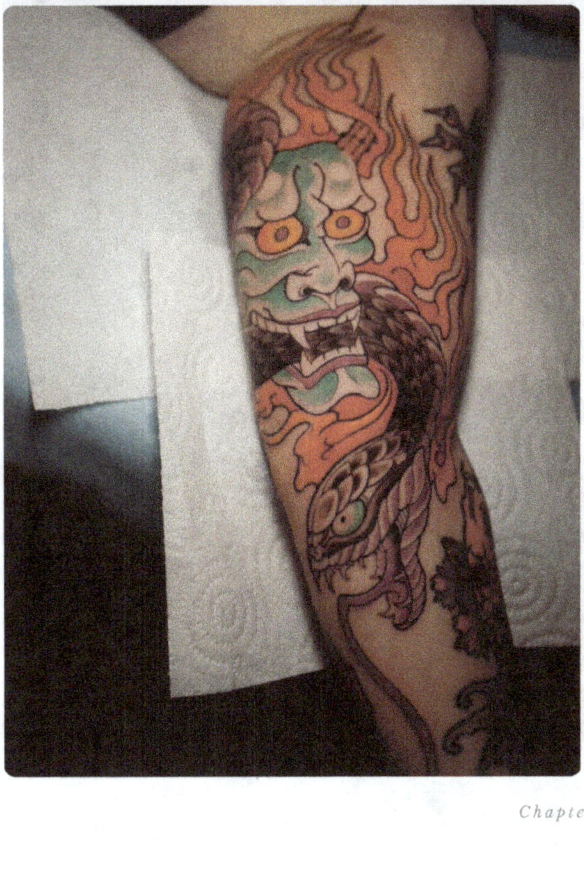

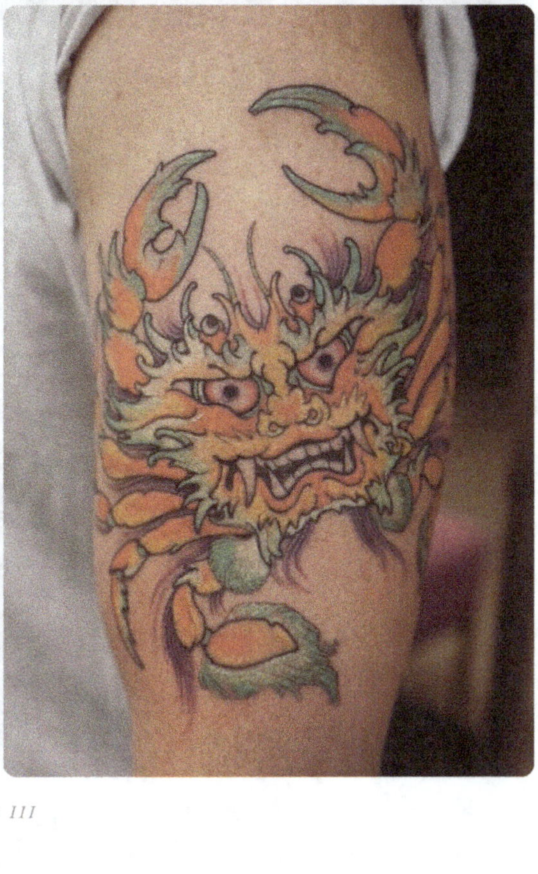

Chapter III

Global Tattoo Magazine

ANGELA FLORIS

BLACK APPLE TATTOO STUDIO | @ANGELA.FLORIS.TATTOO | ITALY, SINISCOLA

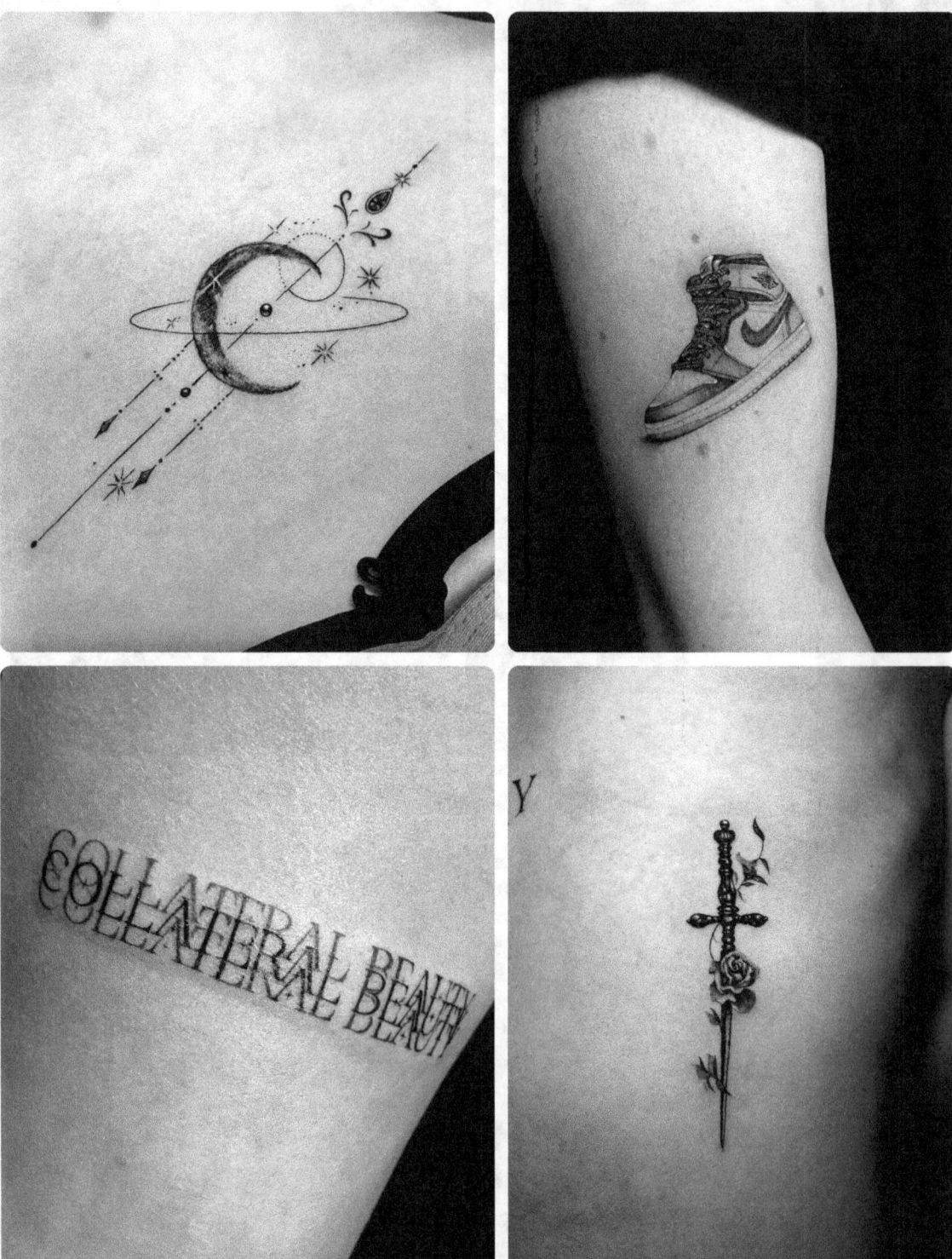

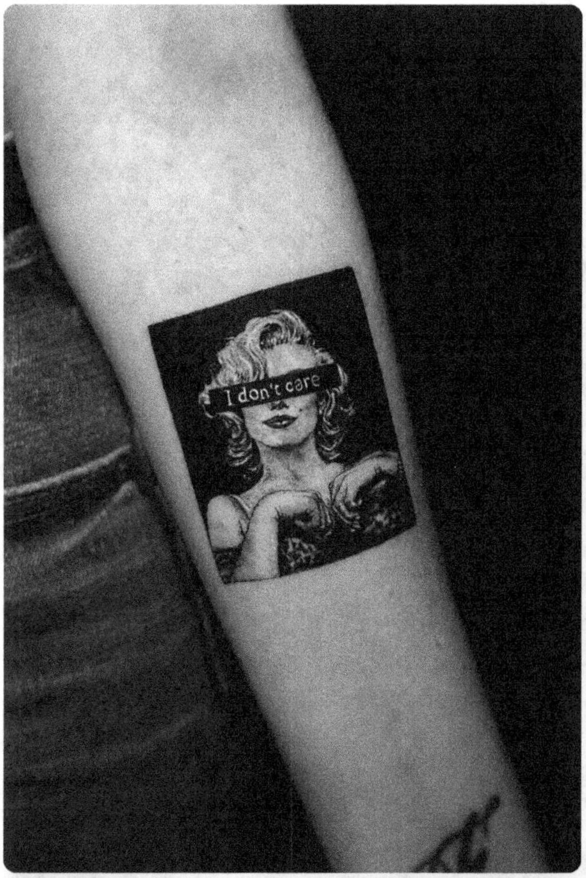

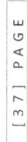

Chapter III

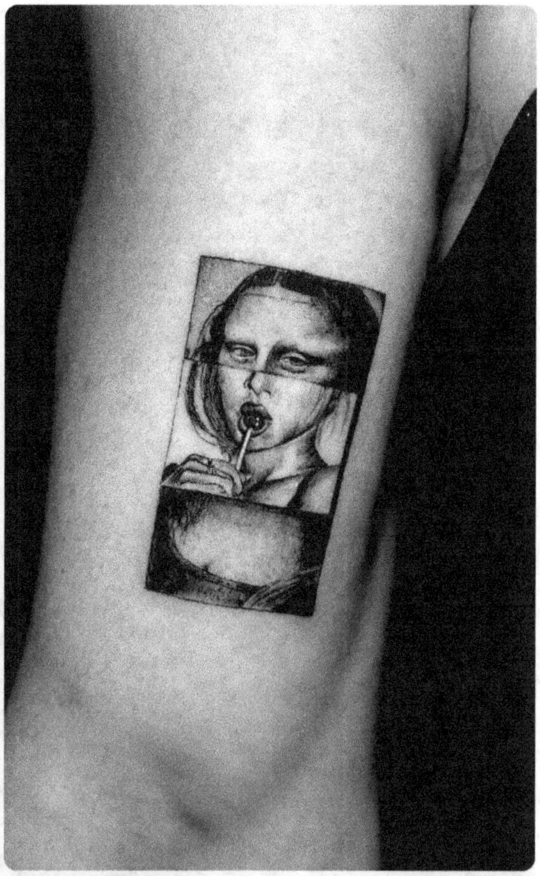

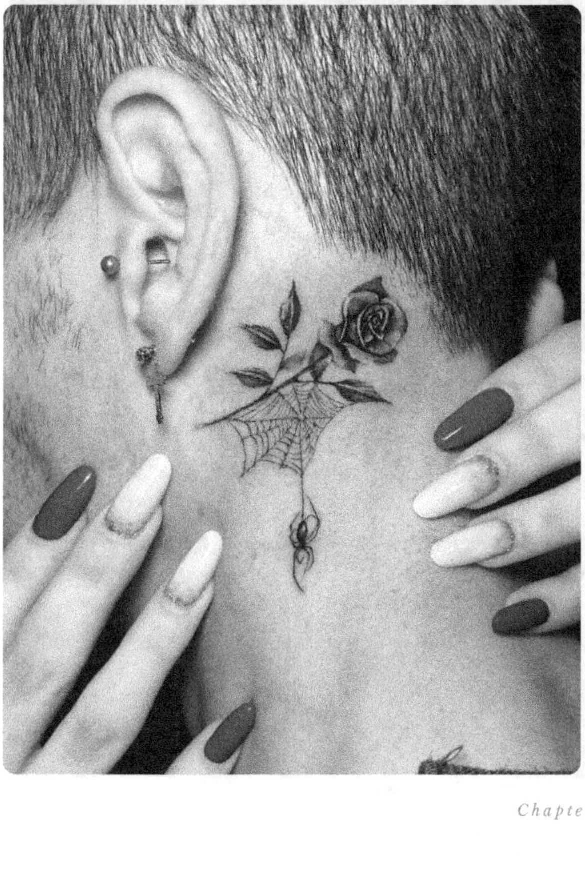

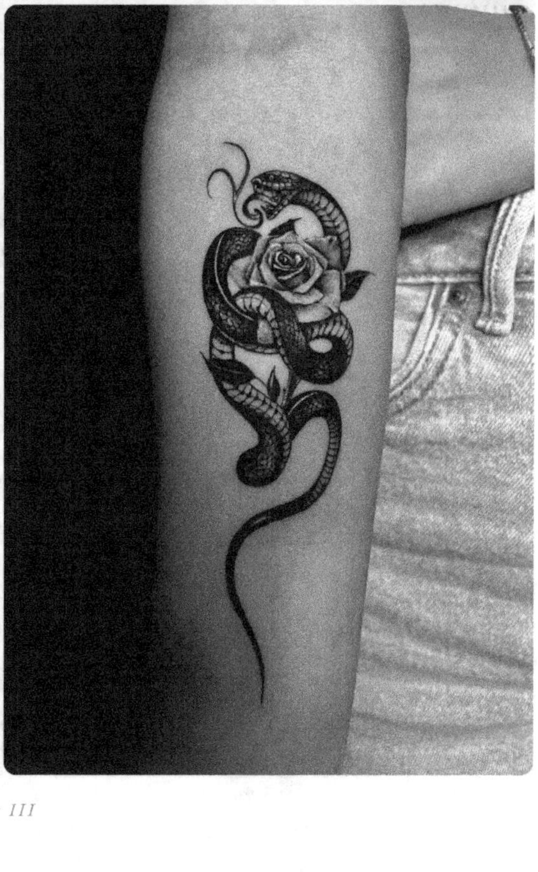

BECCA POTTER

FB: BECCA POTTER TATTOO | @BECCAPOTTERTATTOO | UK, NESTON

[38] PAGE

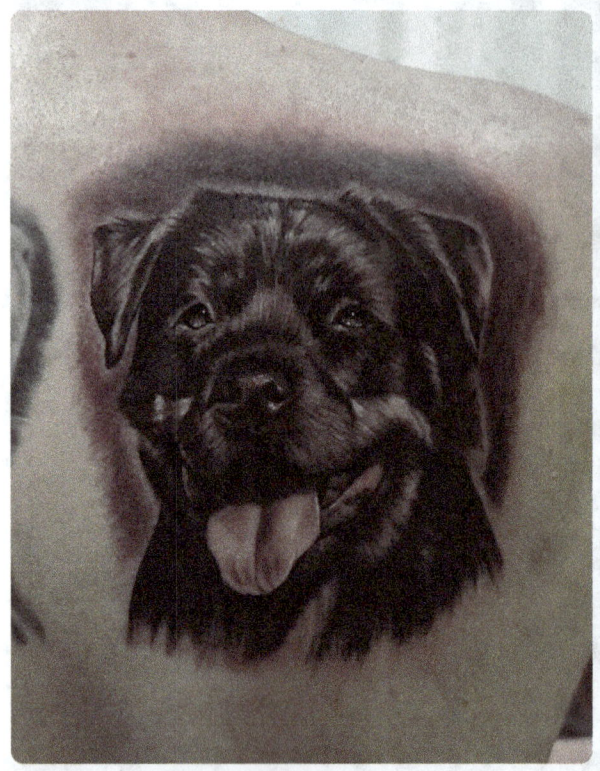
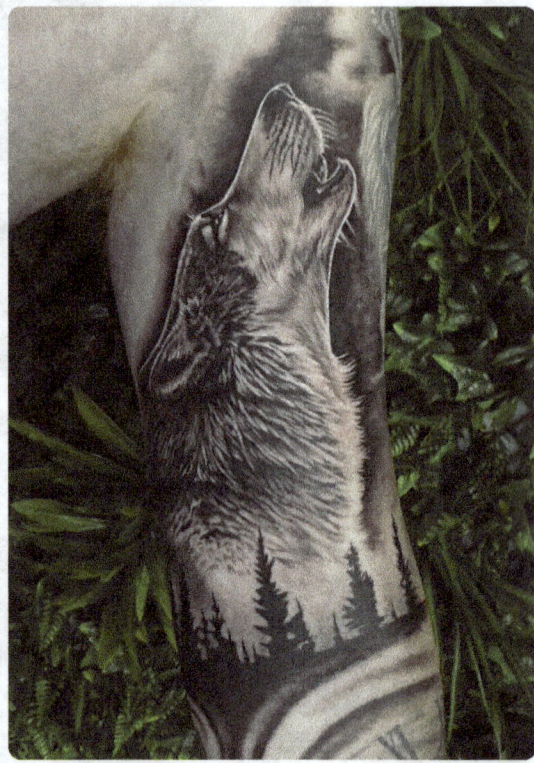
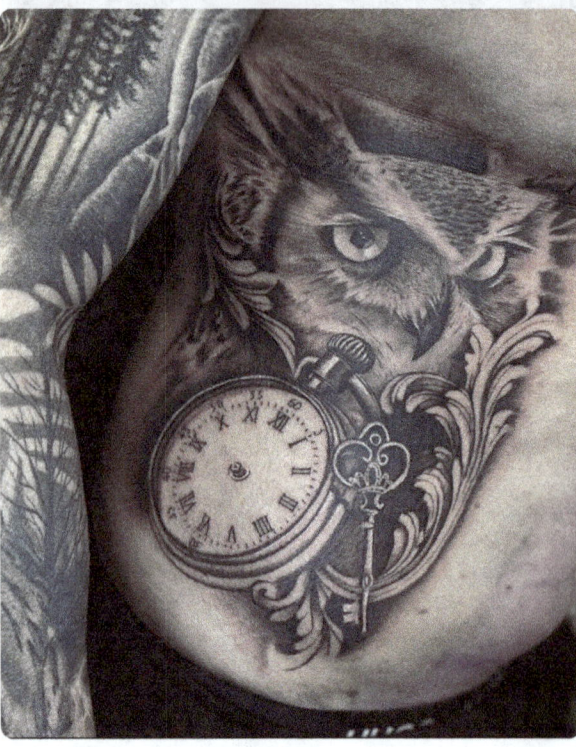
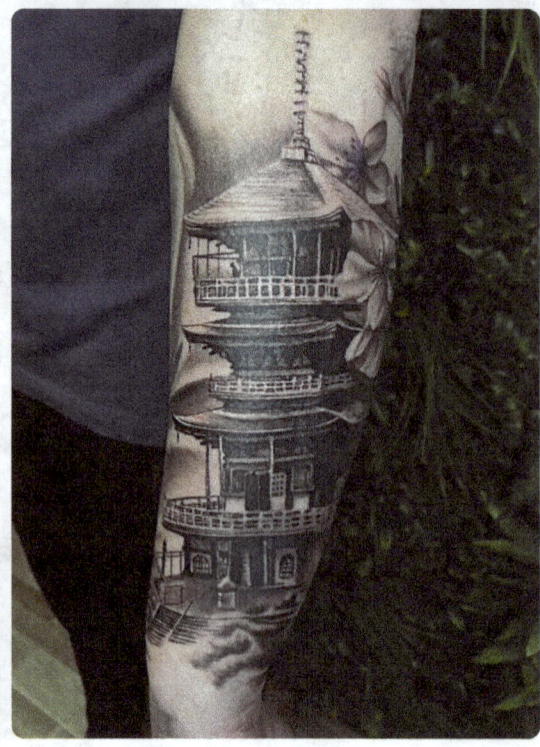

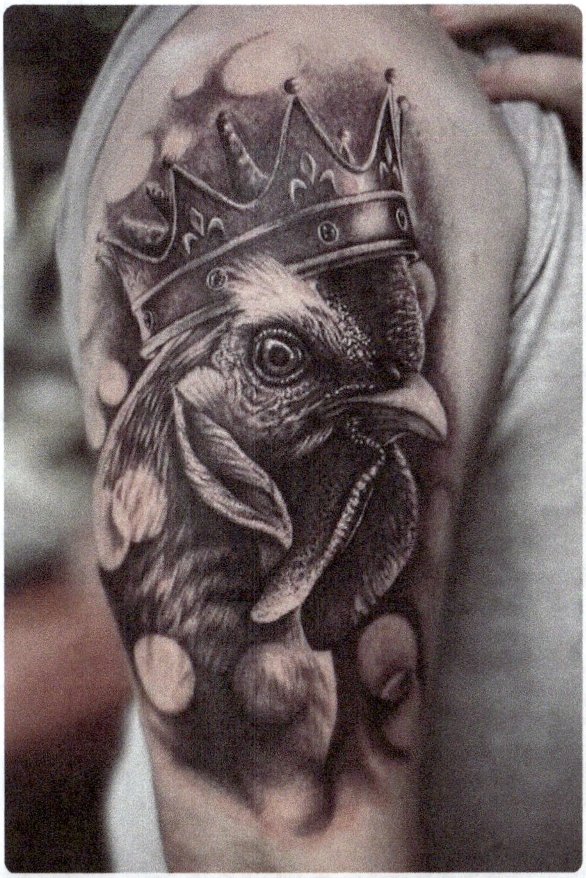

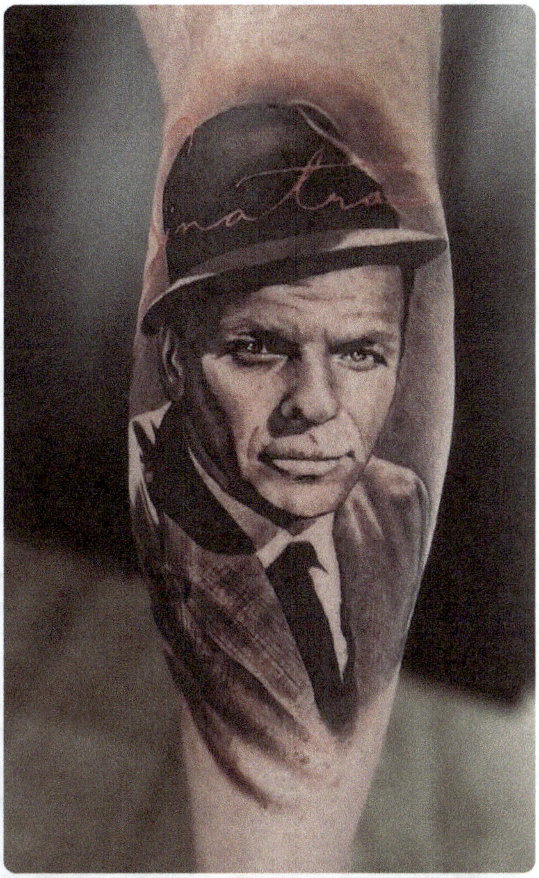

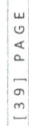

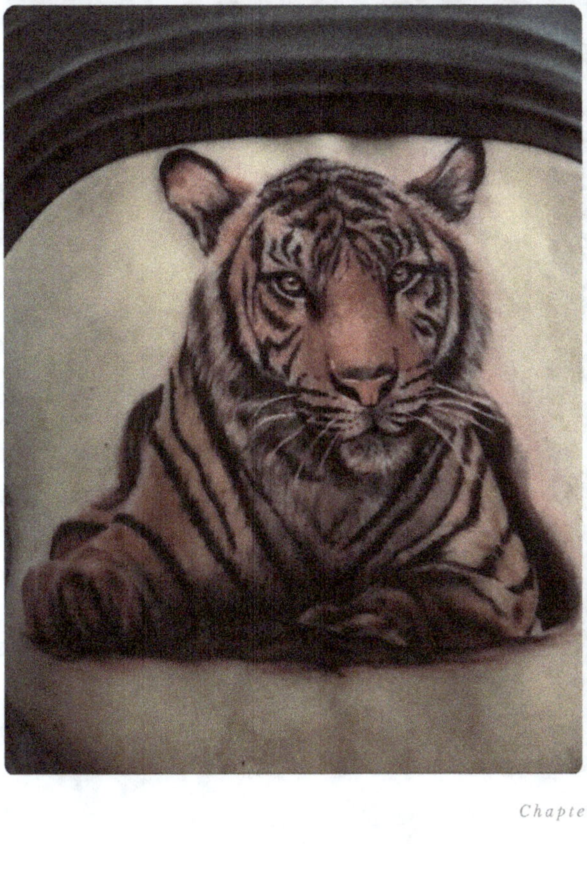

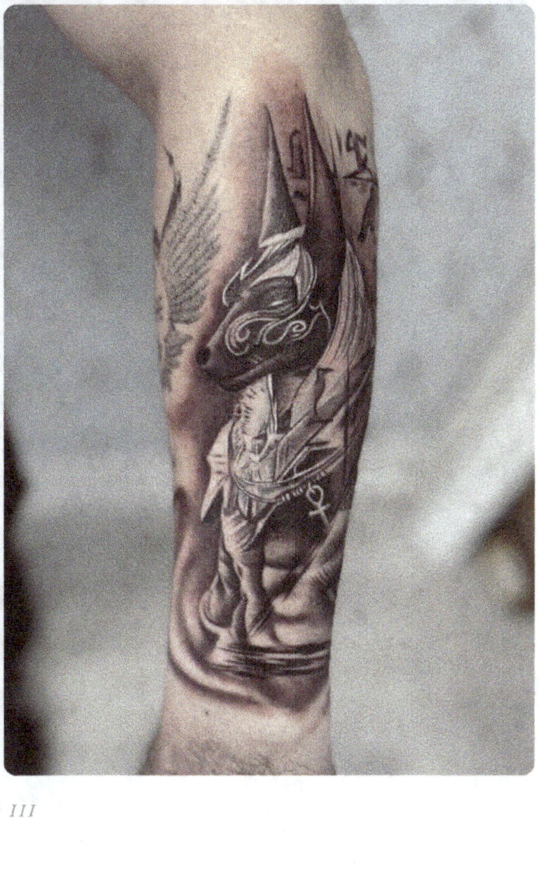

Chapter III

BIGG MEST

FREAK SHOW | FB: FREAK SHOW METZ | @BIGG_MEST | FRANCE, METZ

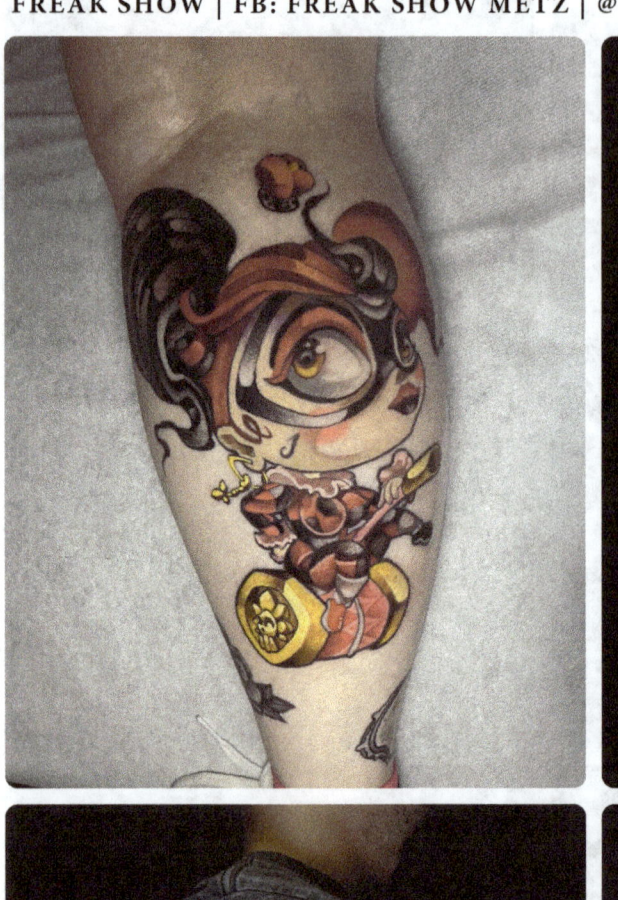
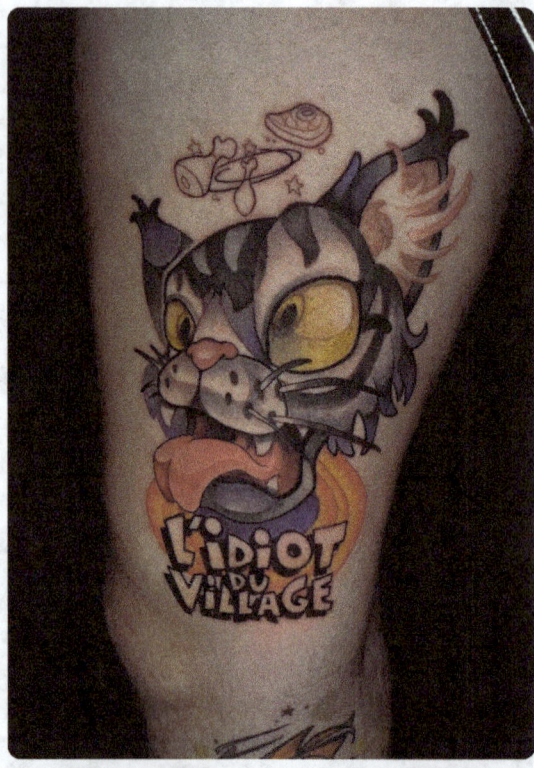
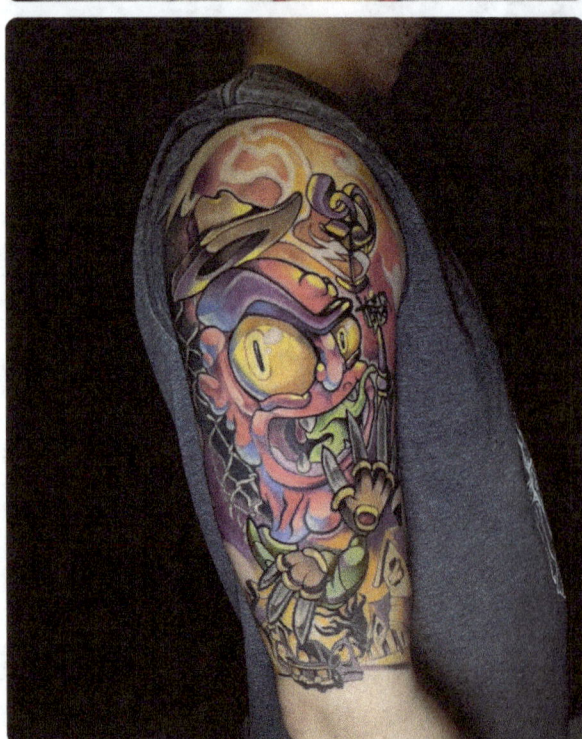
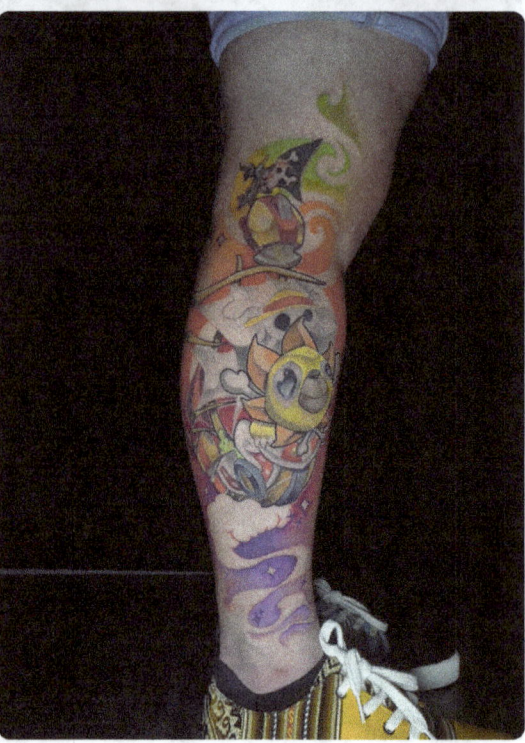

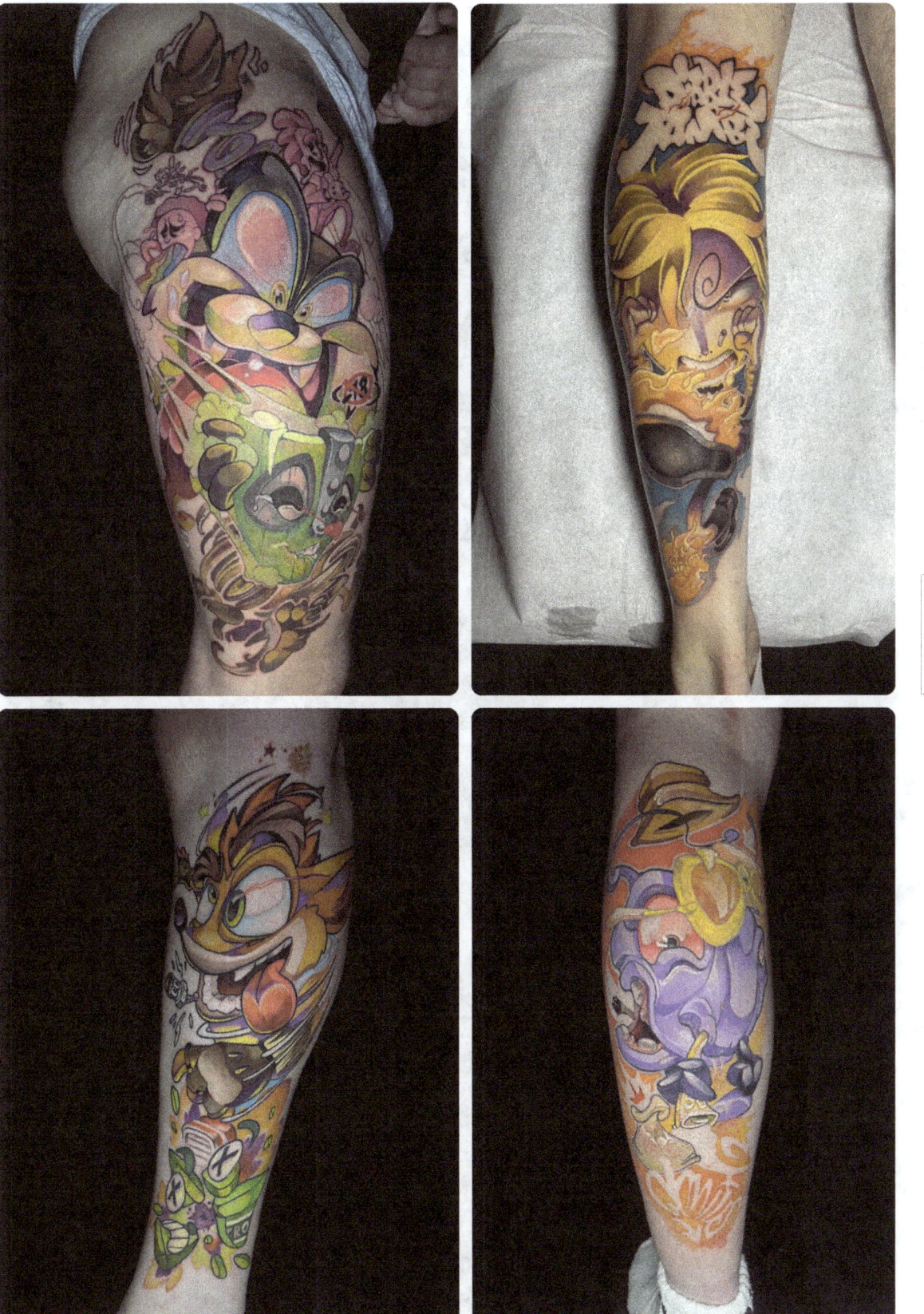

Chapter III

Global Tattoo Magazine

BOYD MACHELESSEN

TATTOOJOEY | @TATTOOJOEY_BOYD | NETHERLANDS, GELDROP

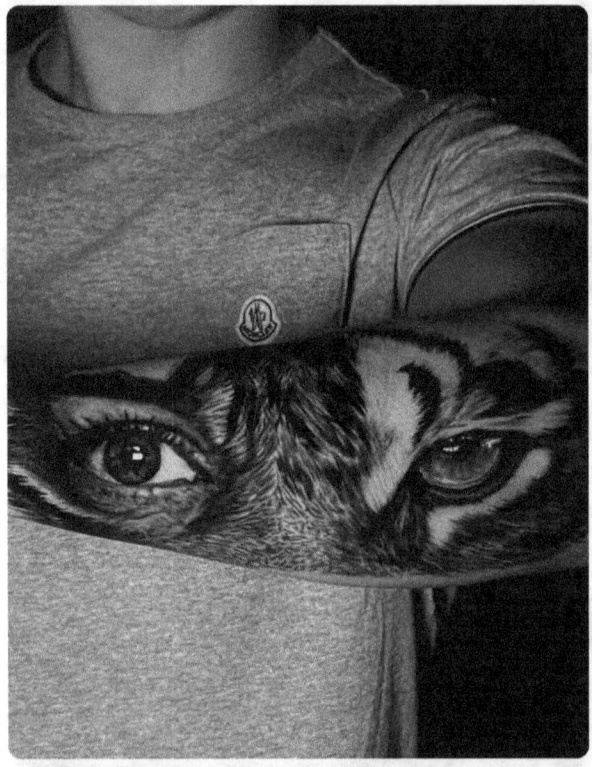

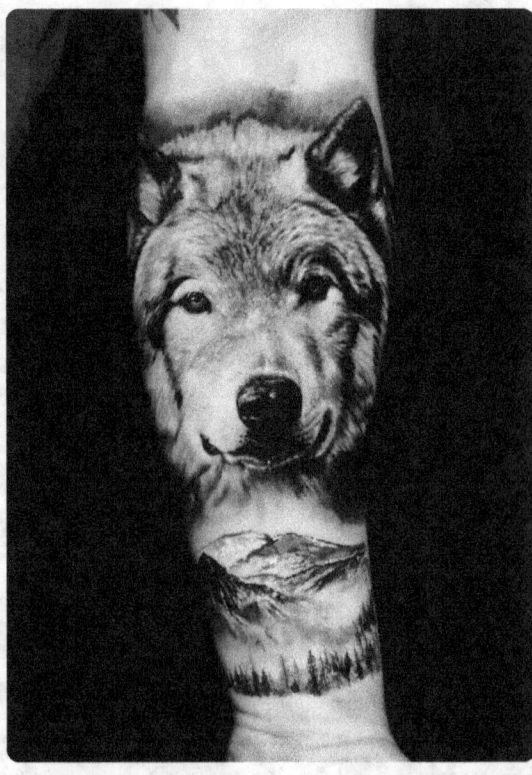

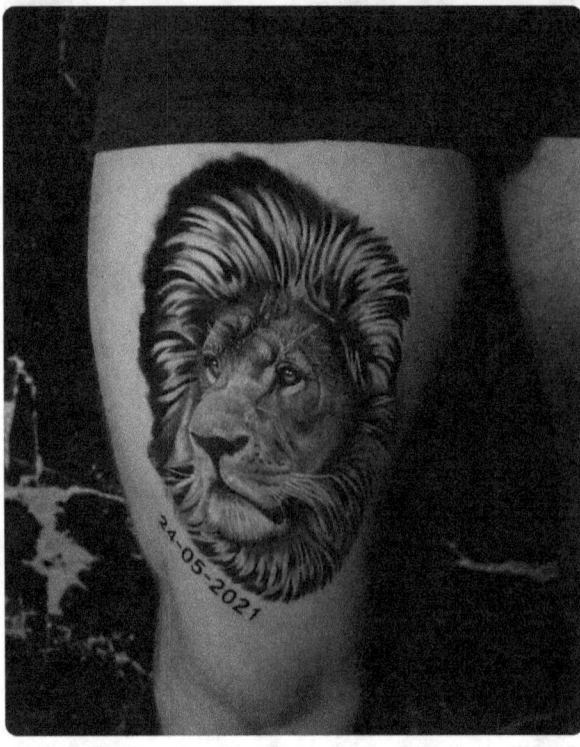

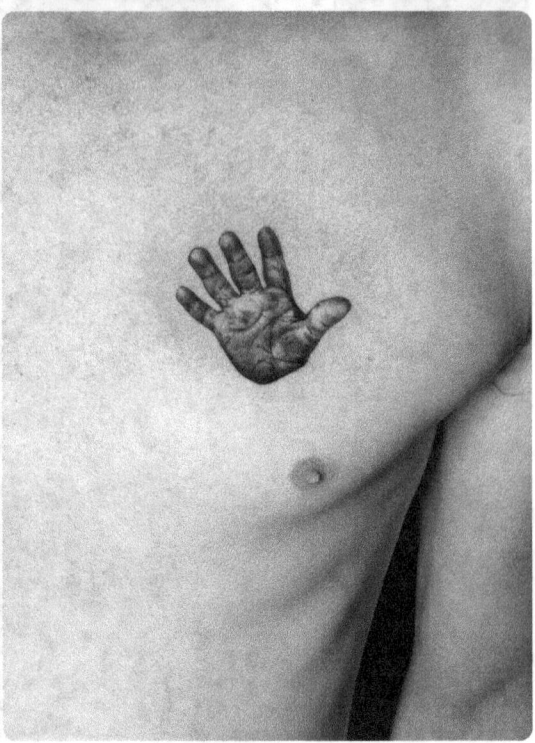

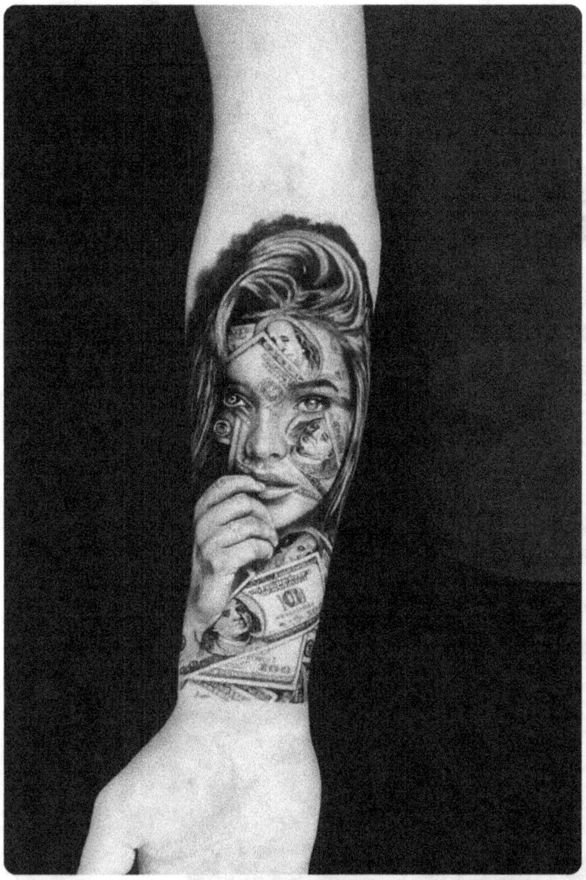

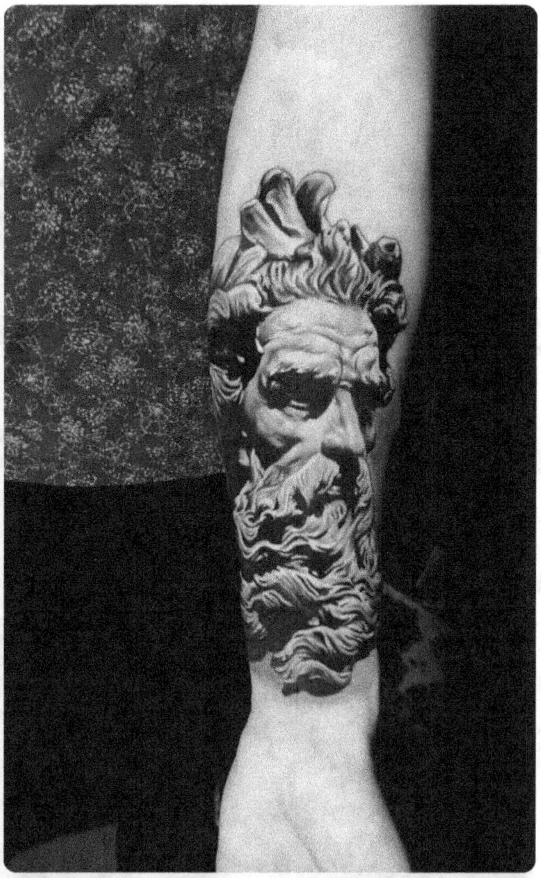

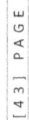

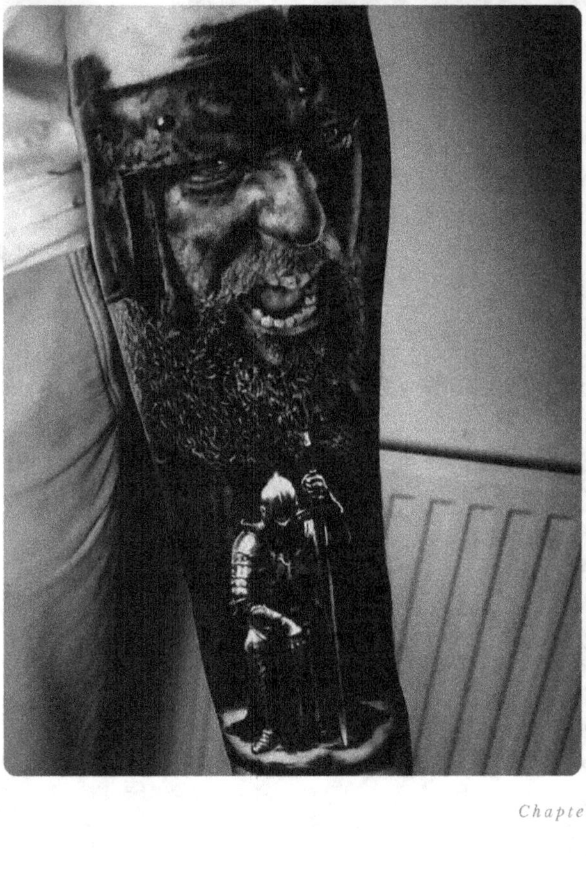

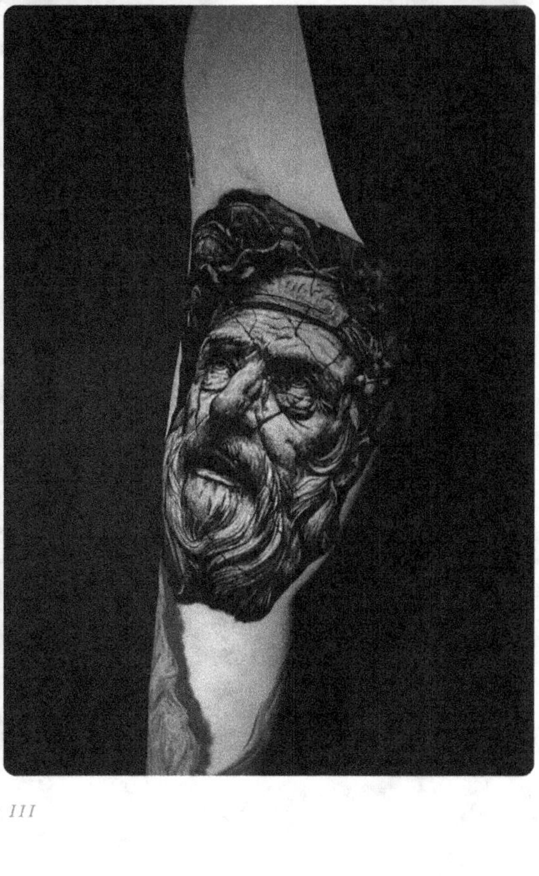

Chapter III

CHOLO SUPREME

SECRET LOTUS TATTOO | @CHOLO_SUPREMETATTOOS | USA, KENTUCKY

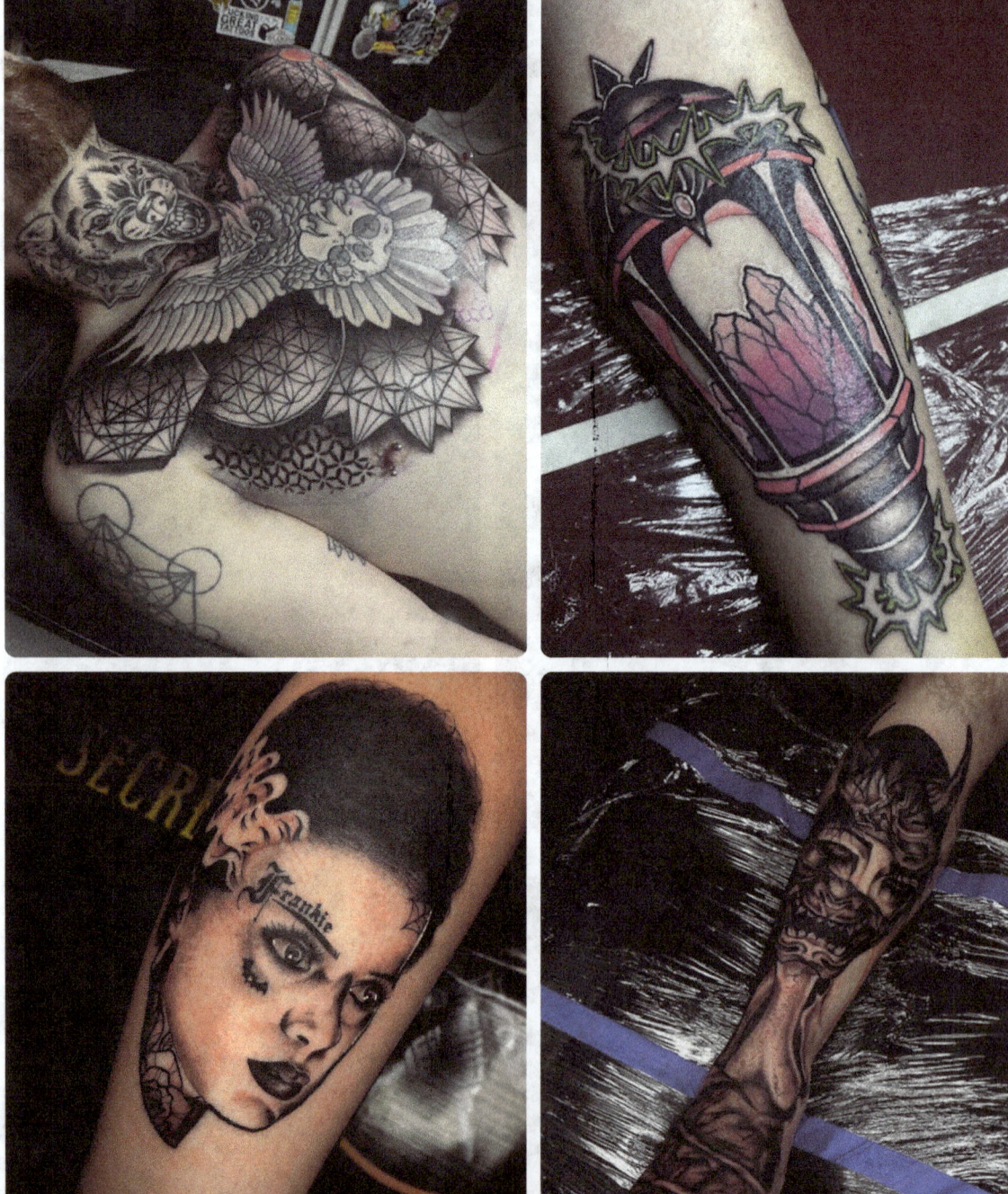

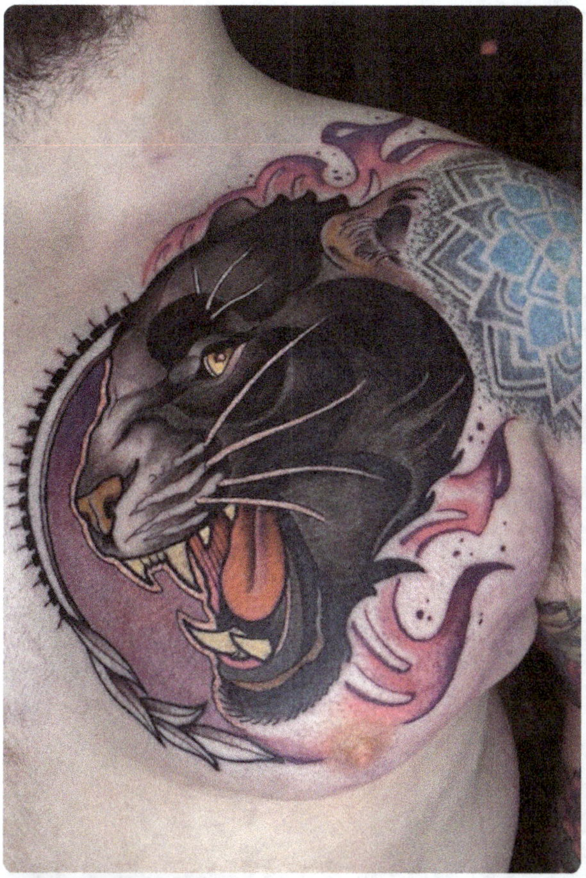

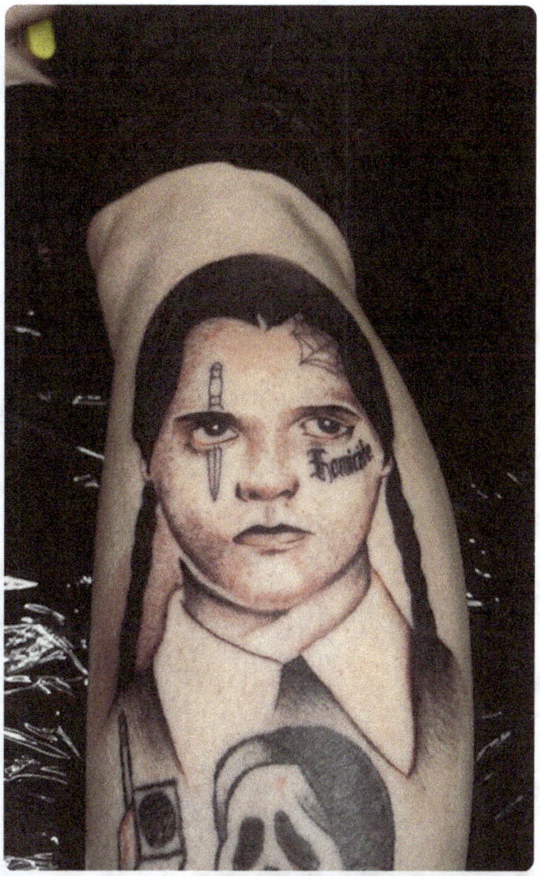

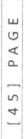

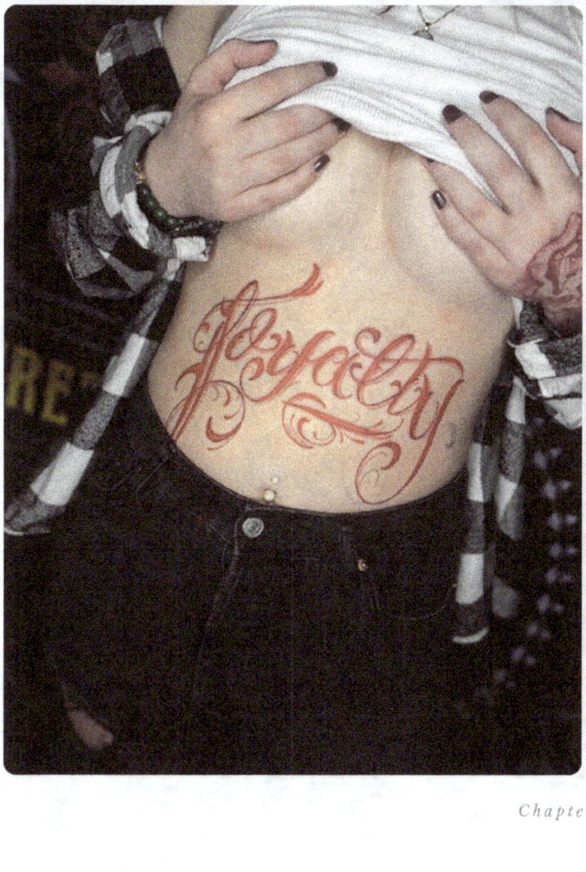

Chapter III

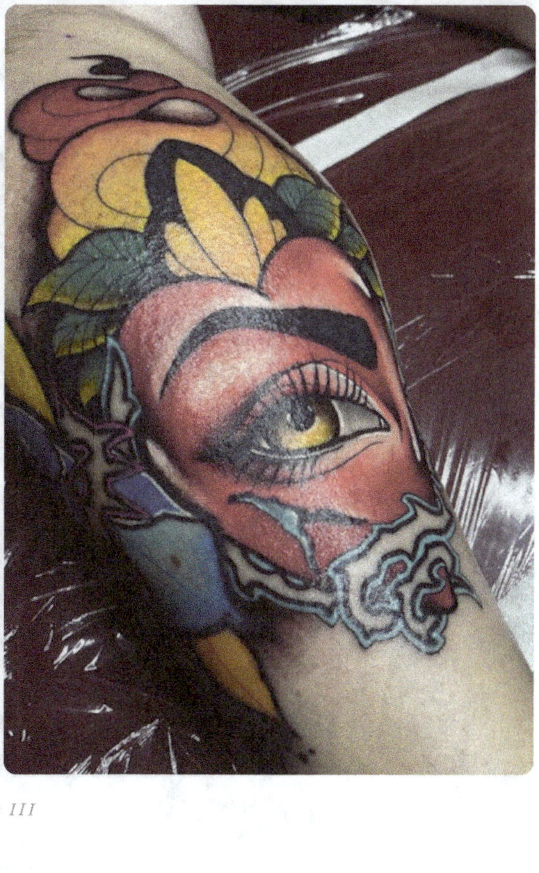

DAAN VERBRUGGEN

FB: @NAMAKUBITATTOO | @NAMAKUBITATTOO | BELGIUM, ANTWERP

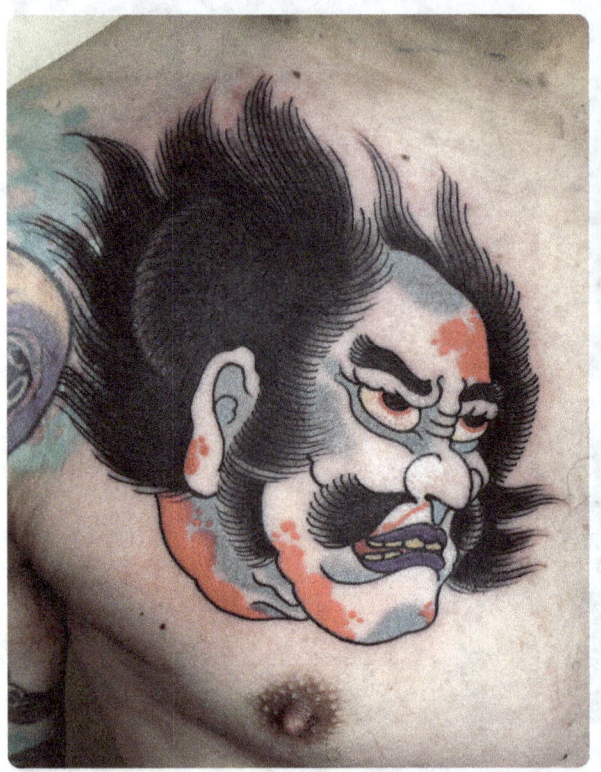
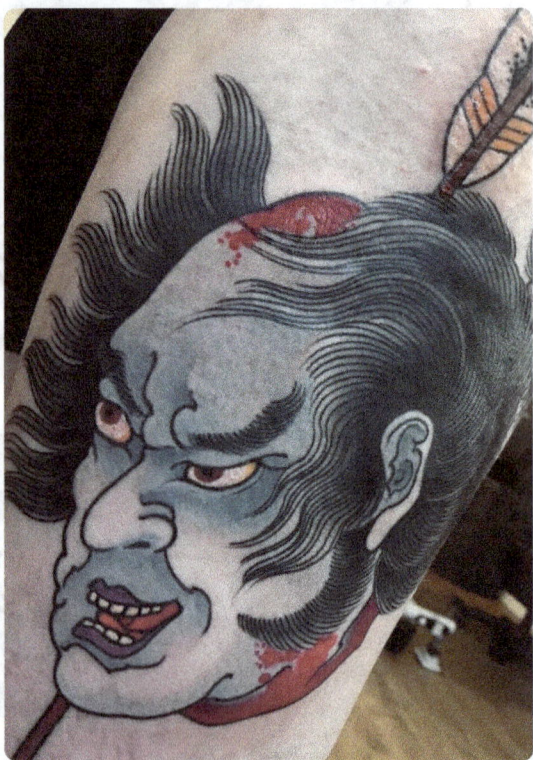
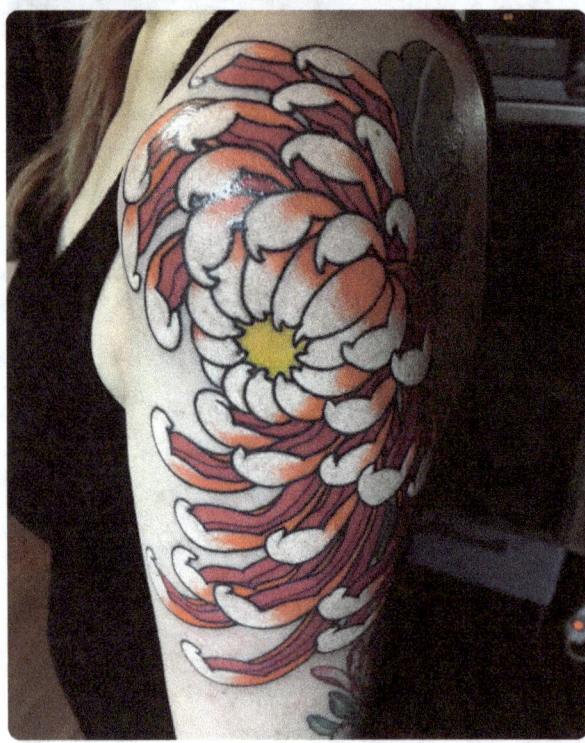
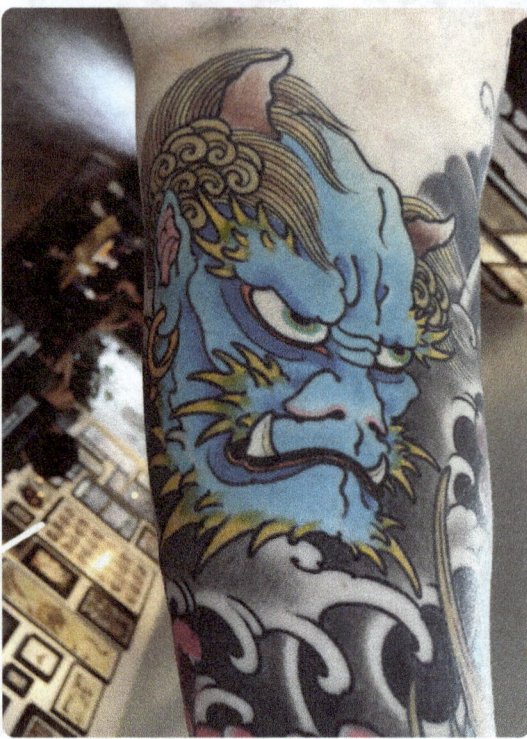

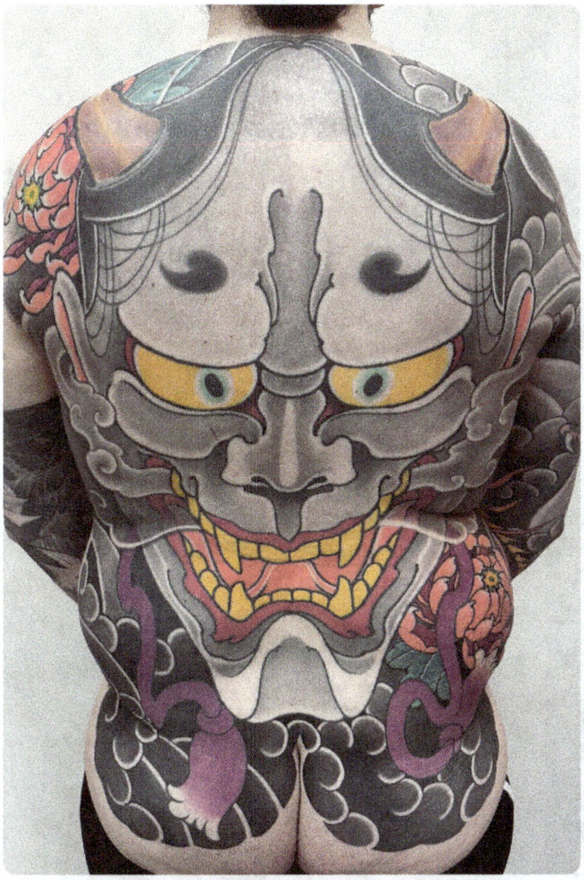

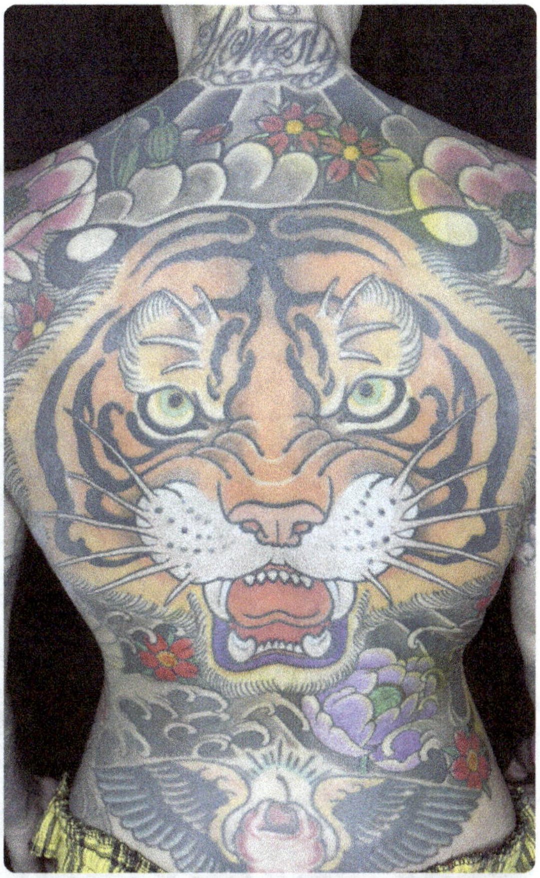

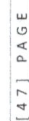

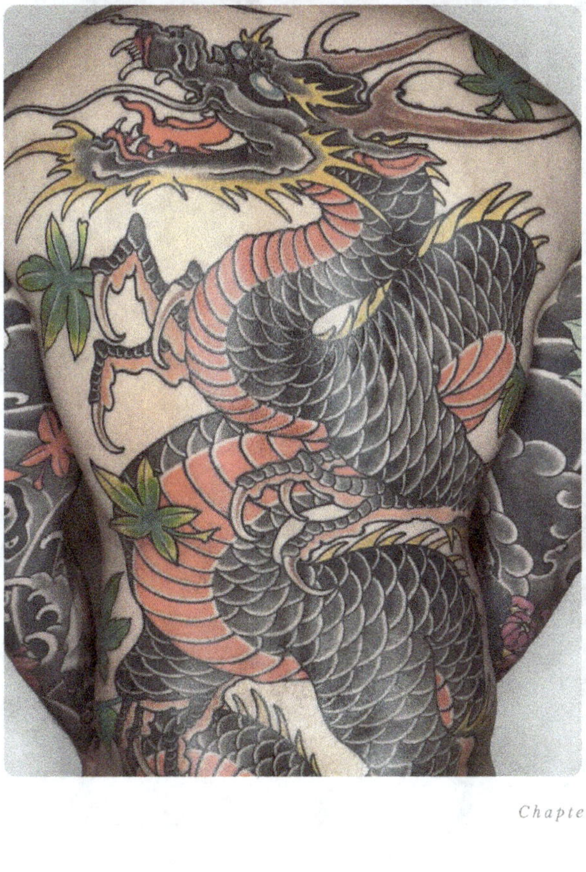

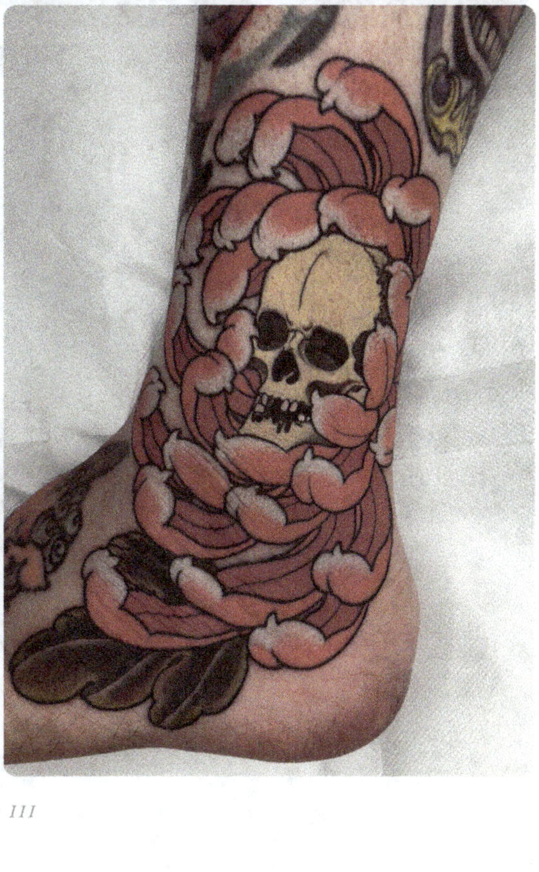

Chapter III

Global Tattoo Magazine

DANIEL HORVAT

INNSIDE INK | @INKED_REBELLX | FB: DAN DI HO | AUSTRIA, INNSBRUCK

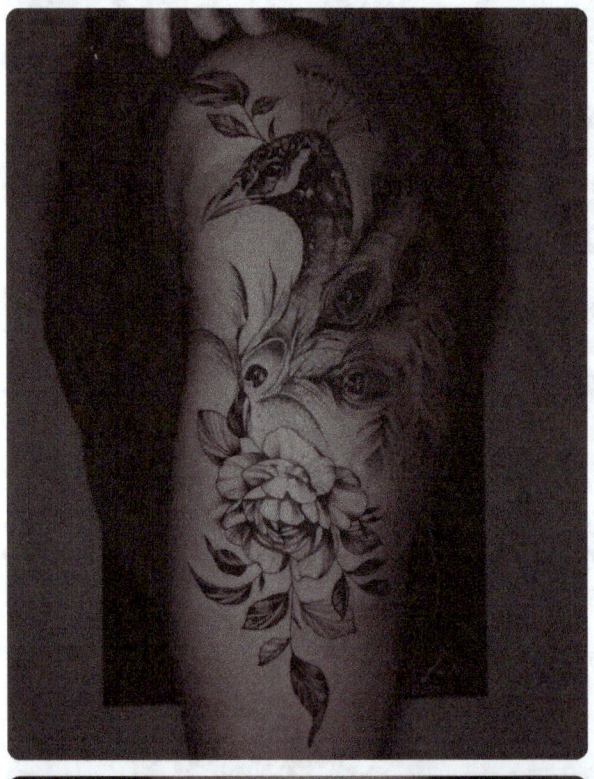
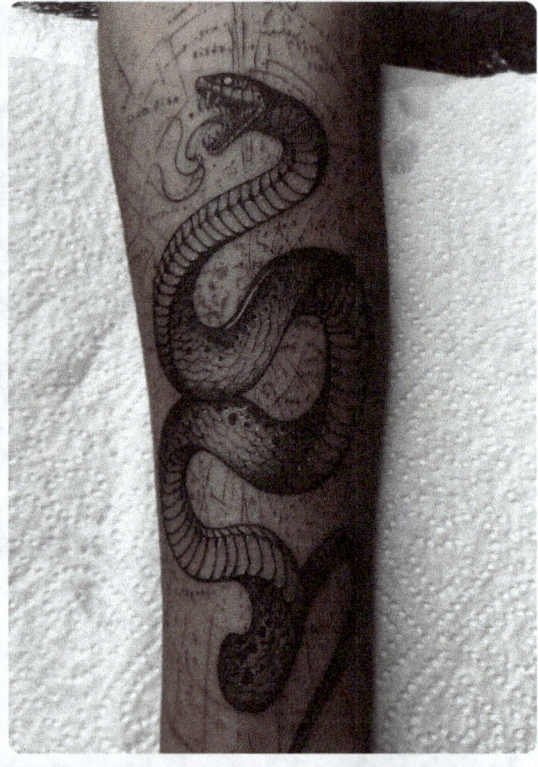
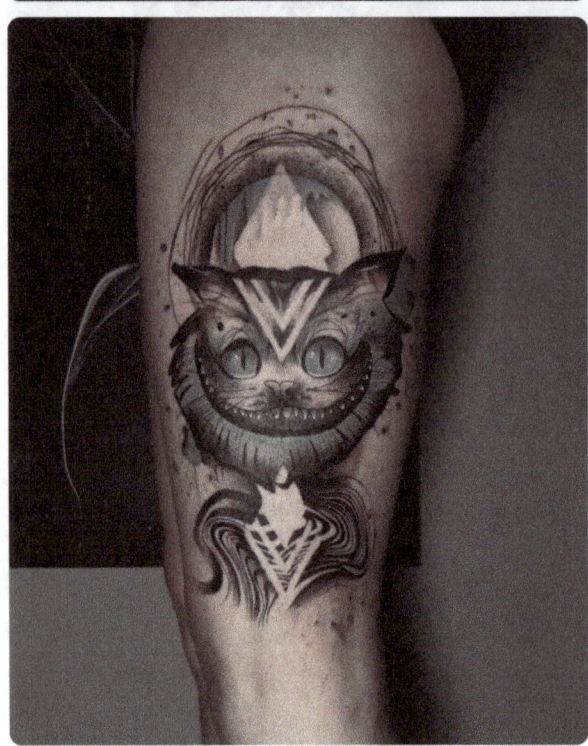
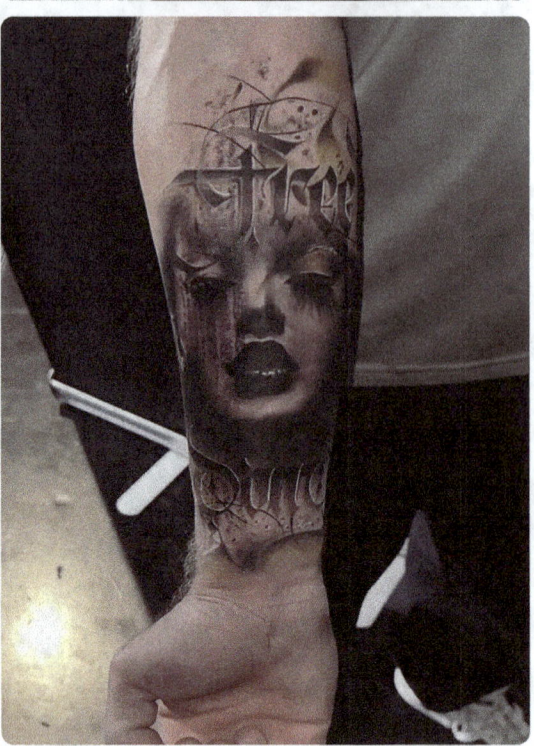

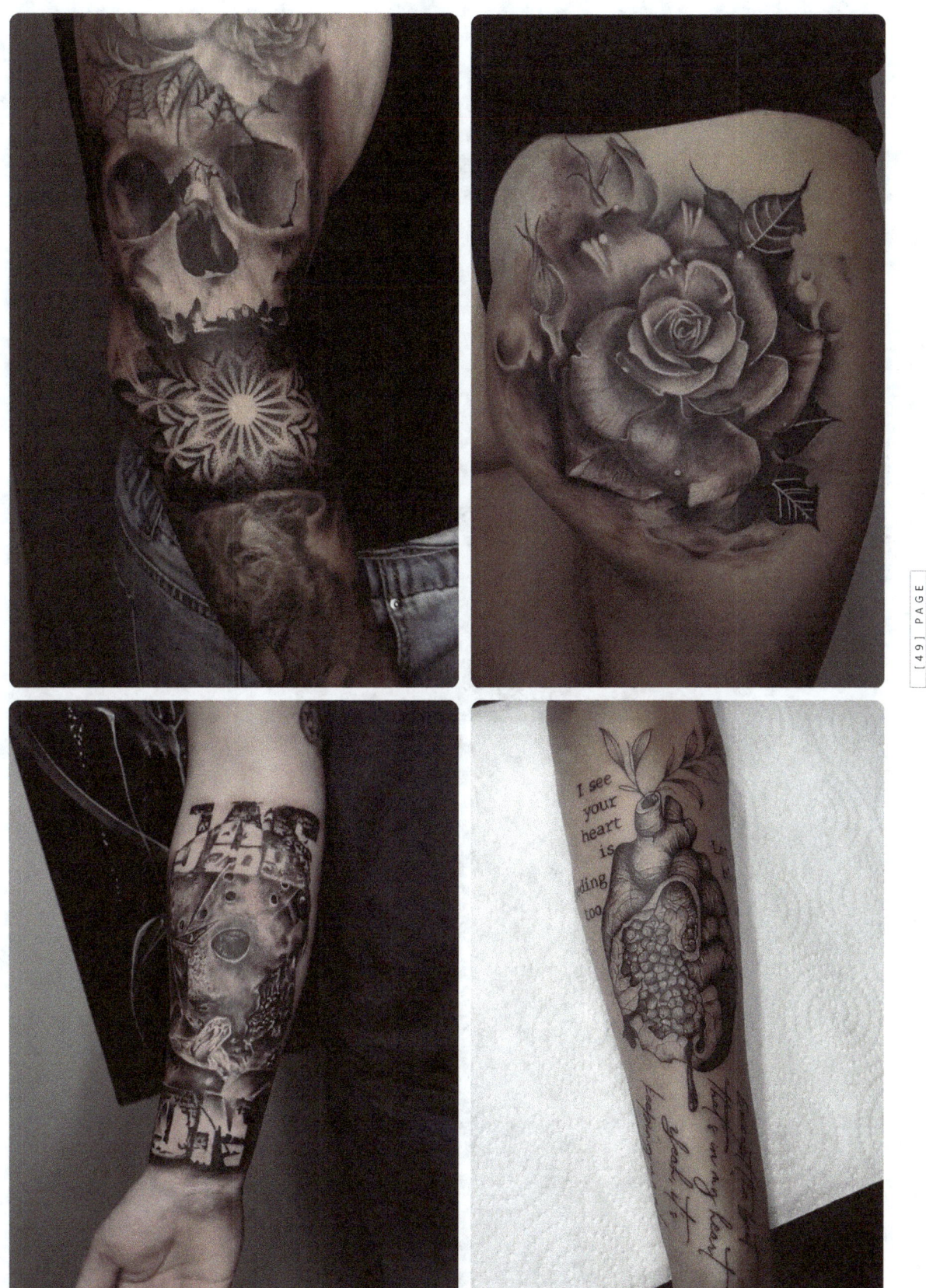

Chapter III

DAVID ZABOS

FB: DAVE ZED'S TATTOOS | @DAVEZEDTATTOO | UK, SHEFFIELD

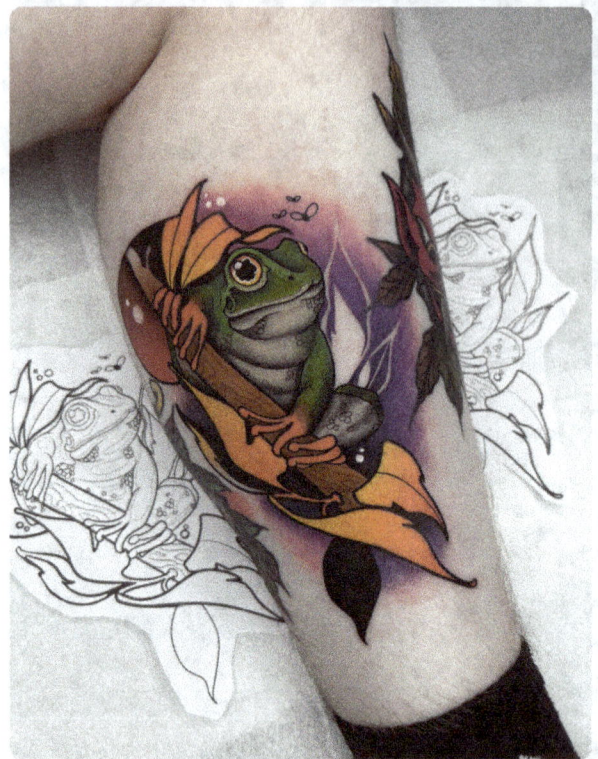
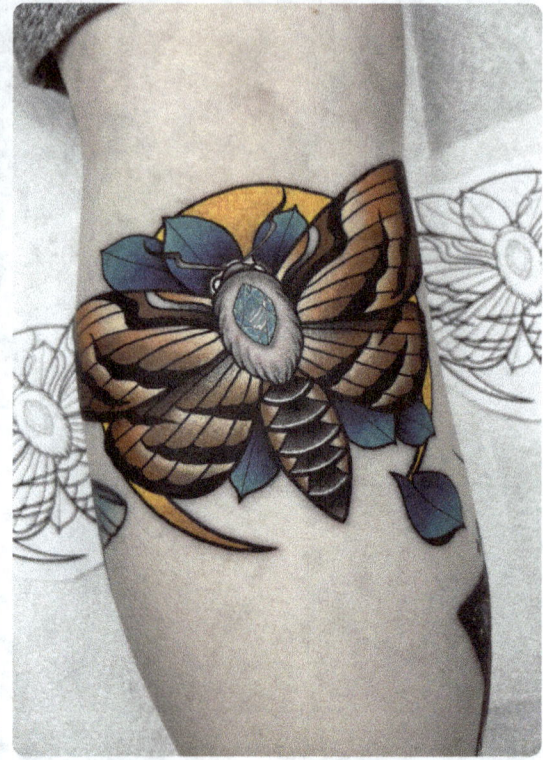
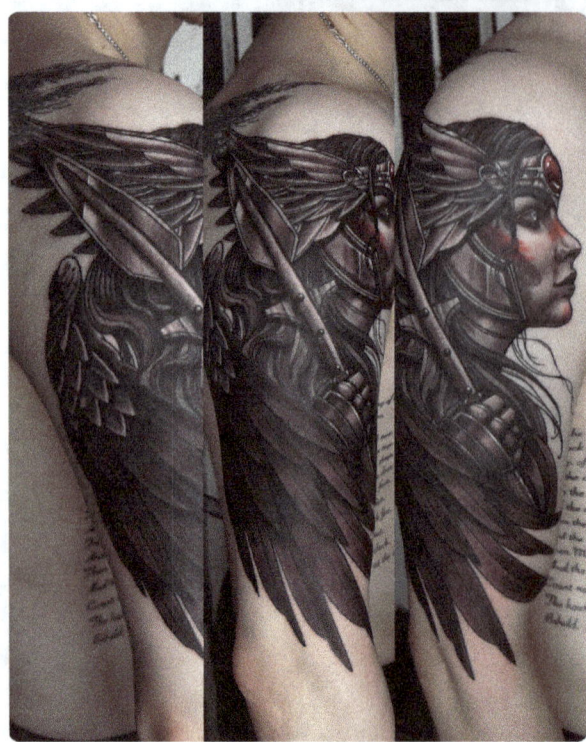
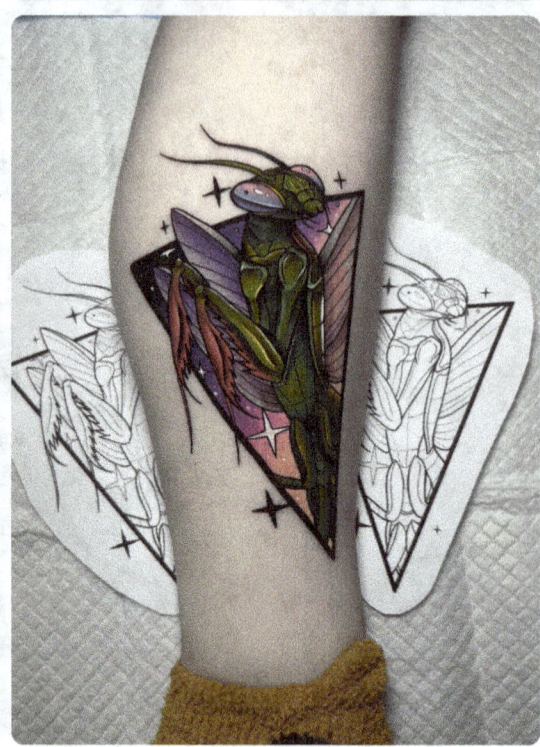

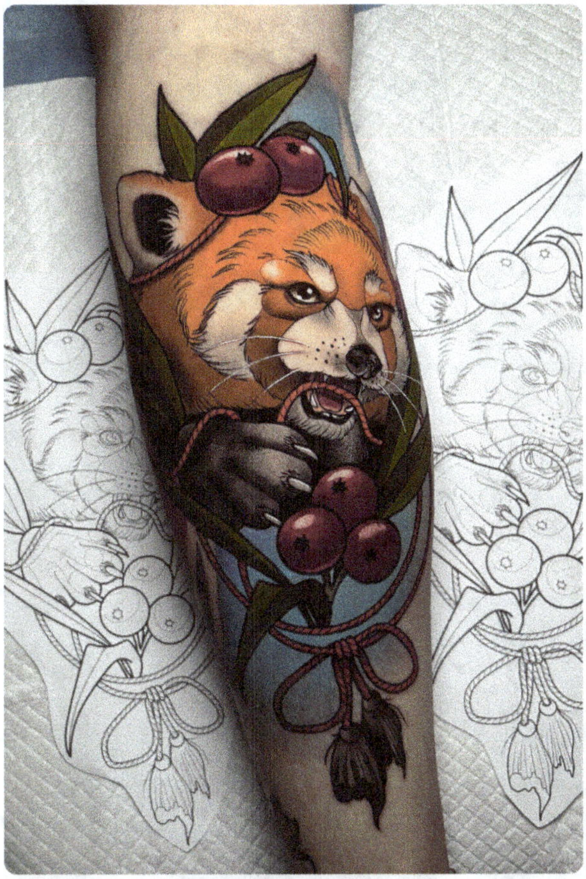

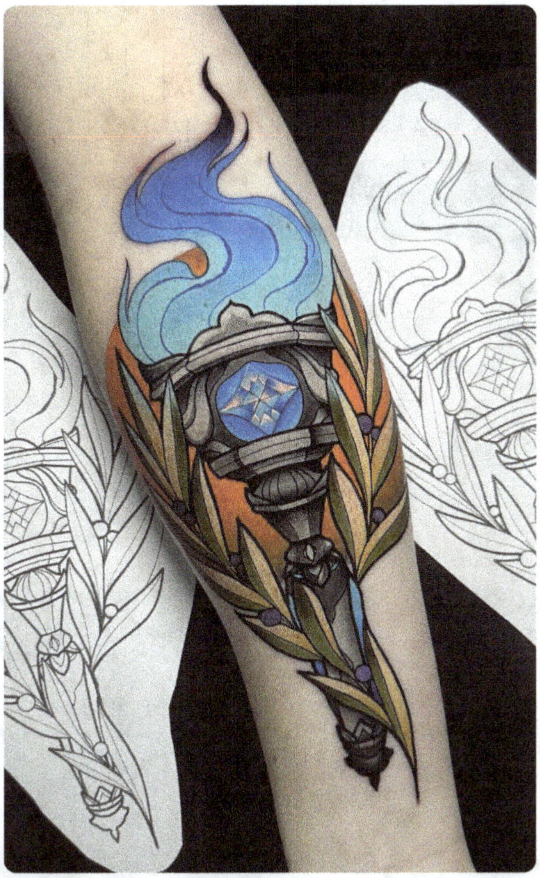

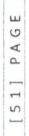

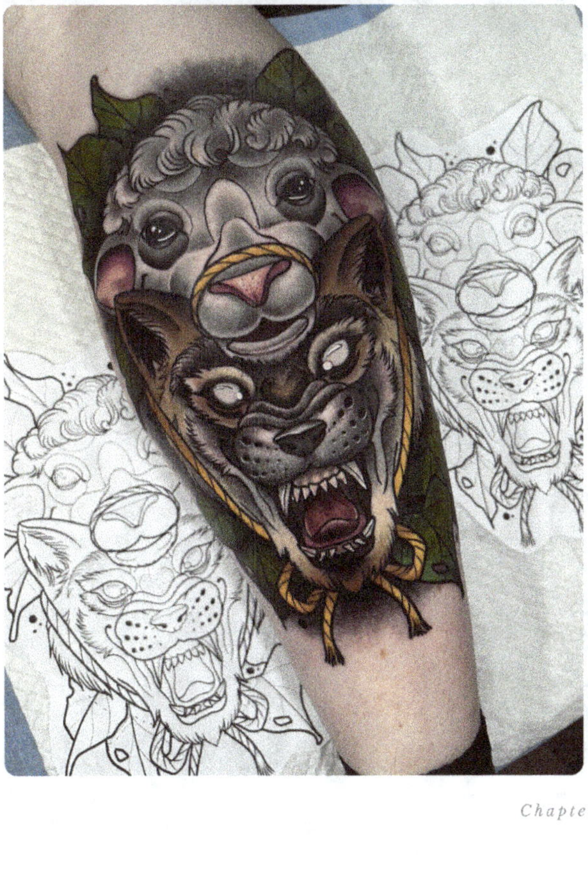

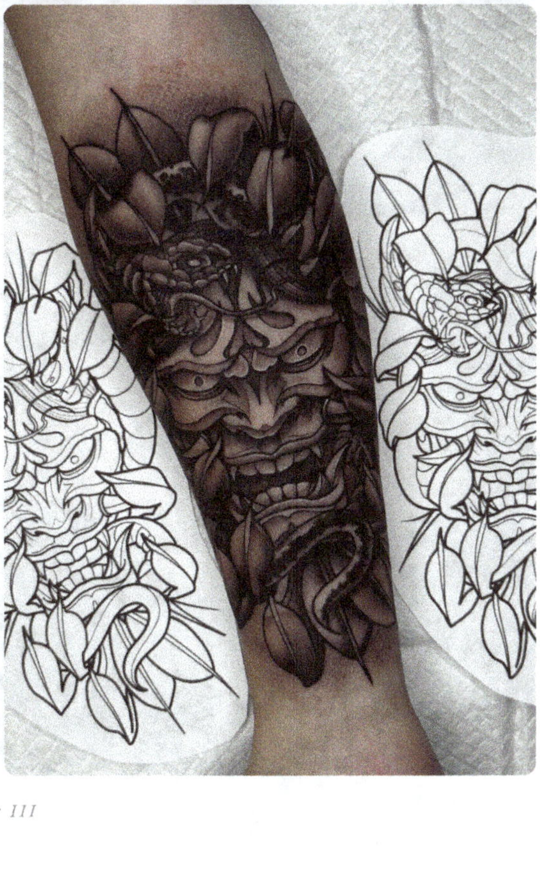

Global Tattoo Magazine

DELPHIN MUSQUET

SANS PATRIE / STUDIO | @DELPHINMUSQUET | UK, LONDON

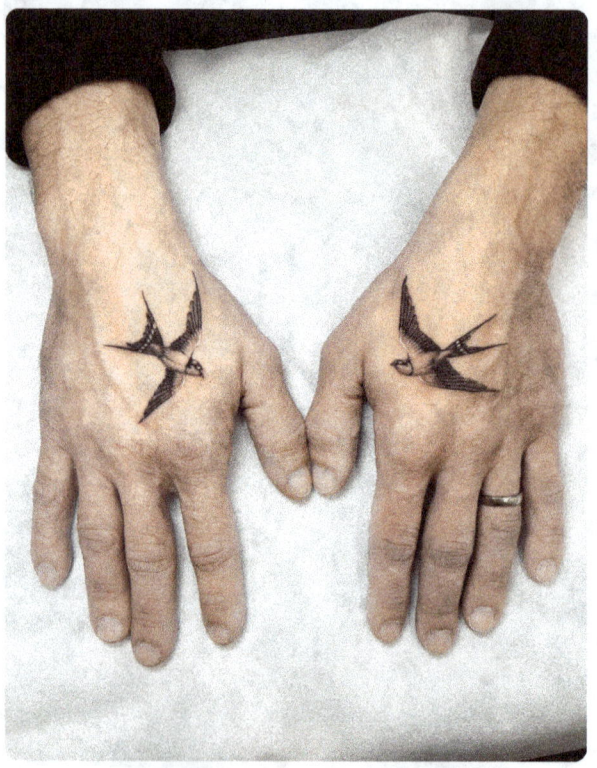

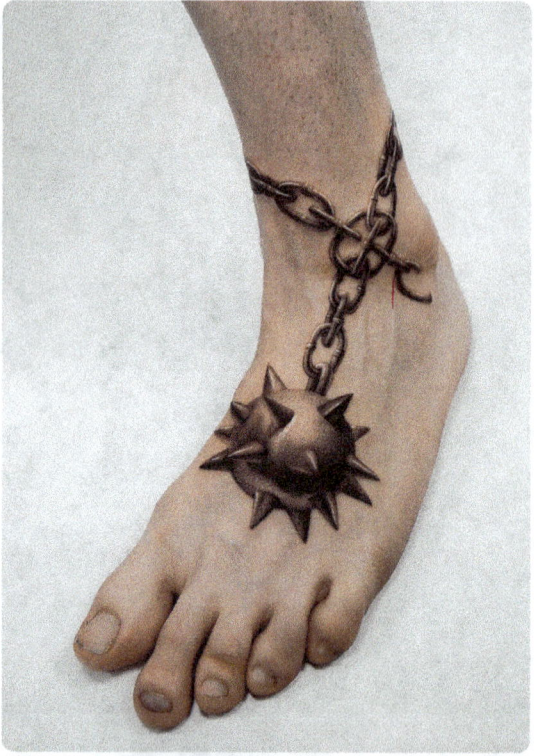

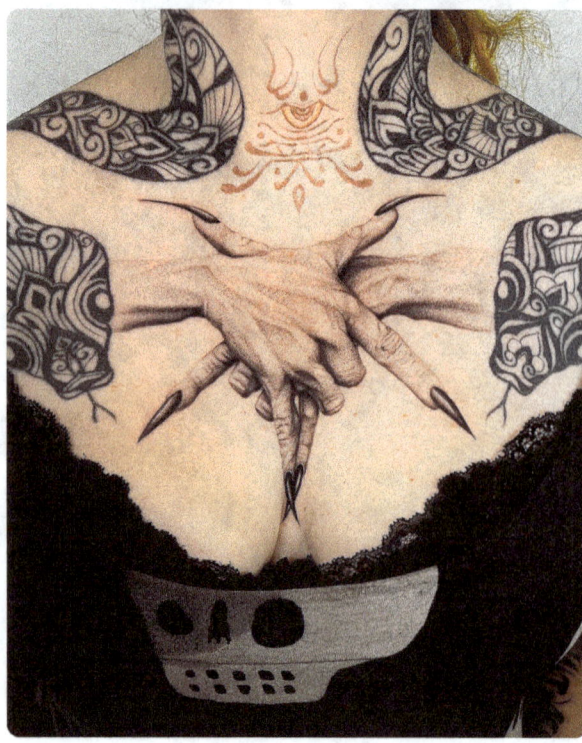

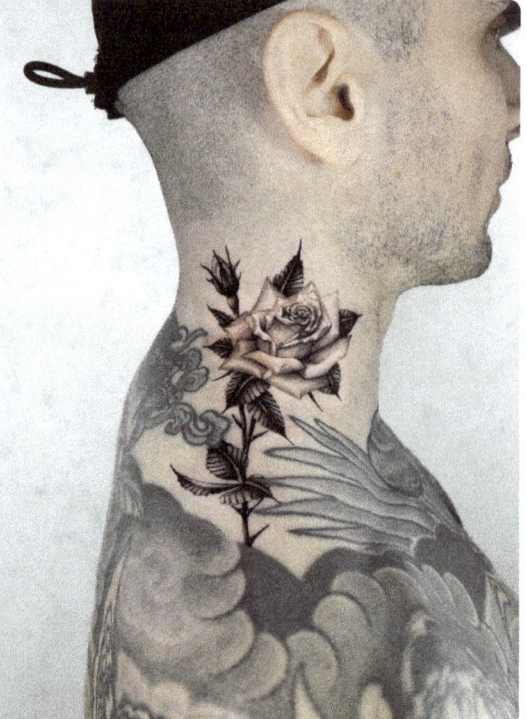

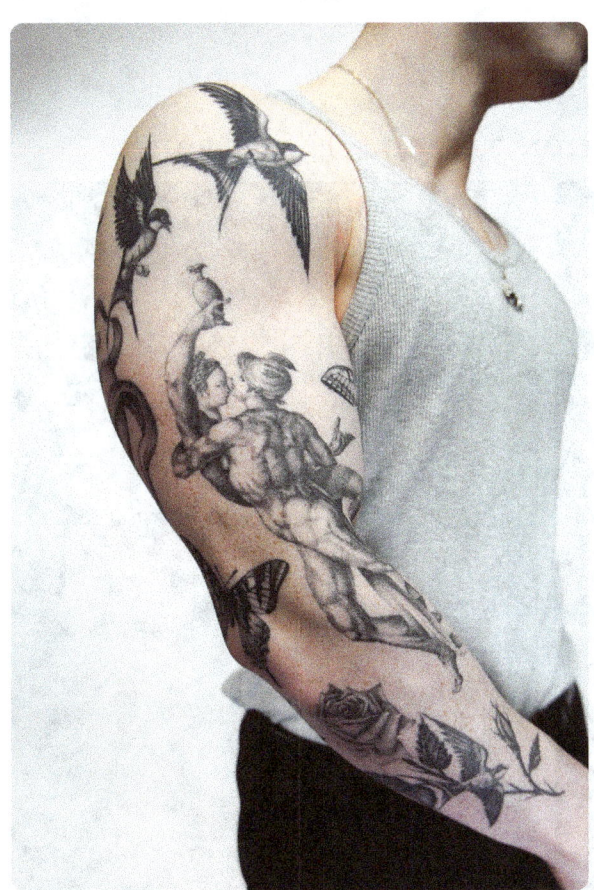

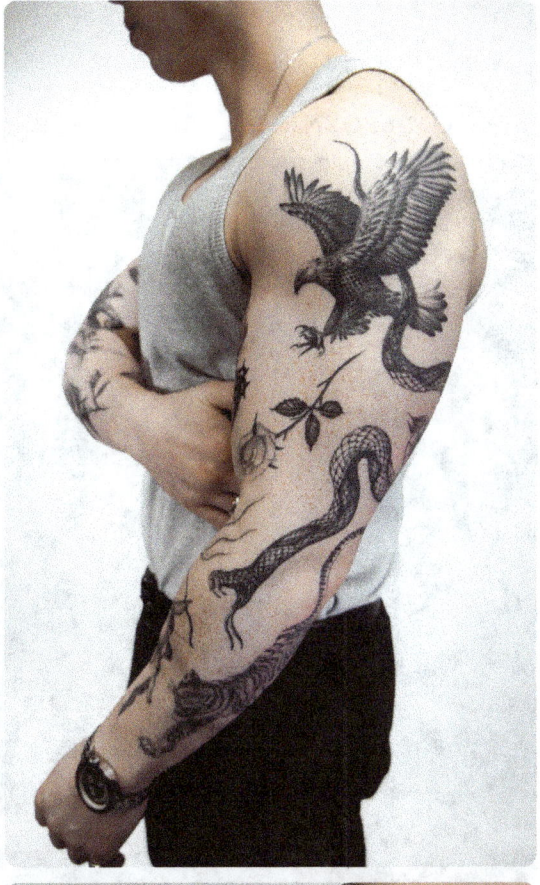

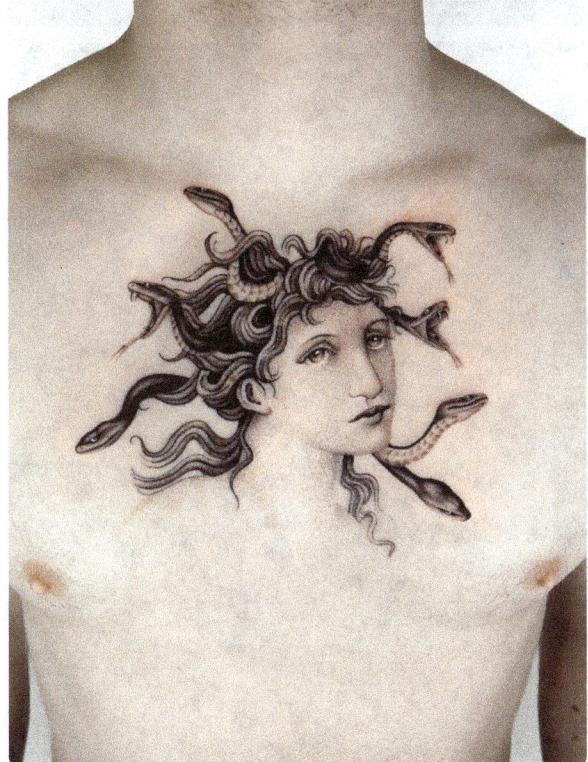

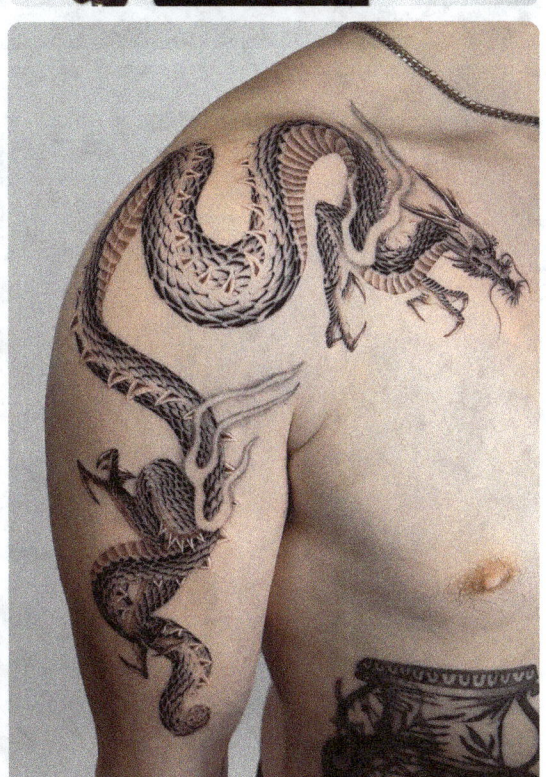

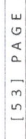

Chapter III

DOM

FB: DOM LEGENDRE | @DOM_LA_STATION_TATTOO | FRANCE, ROISEL

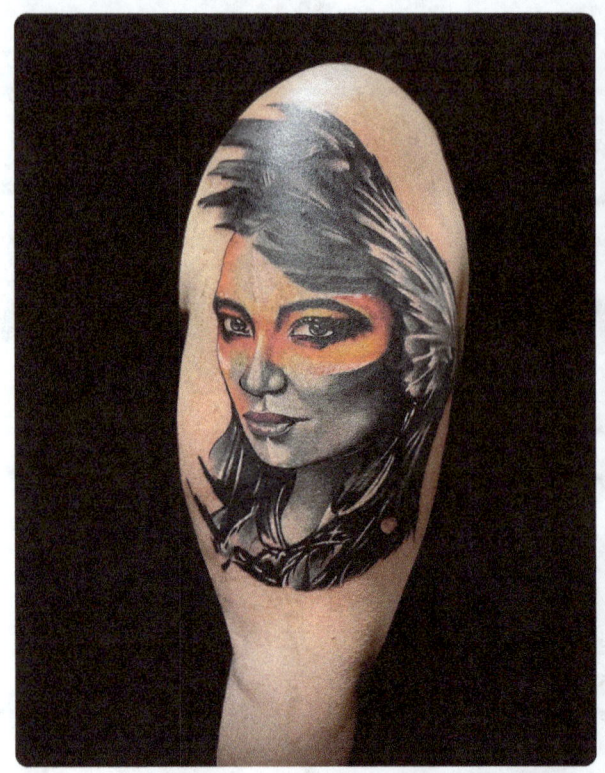
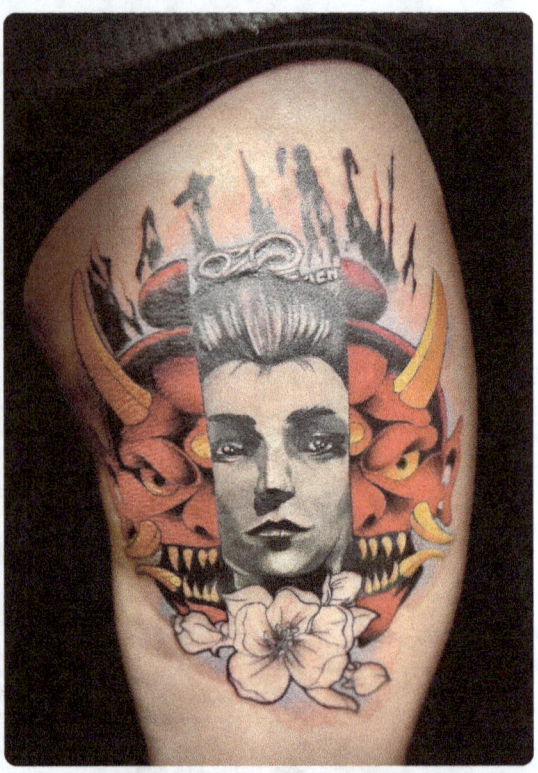
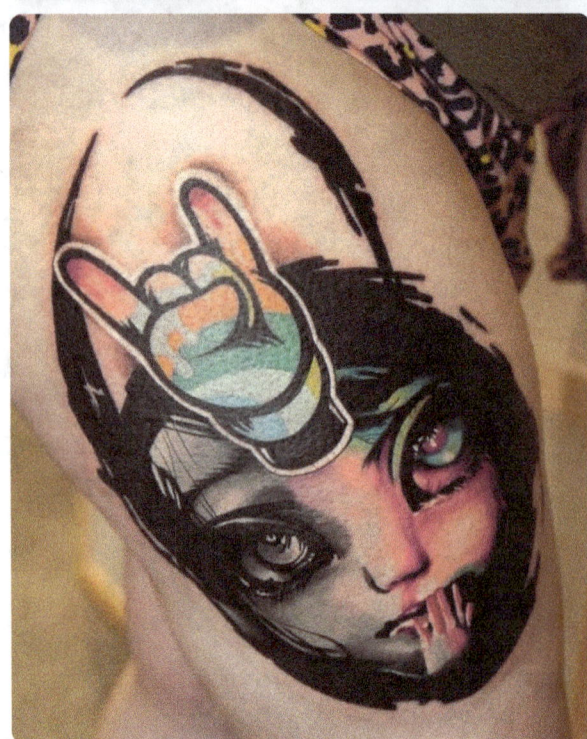
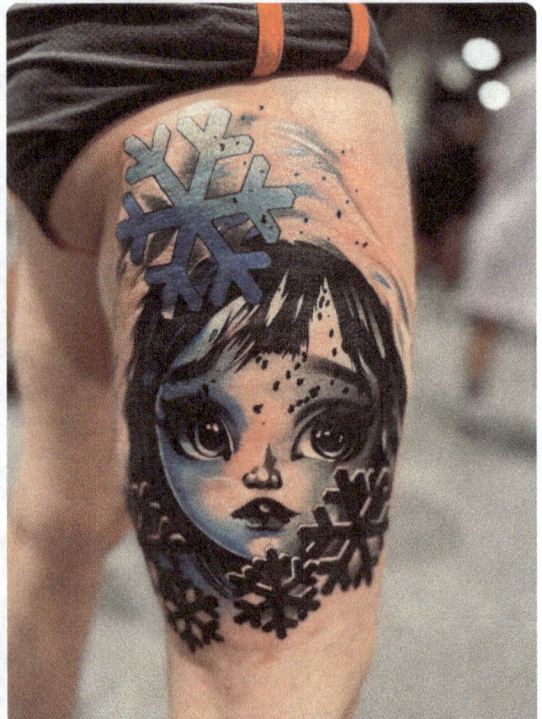

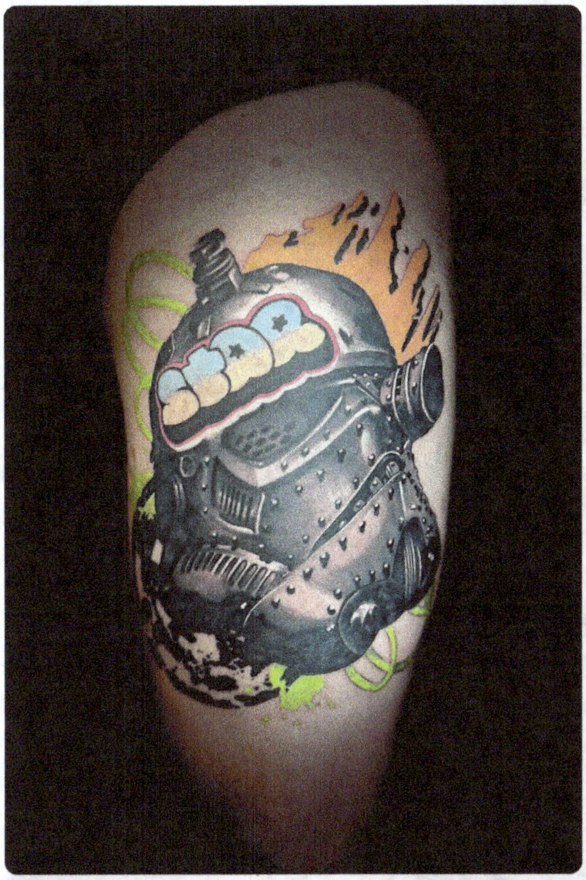

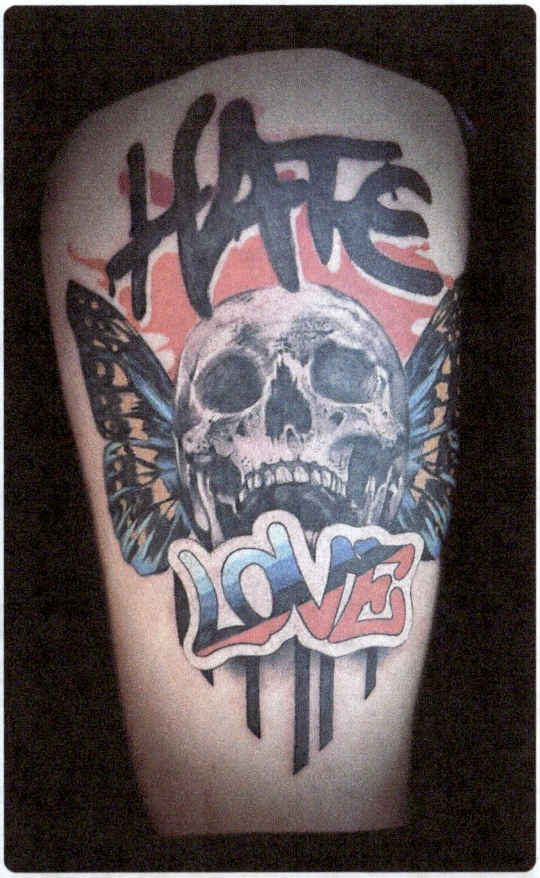

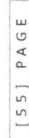

Chapter III

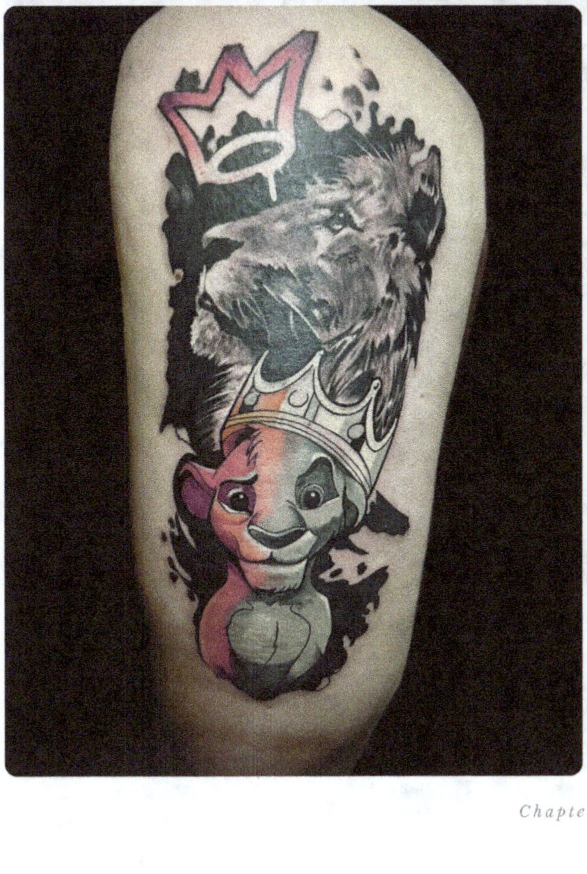

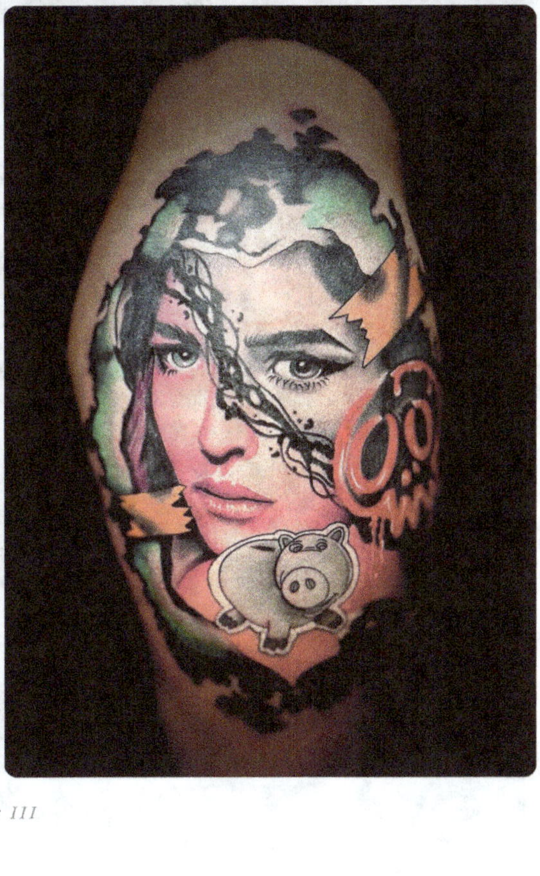

GUHIM TATTOO

BLACKLINETATTOO | @GUHIMTATTOO | FRANCE, ROUEN

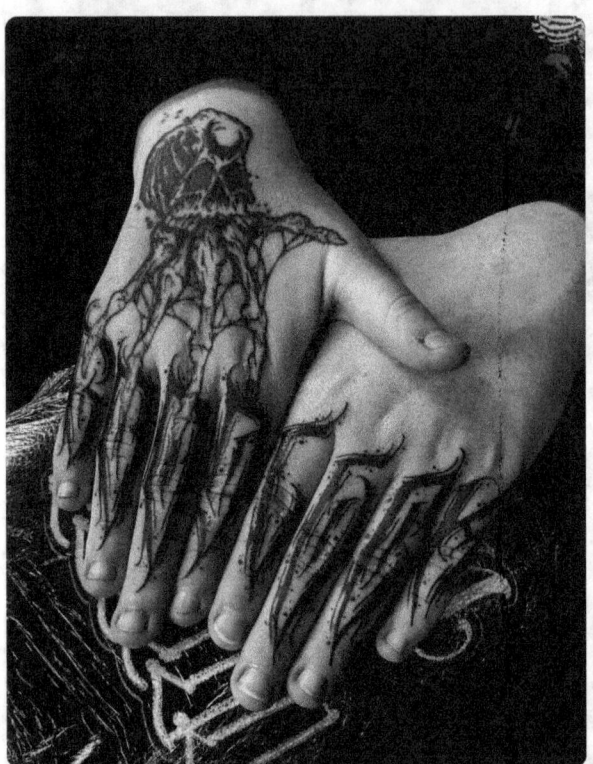

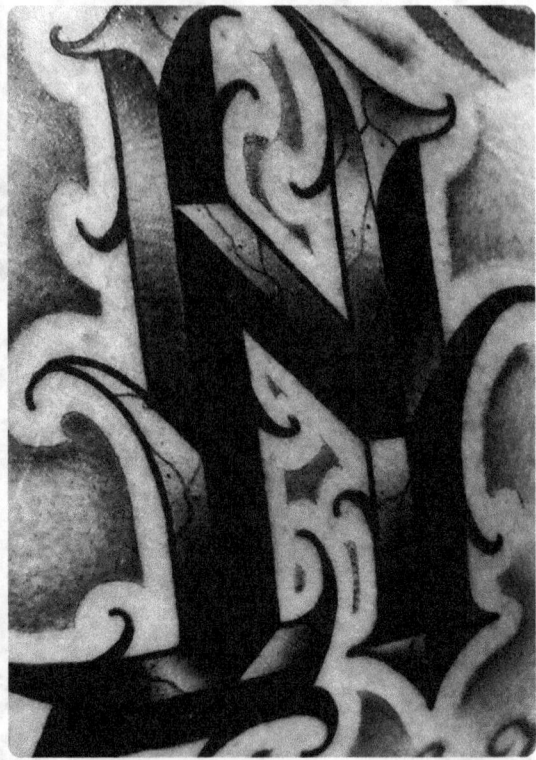

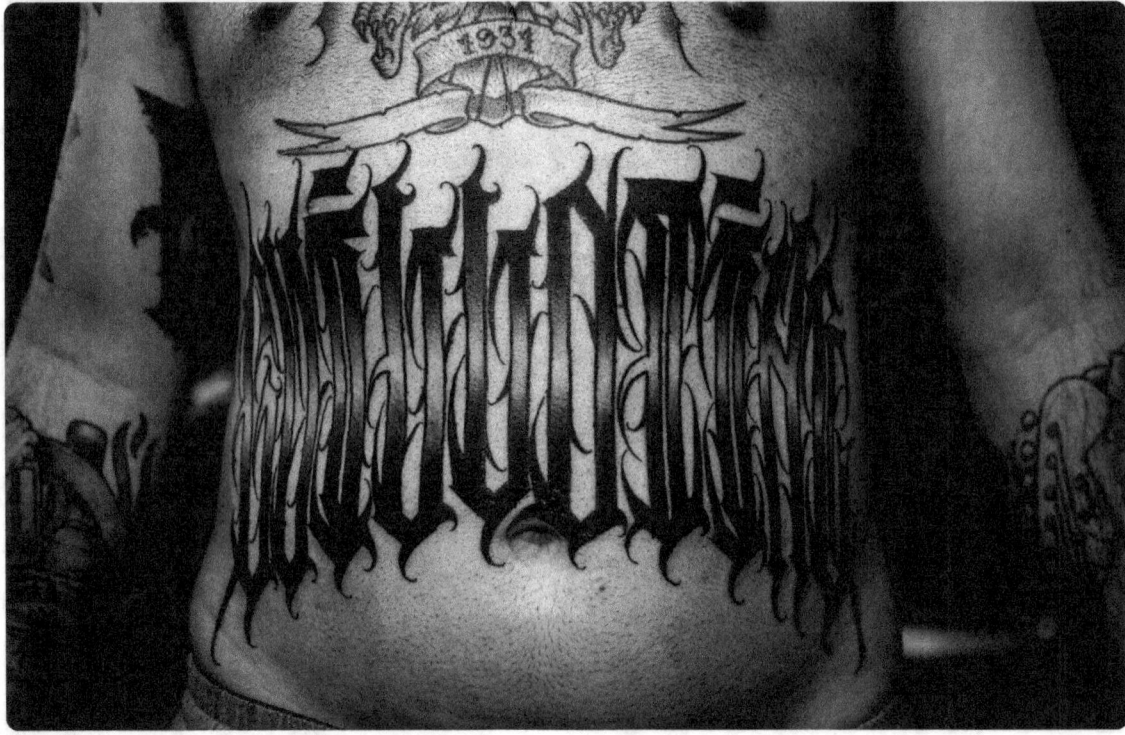

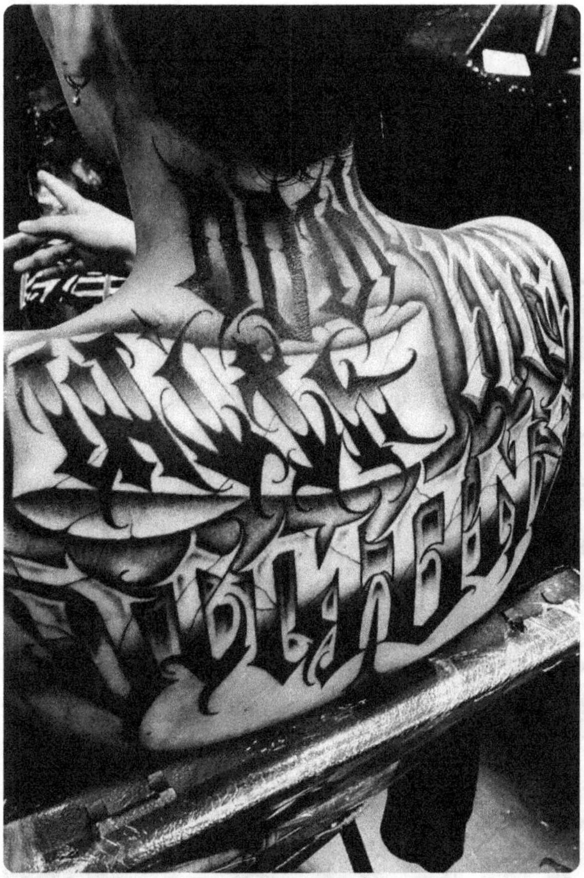

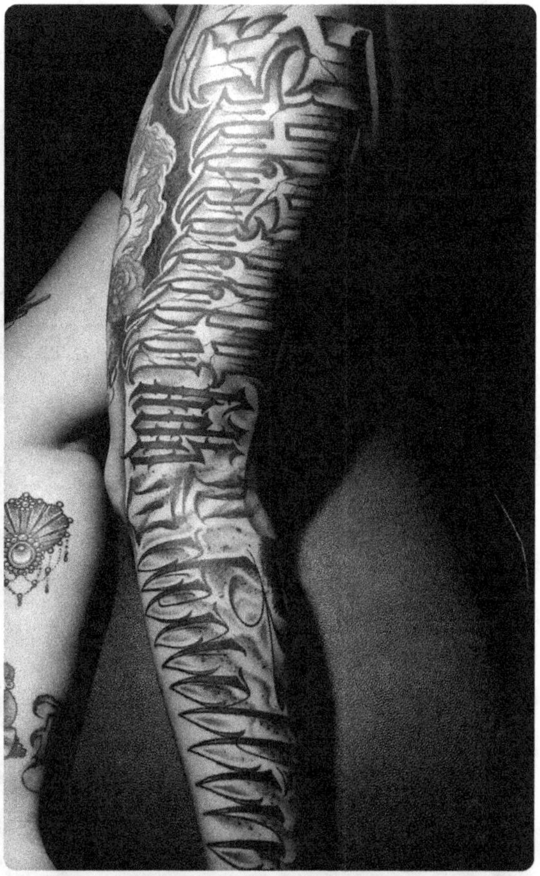

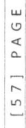

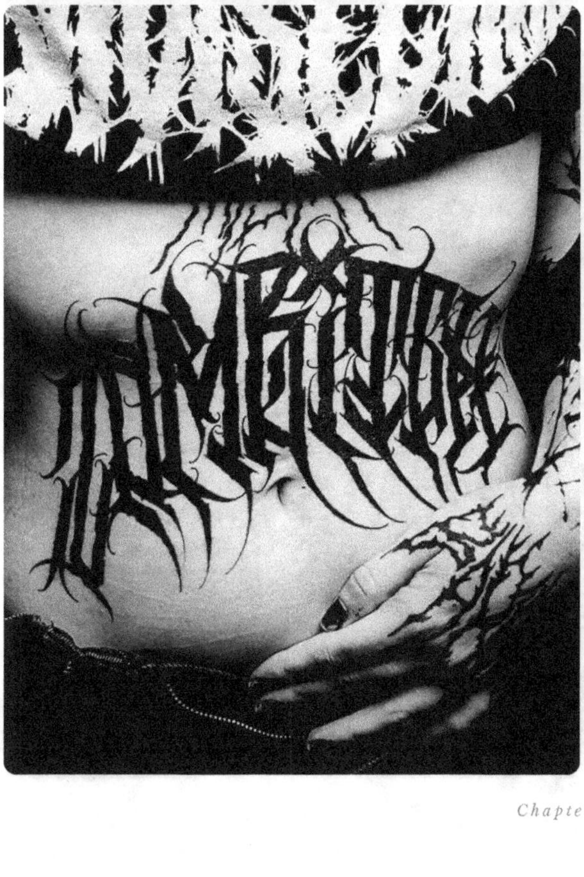

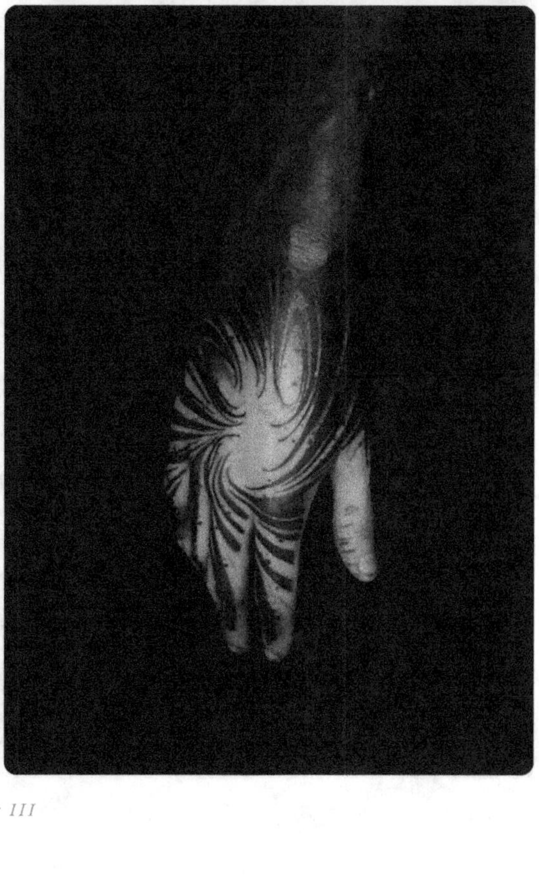

Chapter III

HOLLY SWAN

HOLLY SWAN TATTOOS | @HOLLYSWANTATTOOS | NORTHERN IRELAND, ENNISKILLEN

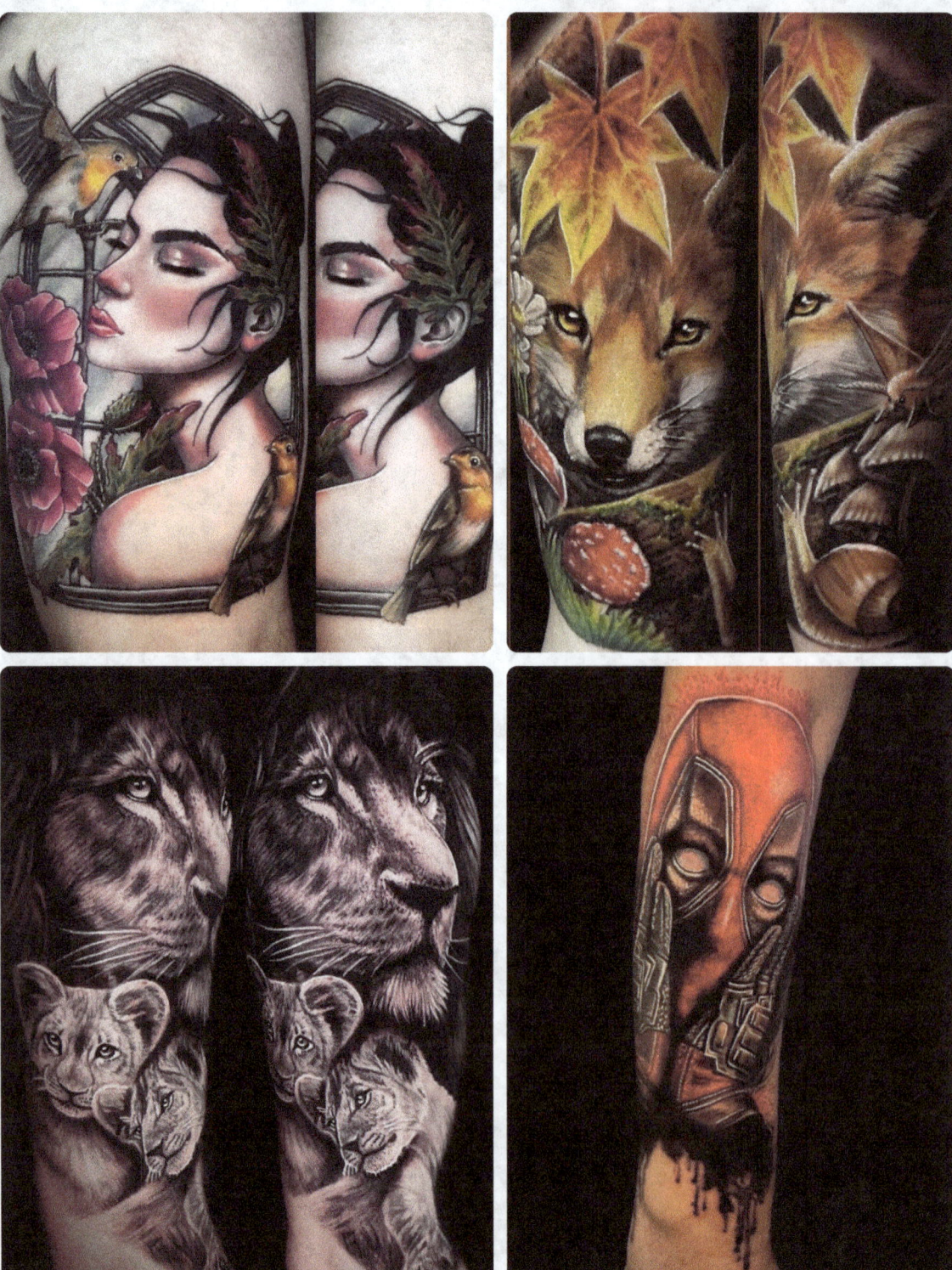

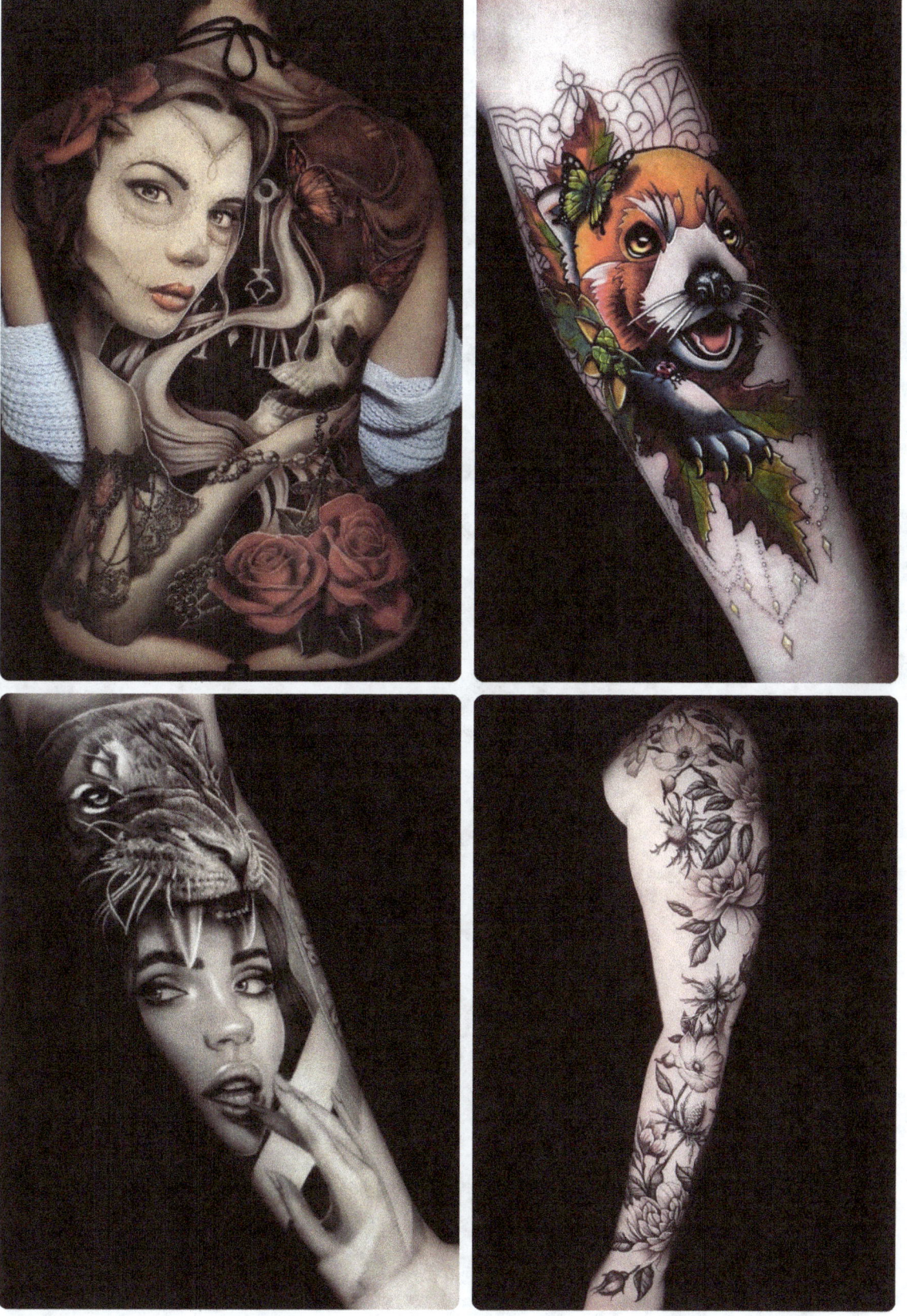

Chapter III

IVAN ANDROSOV

CROWN&ANCHOR | ANDROSOVTTTS.COM | @JOHNBRASS | USA, NEW JERSEY

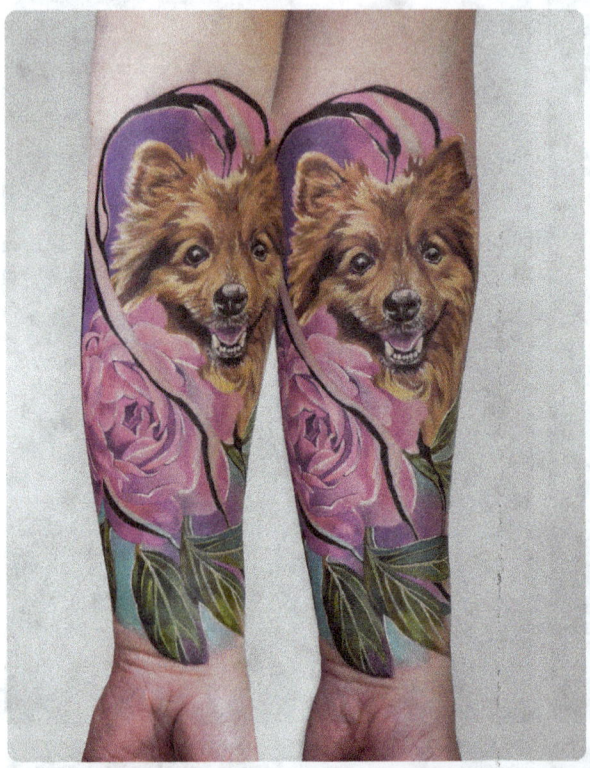
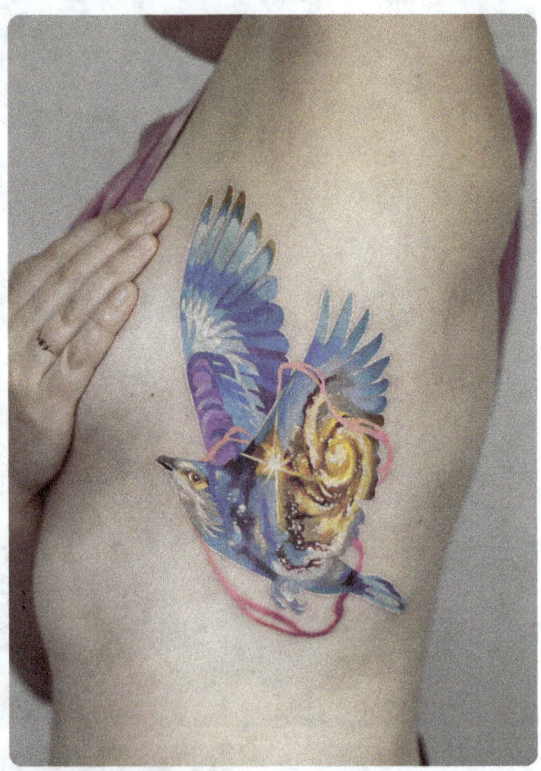
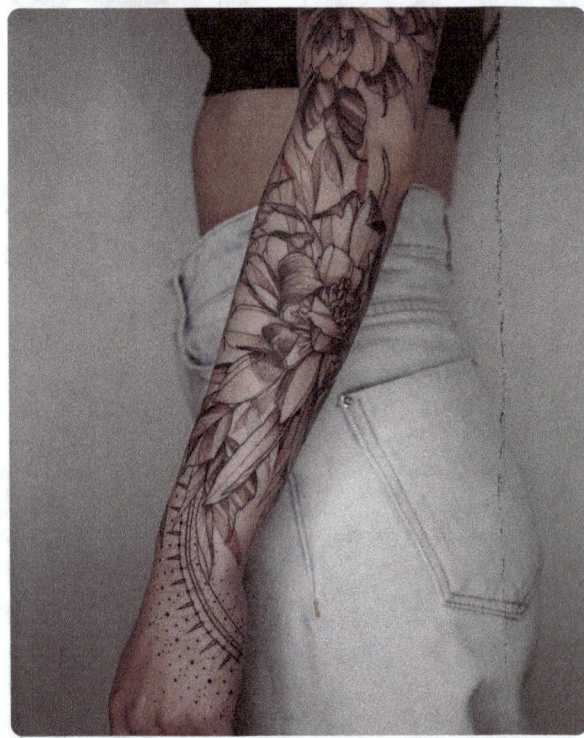
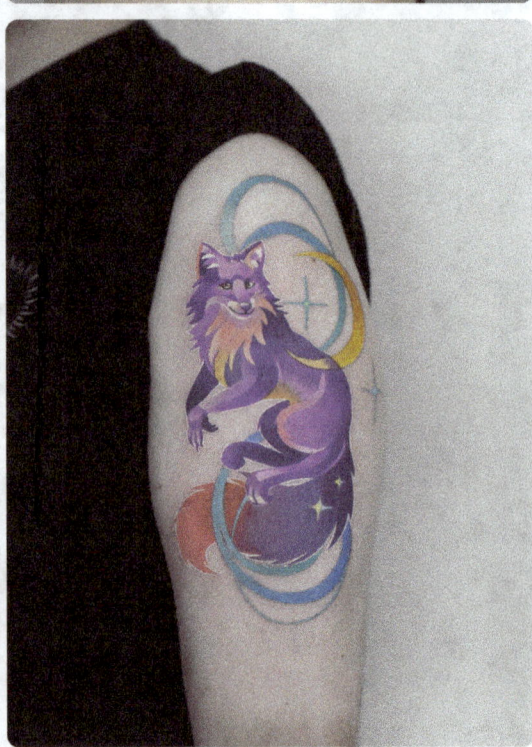

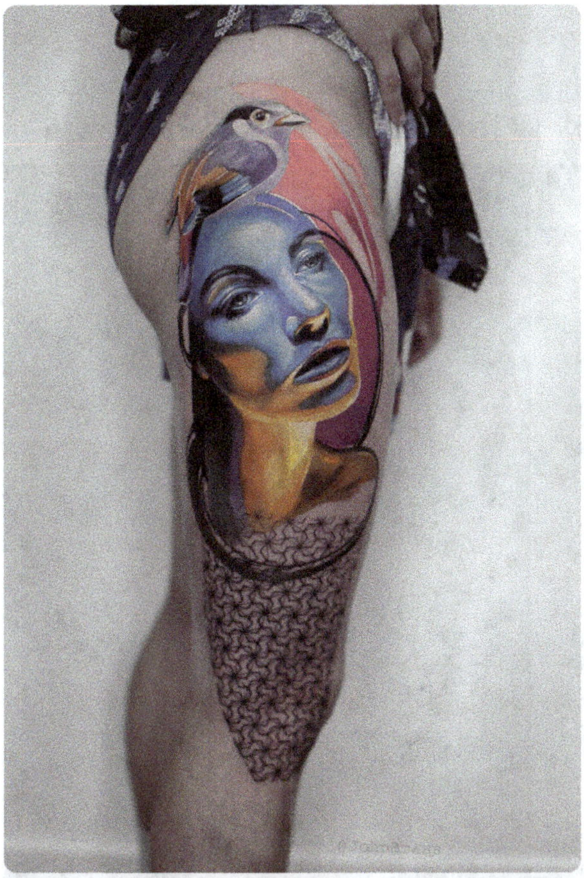

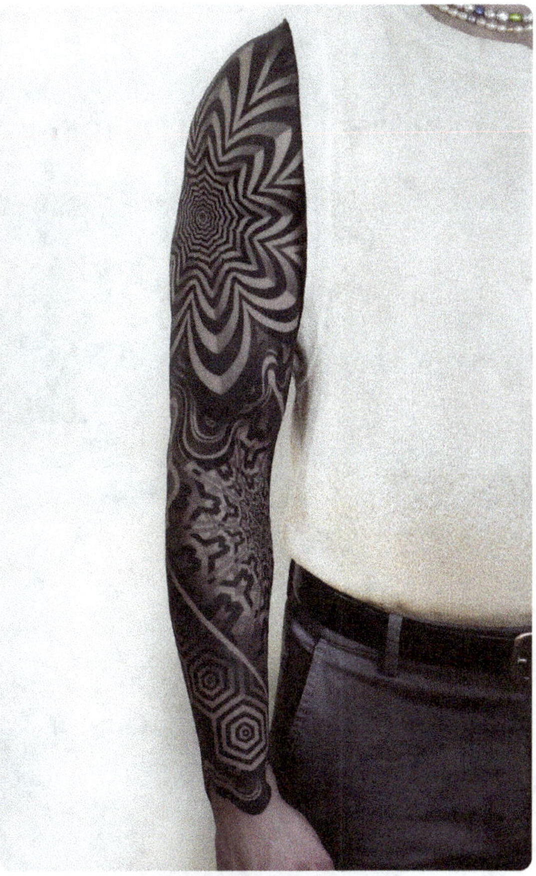

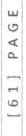

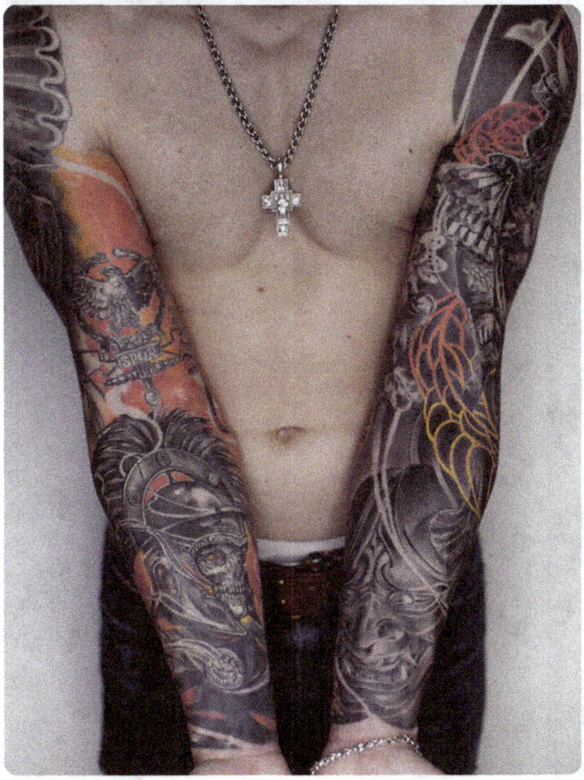

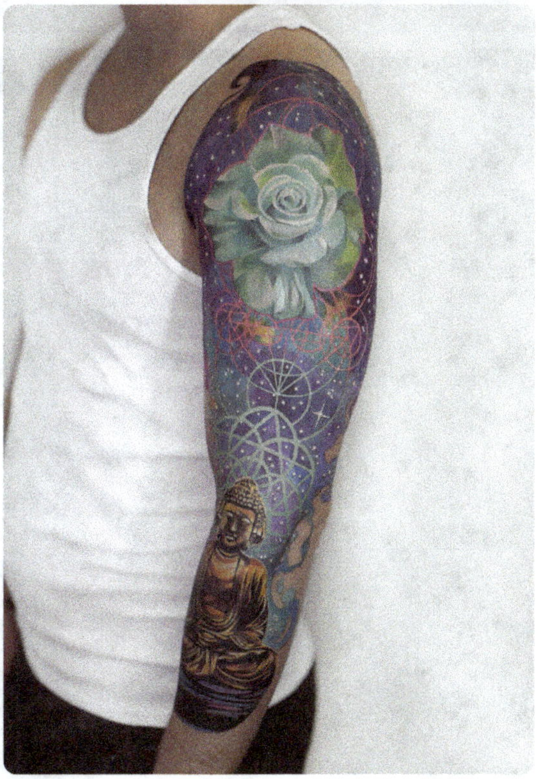

JONARTON

DARK HORSE GALLERY | FB: JONARTON | @JONARTON | UK, BIRMINGHAM

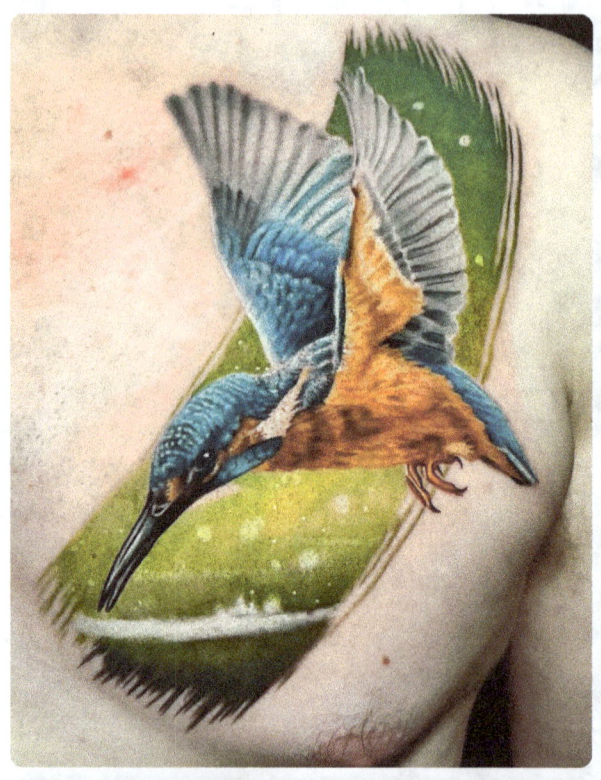
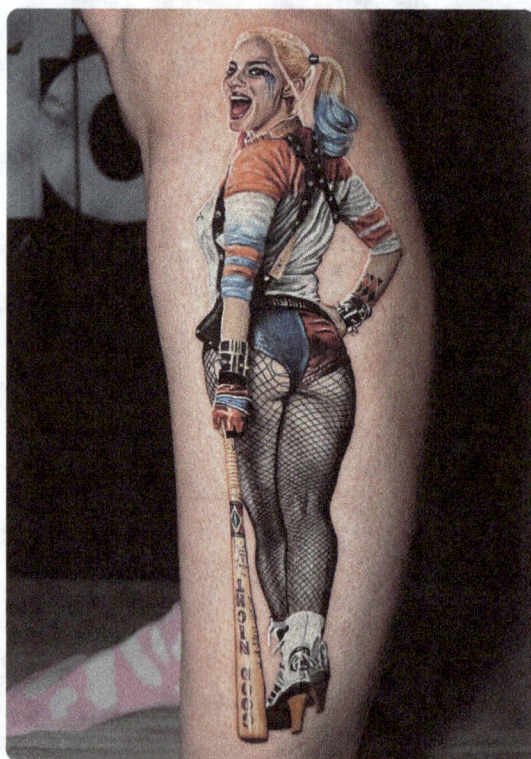
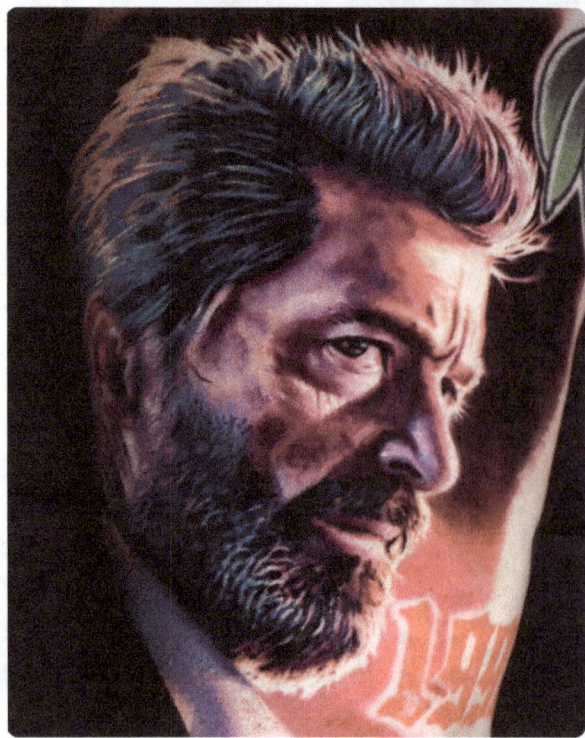
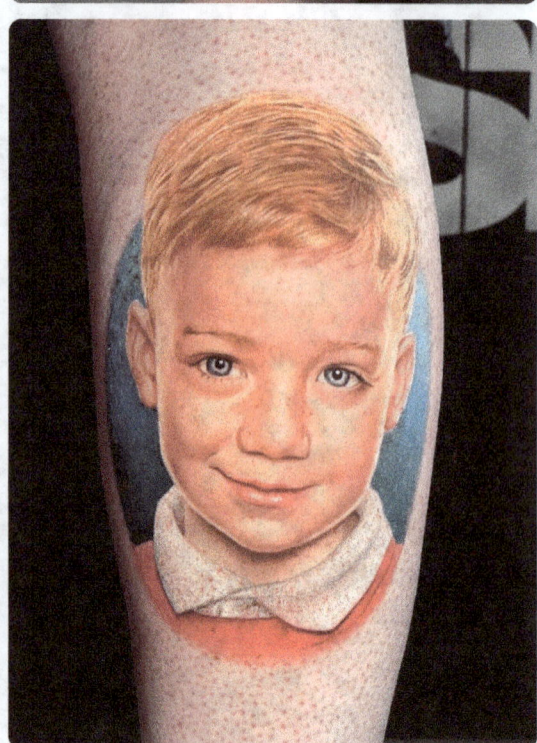

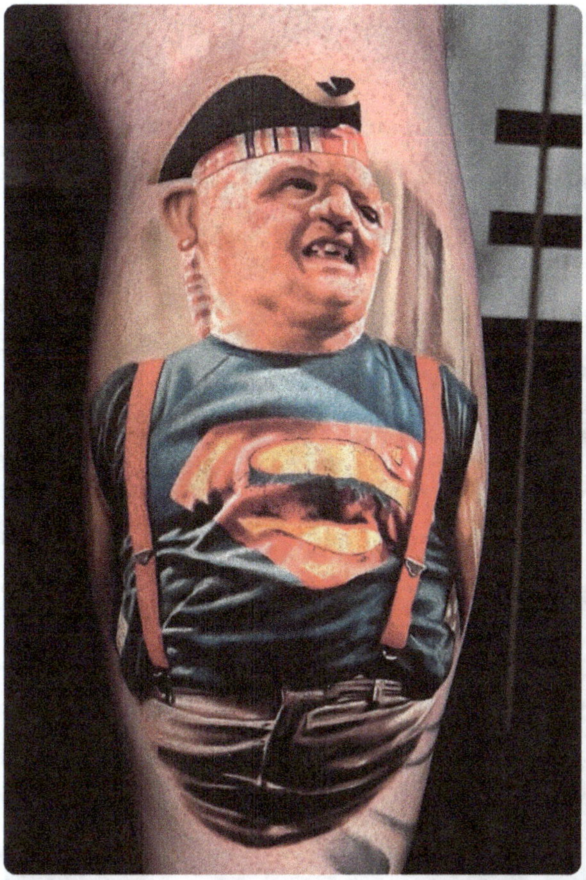

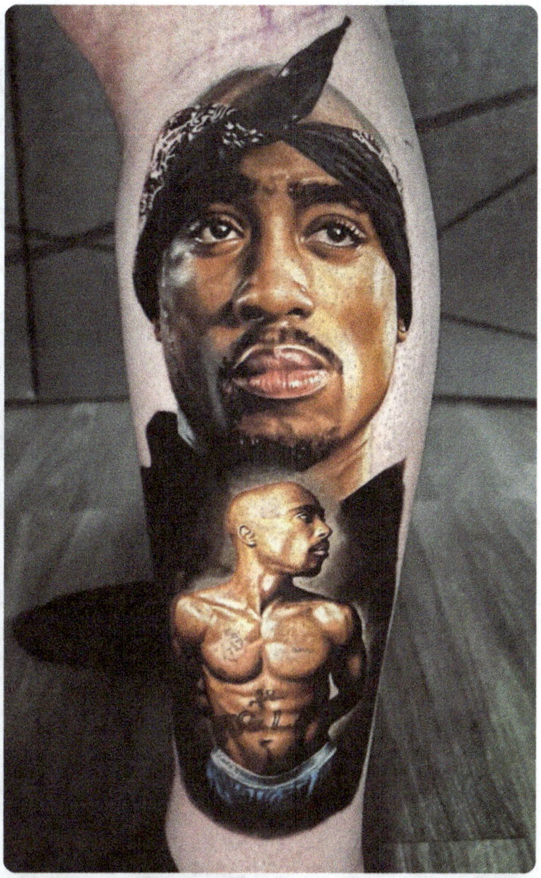

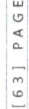

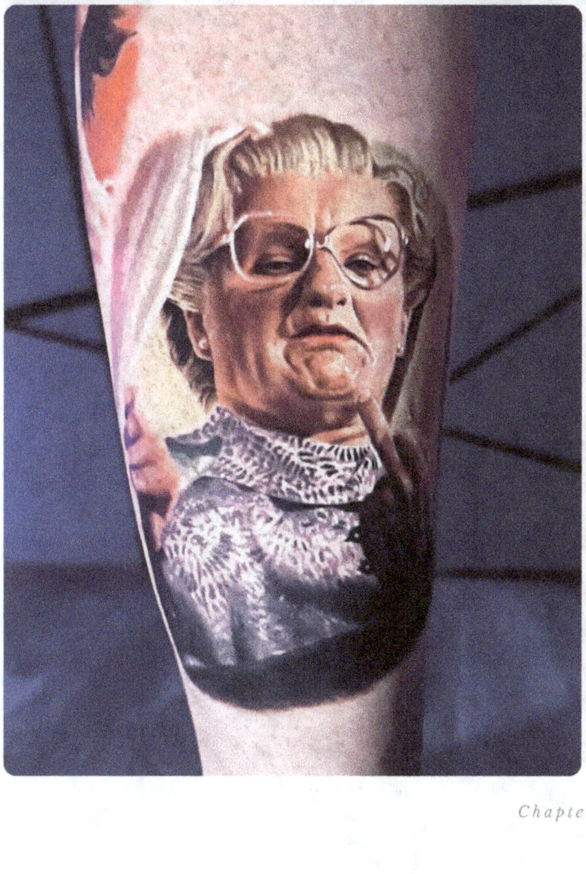

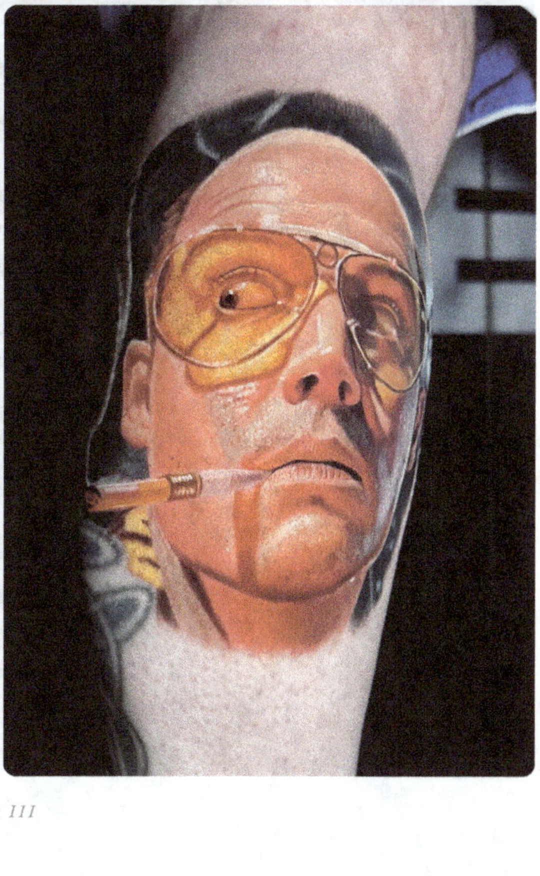

Chapter III

JOSHUA SHORT

TATTOOSSAVEDMYLIFE.COM | @JOSHSHORTTATTOOS | USA, INDIANA

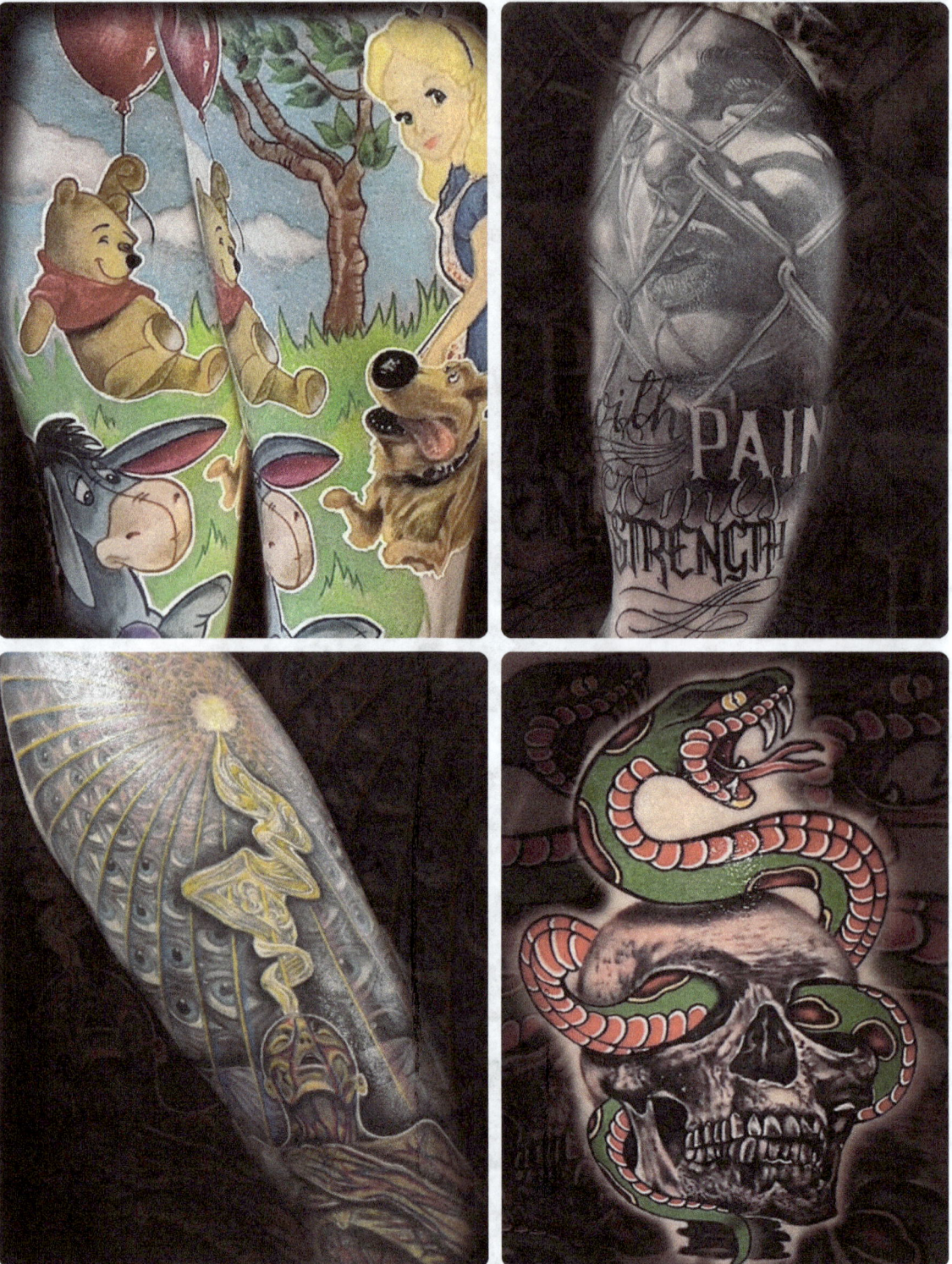

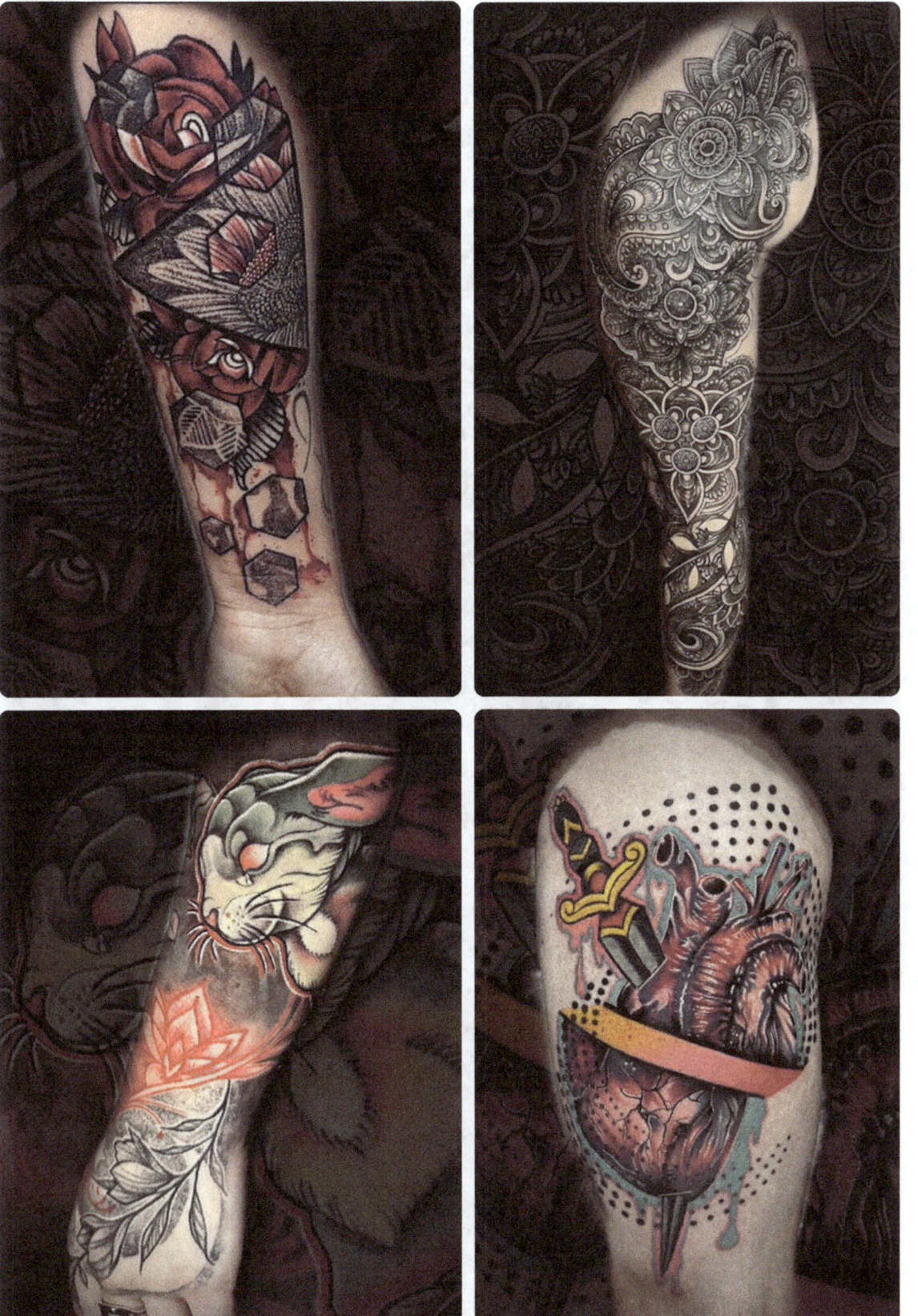

Chapter III

JUANCA GALLO

GOLDEN CAT TATTOO | @JUANCA_GALLO | SPAIN, BARCELONA

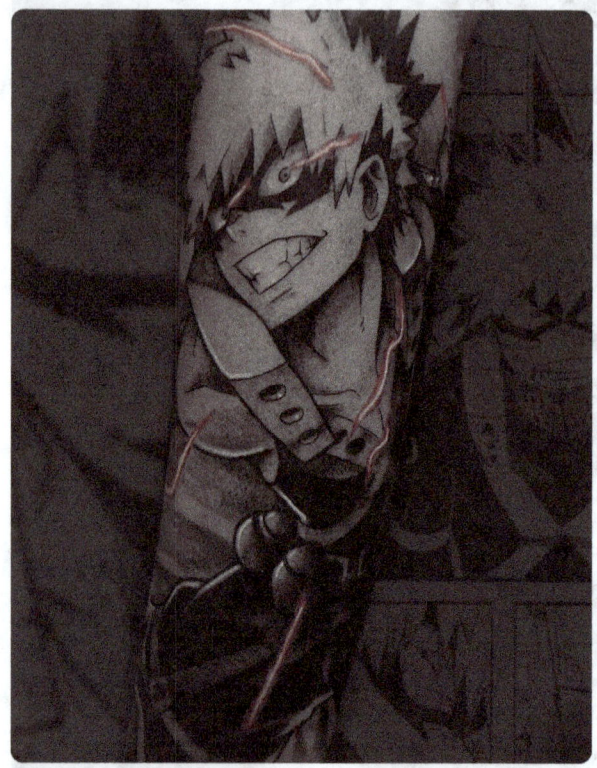
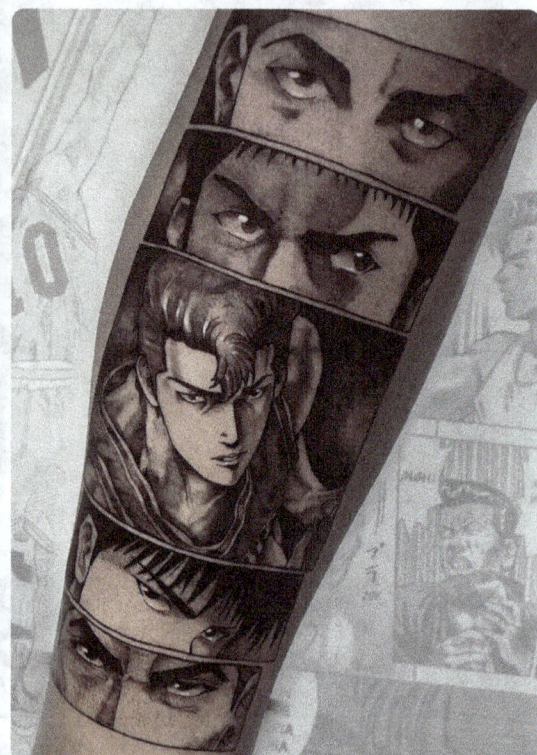
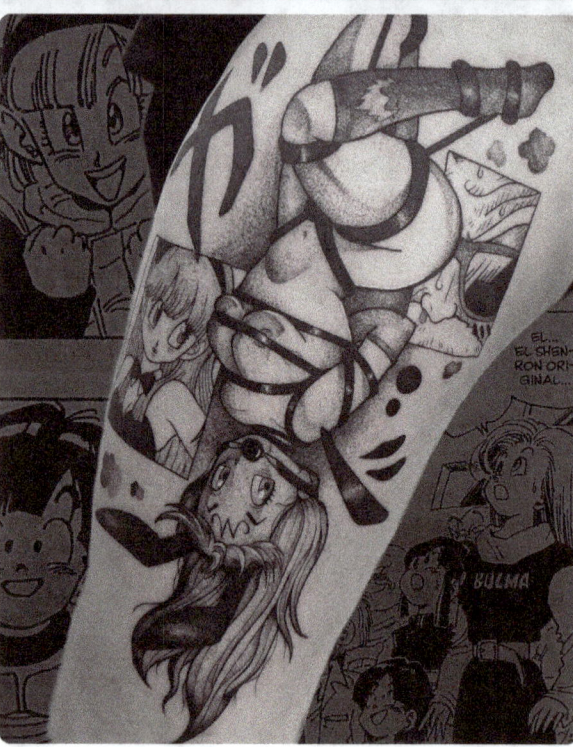
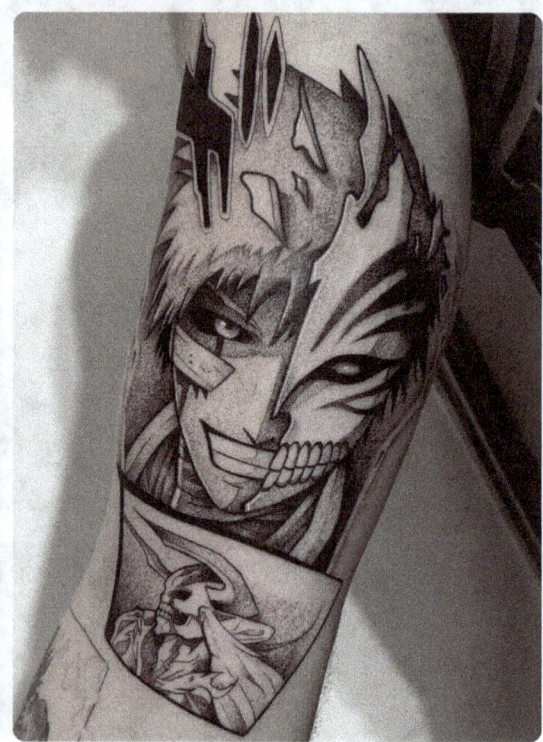

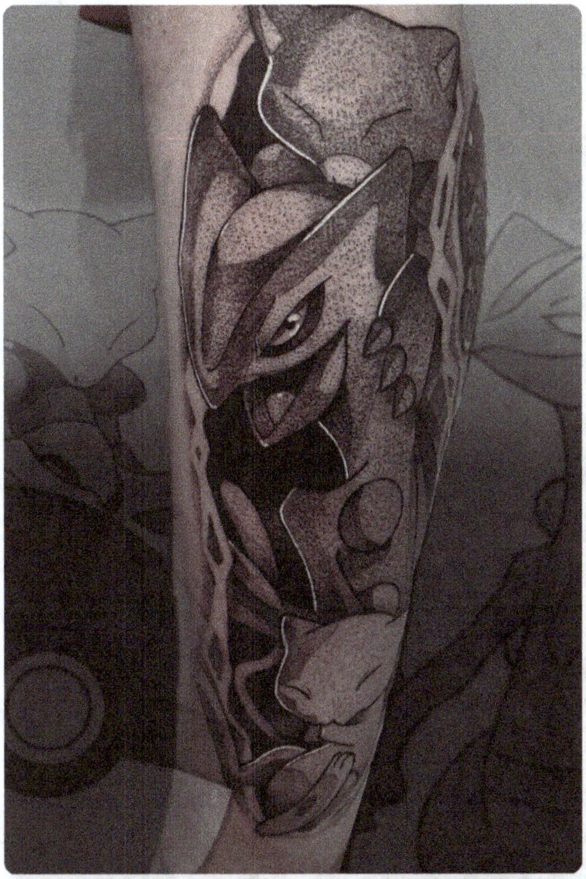

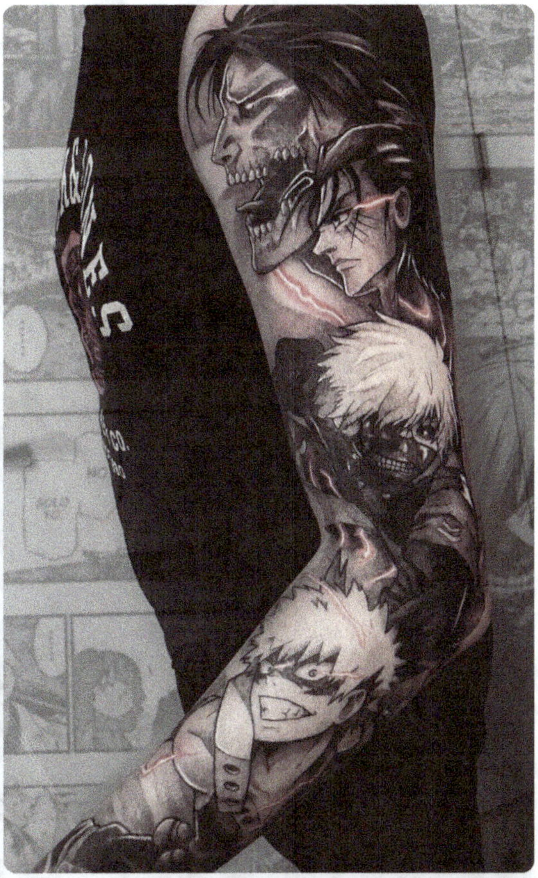

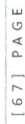

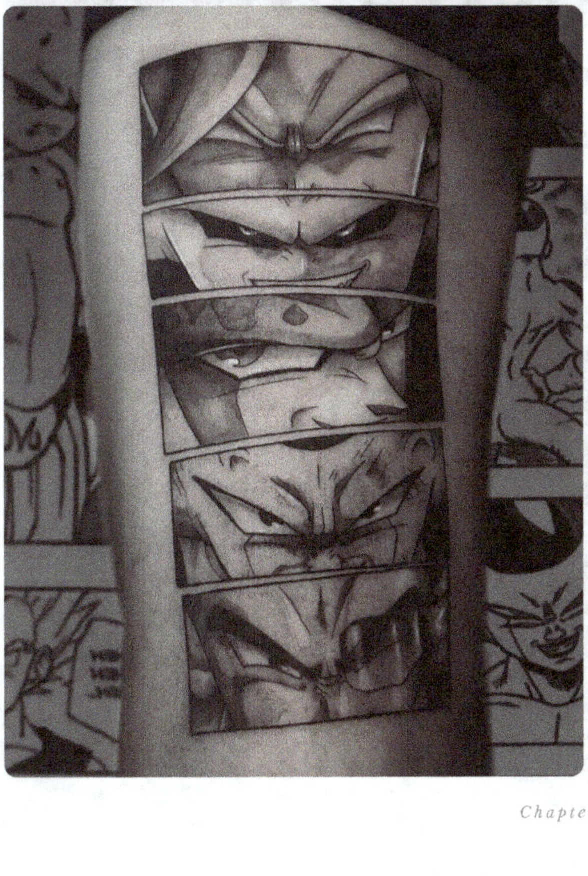

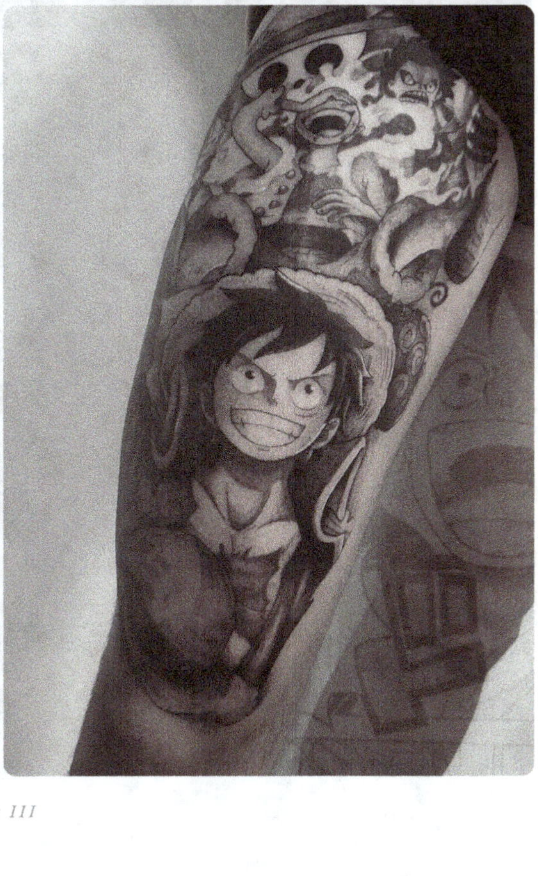

Chapter III

JULIEN DELHAYE

YAMA TATTOO | @JULIENDELHAYE | FRANCE, SAINT-CHAMOND

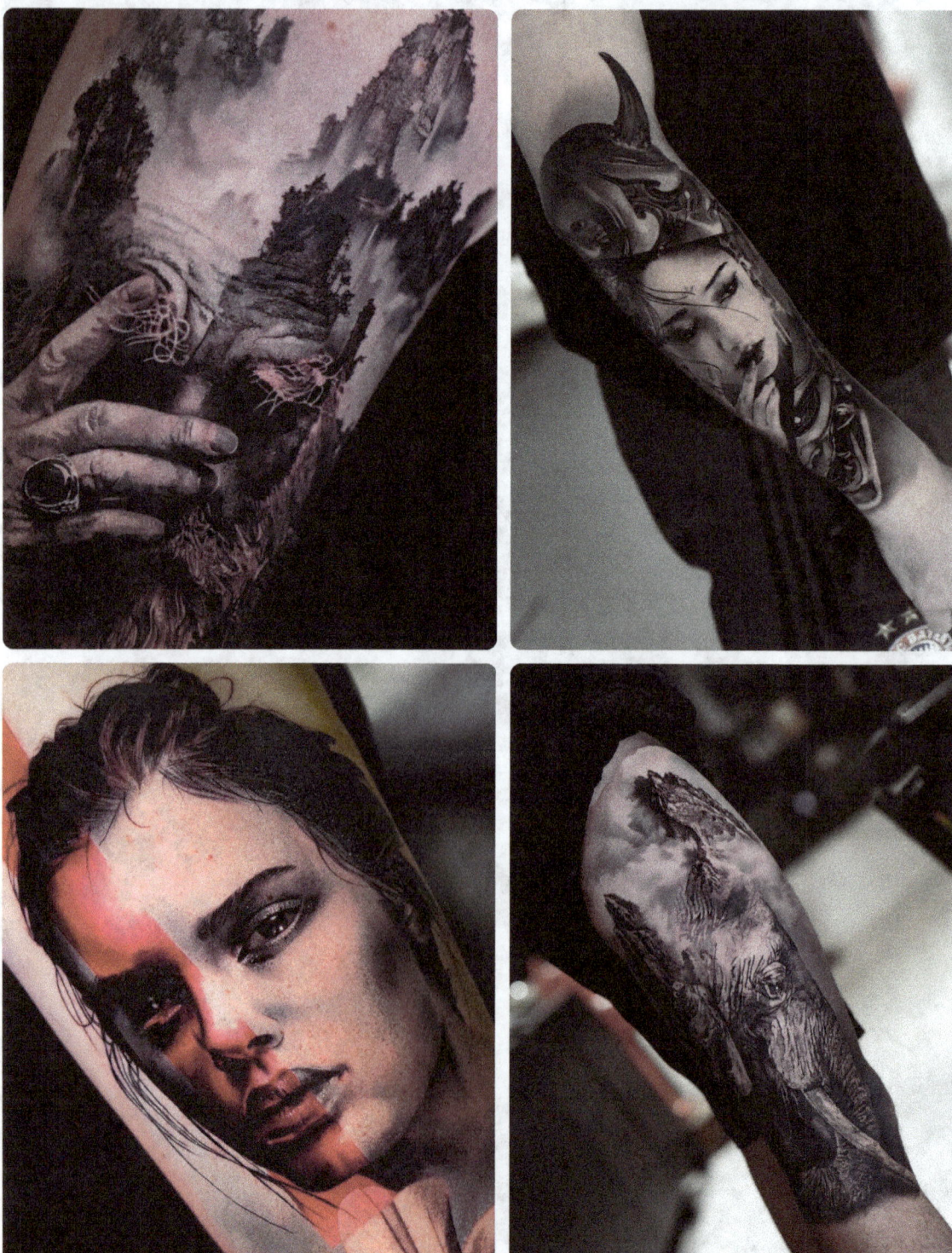

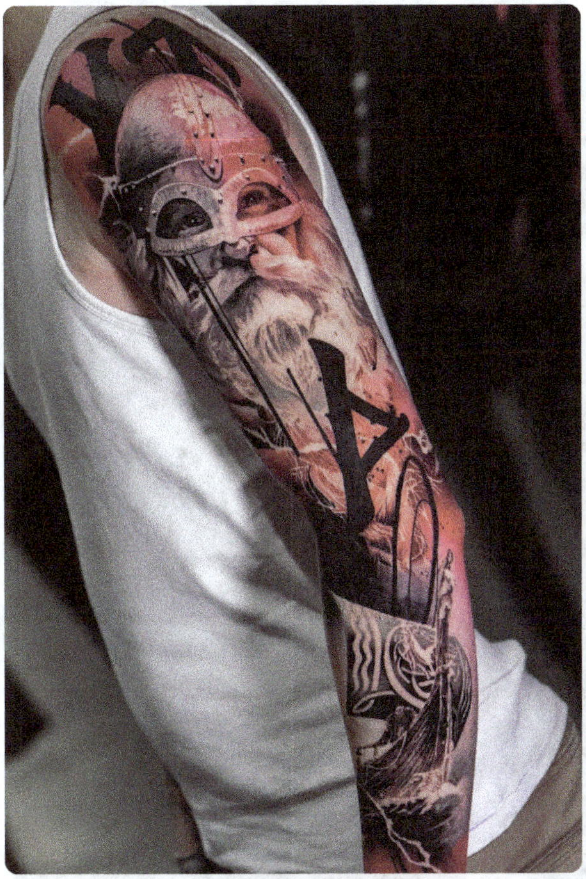

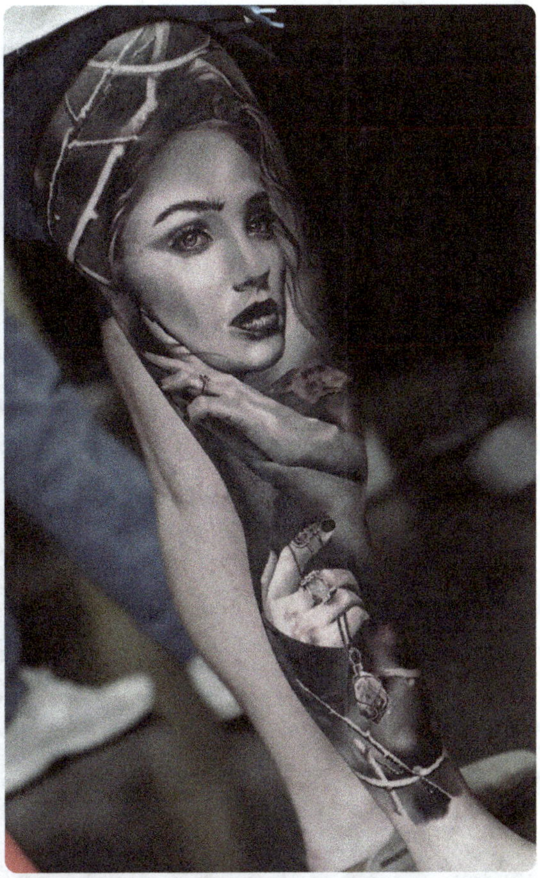

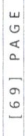

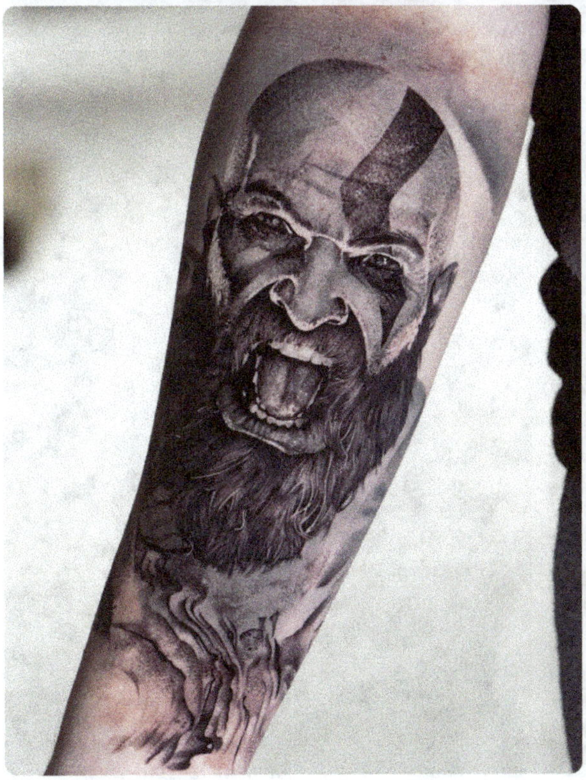

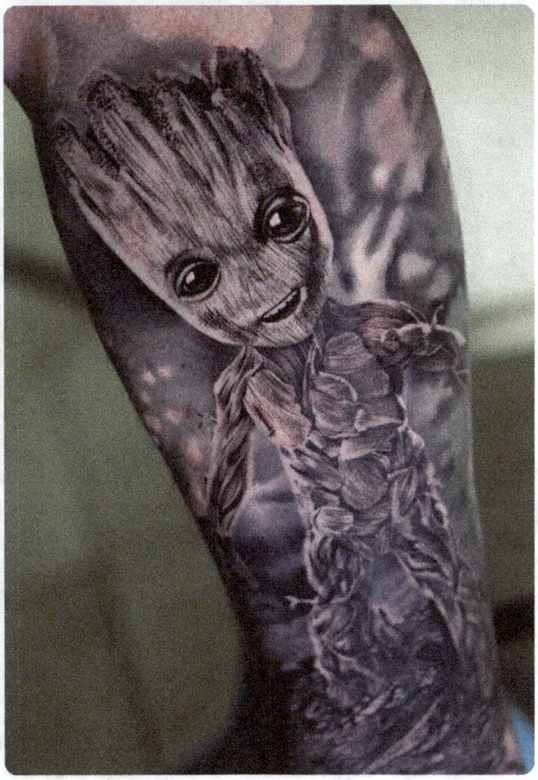

Chapter III

JULO ART

FB: JULO ART | @JULO.ART | FRANCE, LILLE

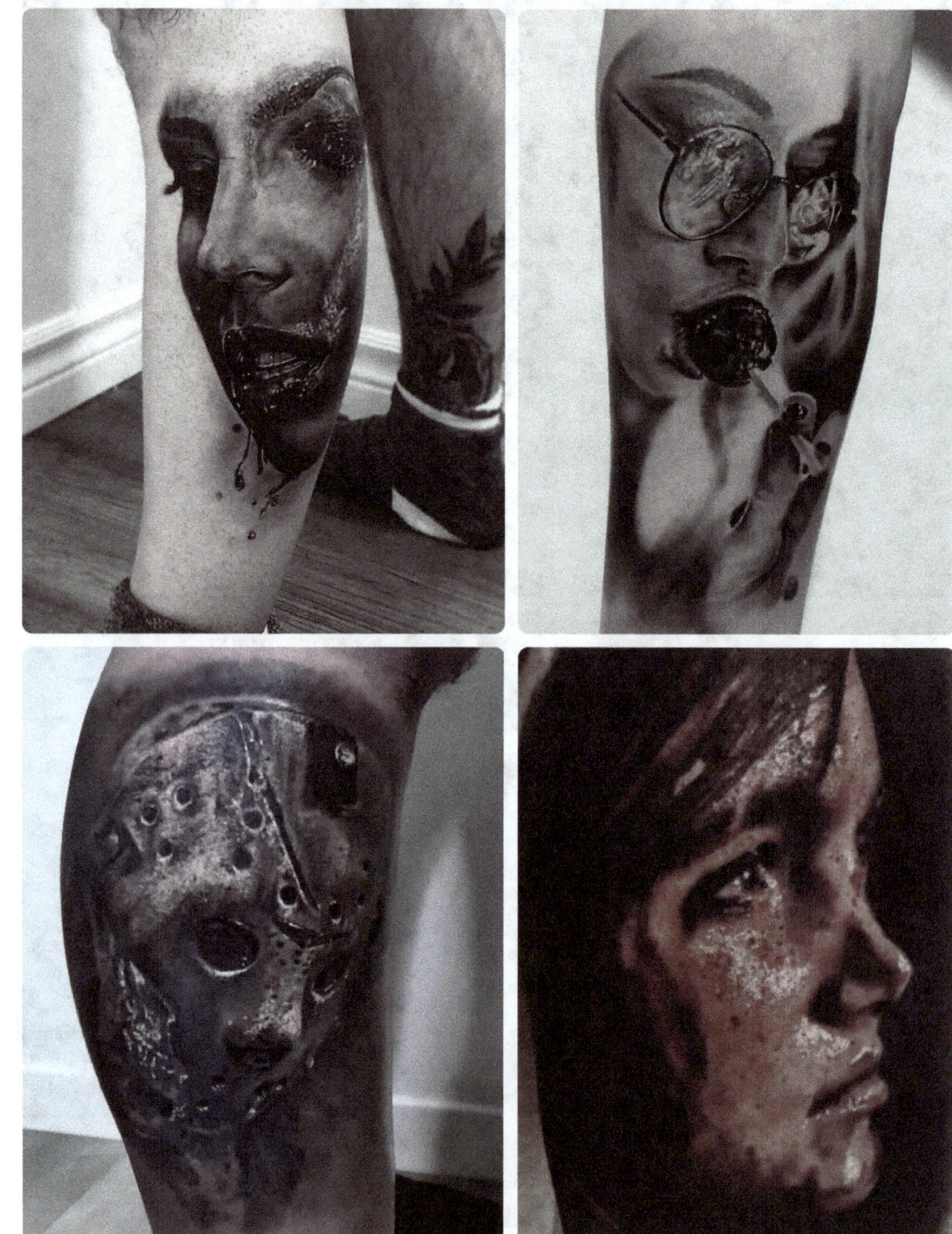

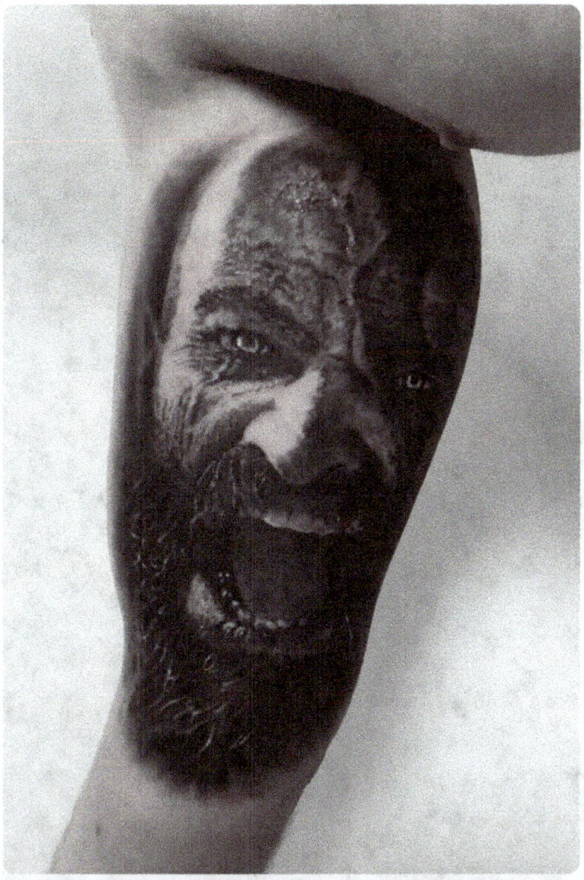

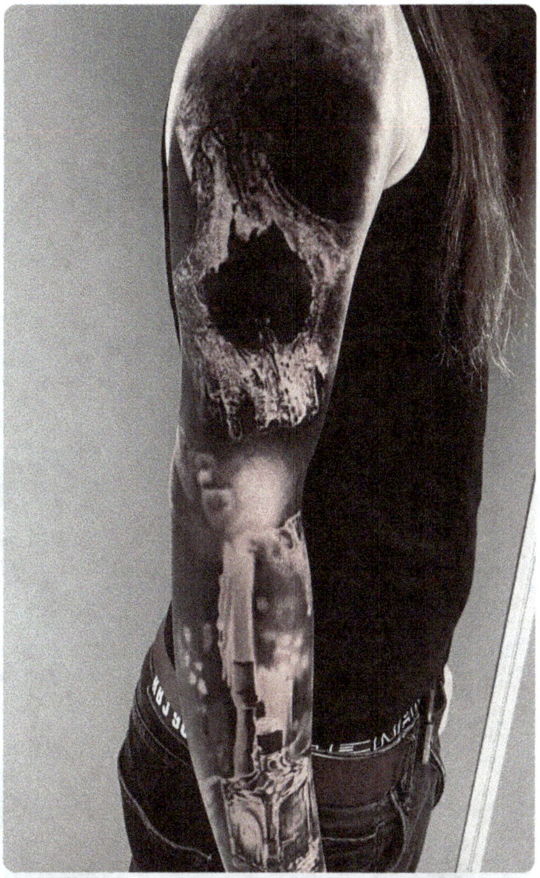

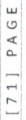

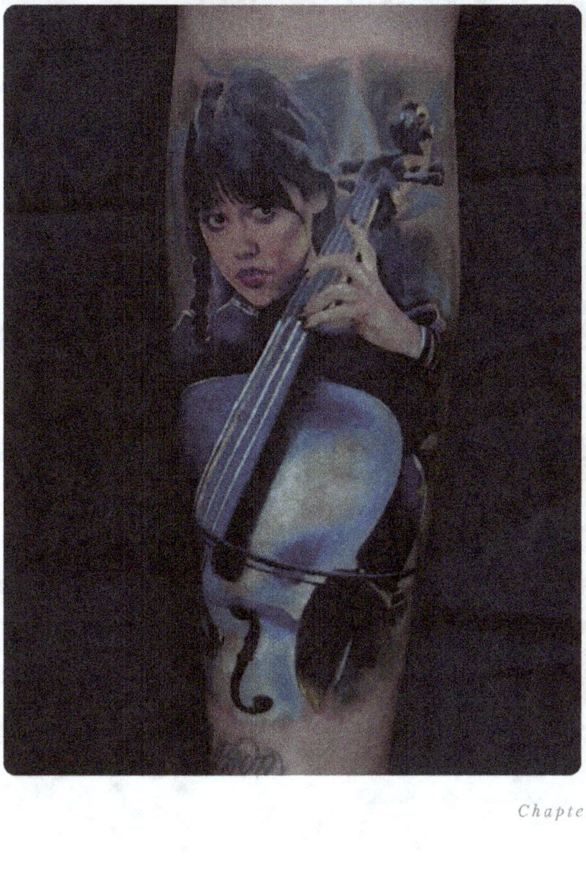

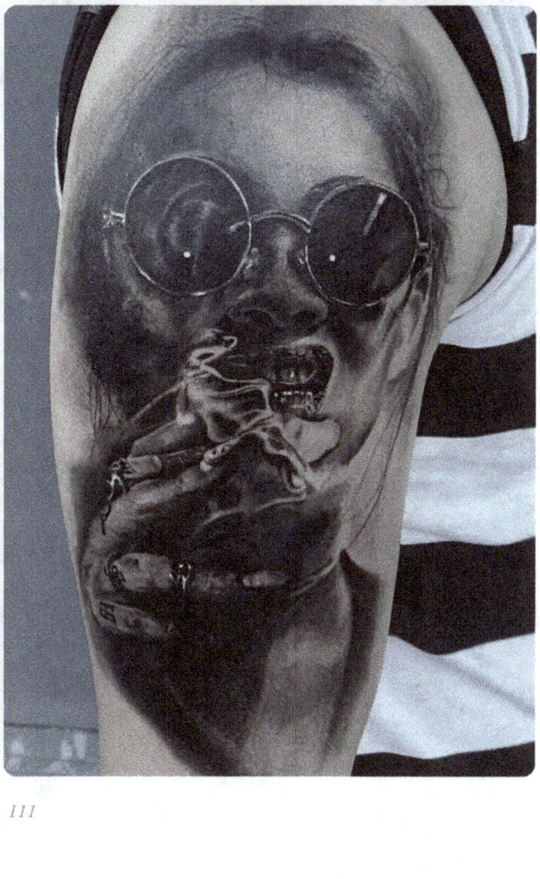

KAJA NIJSSEN

FB: INK BY KAJA | @INK_BY_KAJA | THE NETHERLANDS, SEVENUM

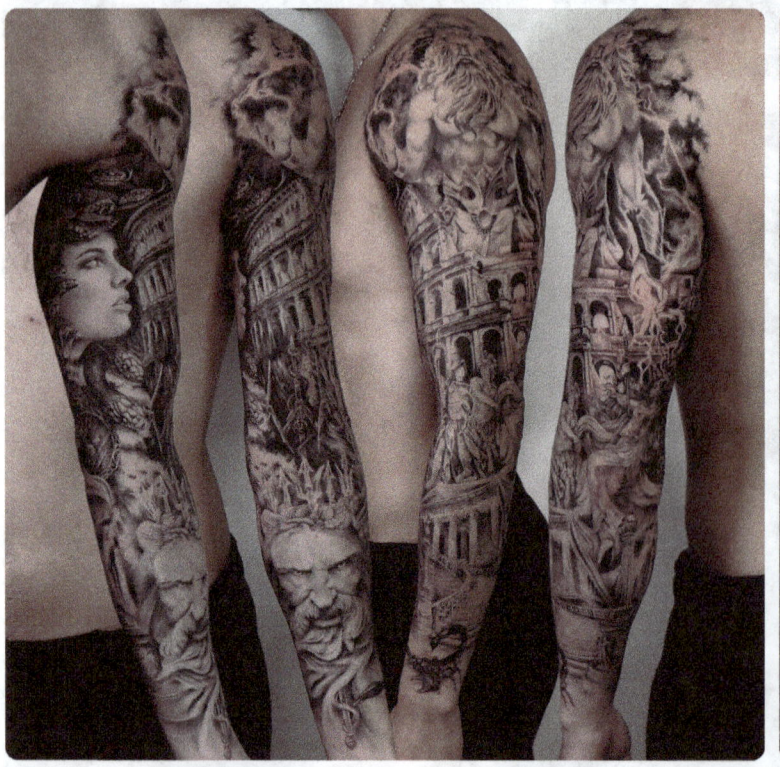

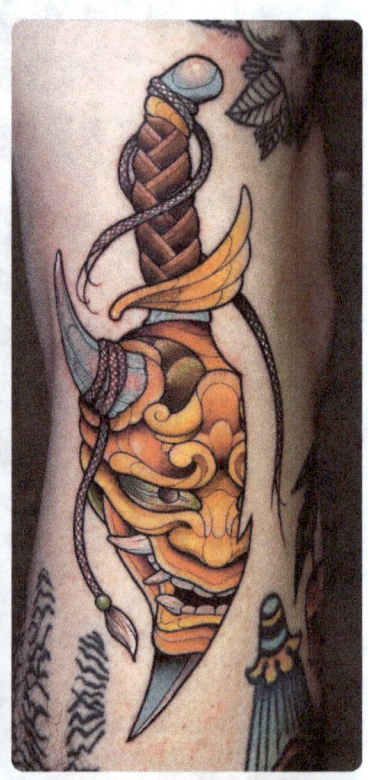

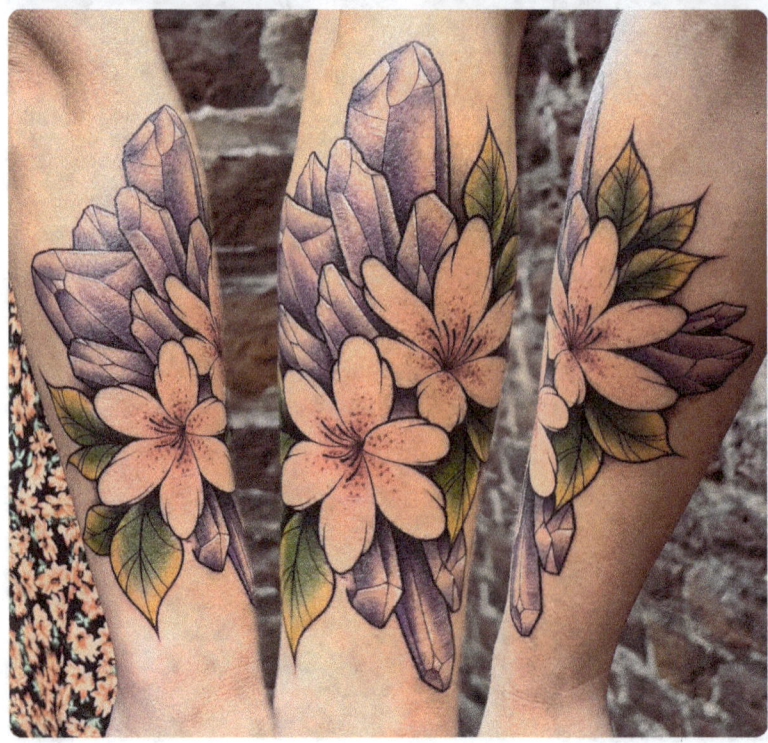

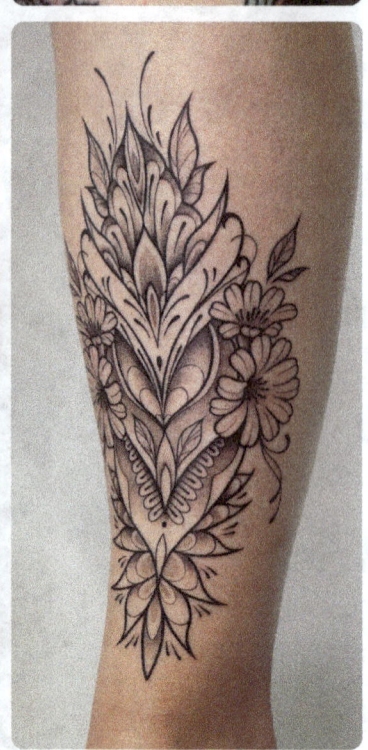

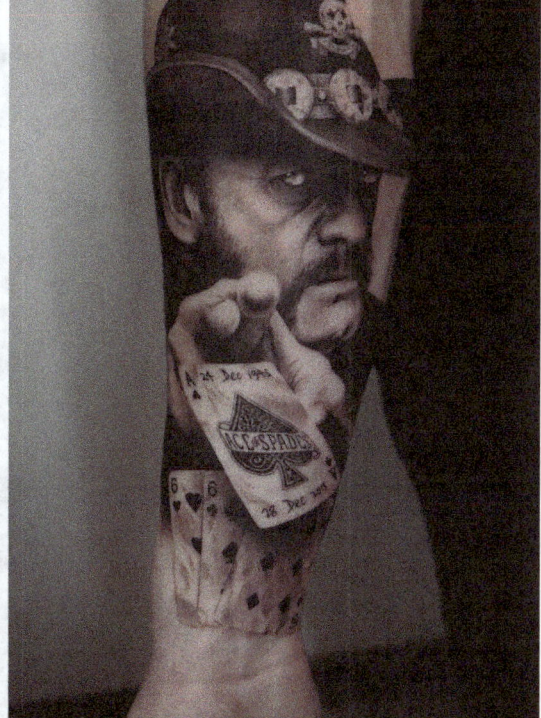
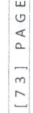
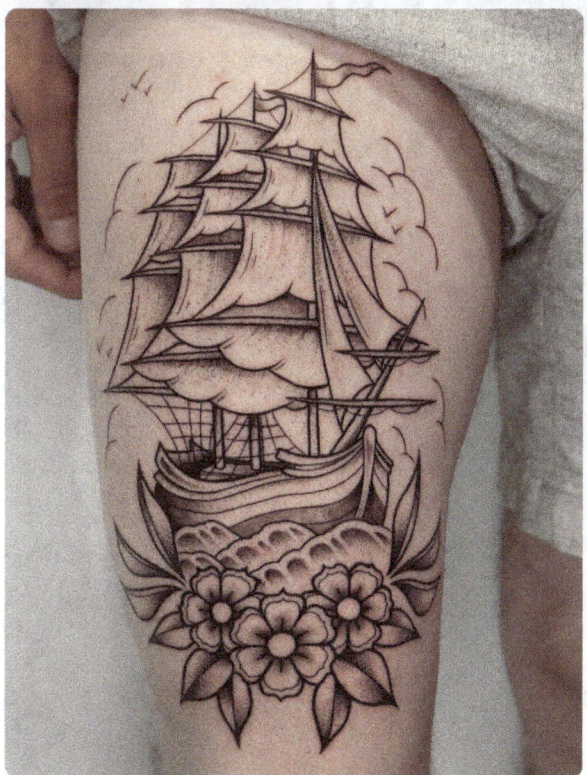
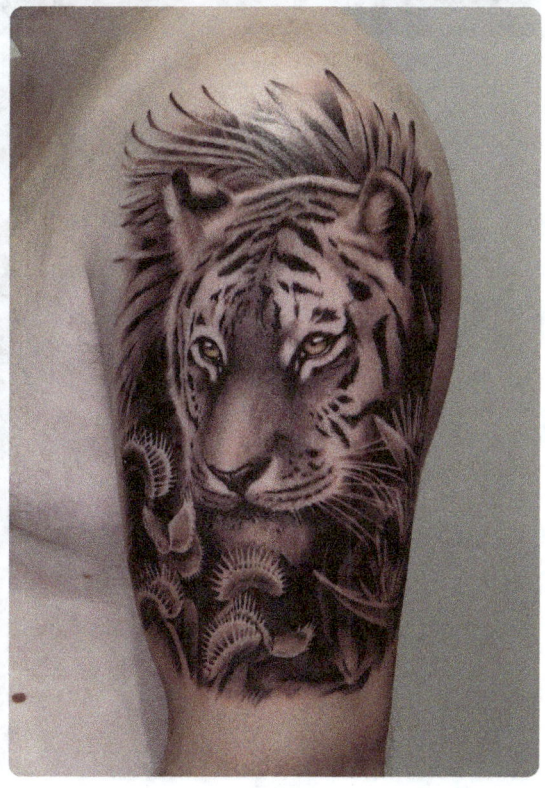

Chapter III

Global Tattoo Magazine

KEVIN HANKS

INCREDIBLE INK TATTOO STUDIO | @KEVHANKS_TATTS | UK, STOKE ON TRENT

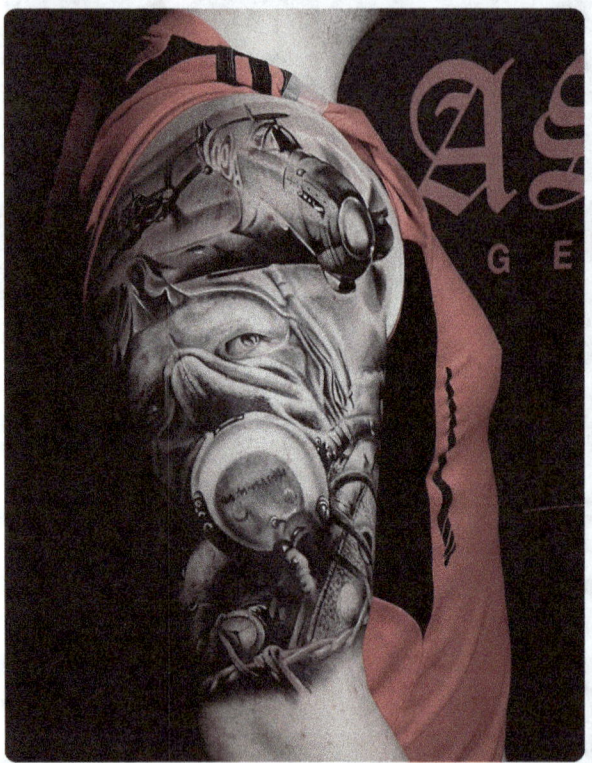
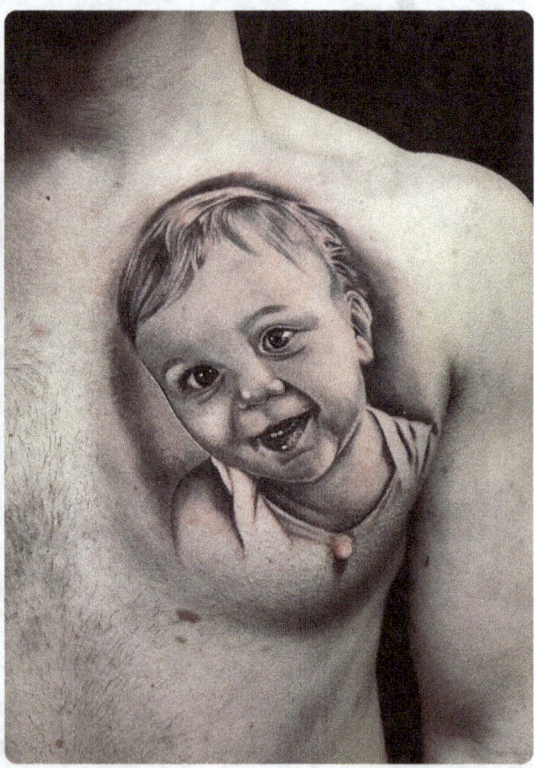
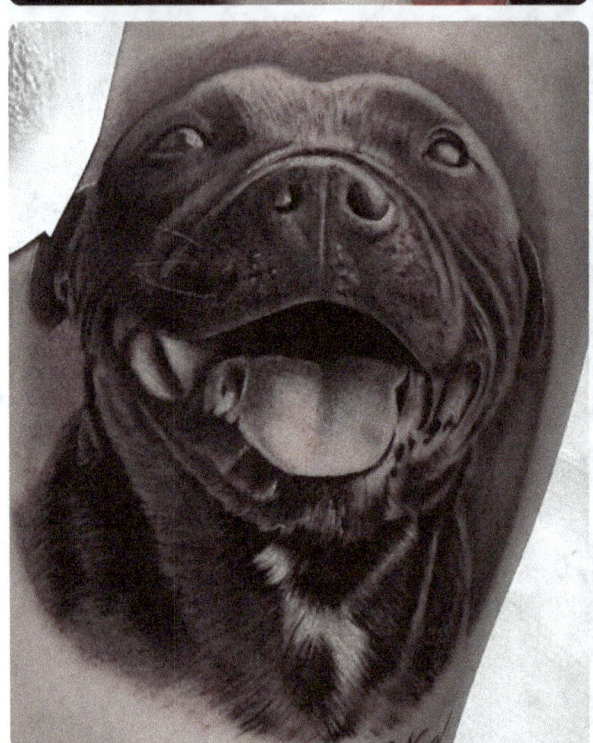
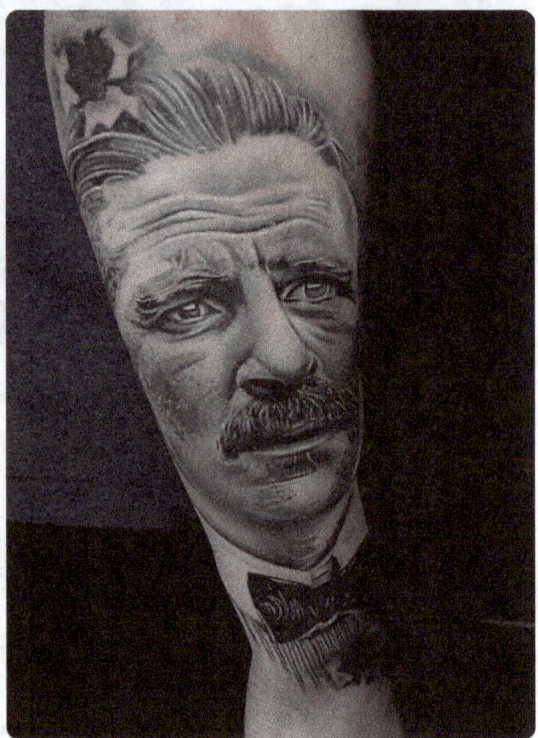

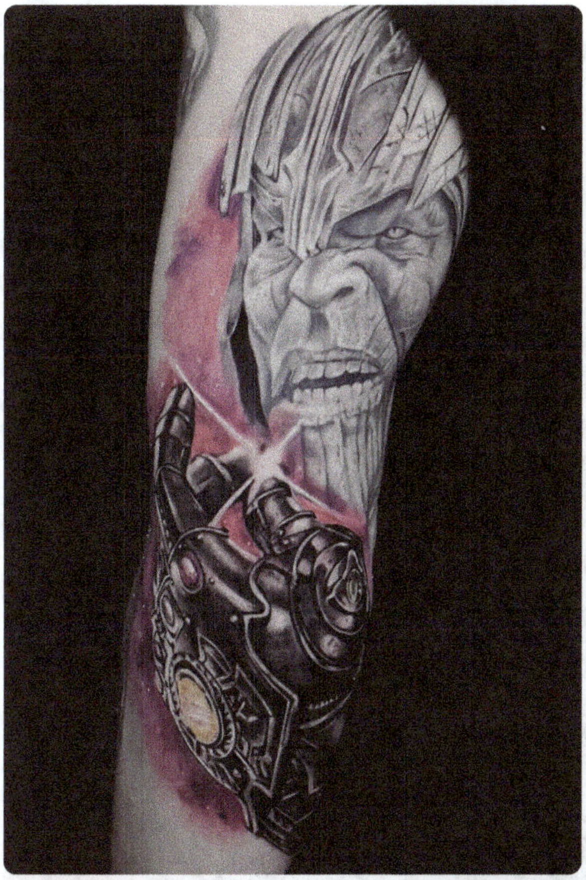

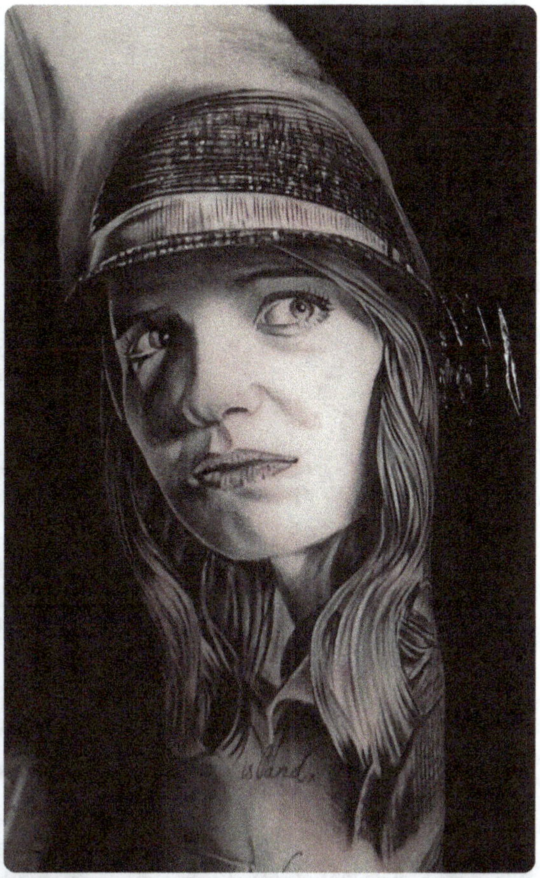

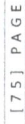

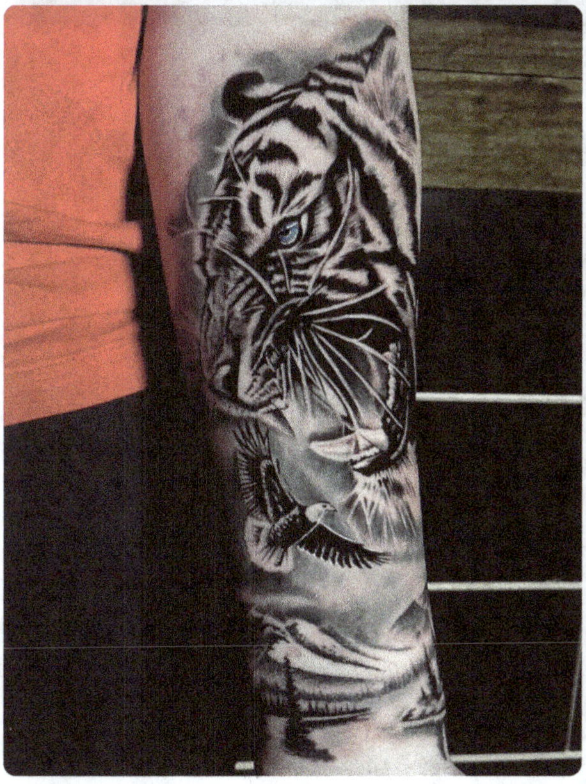

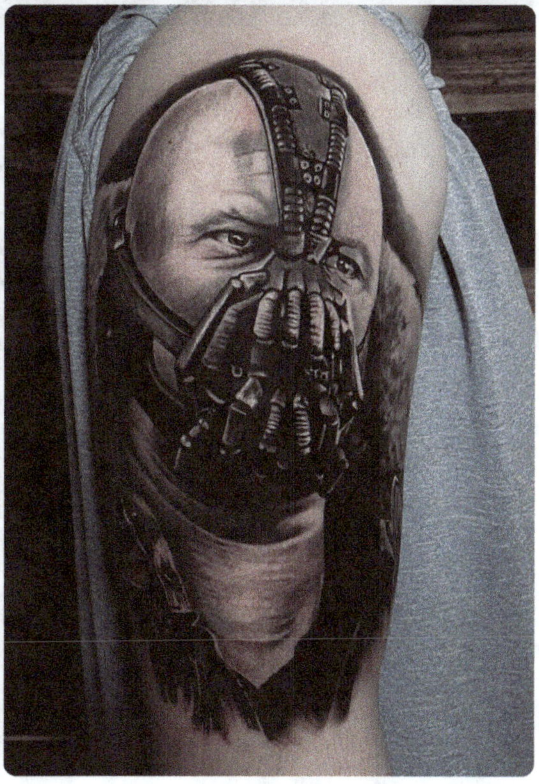

Global Tattoo Magazine

L'HERBE ROUGE

TERRE NOIRE | @LHERBEROUGETATTOO | FRANCE, SION LES MINES

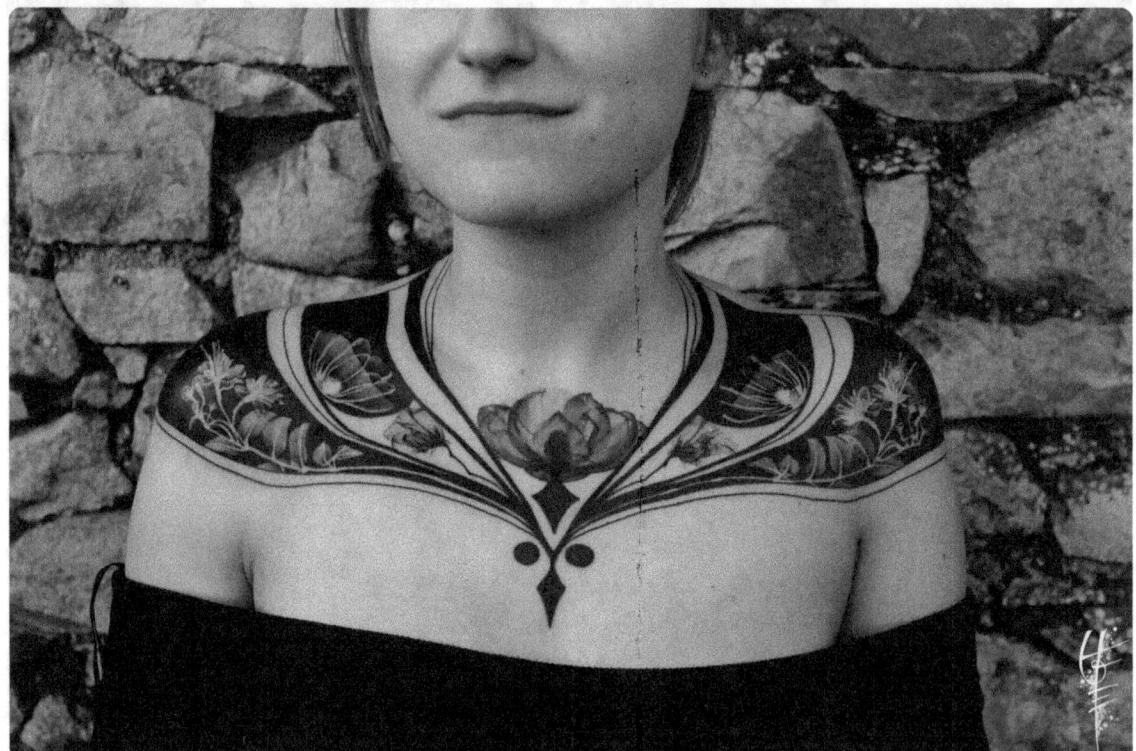

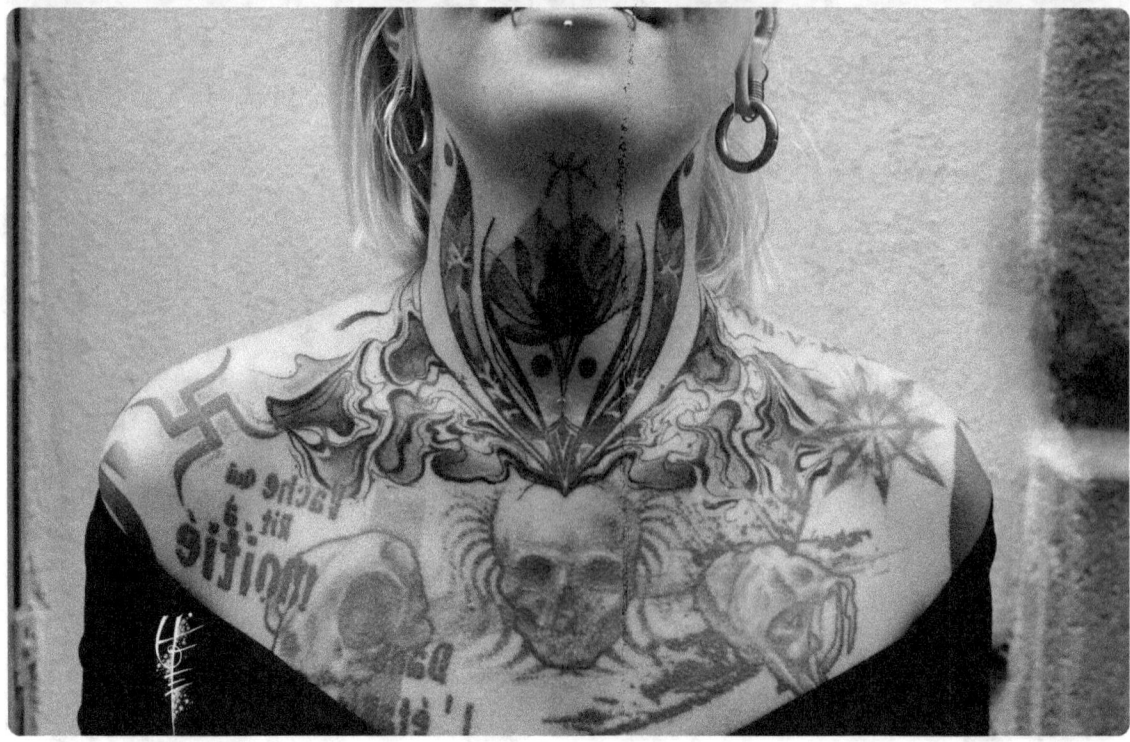

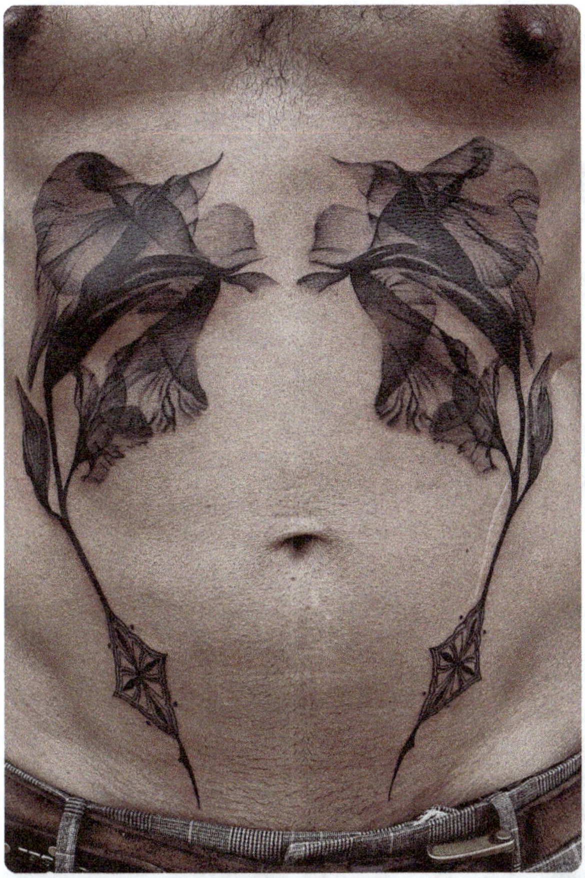

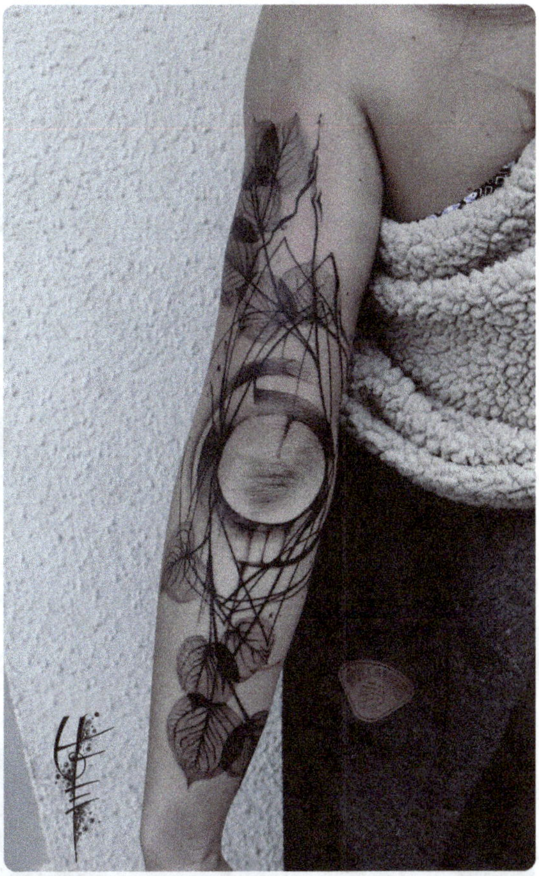

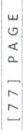

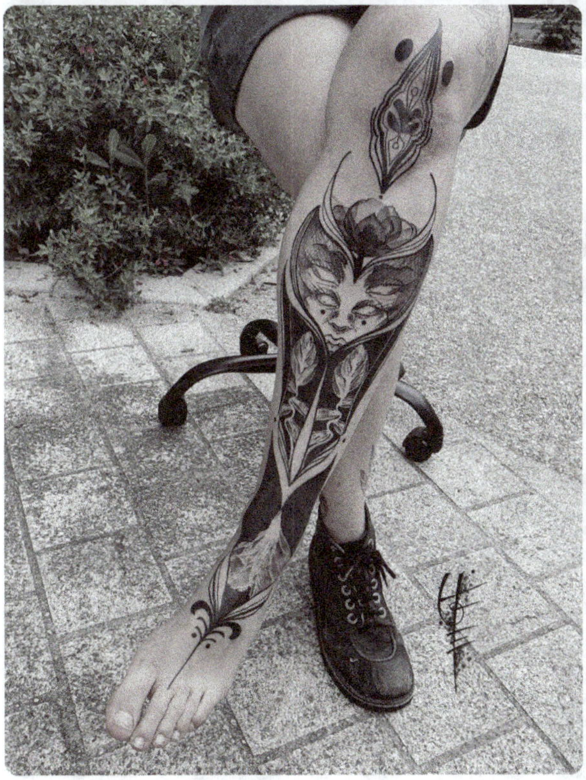

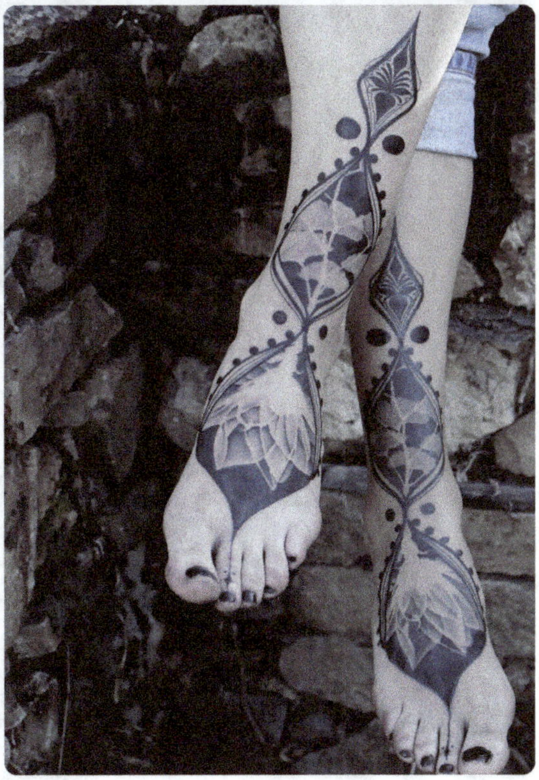

Chapter III

LAUREN DUNLOP

BRASS BUDDHA TATTOOS | @PEPAMALLOWTATTOO | SCOTLAND, EAST LOTHIAN

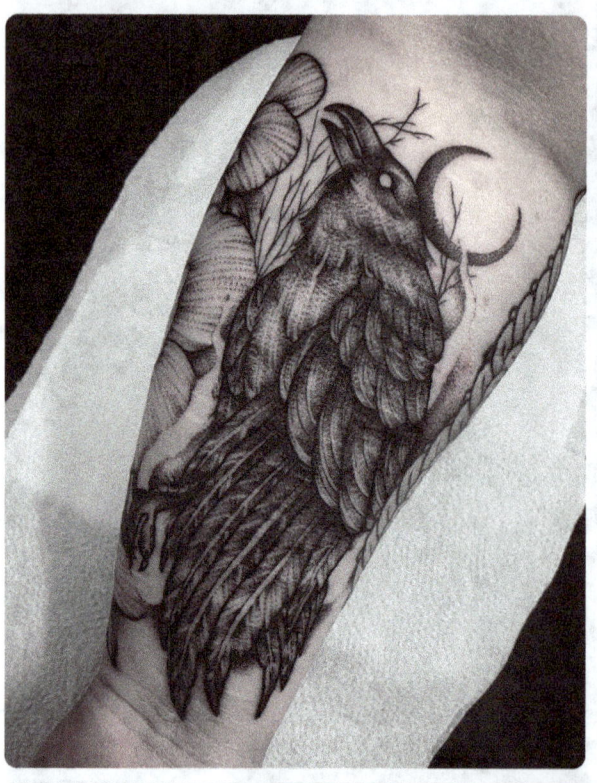

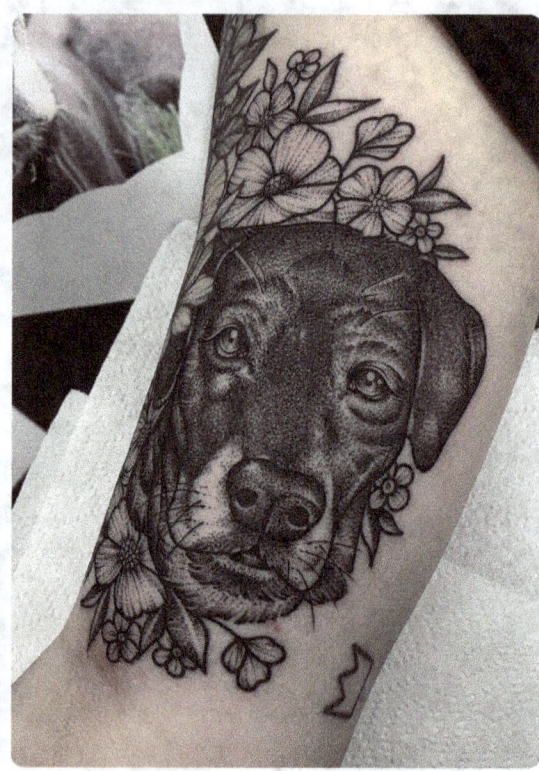

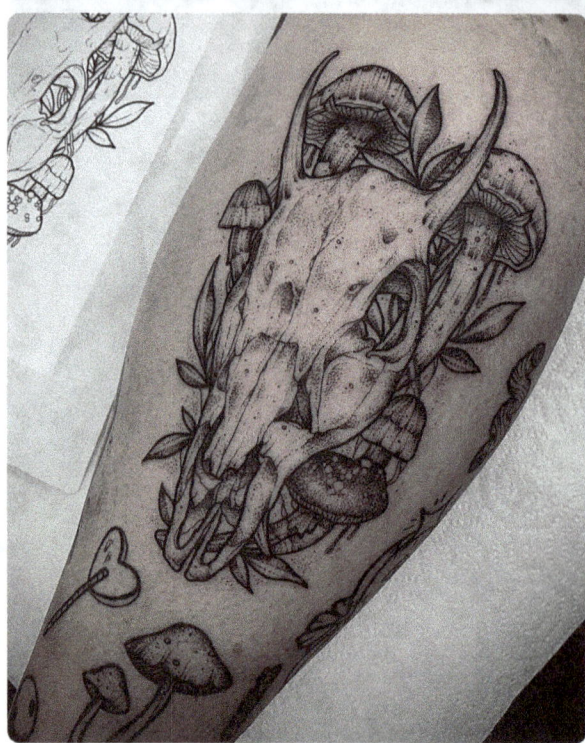

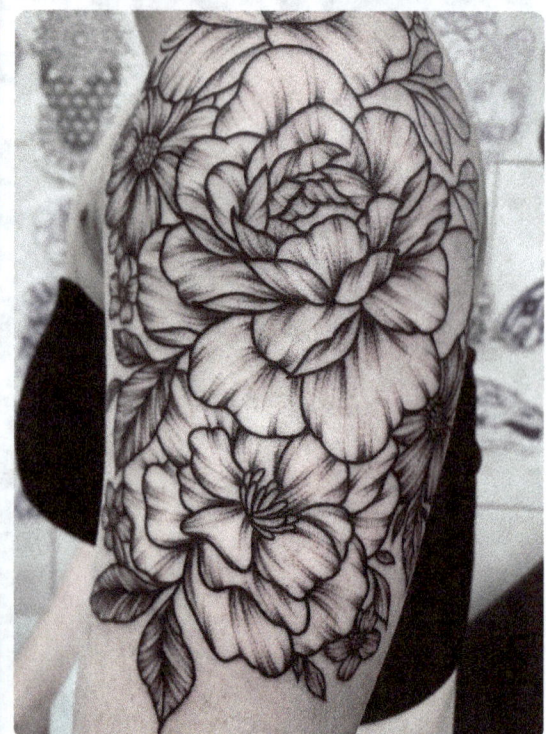

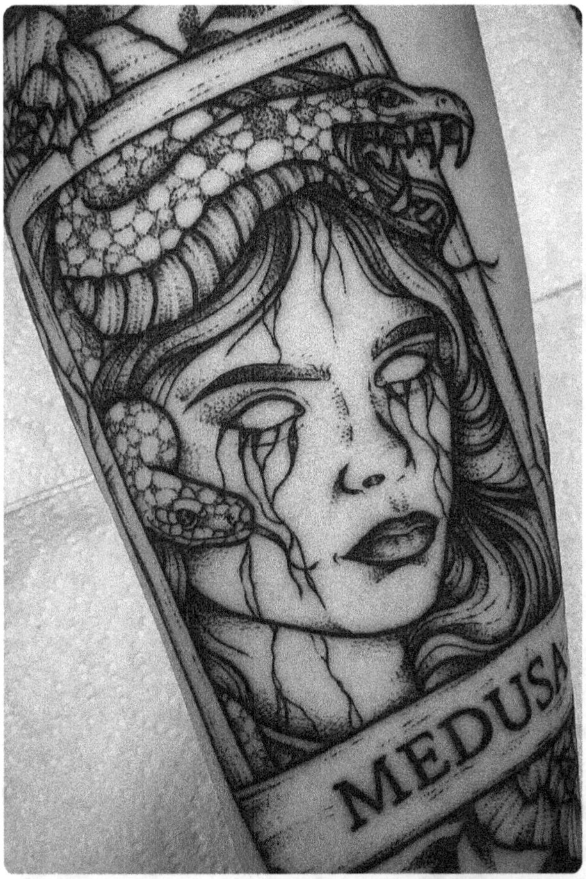

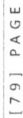

Chapter III

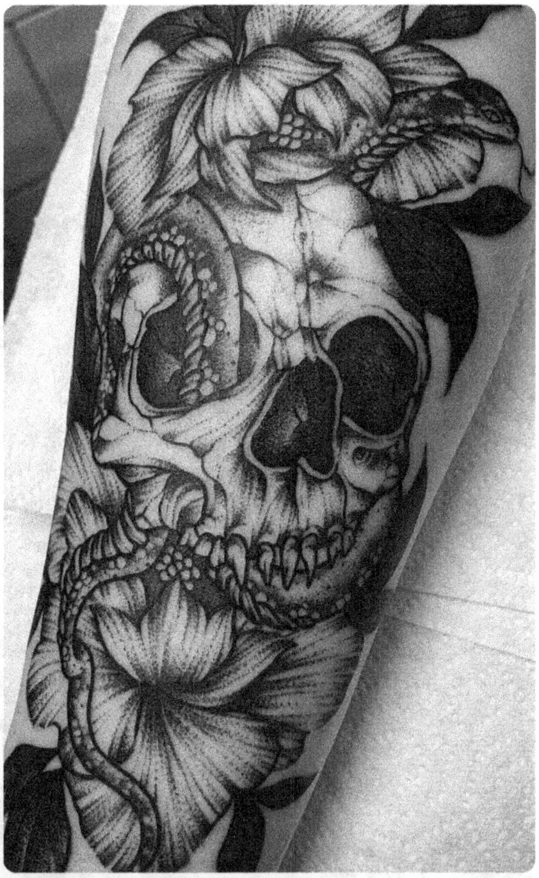

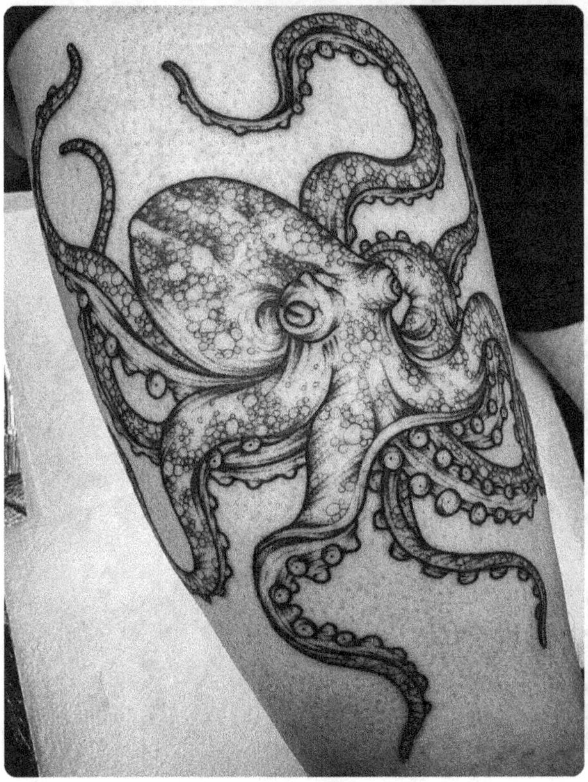

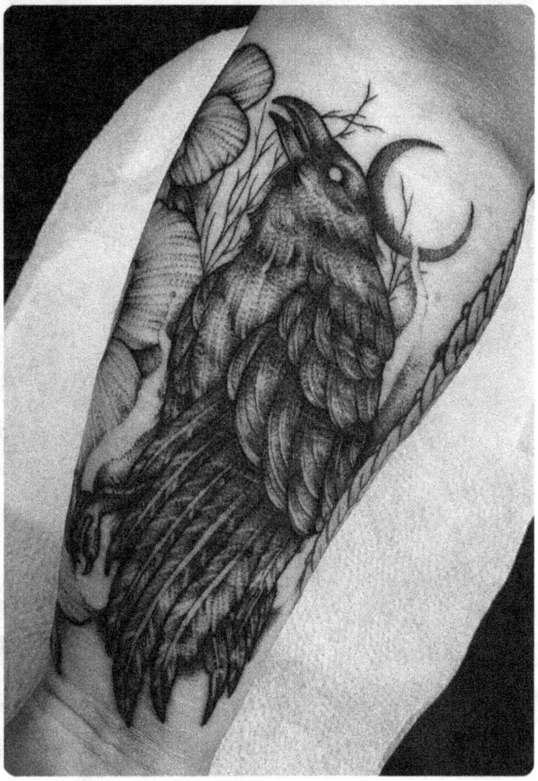

Global Tattoo Magazine

LI WANG

TATTOOCITY BY ONNY'S | @LIWANG.INK | NETHERLANDS, NIJMEGEN

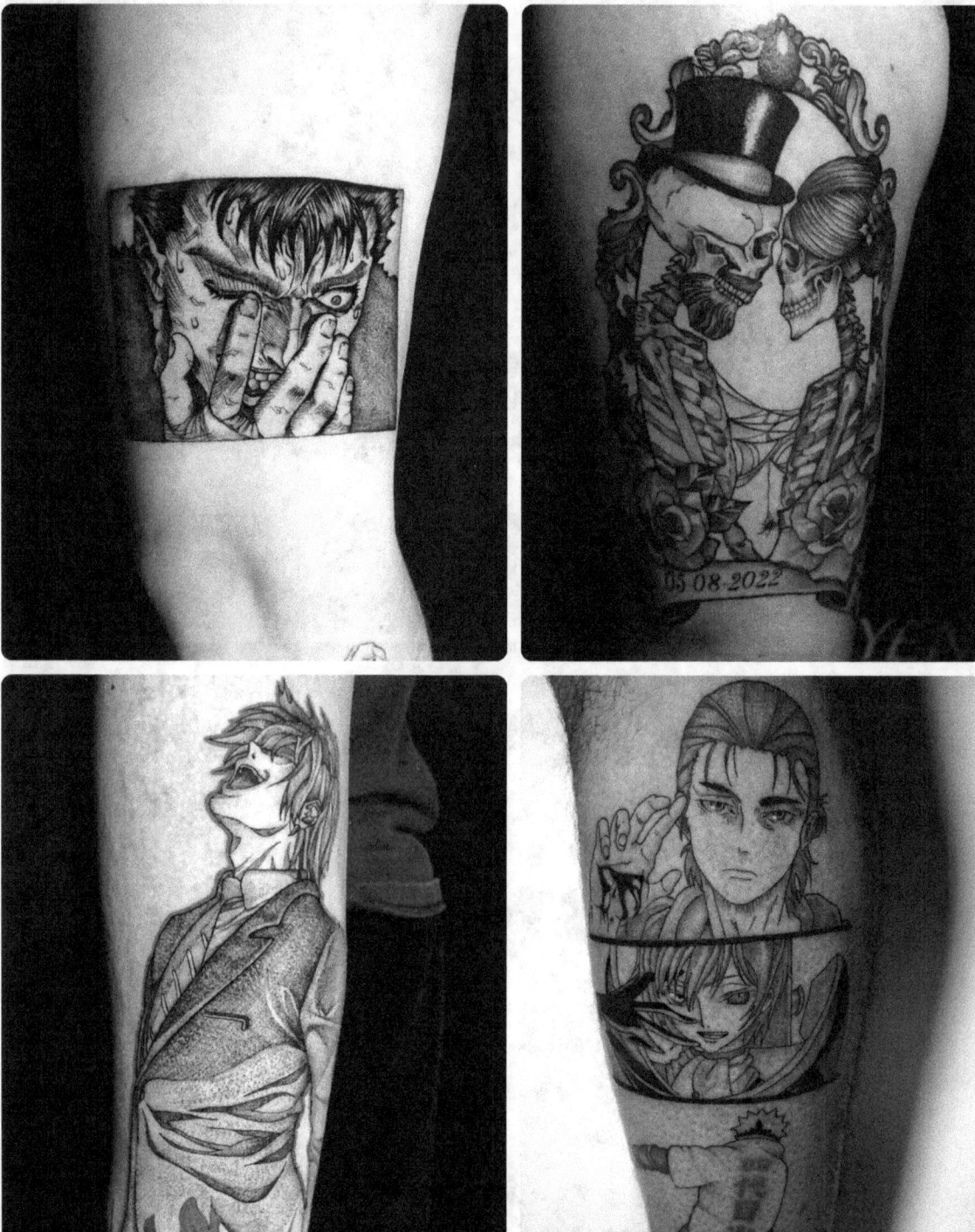

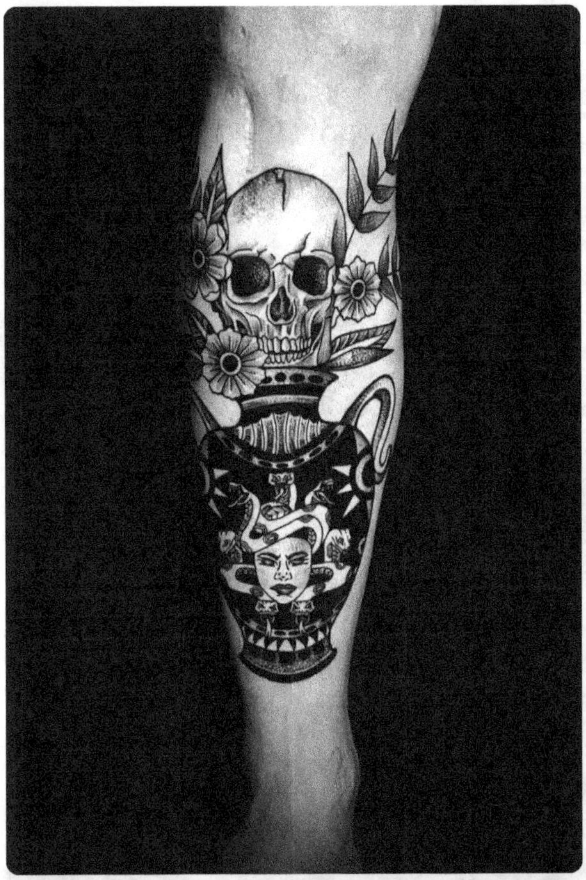

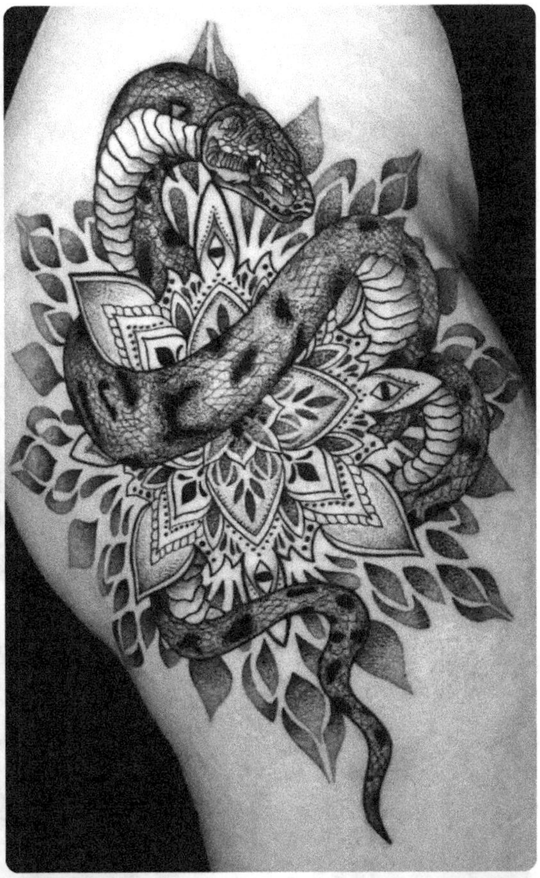

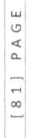

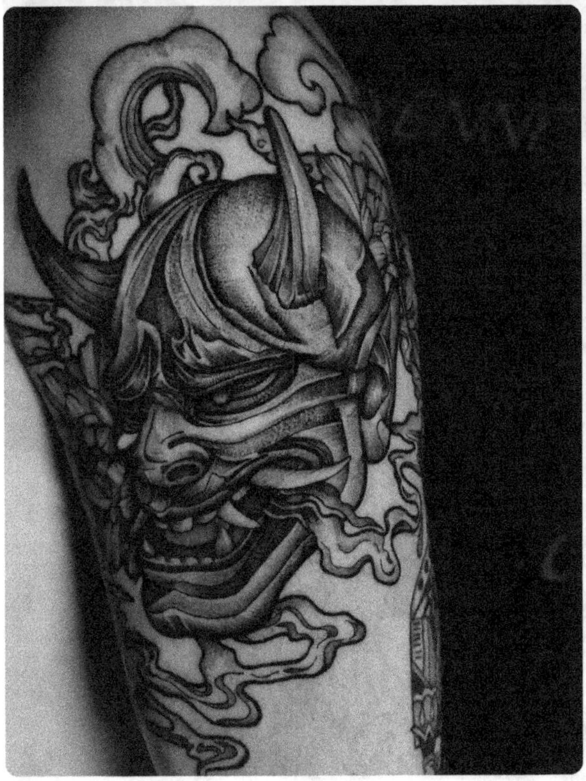

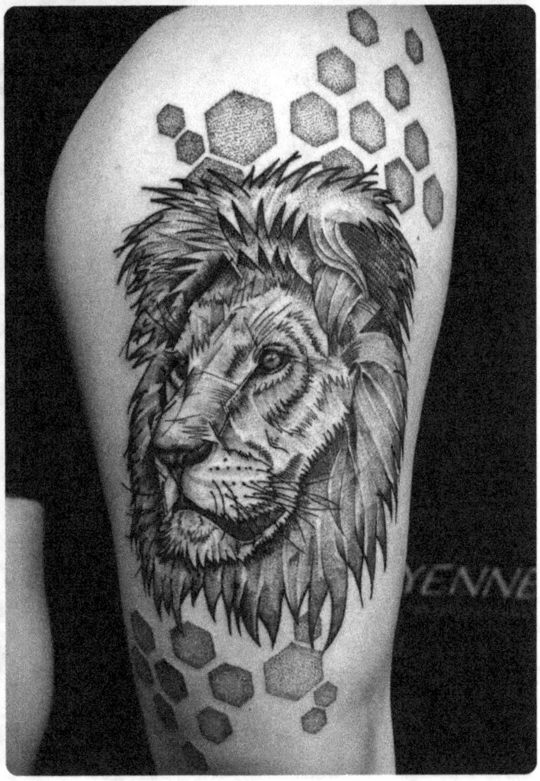

Chapter III

Global Tattoo Magazine

LINDSEY THOMAS

THE TATTOO STATION | @LINDSEY_M_THOMAS | UK, NEWCASTLE UPON TYNE

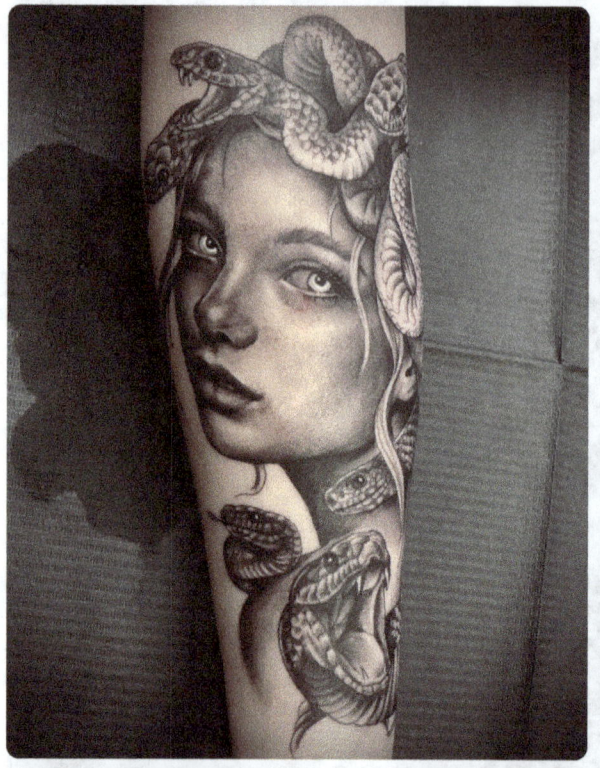
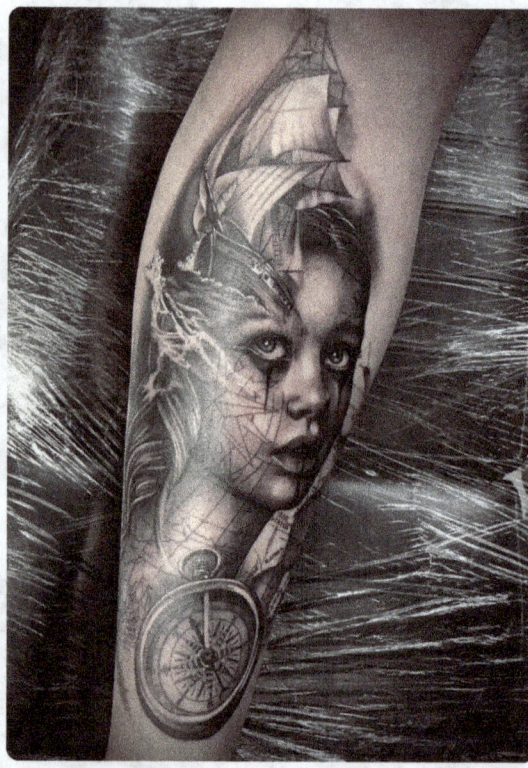
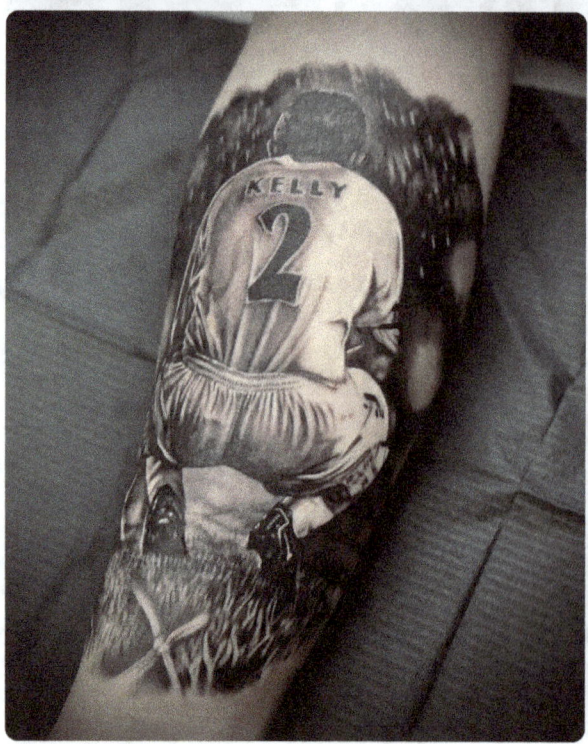
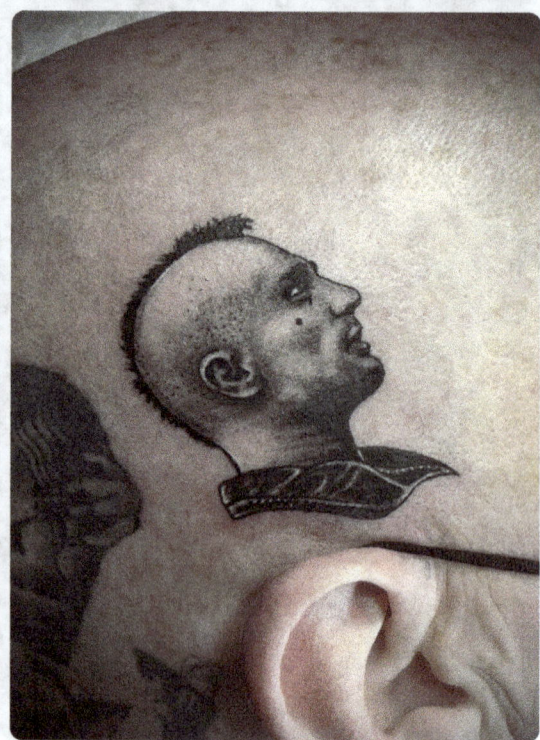

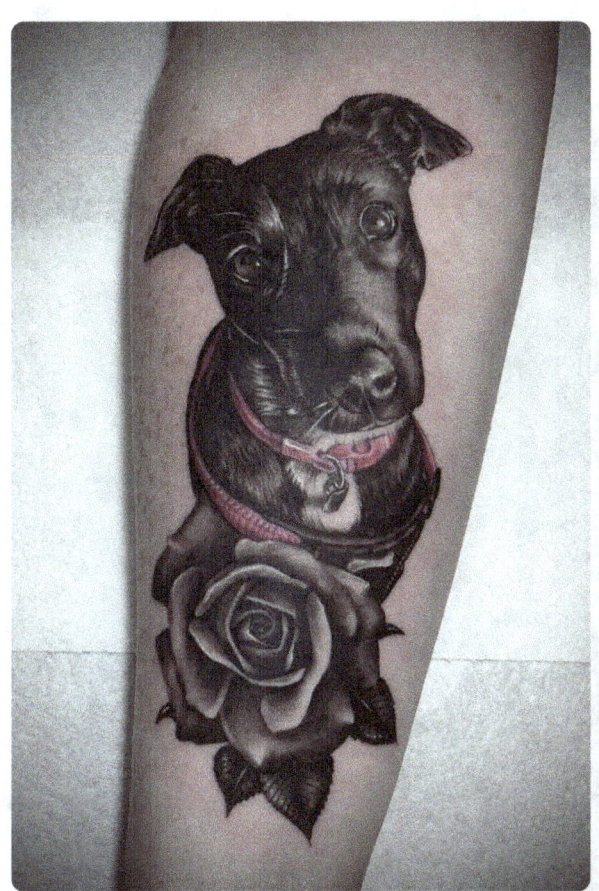

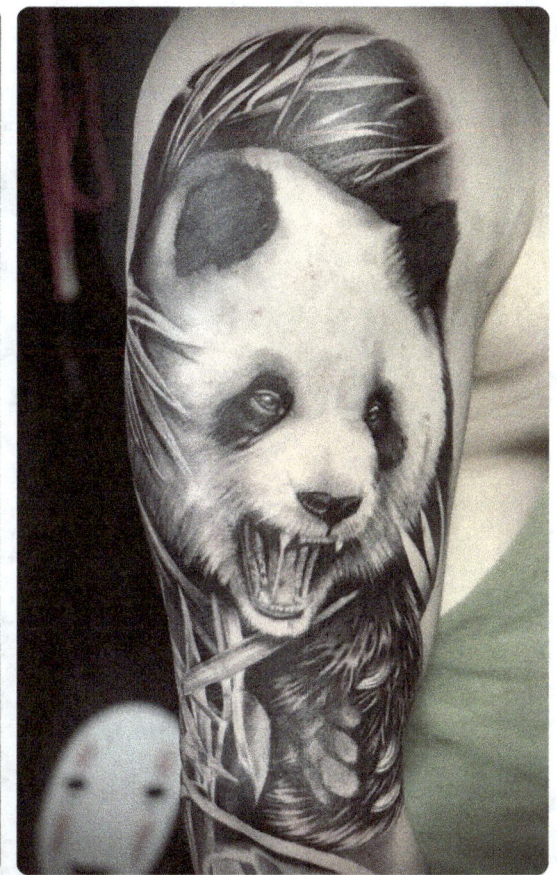

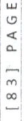

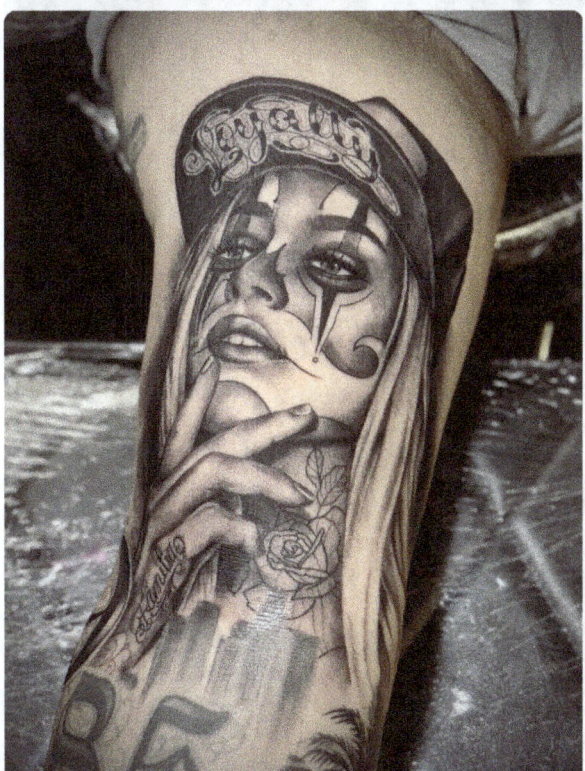

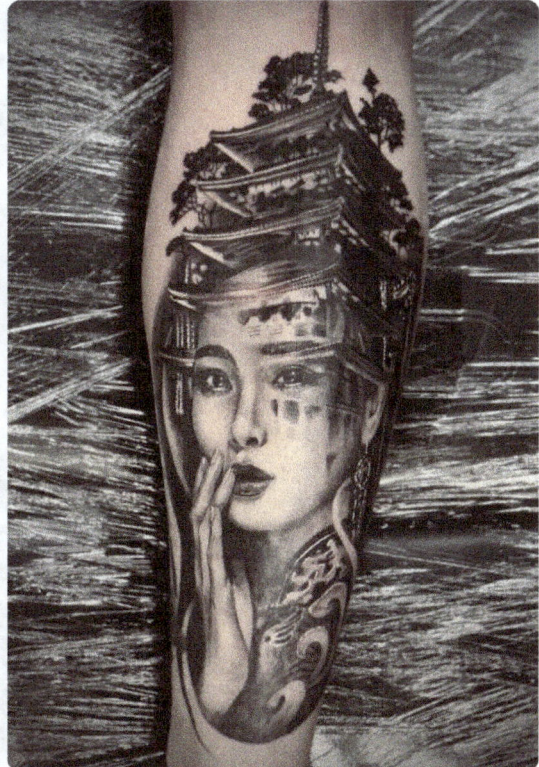

Chapter III

LORENZO CASAGRANDE

WHITELABELTATTOO | @_CASITOSTATTOO_ | ITALY, CESANO MADERNO

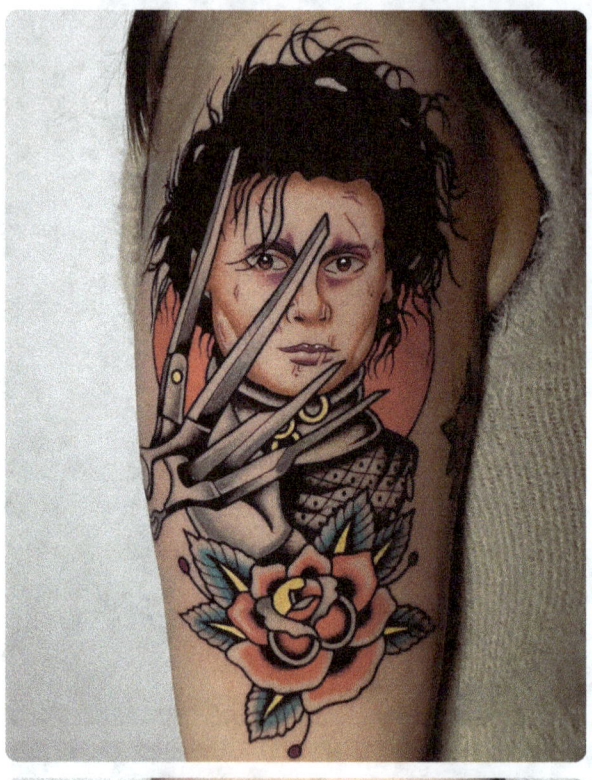
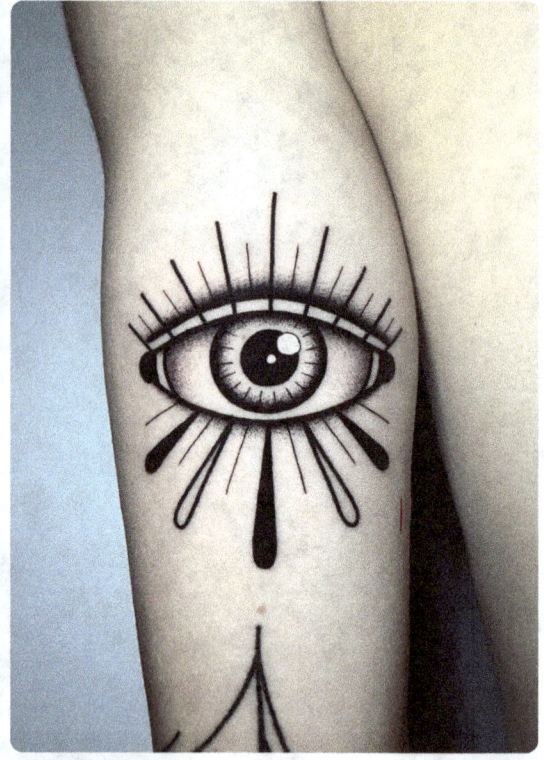
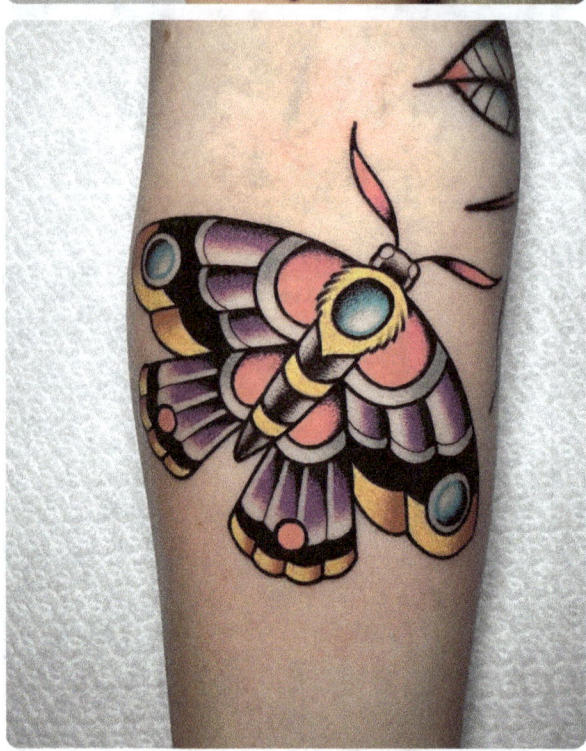
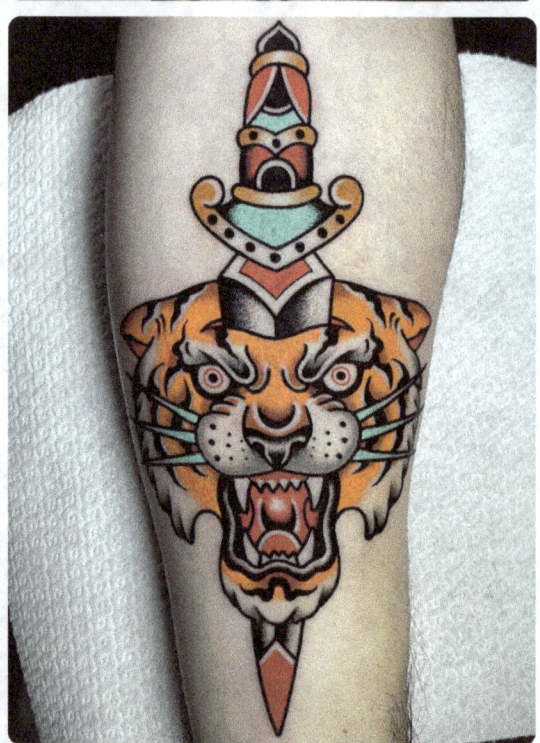

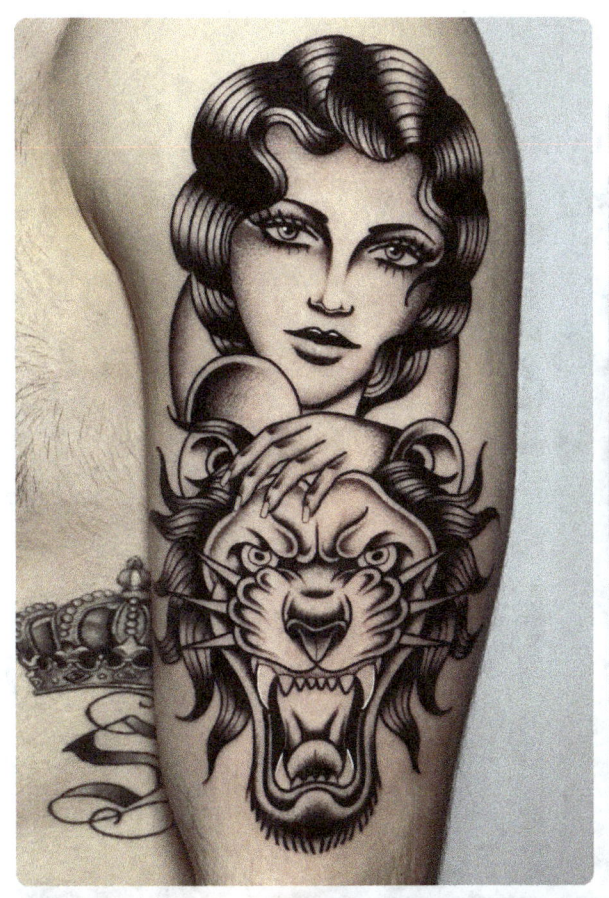

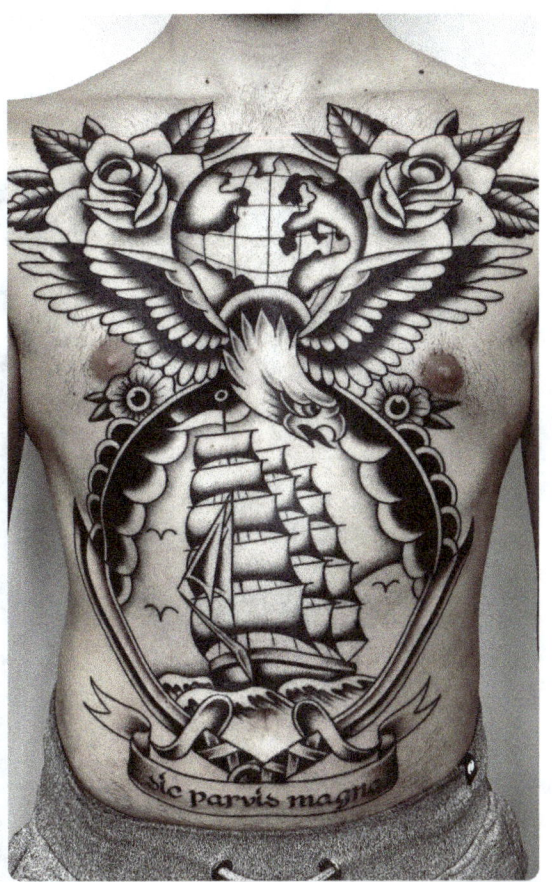

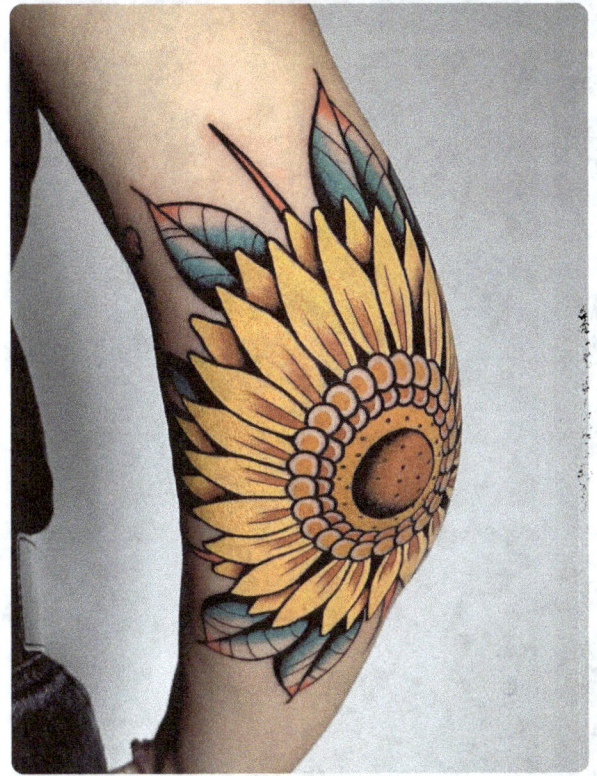

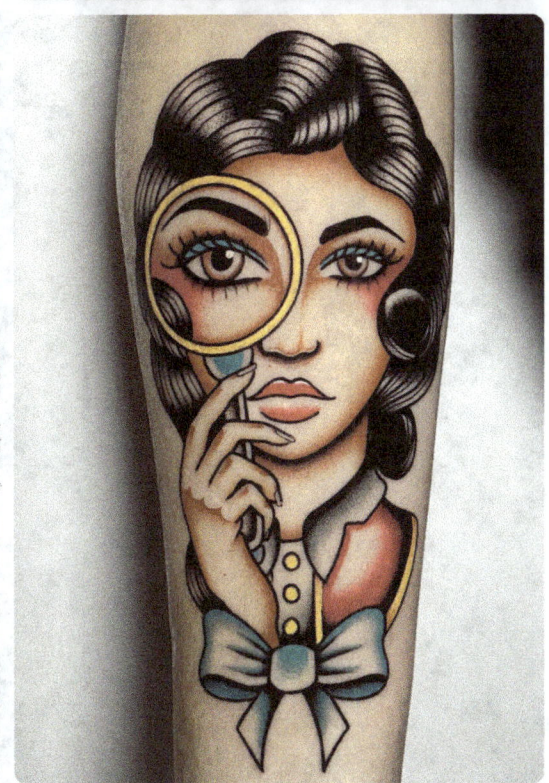

Chapter III

LUCAS SLEVIN

WTF TATTOO GALLERY | @LUCAS_SLEVIN | FRANCE, LYON

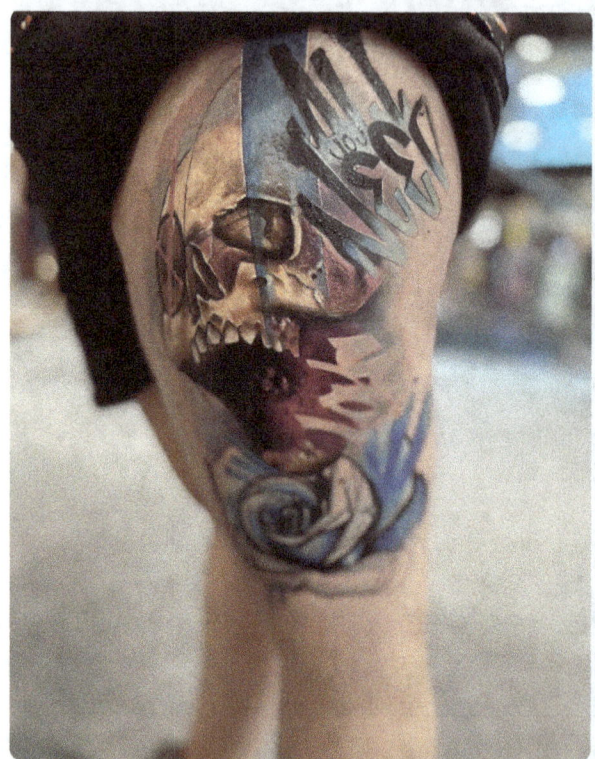
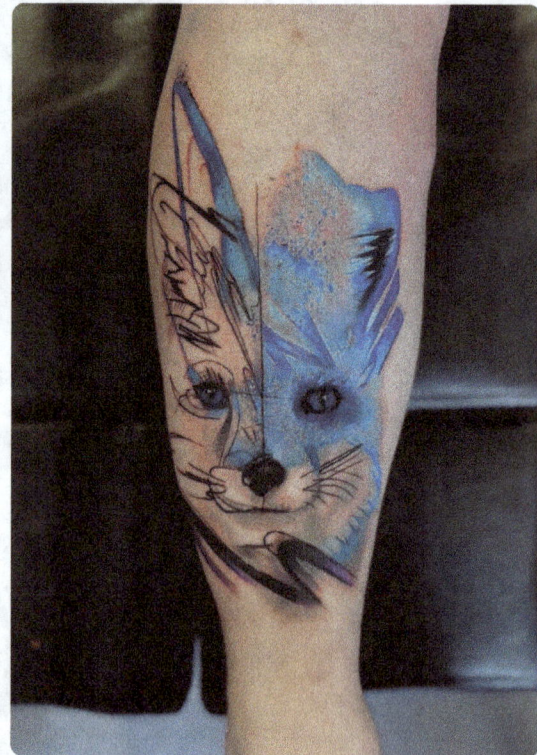
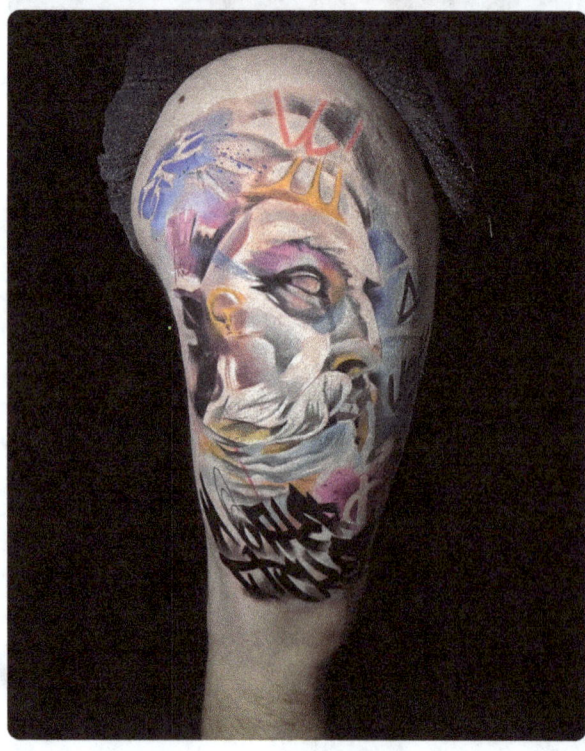
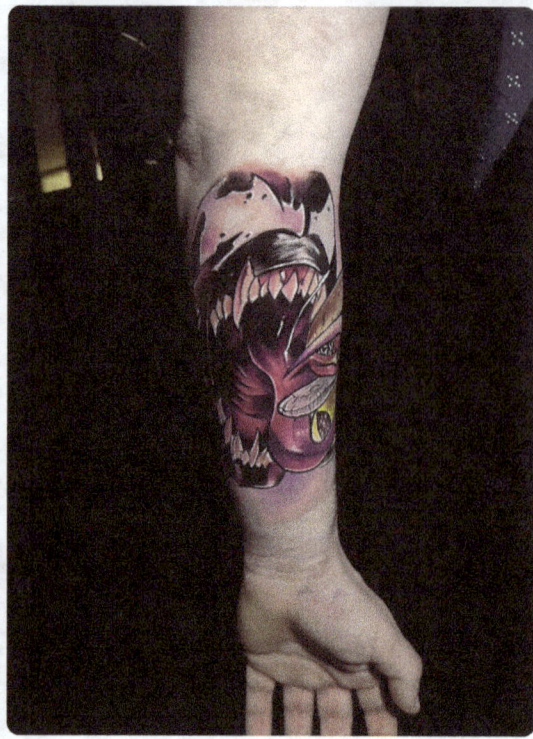

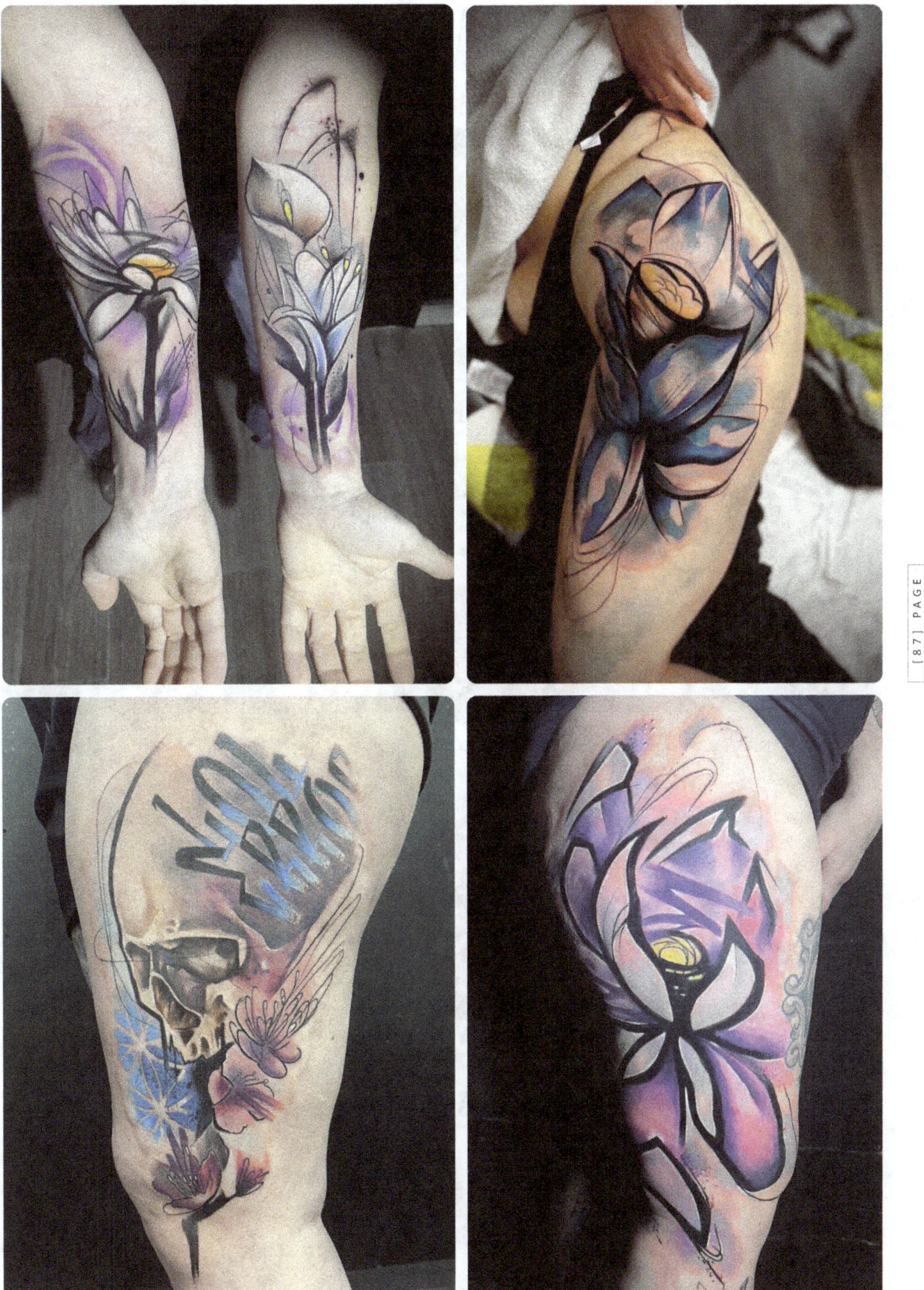

Chapter III

LUKE EDWARDS

FB: LUKE EDWARDS | @LUCASEDWARDO_TATTOOS | UK, LEIGH-ON-SEA

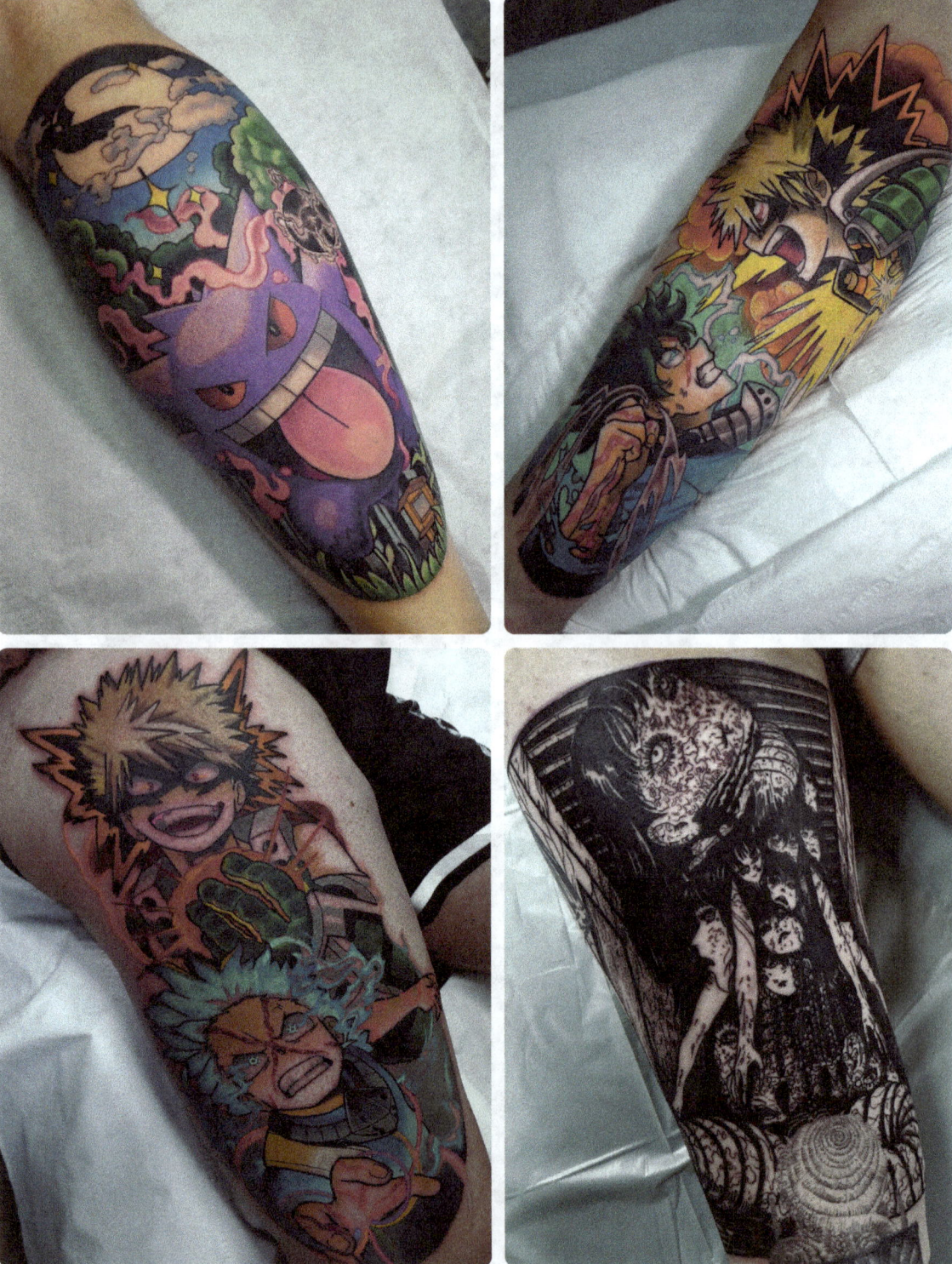

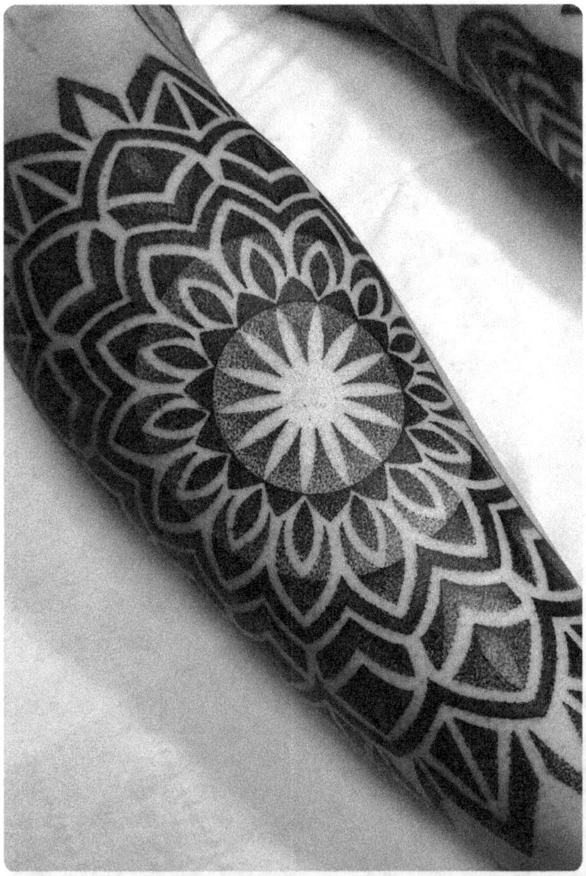

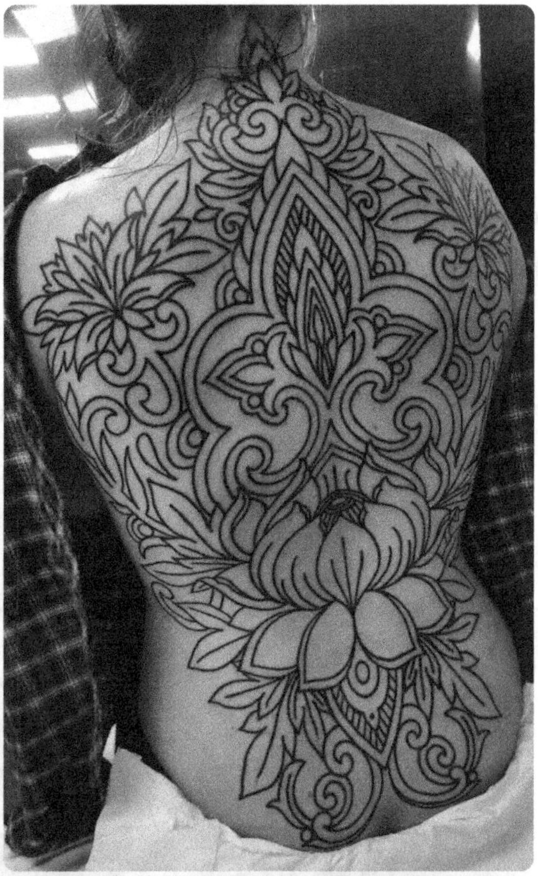

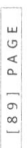

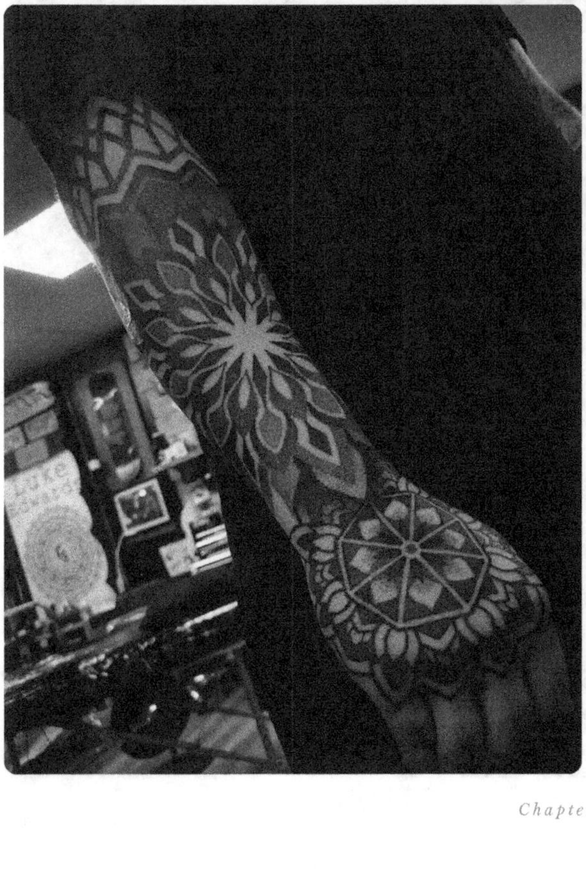

Chapter III

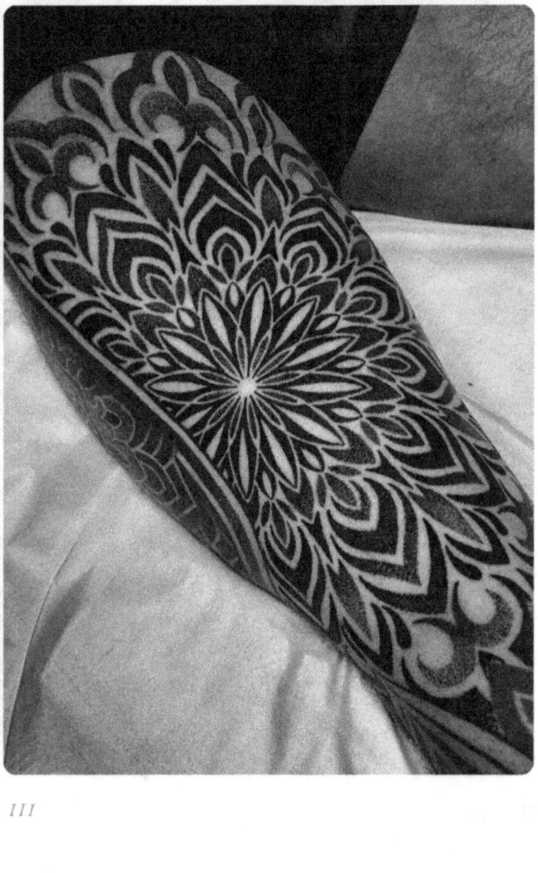

LYCANA ART

GOLDEN CAT TATTOO | @LYCANA.ART | SPAIN, BARCELONA

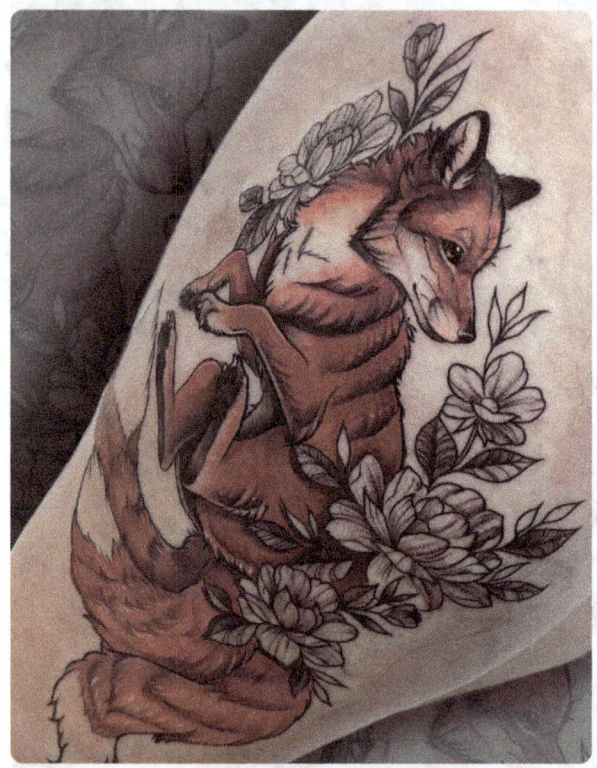
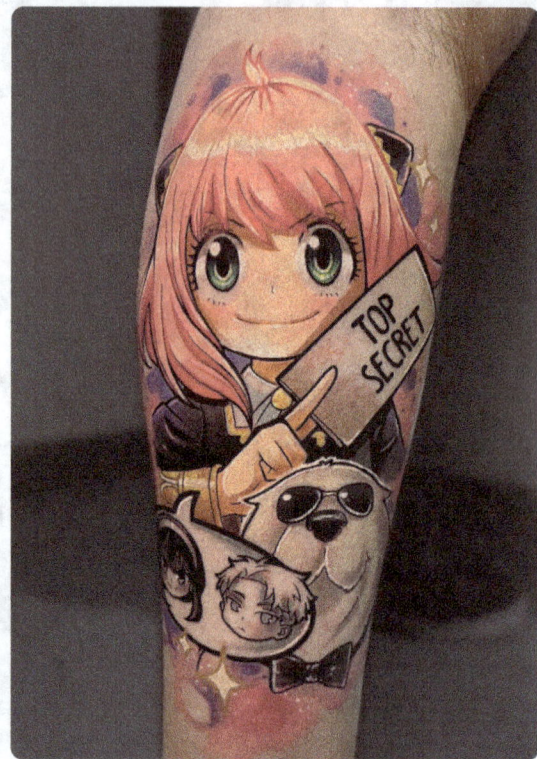
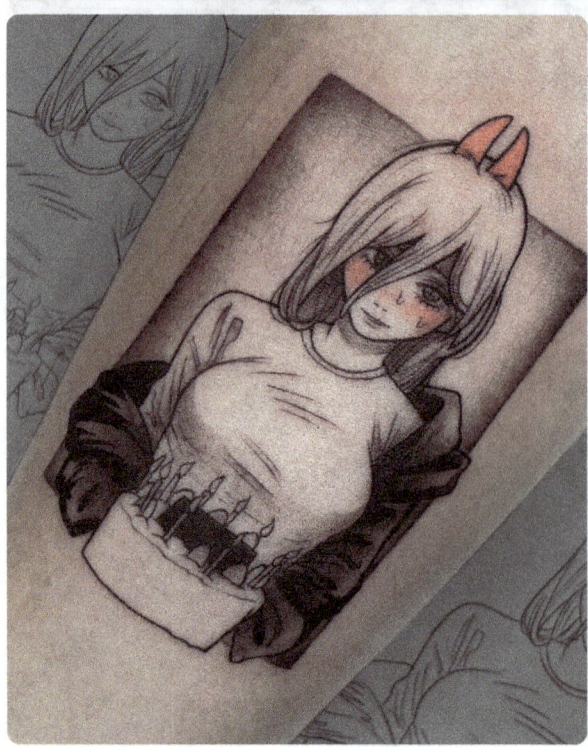
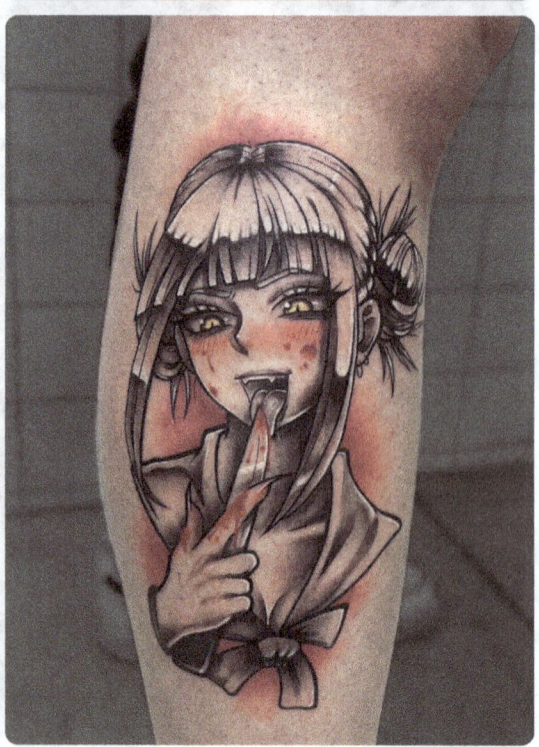

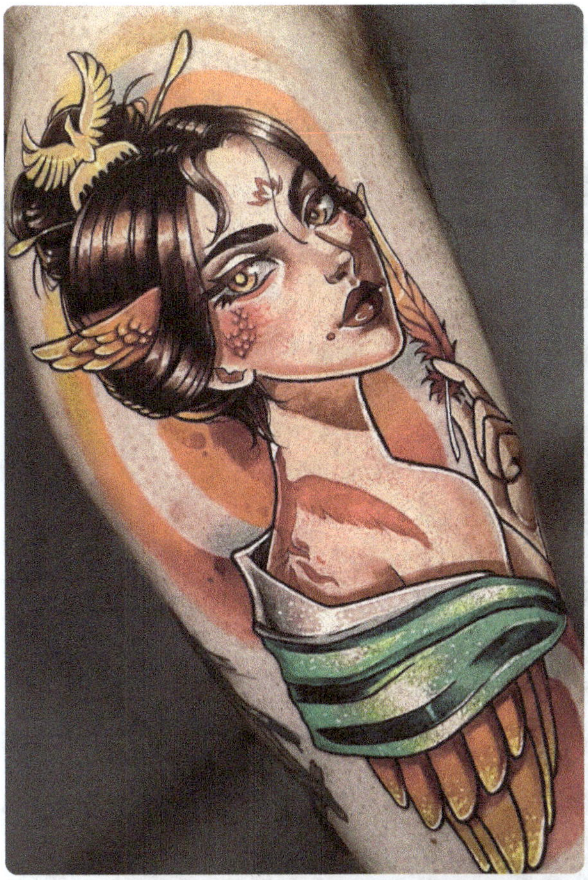

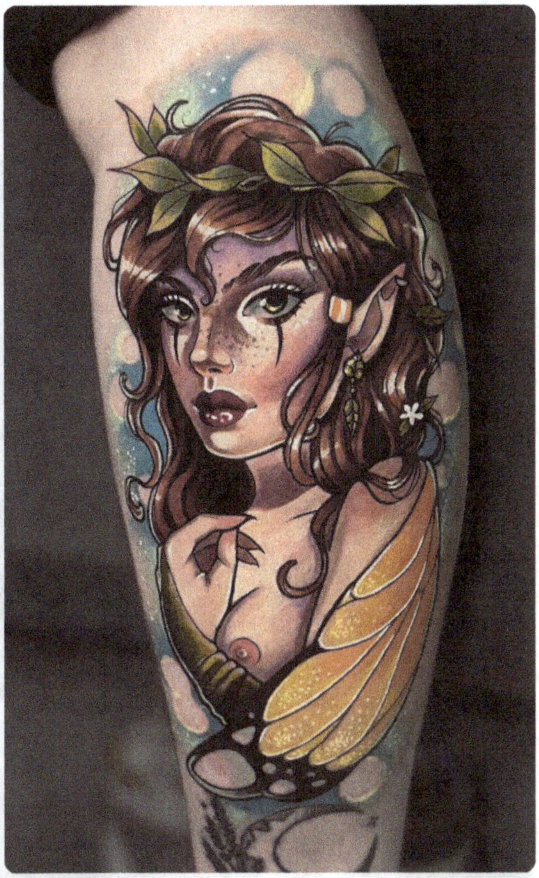

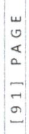

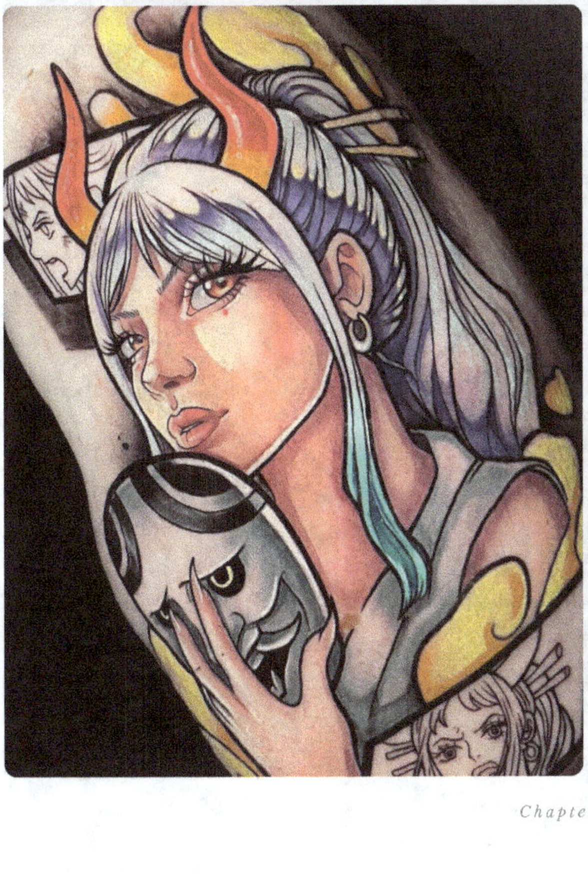

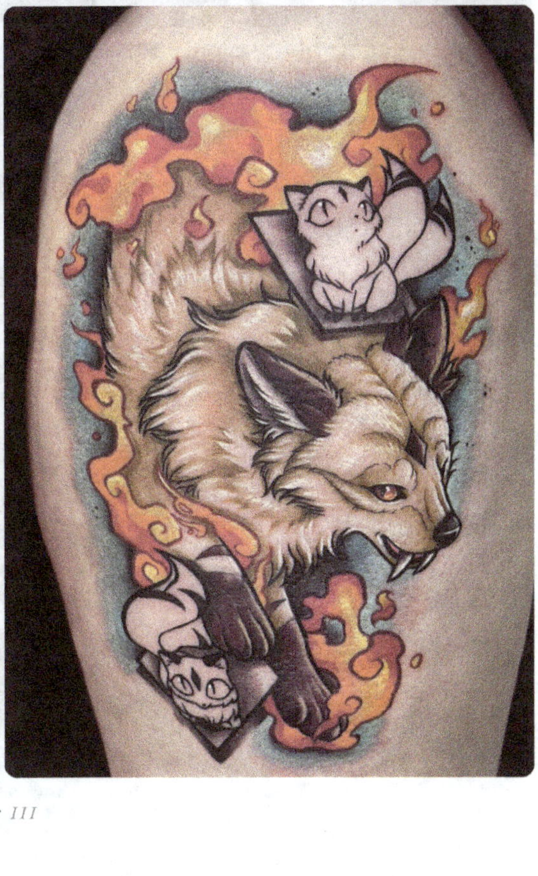

Chapter III

MADAME RED

STUDIO FREAK SHOW | @MADAME_RED_TATTOO | FRANCE, METZ

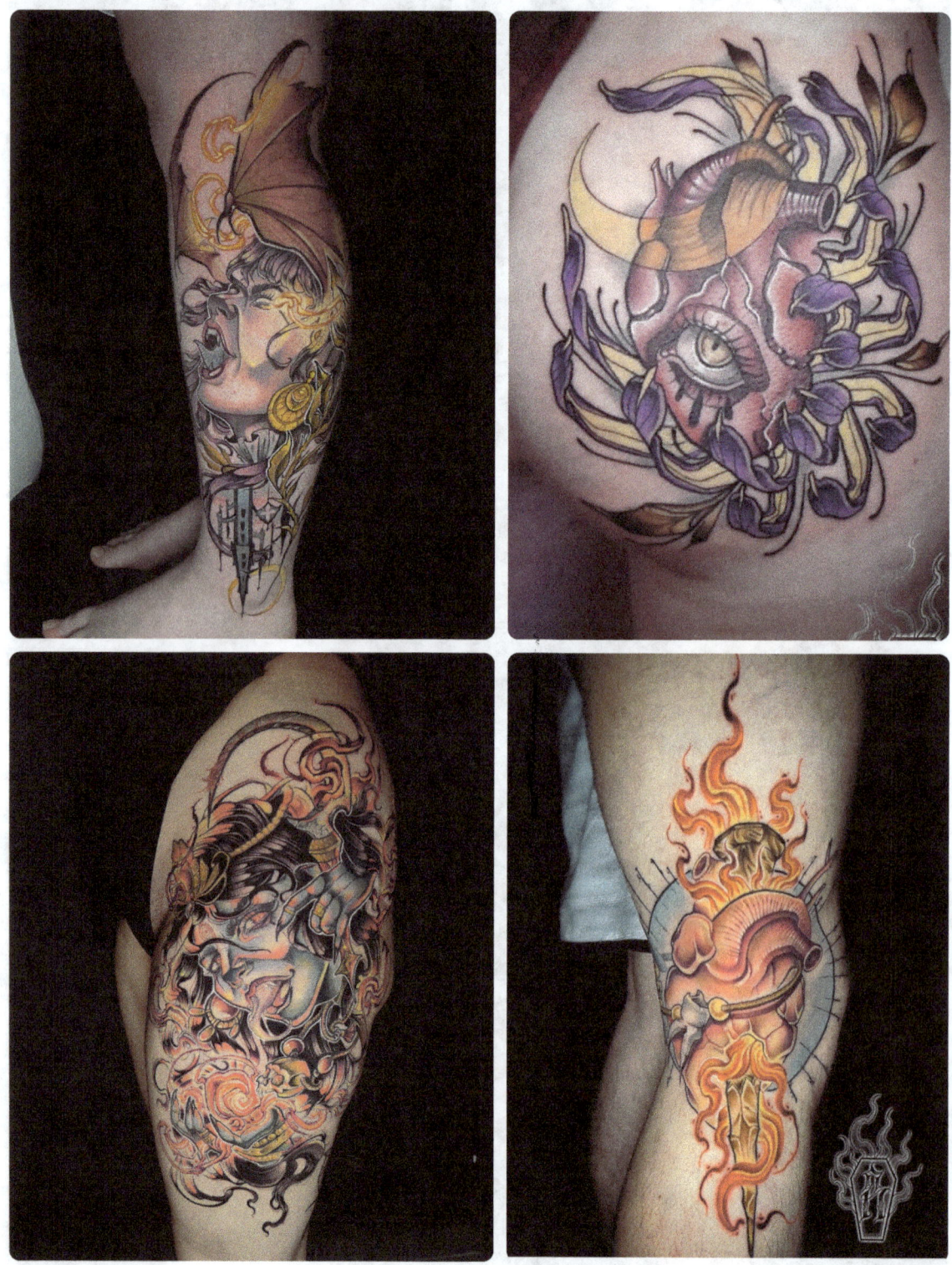

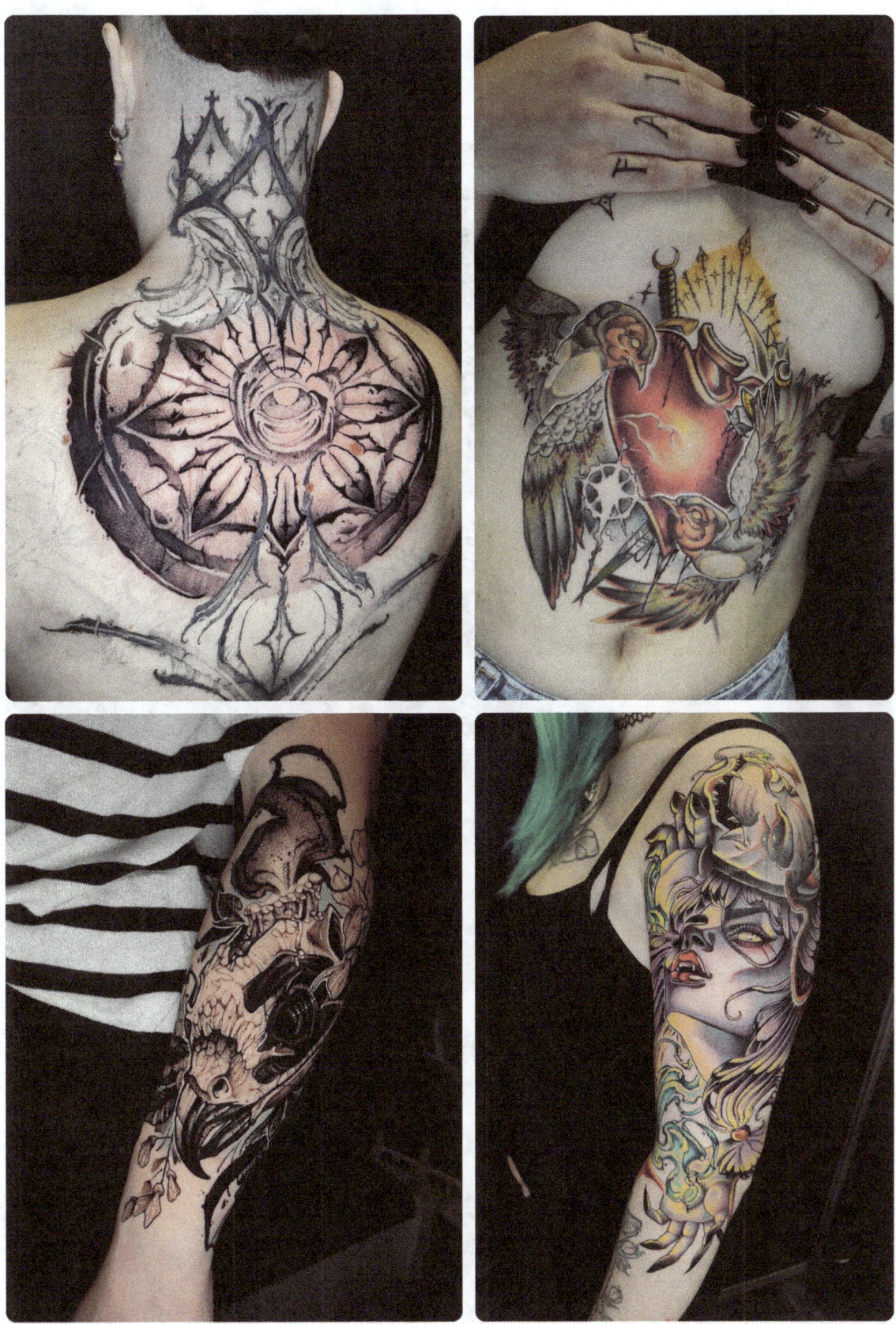

Global Tattoo Magazine

MADISON STANWAY

INCREDIBLE INK TATTOO STUDIO | @MADI.TATTOOS | UK, STOKE-ON-TRENT

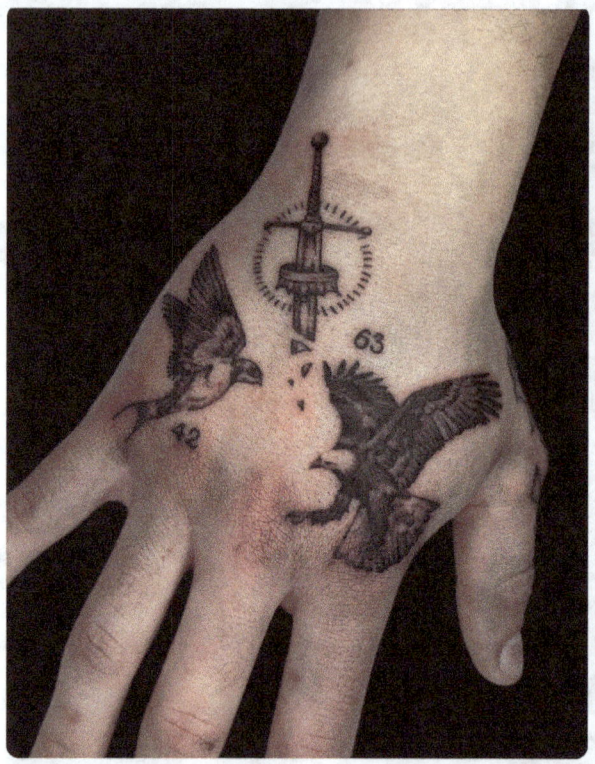

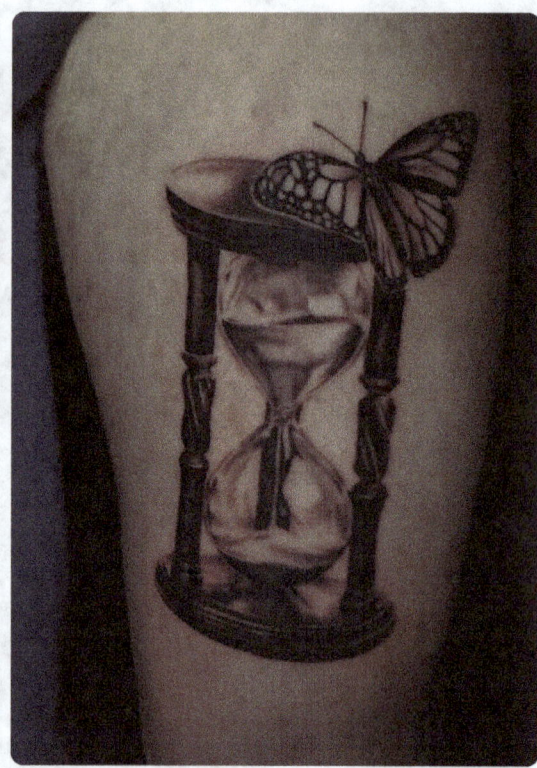

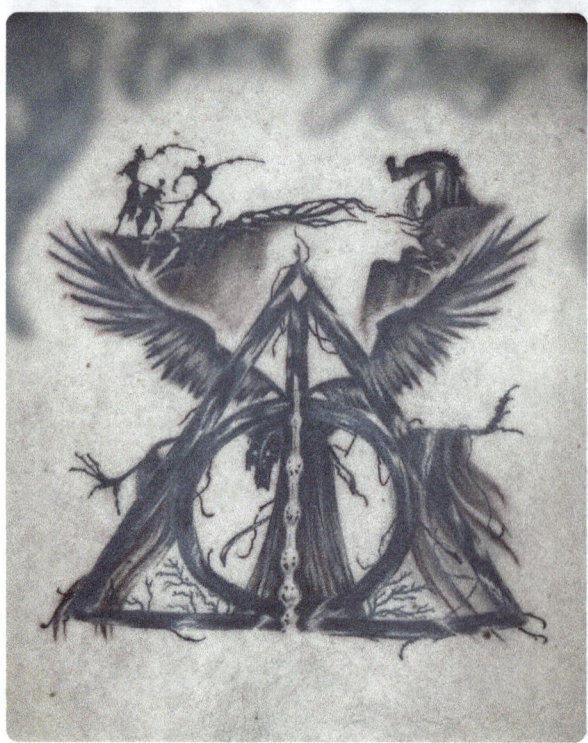

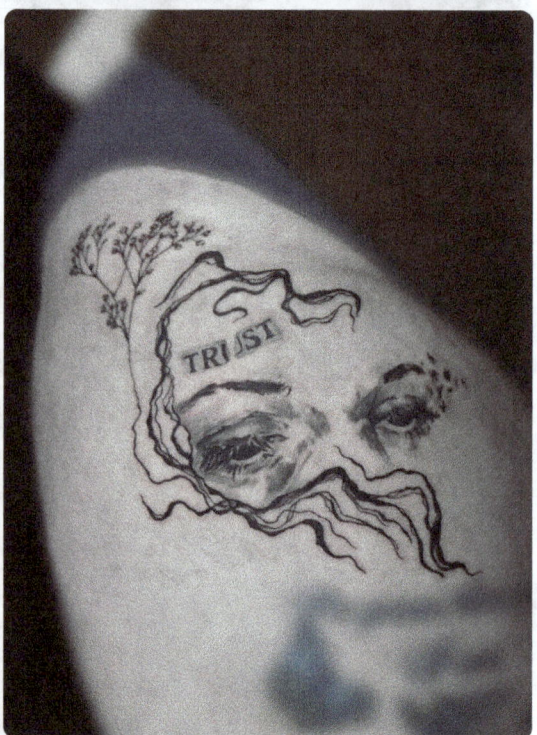

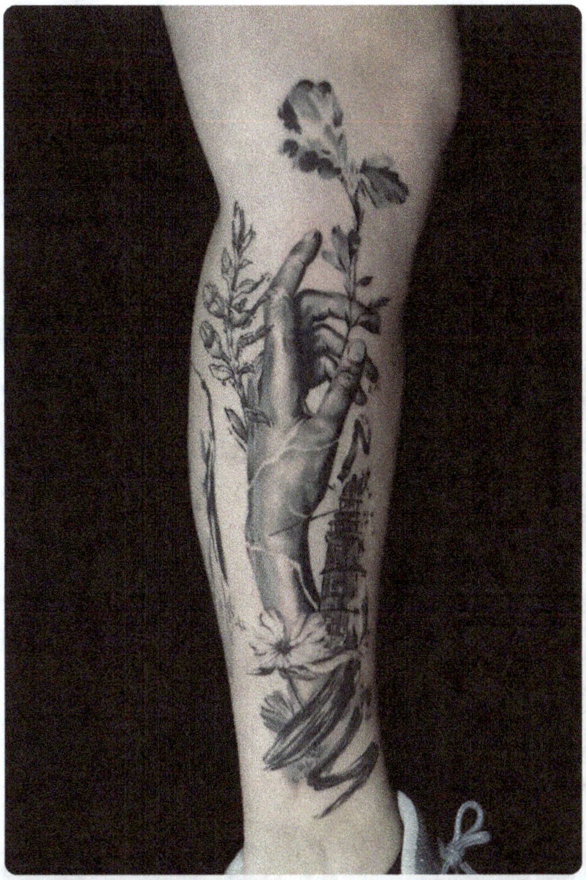

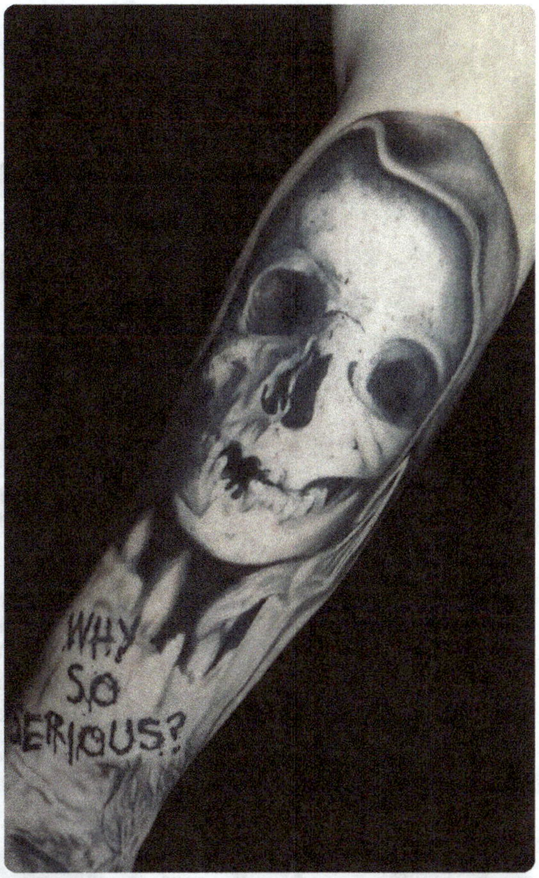

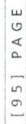

Chapter III

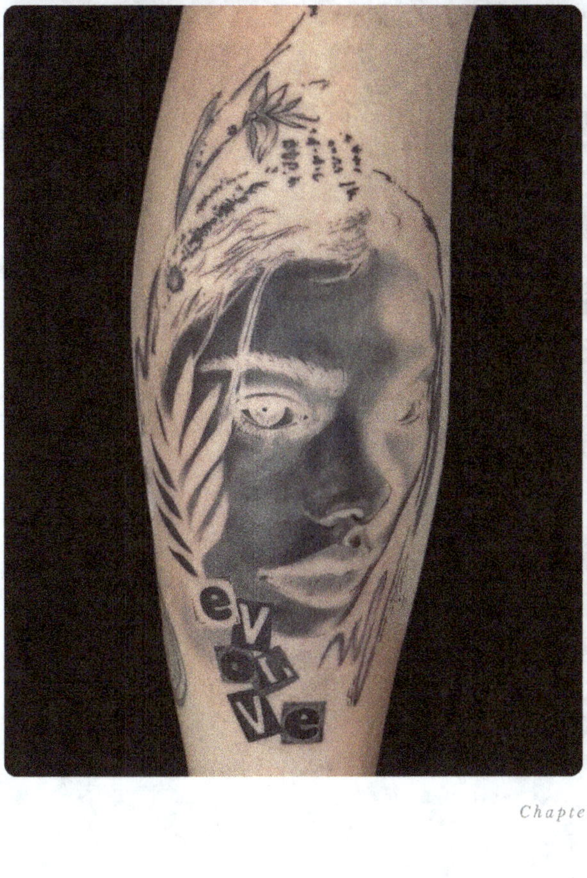

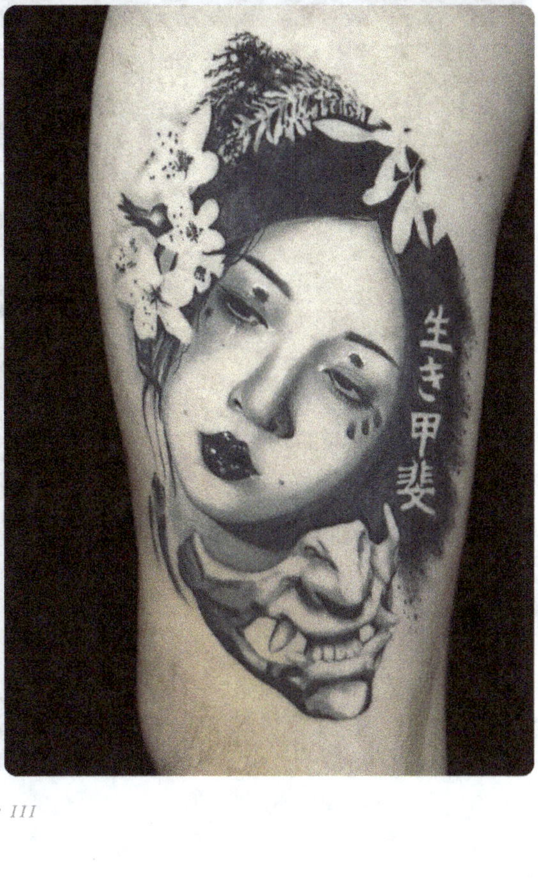

MAKSIM CHANISHEV

SHIFU SOSET | @CHANISHEV_MXM | RUSSIA, KRASNODAR

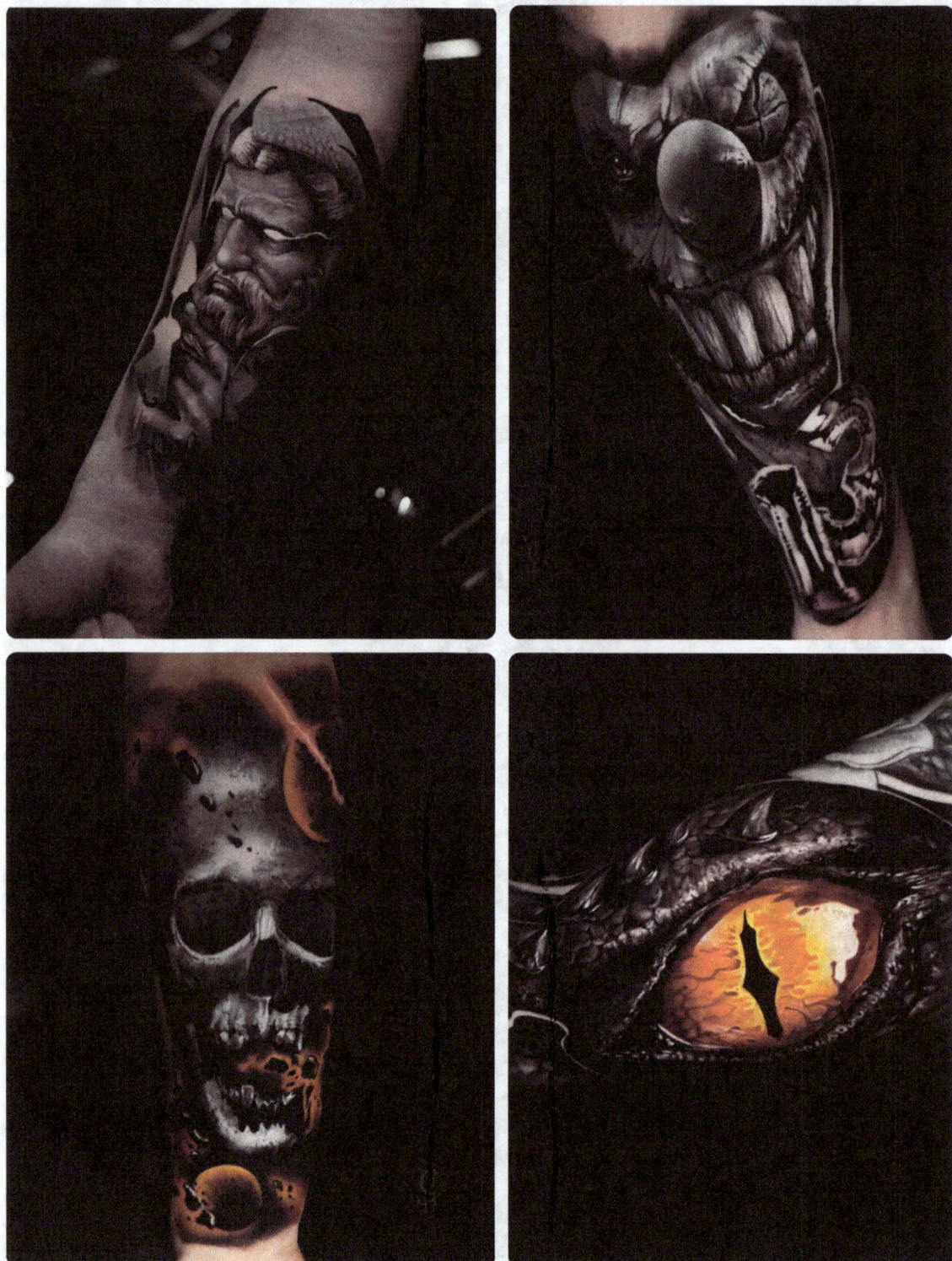

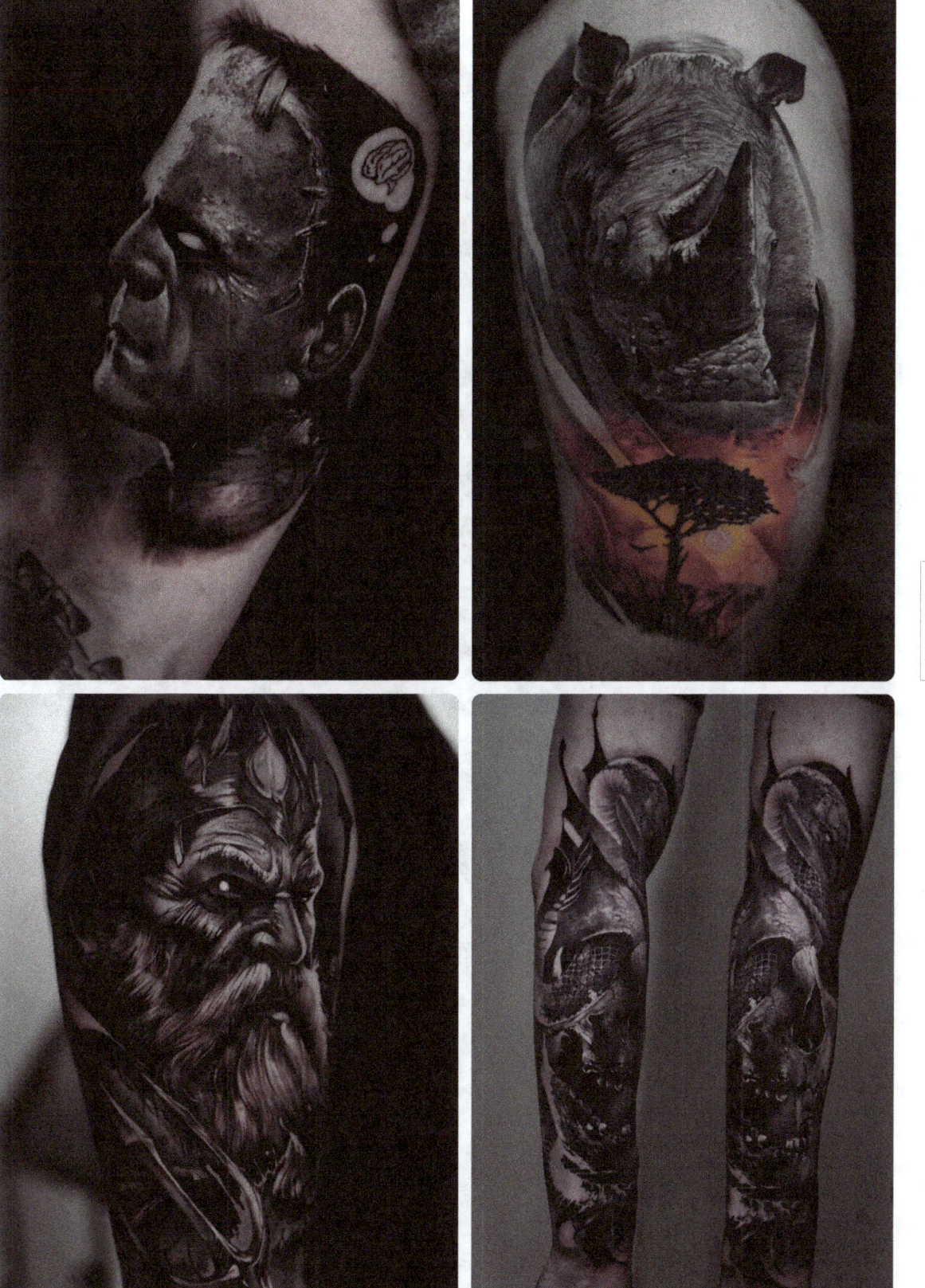

Chapter III

MATHEW PRICE

SURSUM TATTOO | @MATHEWPRICETATTOO | PEMBROKESHIRE, WEST WALES

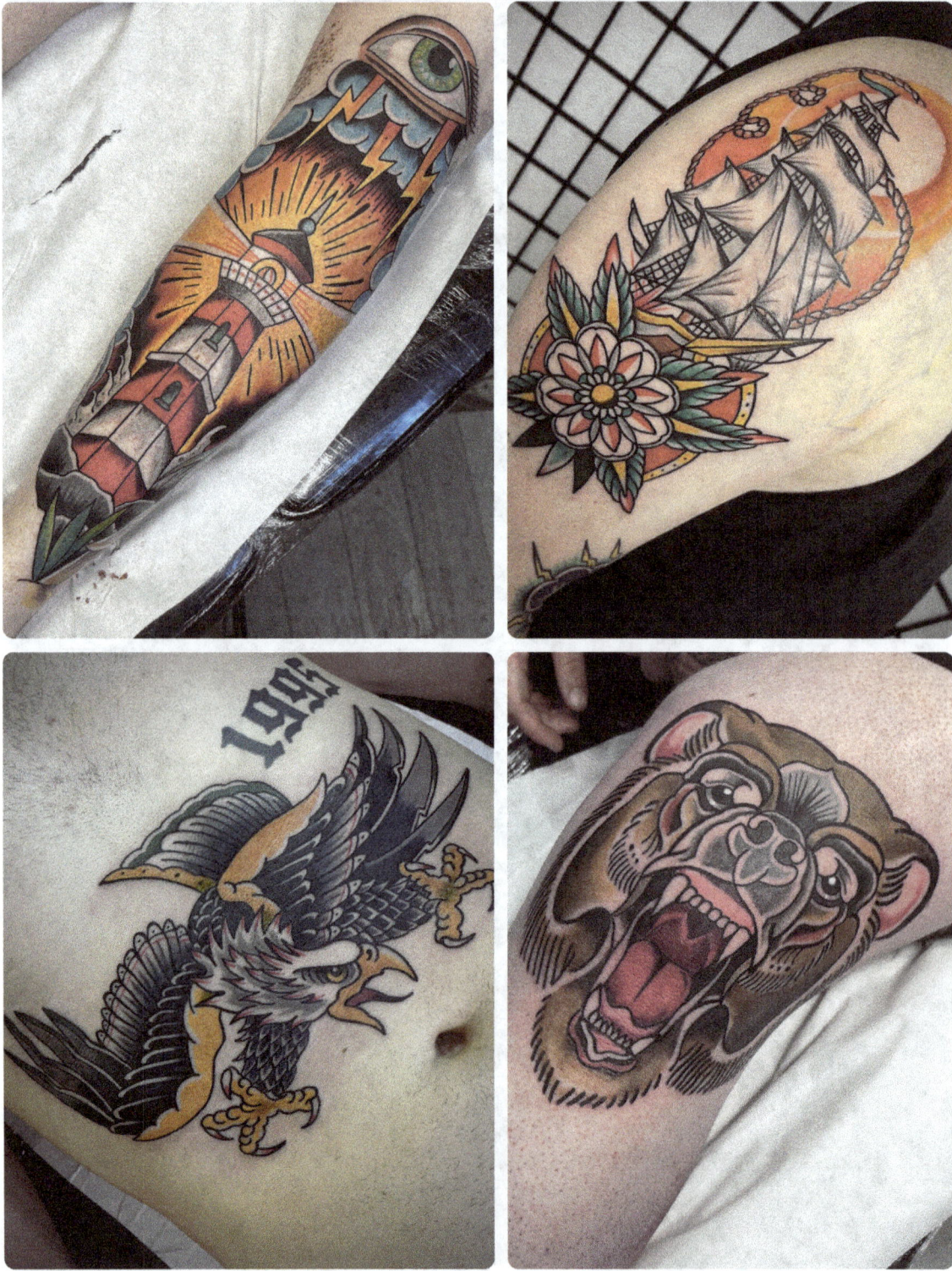

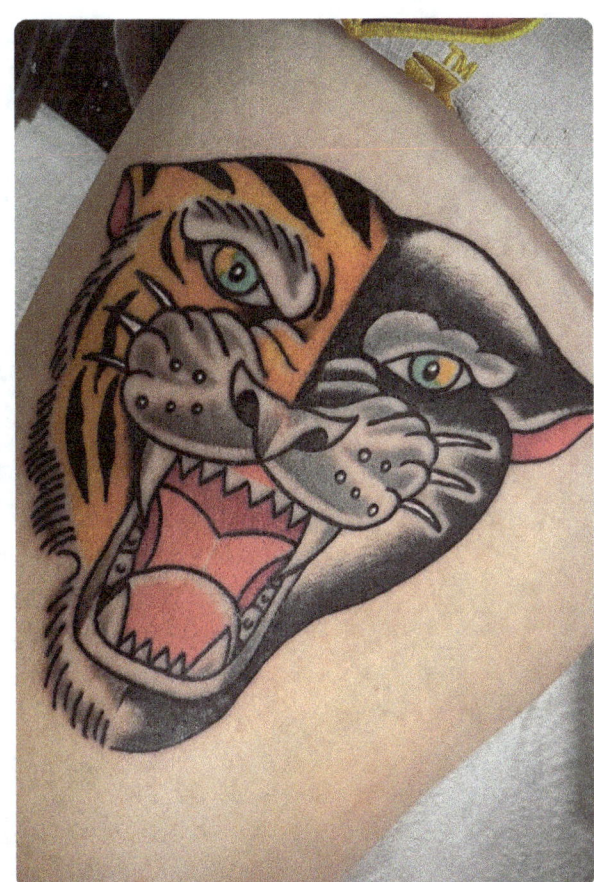

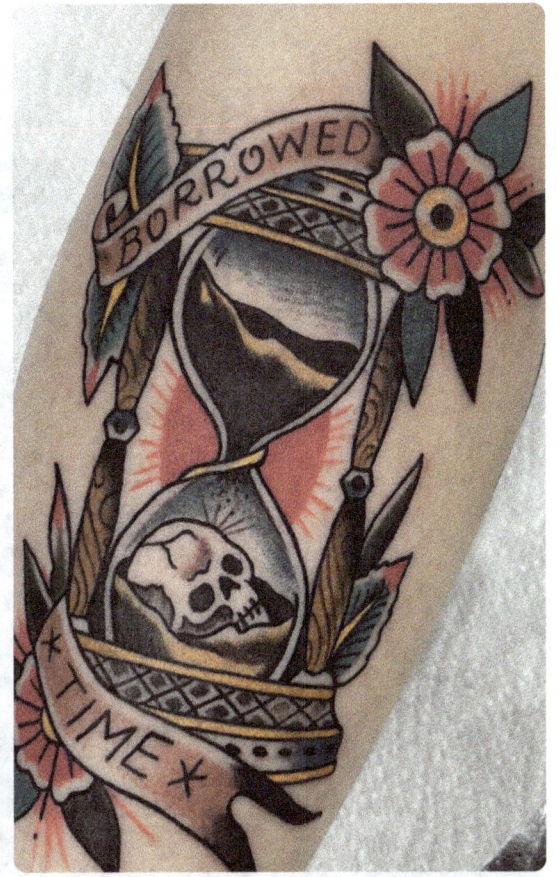

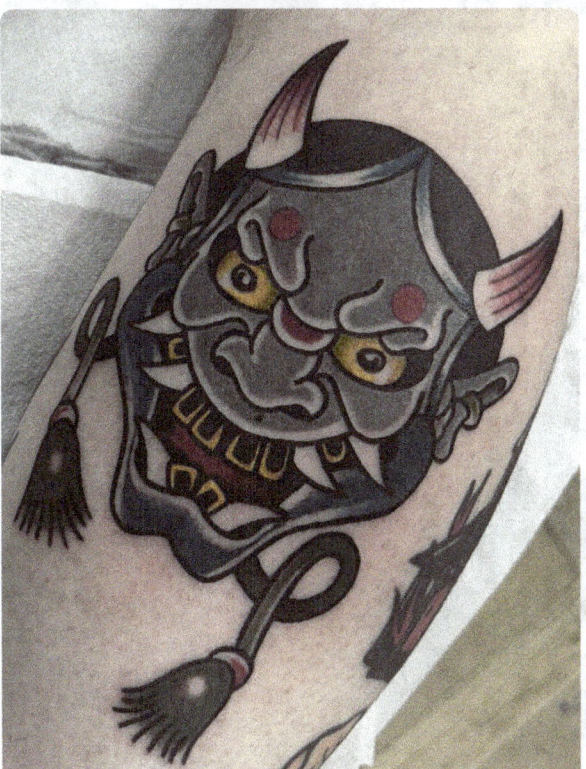

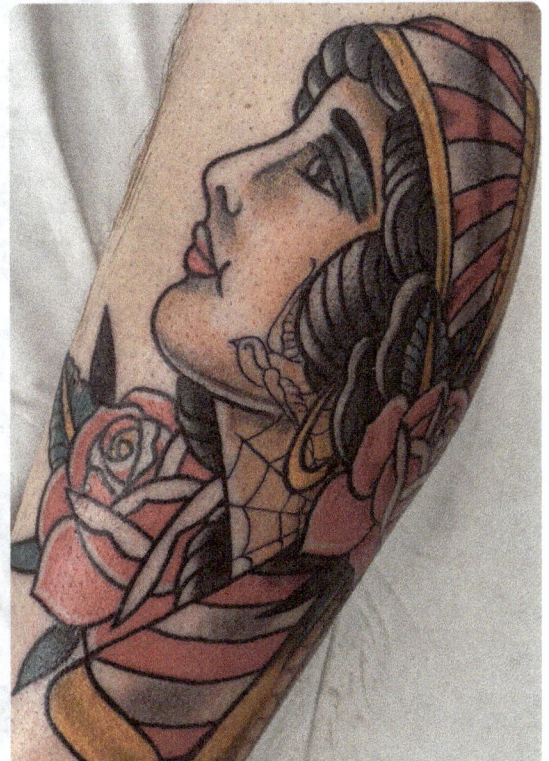

Chapter III

MIST.INK

INKMOB | FB: @MIST.TATTOO | @MIST.INK | NORWAY, ÅLESUND

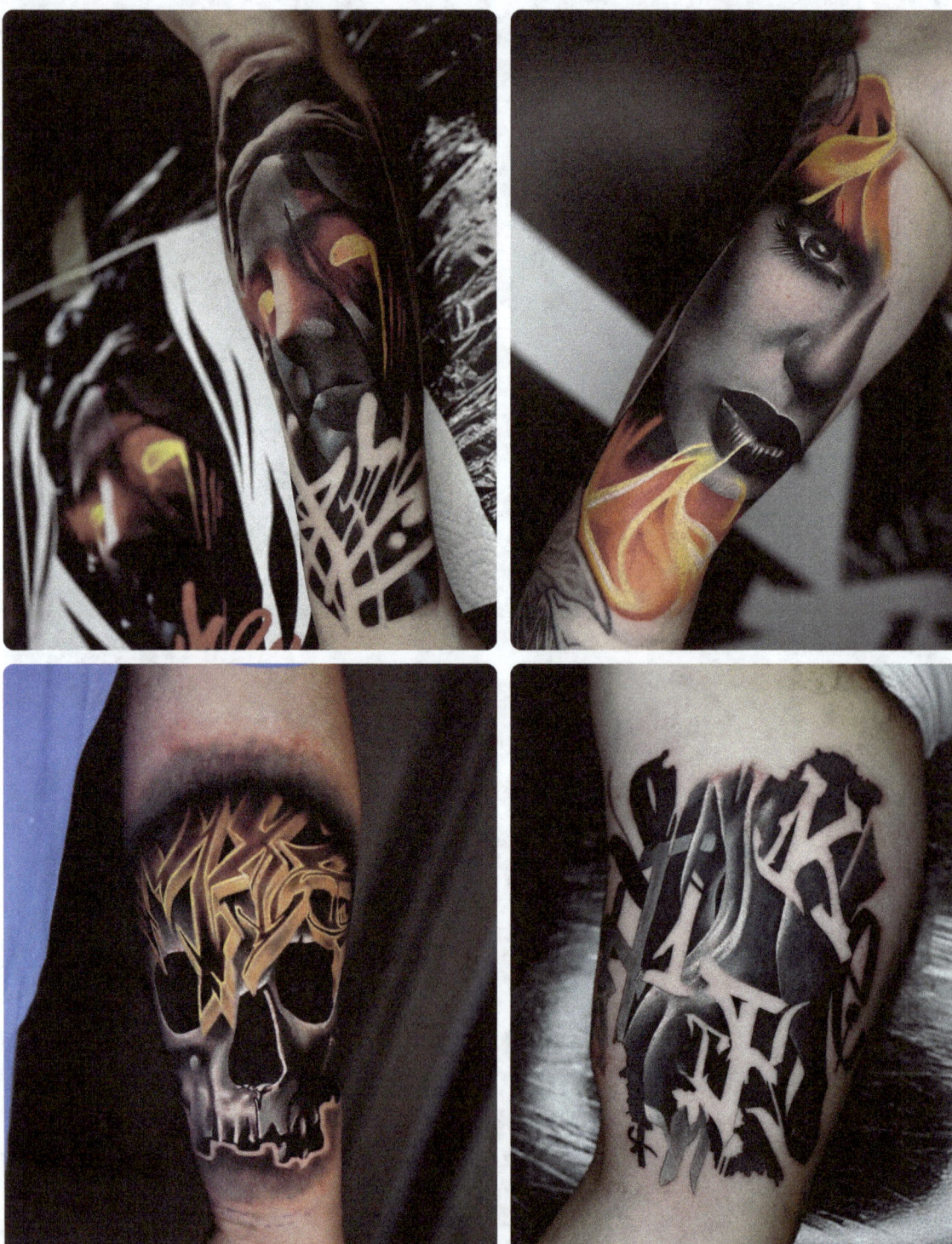

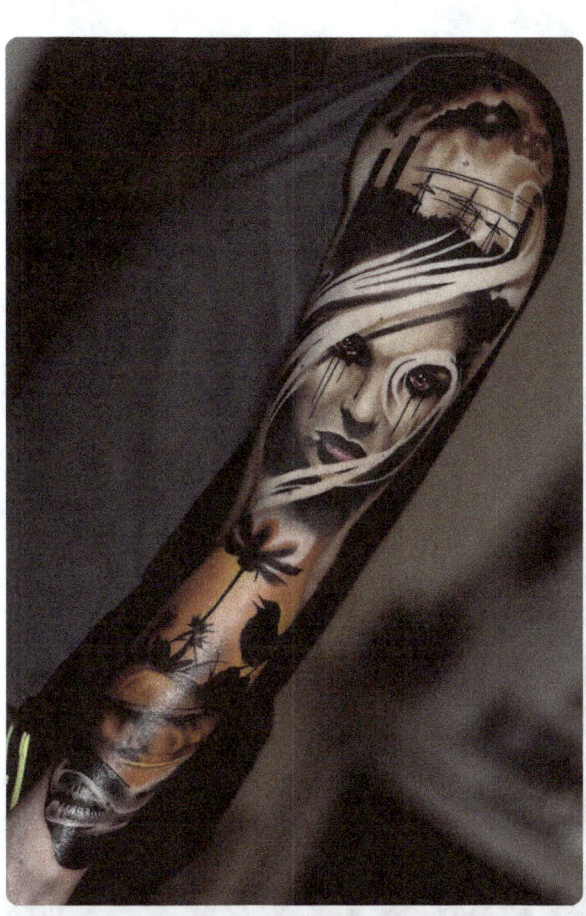

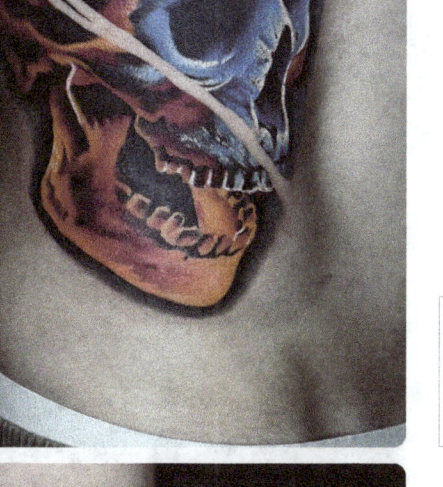
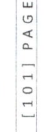
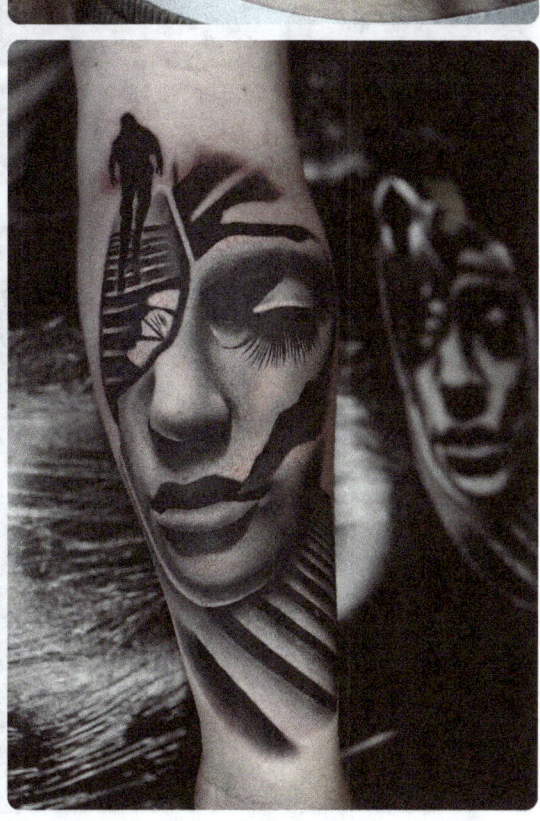

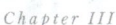

Chapter III

Global Tattoo Magazine

MORGANE DORFFER

VESPERAL | @MORGANE.DORFFER | FRANCE, BESANÇON

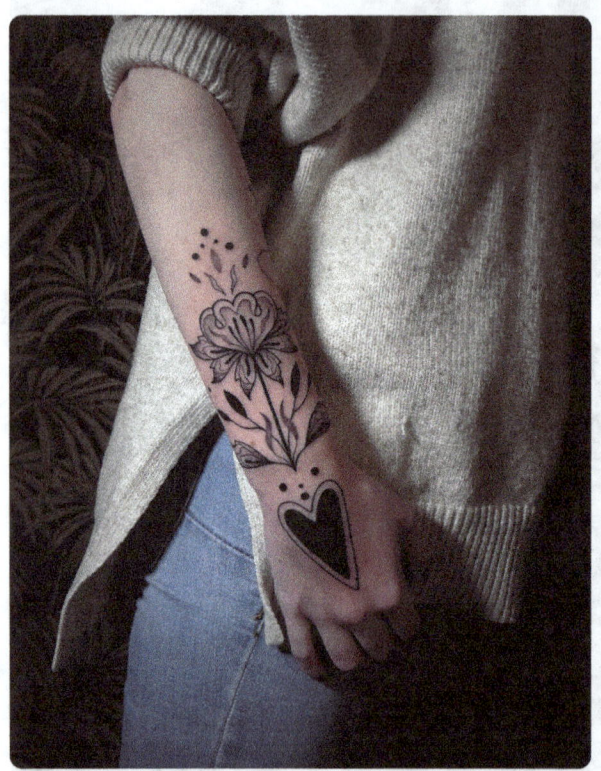
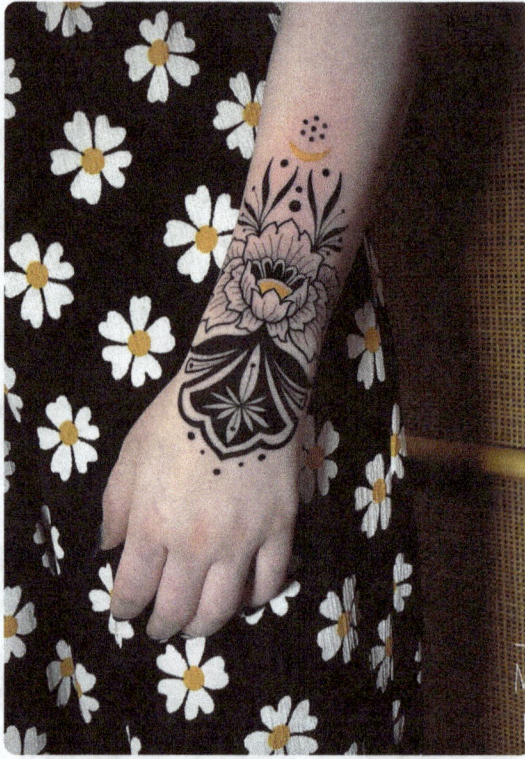
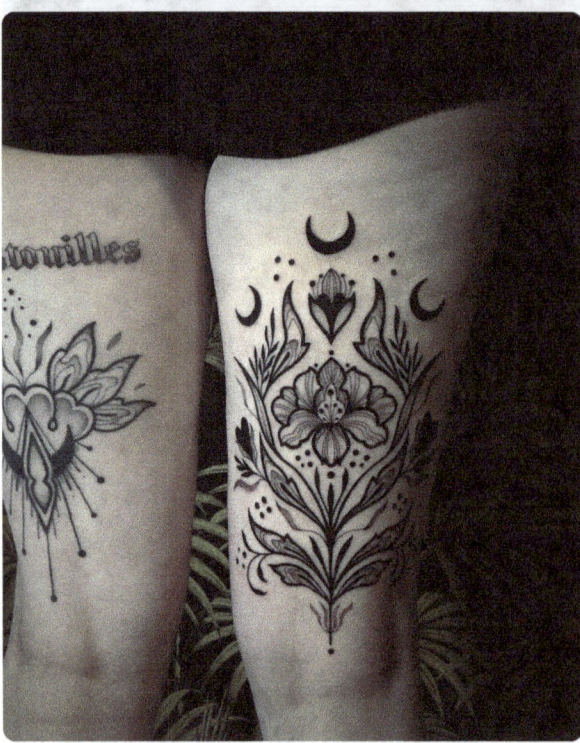
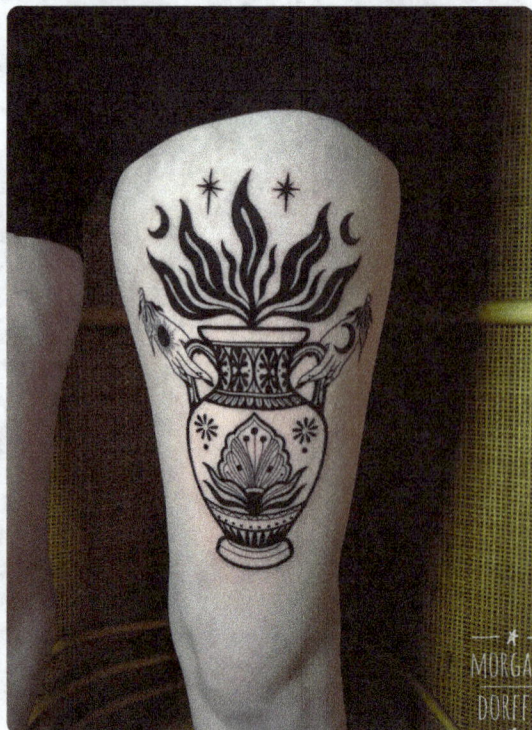

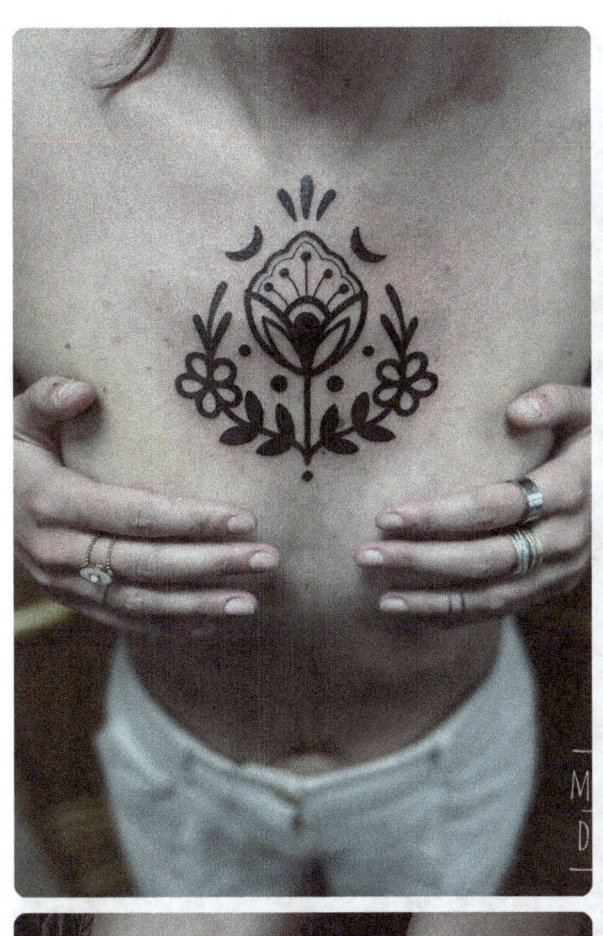

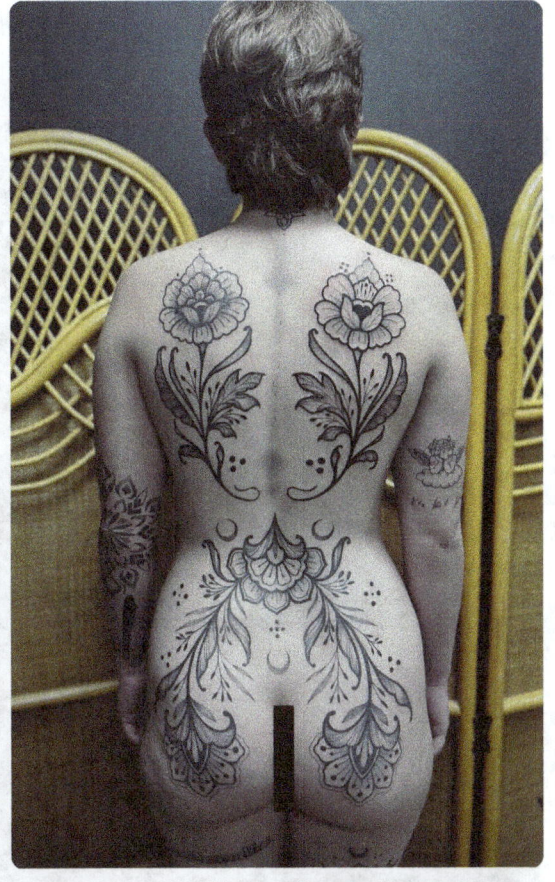

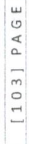

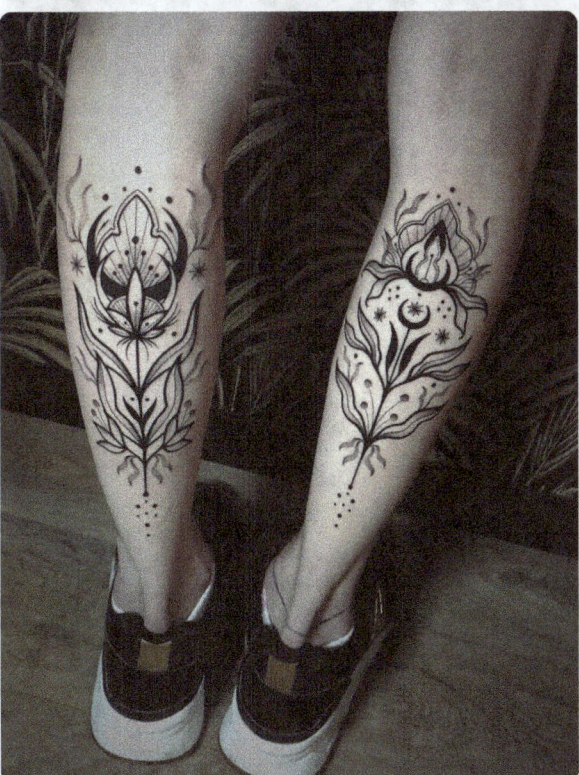

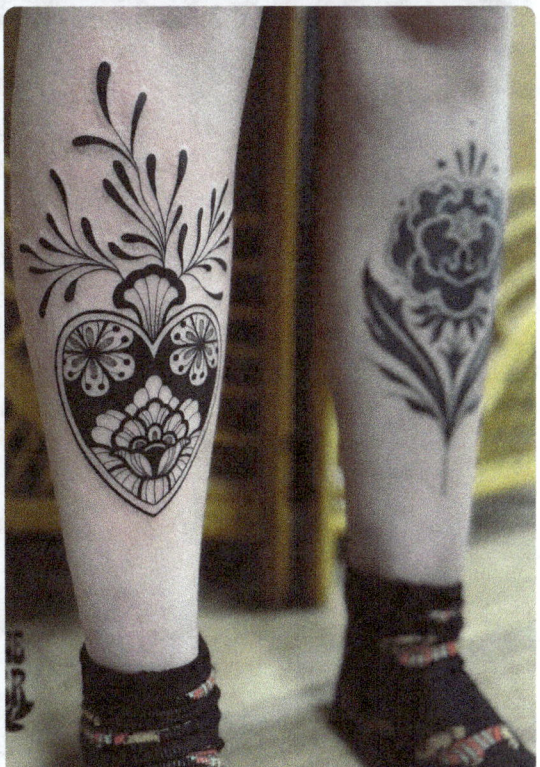

Chapter III

Global Tattoo Magazine

NICCOLÒ CASATI

@NICCOLOCASATITATTOO | FB: NICK BLACK TATTOOING | THE NETHERLANDS, EINDHOVEN

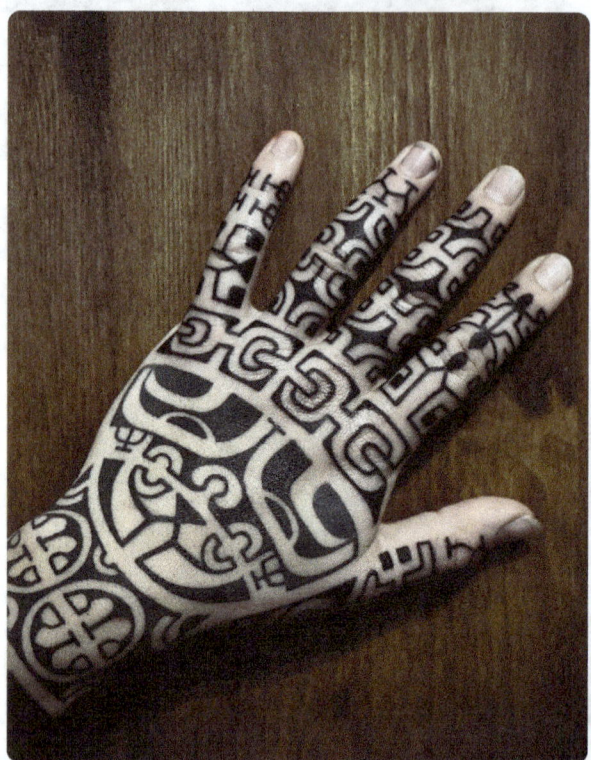
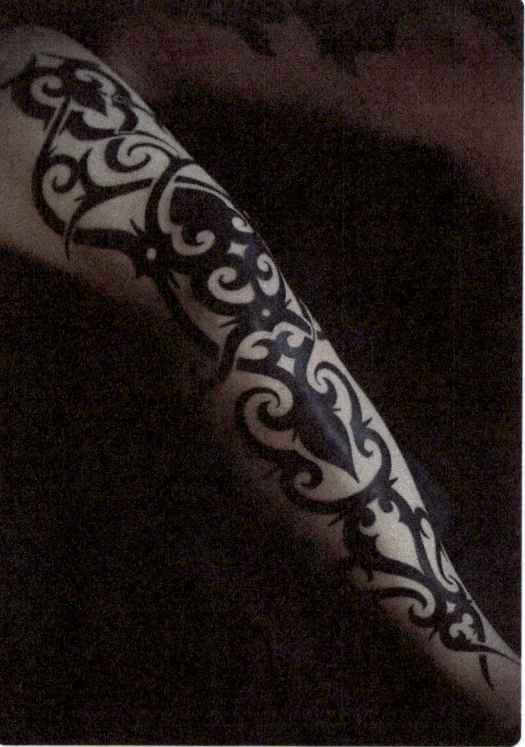
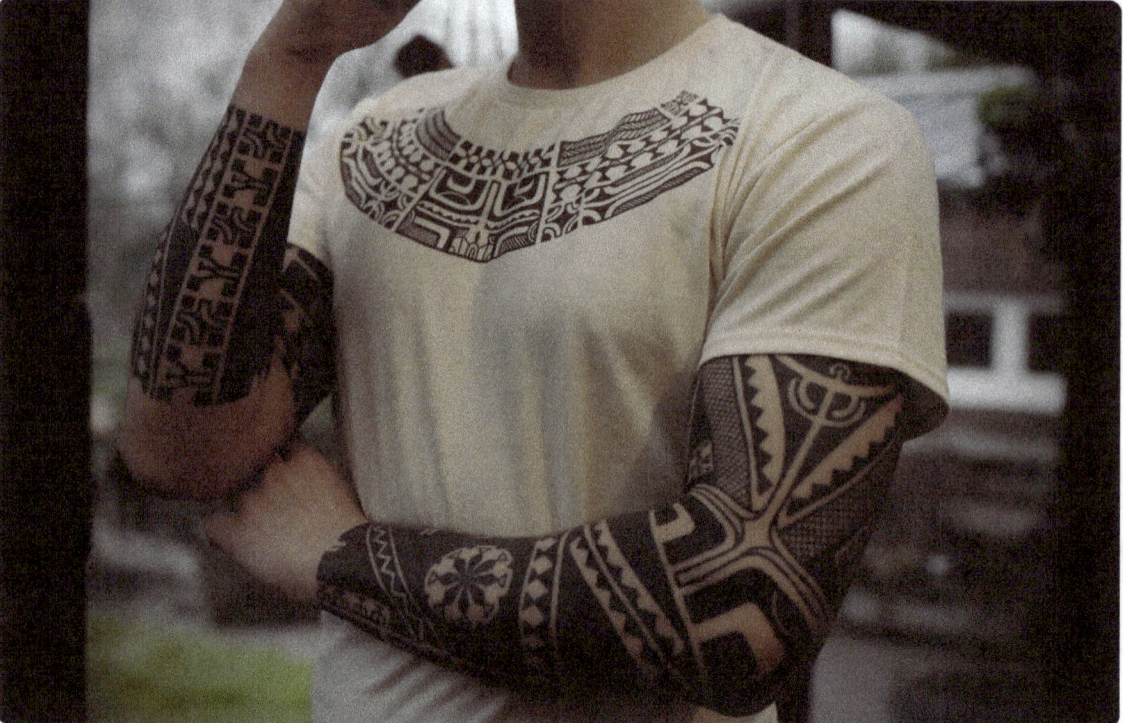

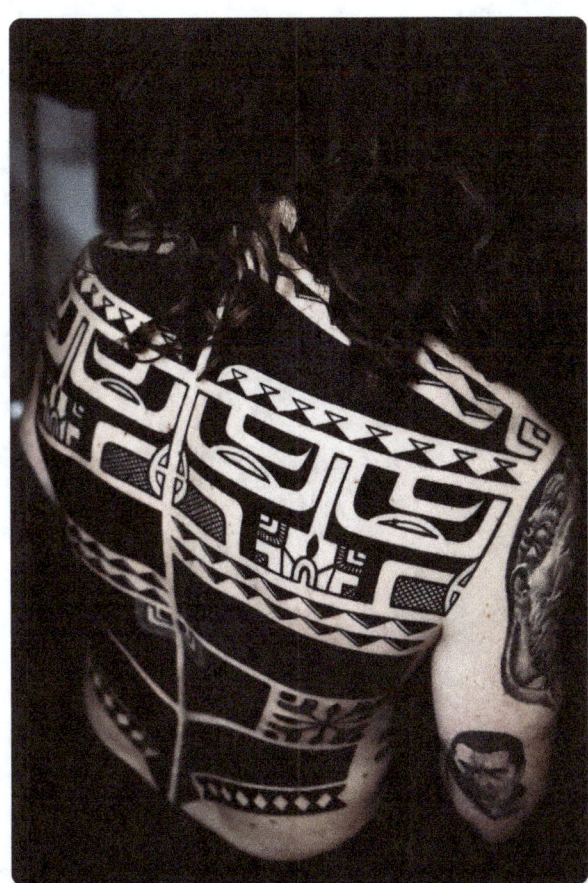

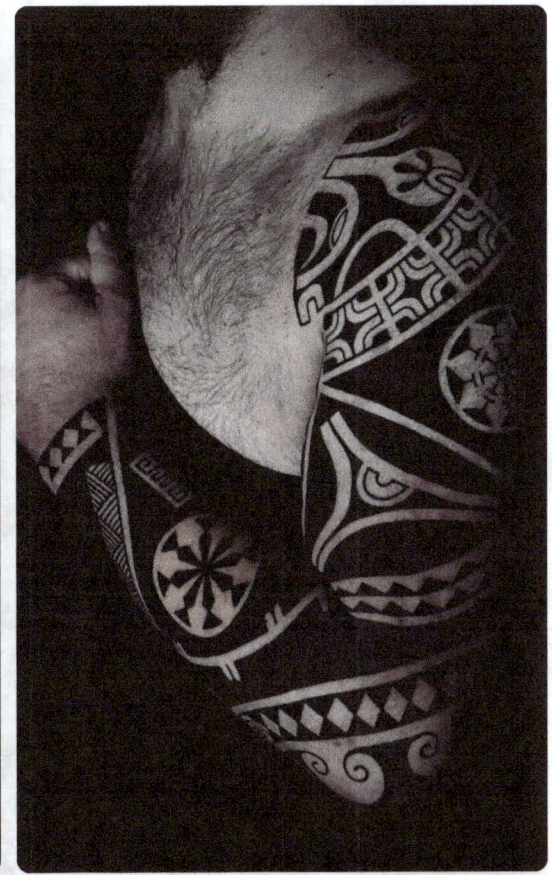

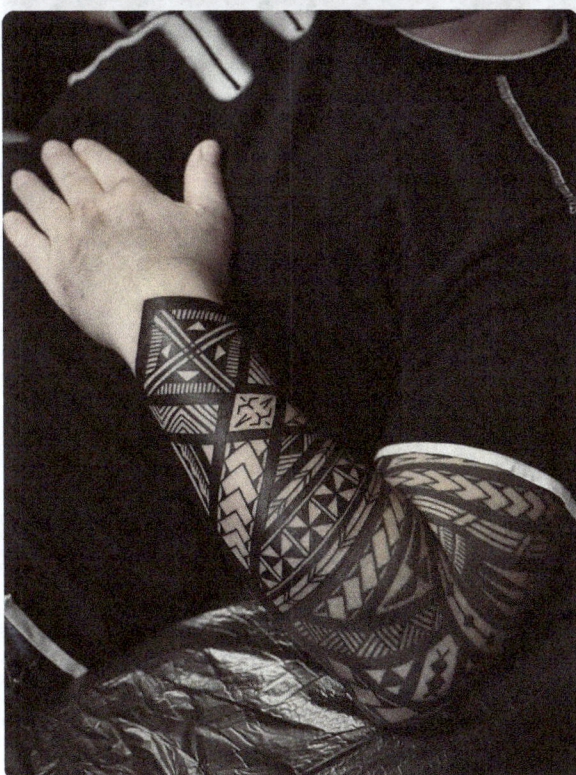

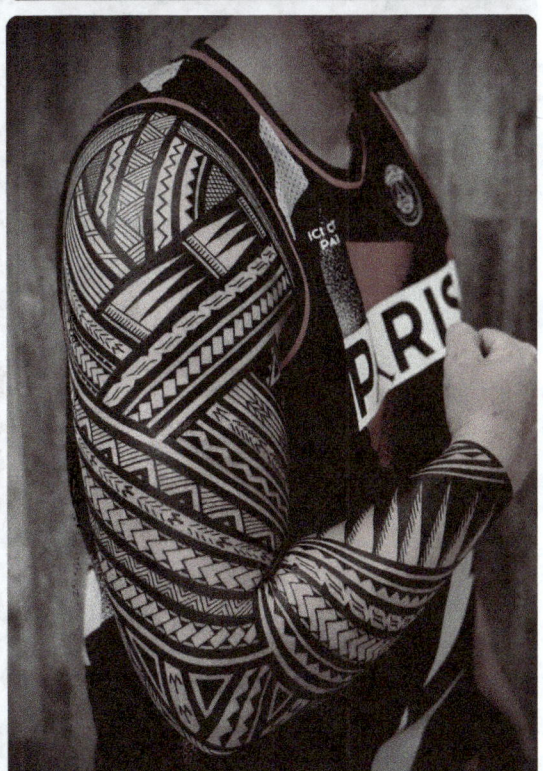

Chapter III

NICK UITTENBOGAARD

INCK TATTOOS | @NICK_INCKTATTOOS | THE NETHERLANDS, CULEMBORG

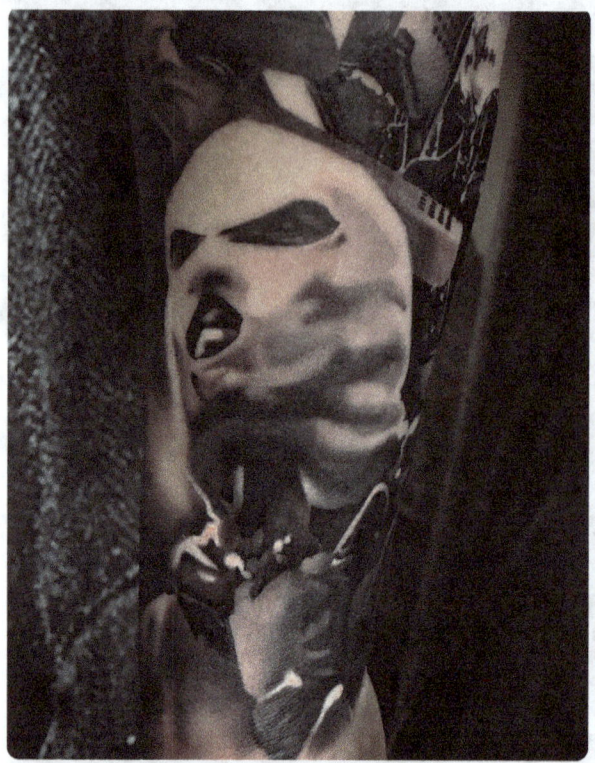

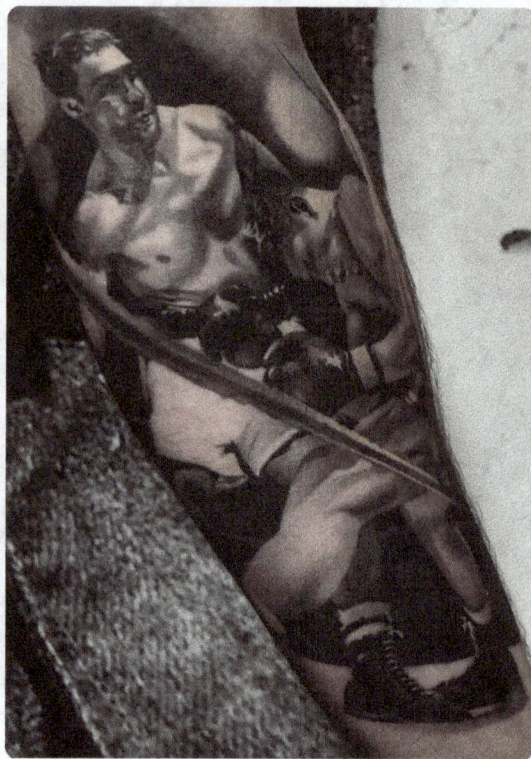

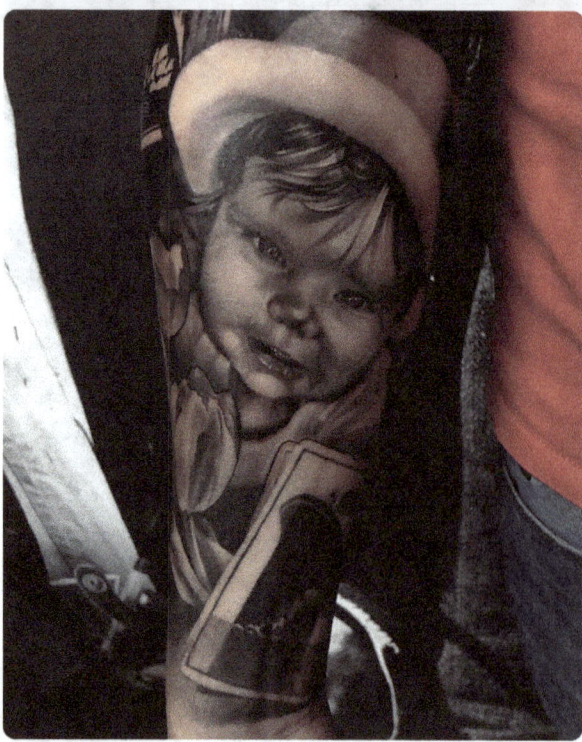

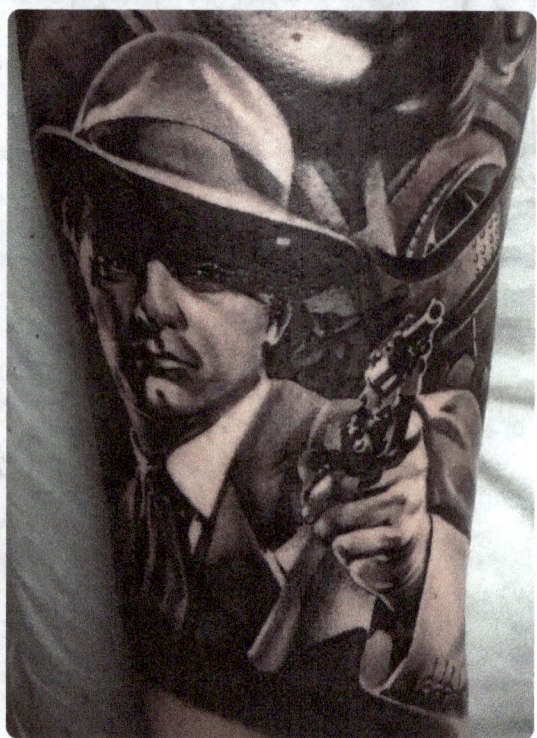

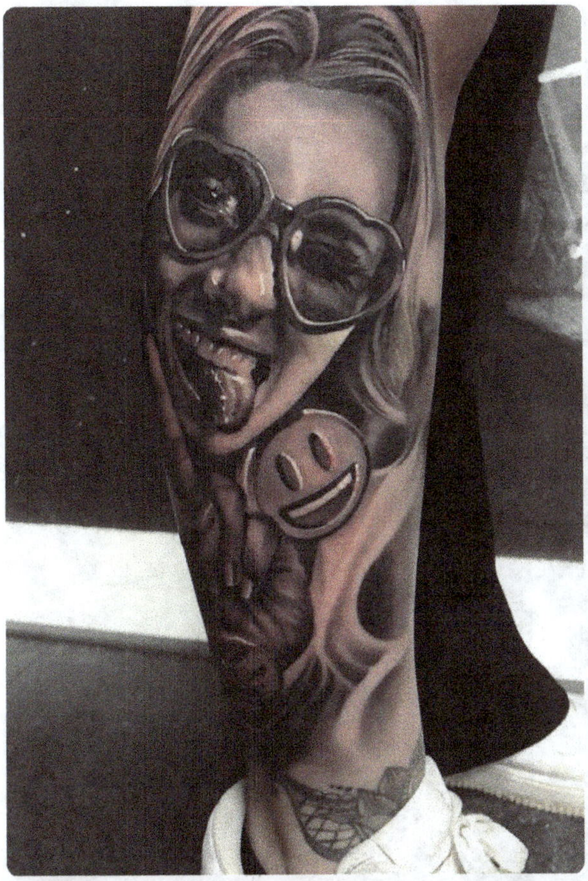

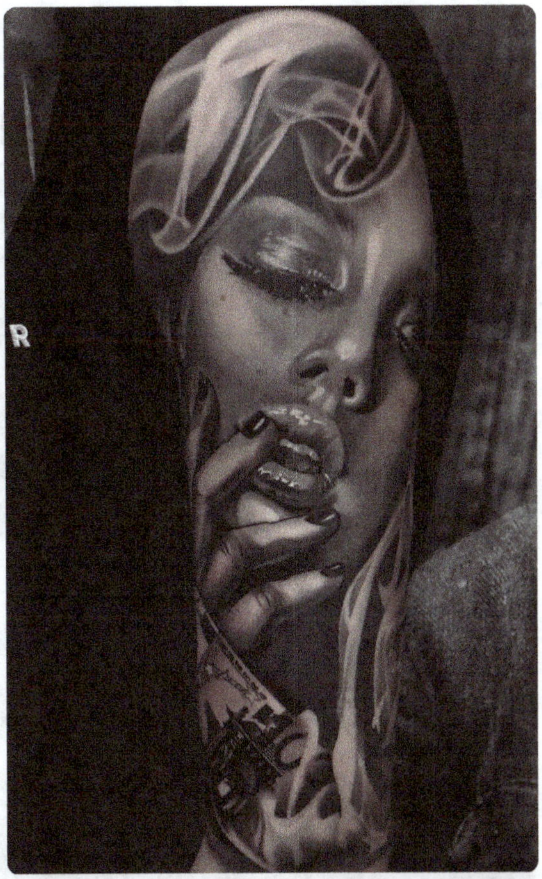

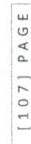

Chapter III

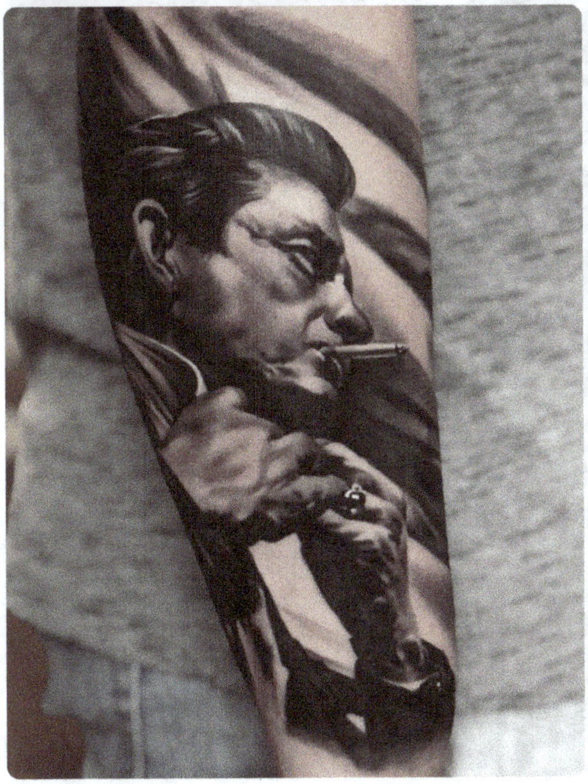

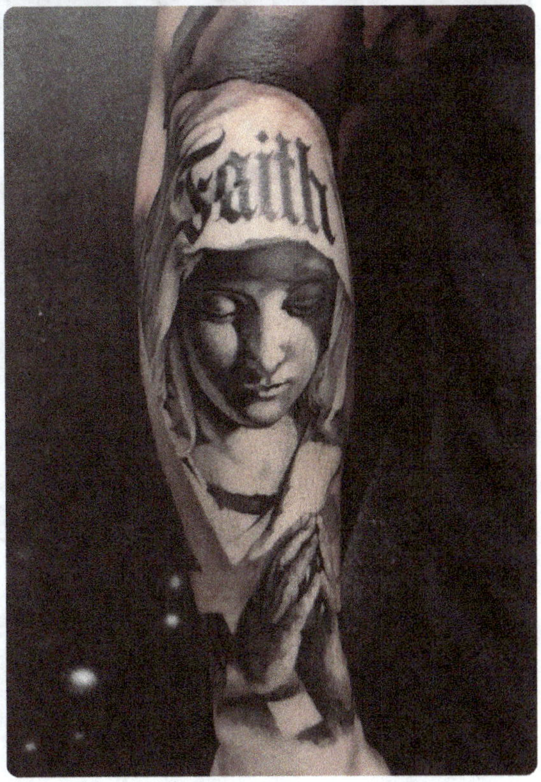

NUNO BATISTA

INK THE SOUL | FB: NUNO.BATISTA.03 | @TRIXTER_INKNART| PORTUGAL, LISBON

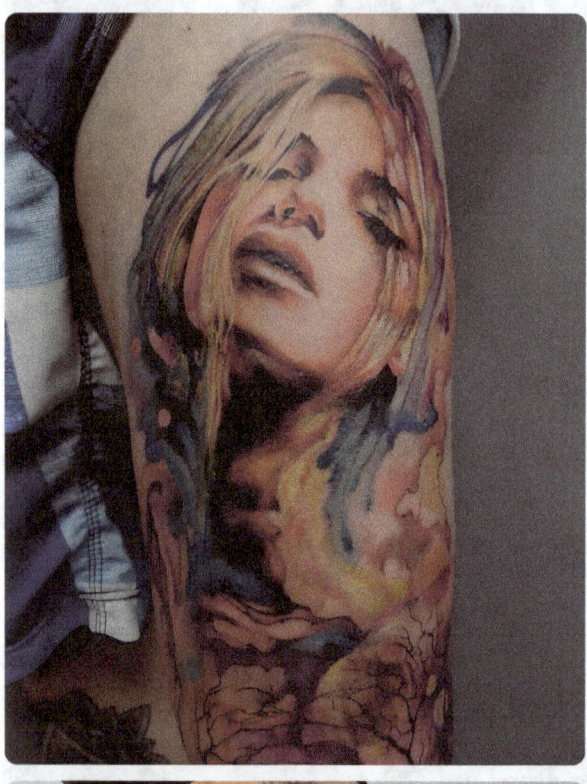
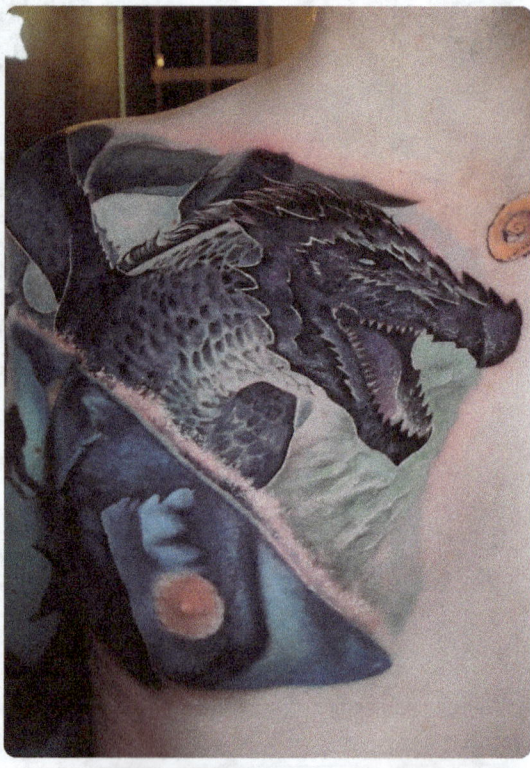
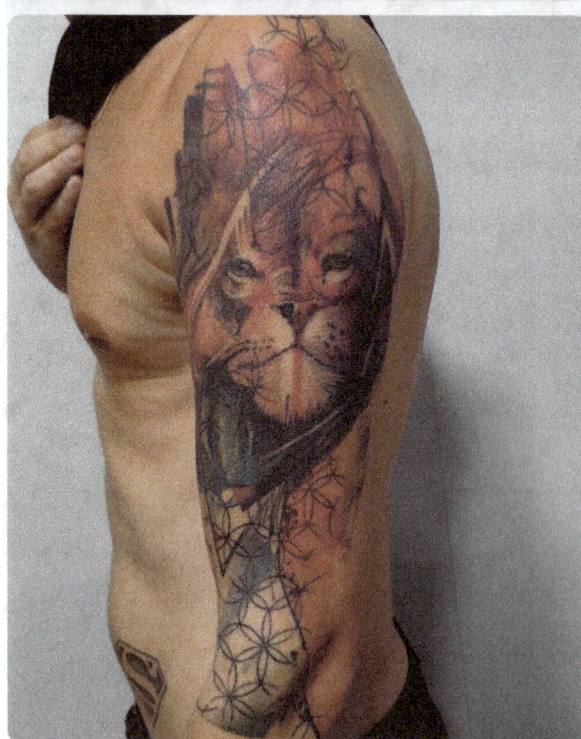
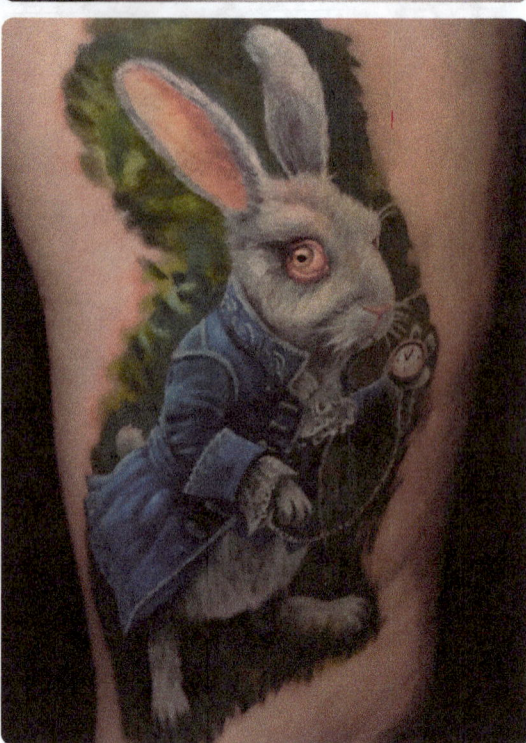

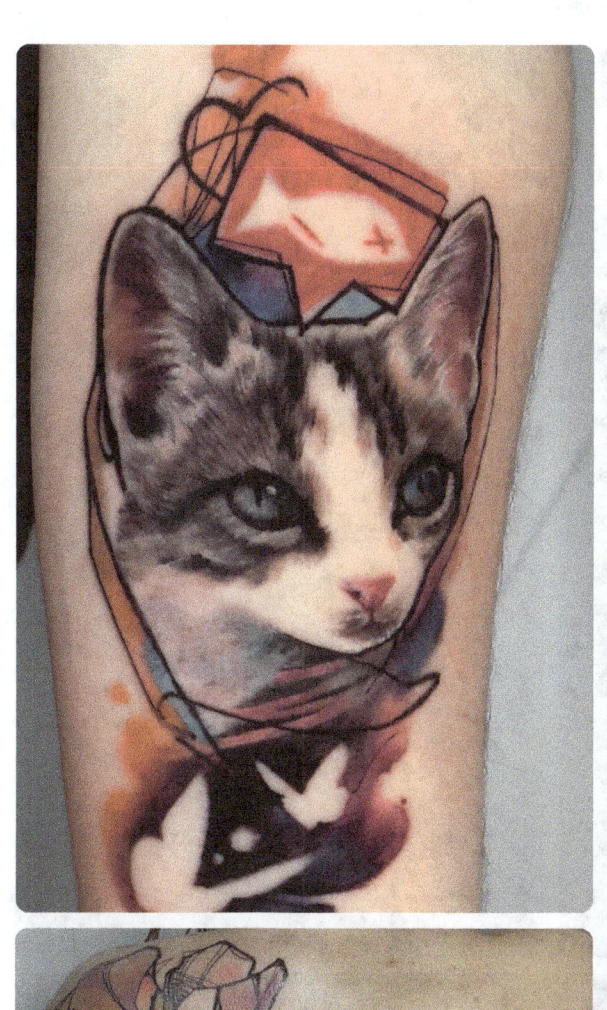

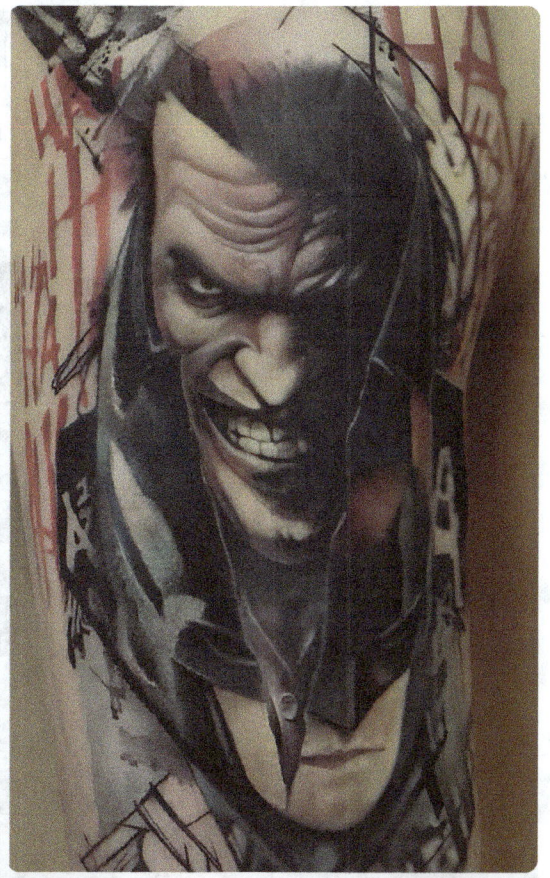

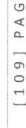

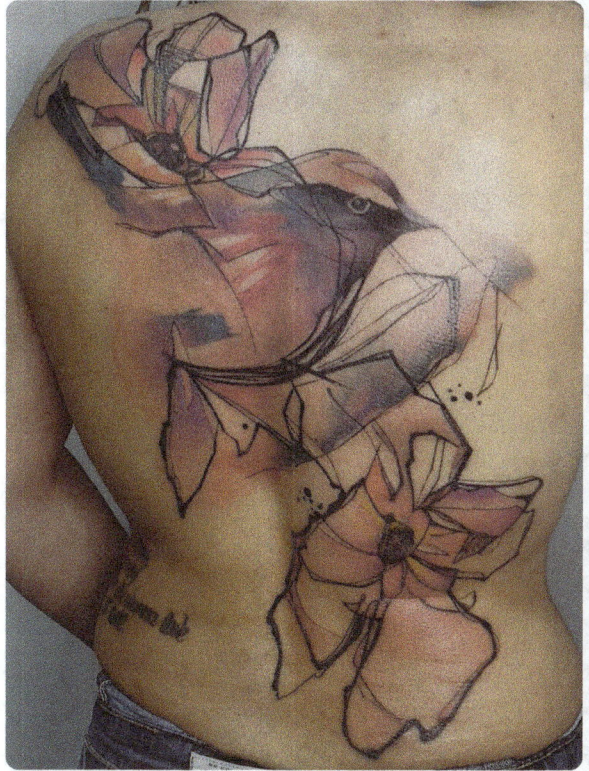

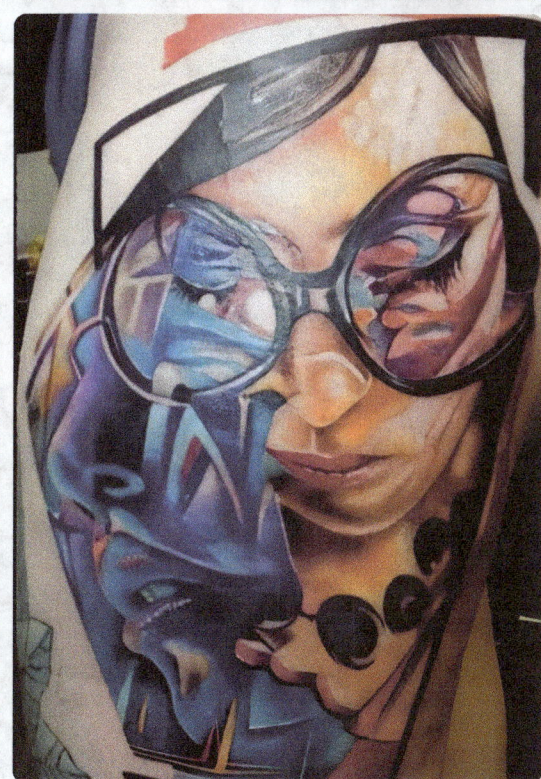

Chapter III

Global Tattoo Magazine

PAWEL POWSTANSKI

TUZ TUSZ TATTOO | @POWSTANSKI.TATTOO | POLAND, POZNAN

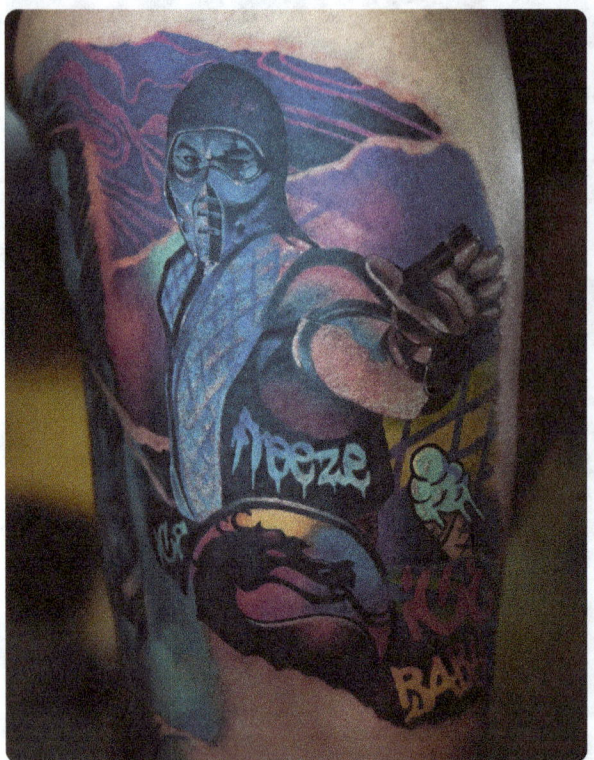

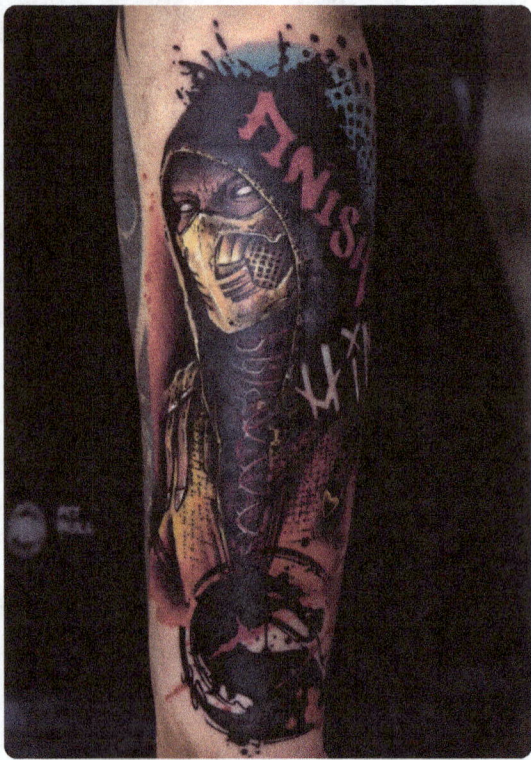

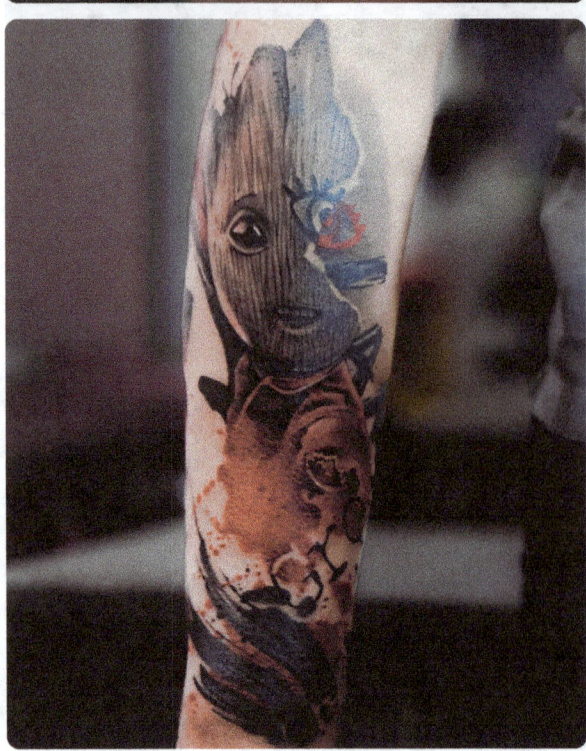

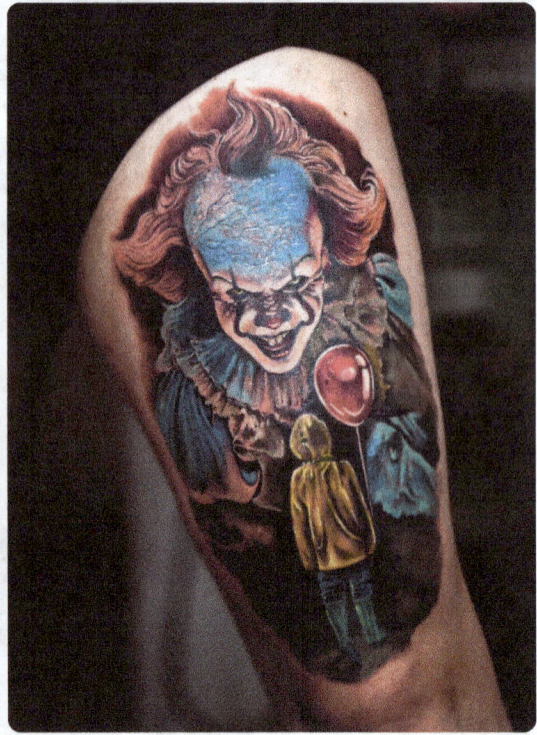

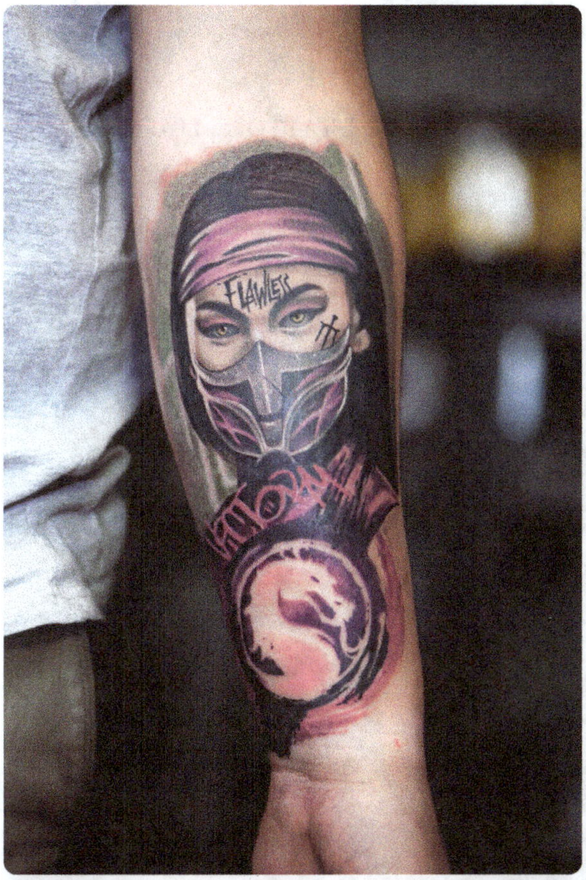

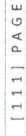

Chapter III

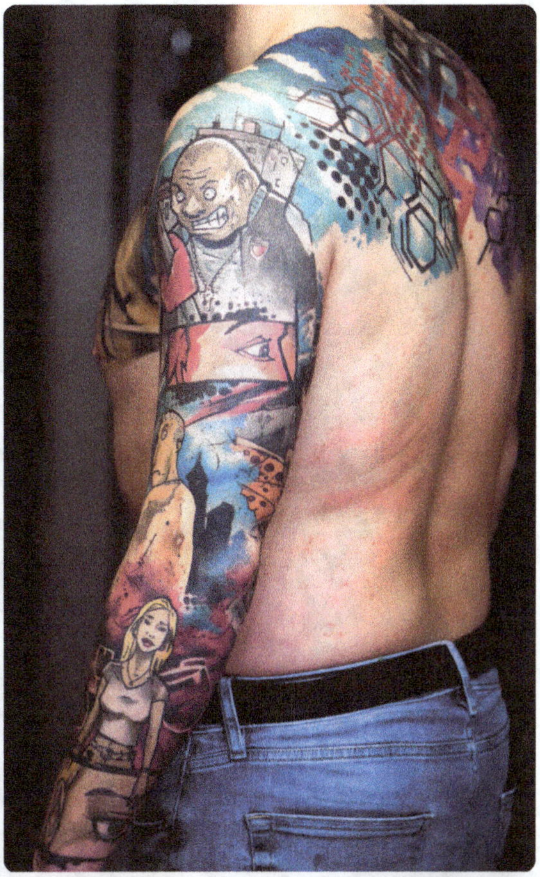

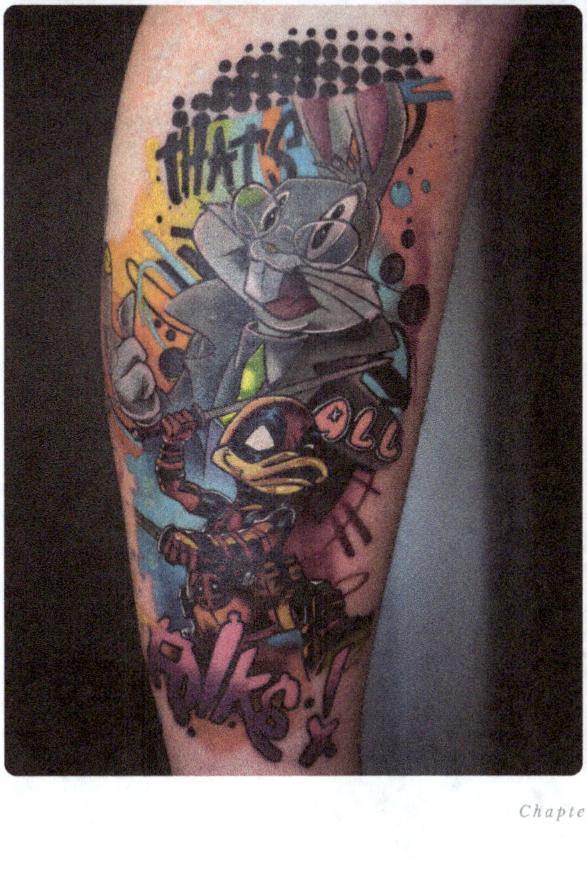

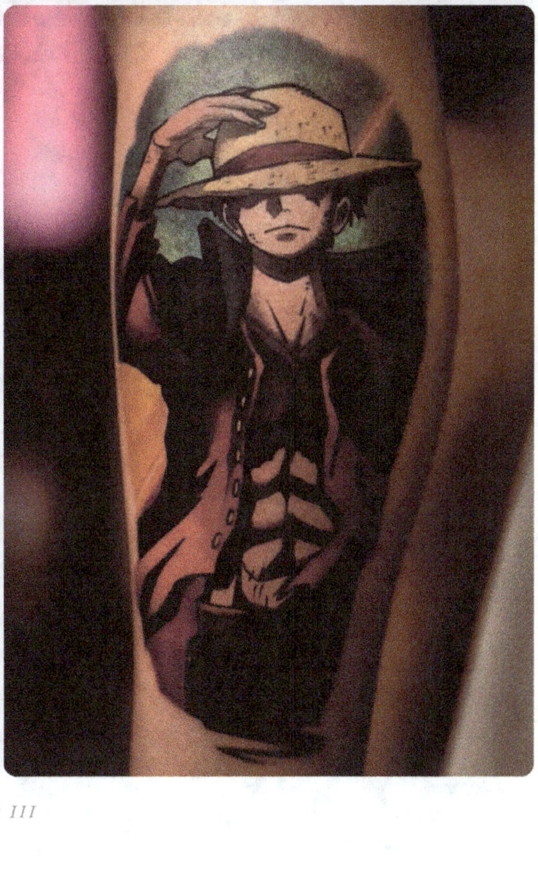

Global Tattoo Magazine

PIETRO STILL

BEST OF TIMES AND NORTH LAKE TATTOO | @PIETRO STILL TATTOO | ITALY, MILANO

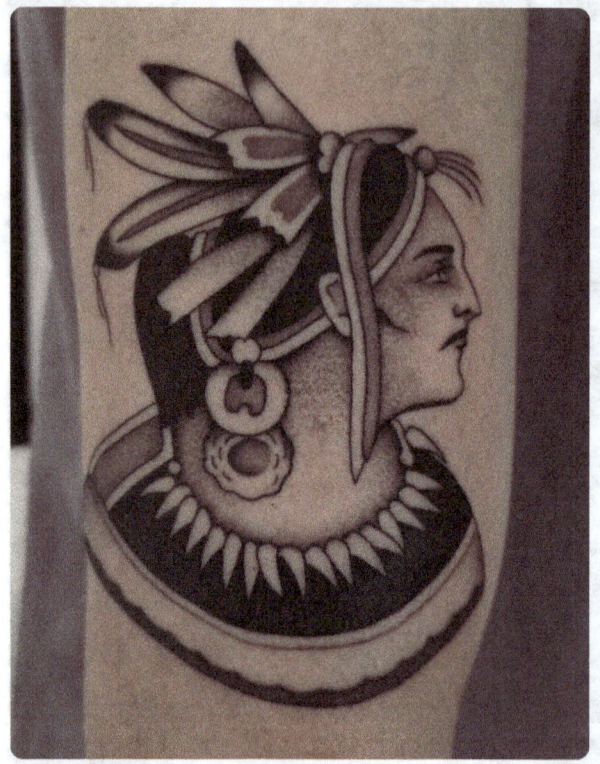

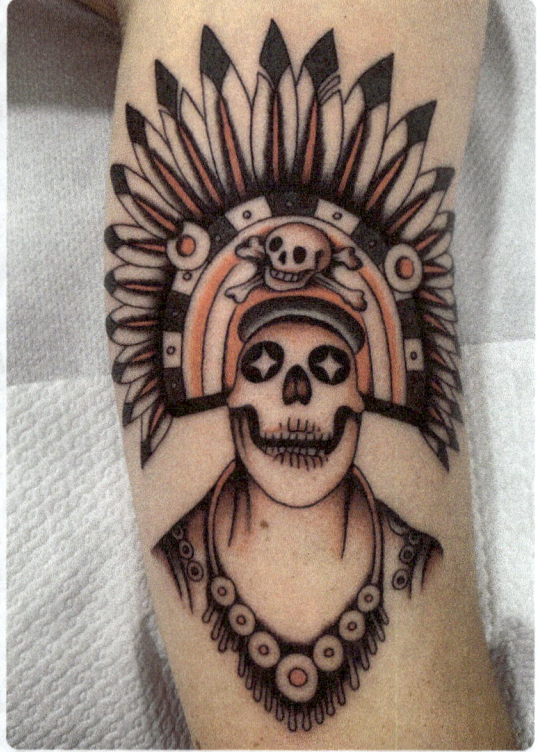

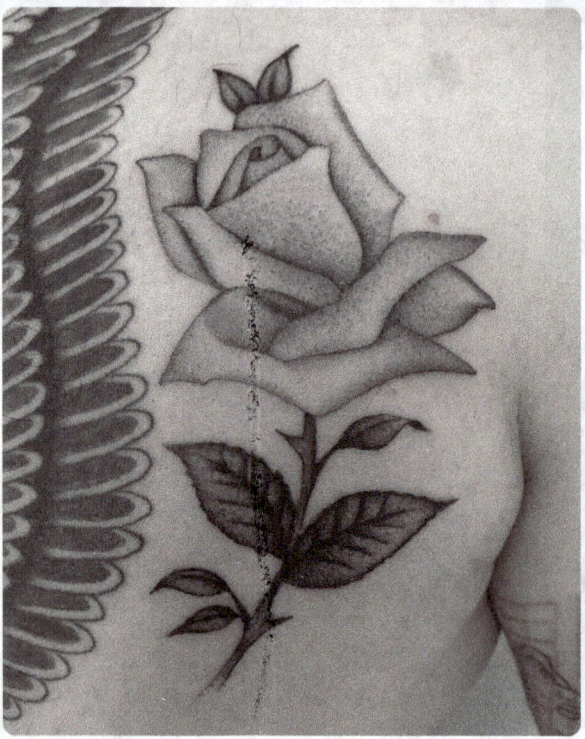

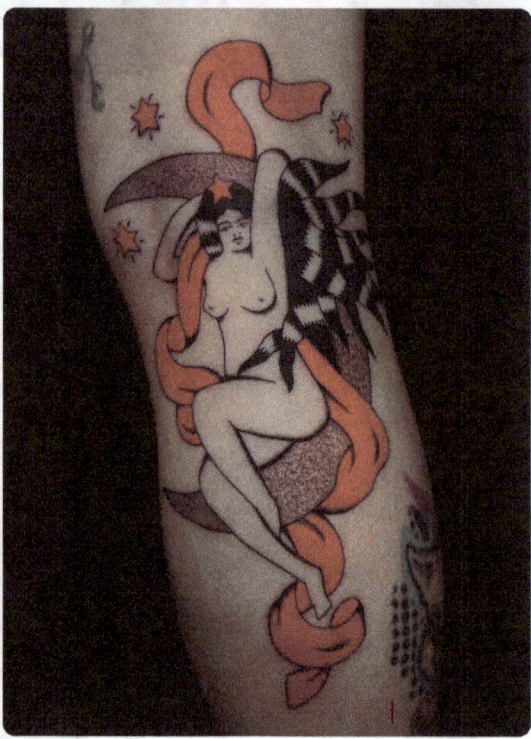

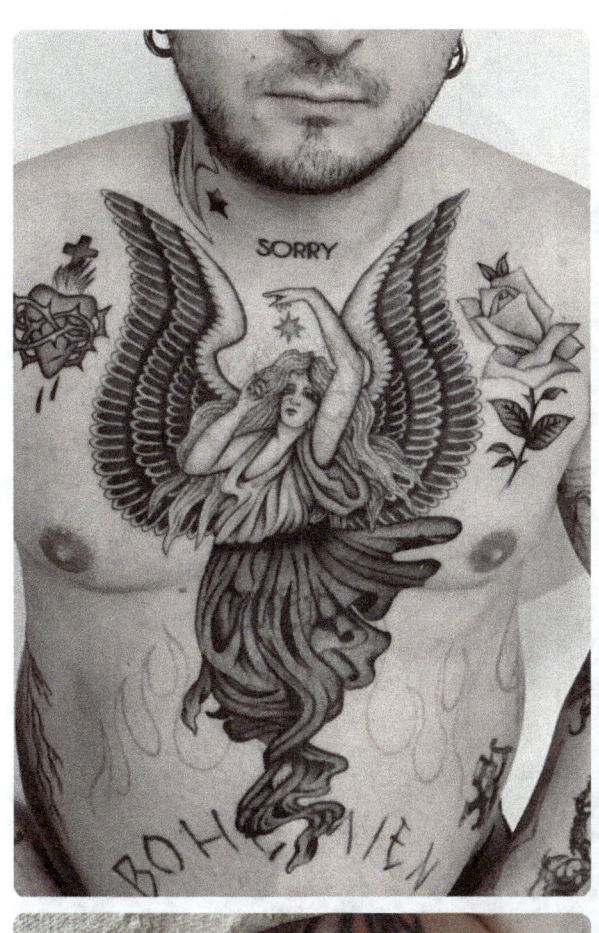

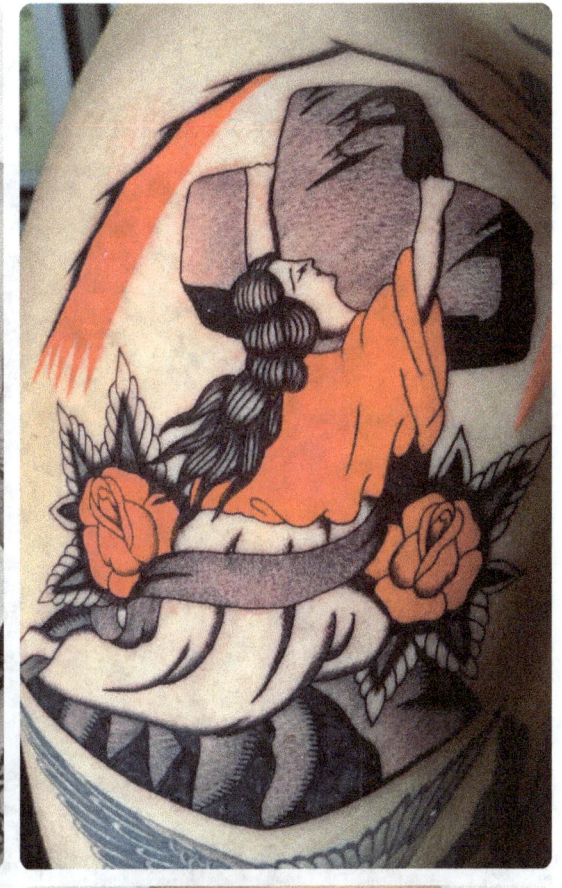

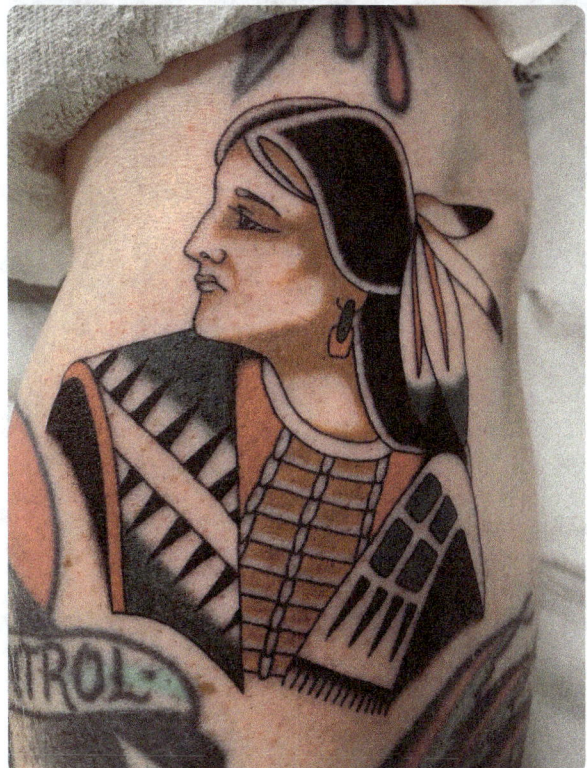

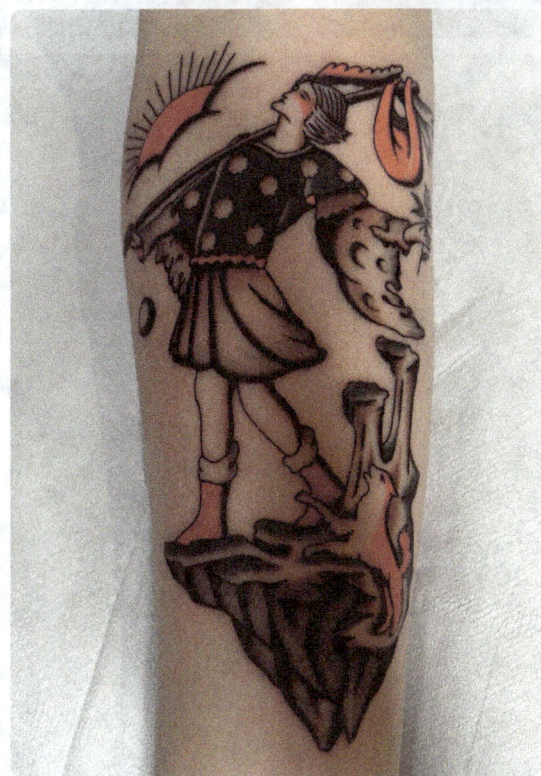

REMY OSKURO

LES ARCHIVES TATTOO SAINTES | @REMY.OSKURO | FRANCE, SAINTES

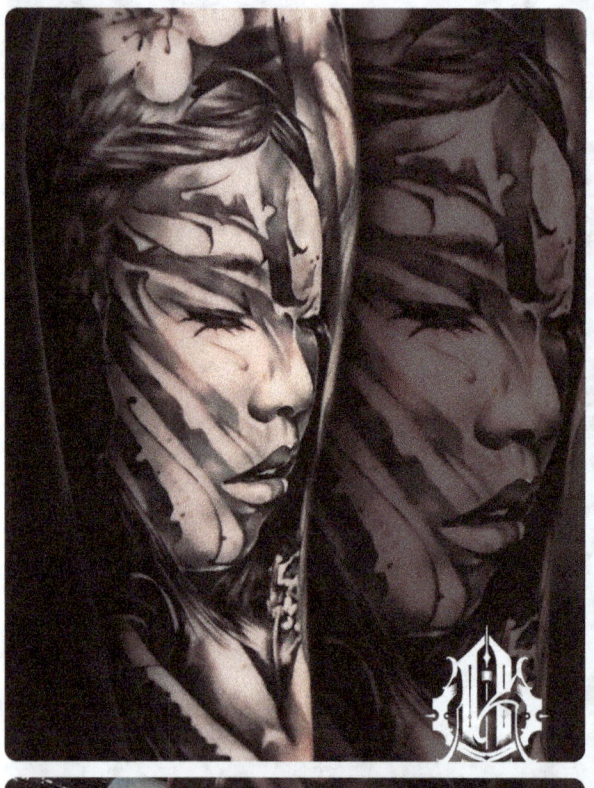
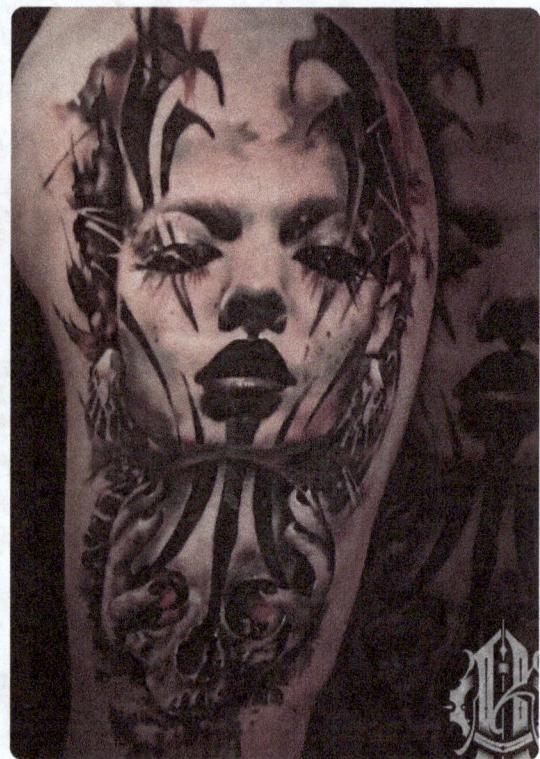
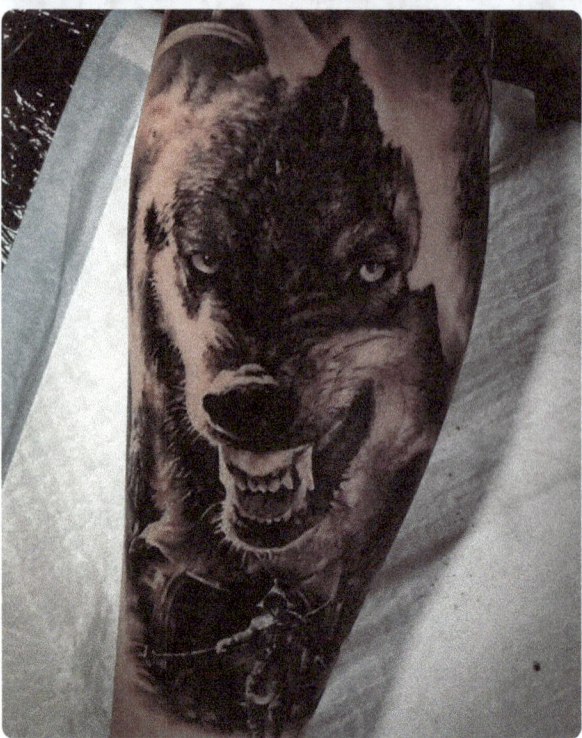
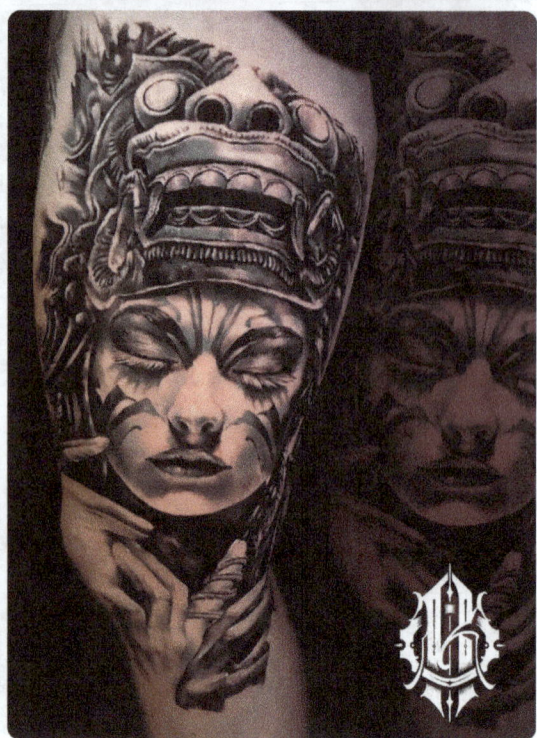

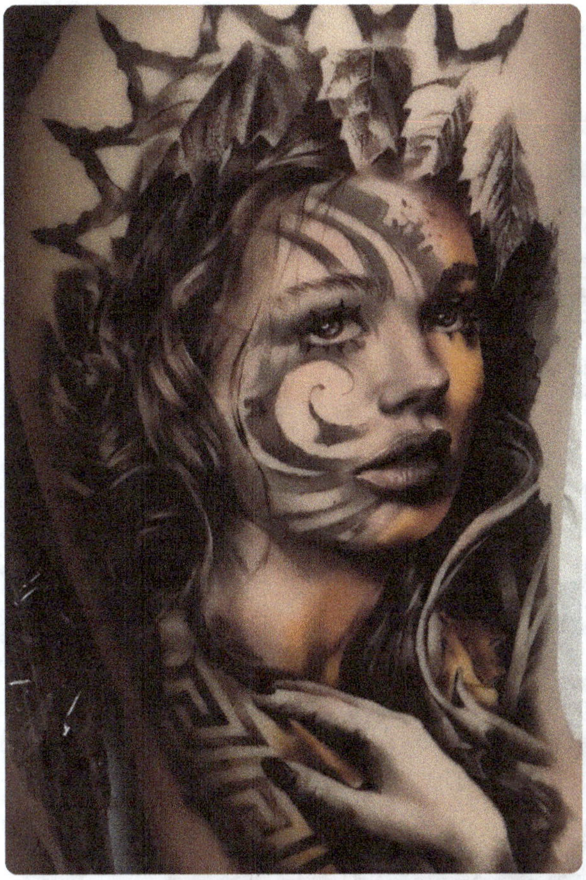

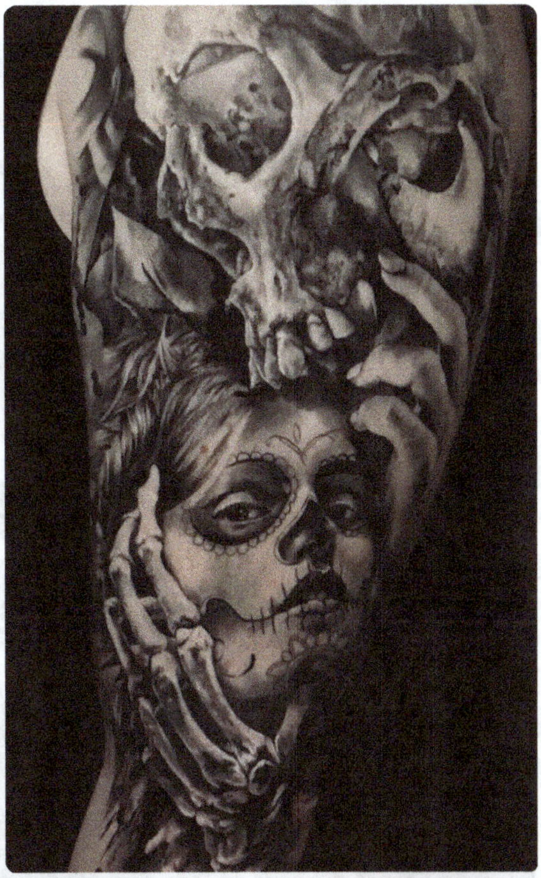

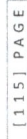

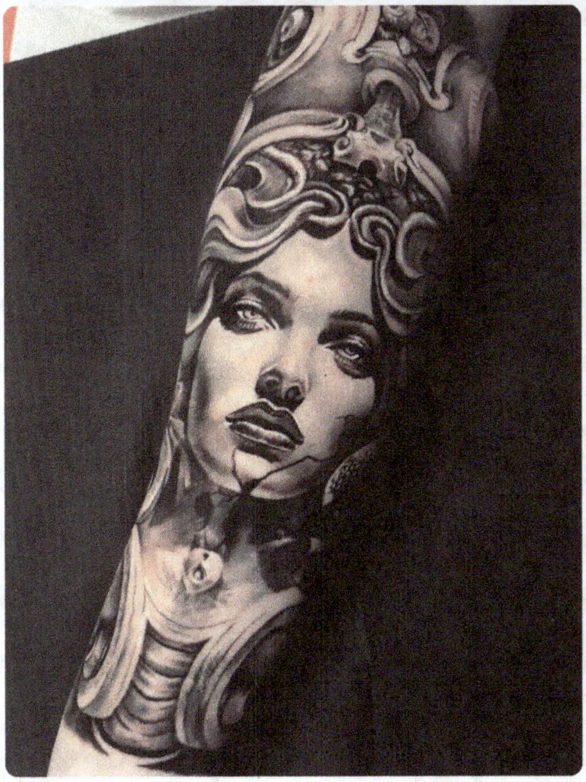

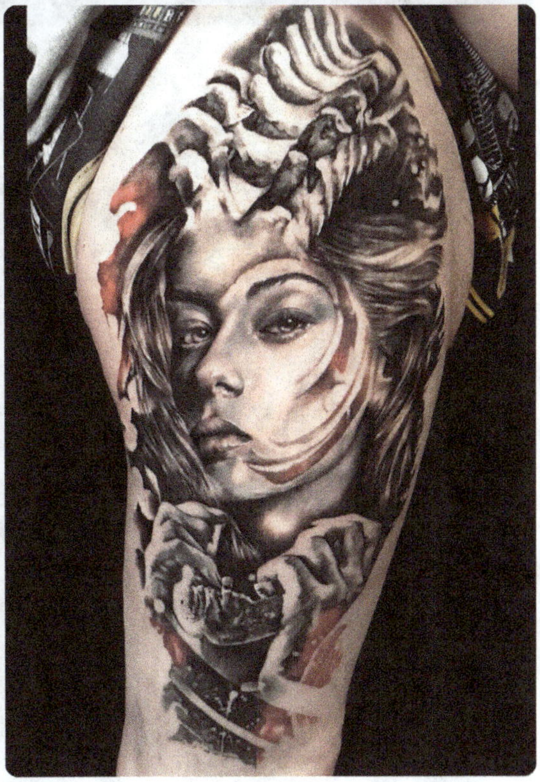

Chapter III

RICARDAS GALECKIS

KARMA ARTS TATTOO | FB: SPOKISTATTOO | @SPOKISTATTOO | UK, LEEDS

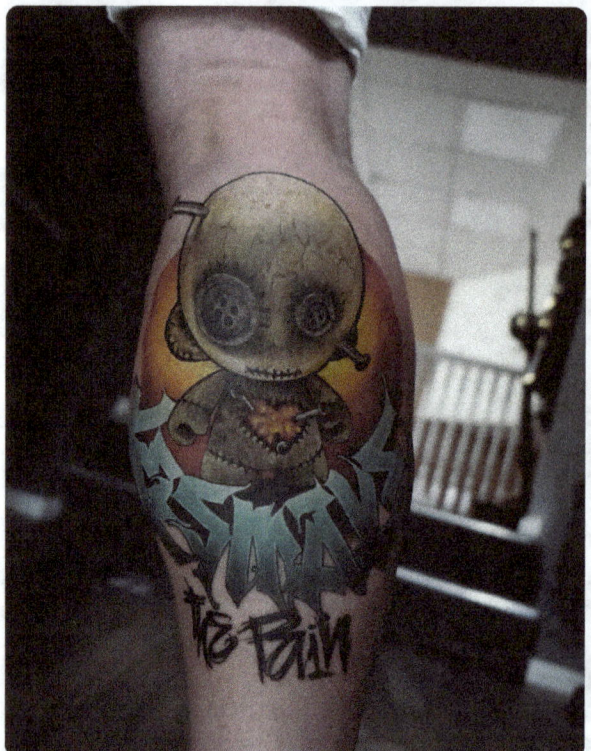

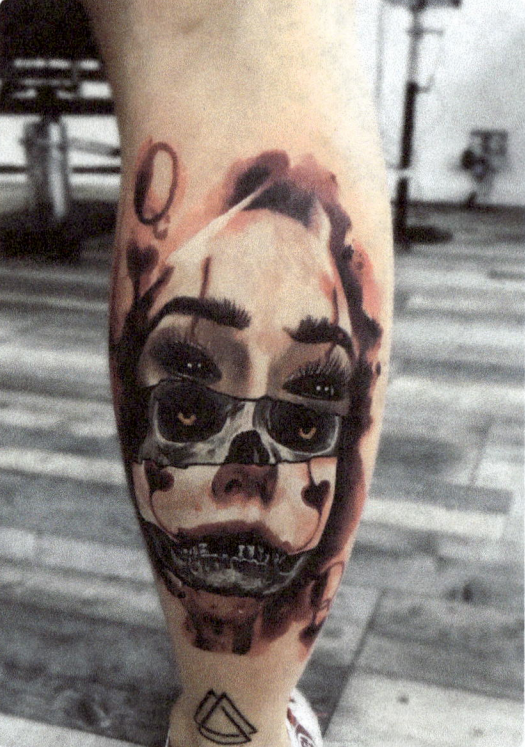

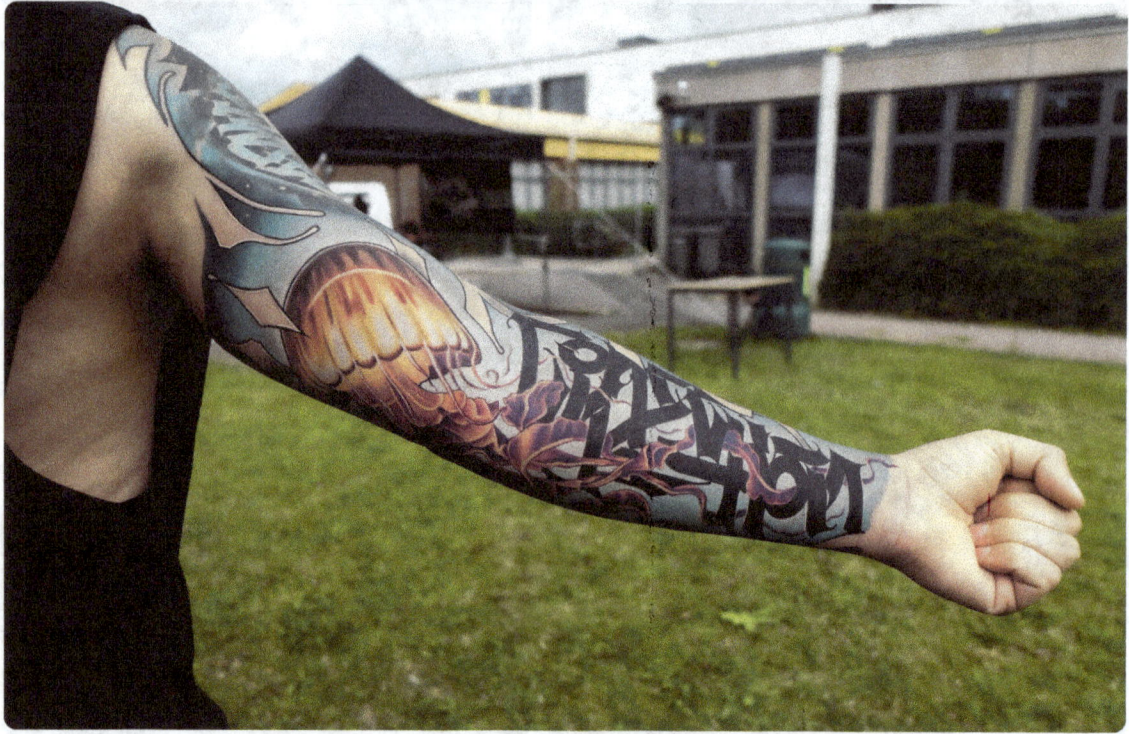

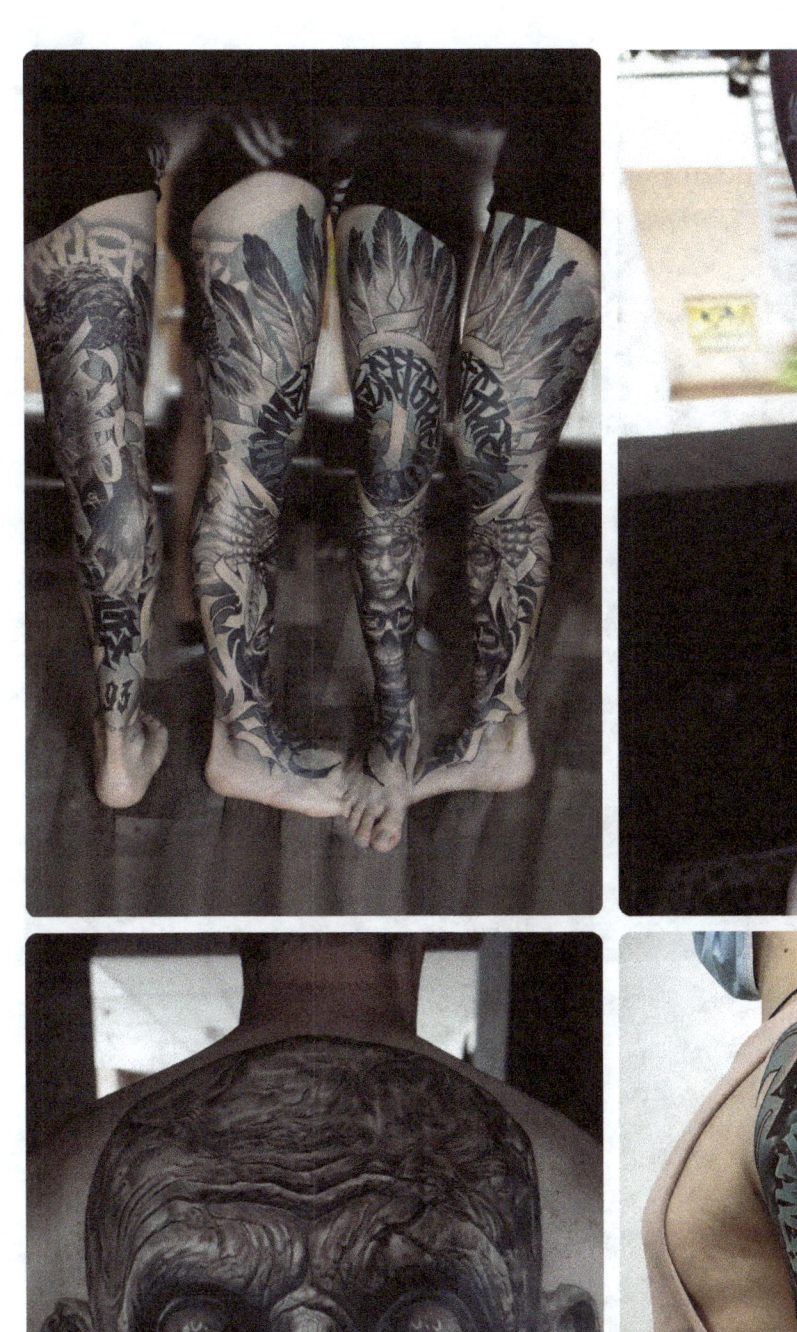
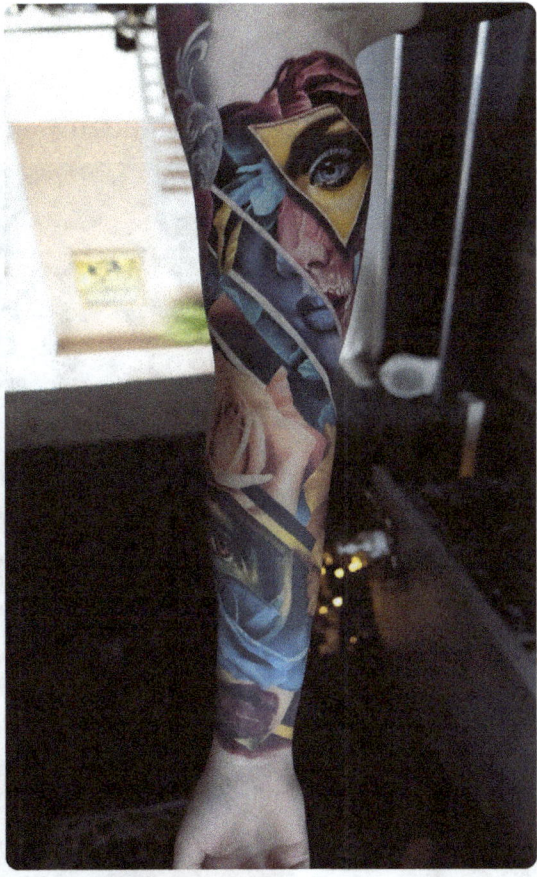

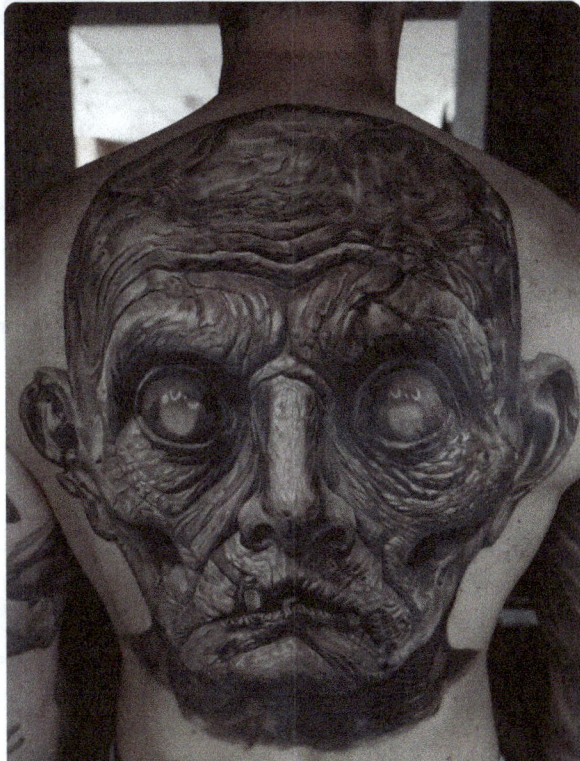
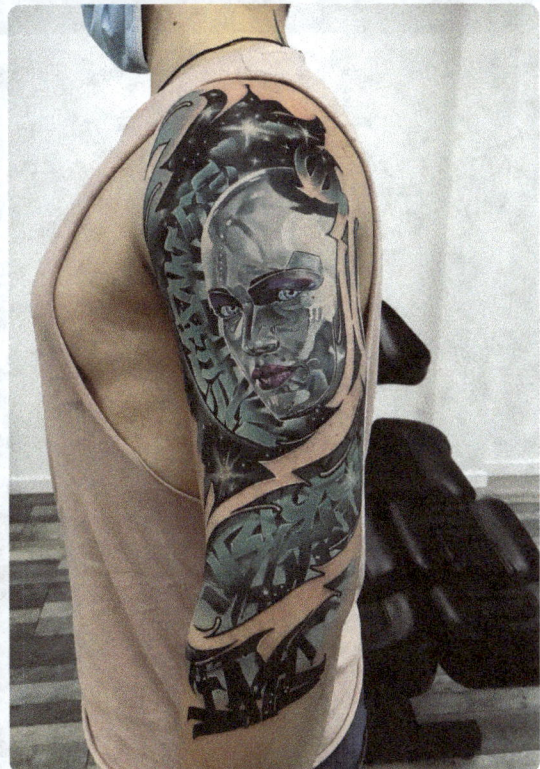

Chapter III

Global Tattoo Magazine

SERGIO VERDUGO

SECRETBANDTATTOO | @SERGIOVERDUGO_TATTOO | SPAIN, MALAGA

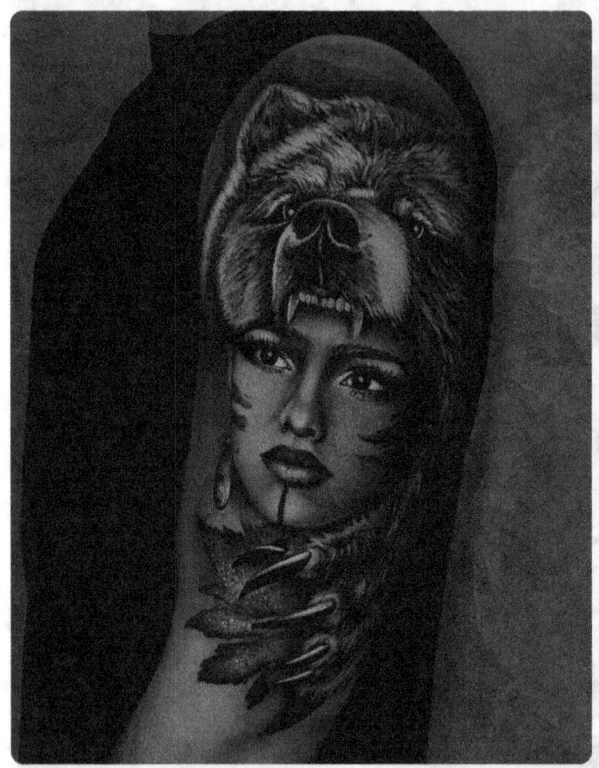
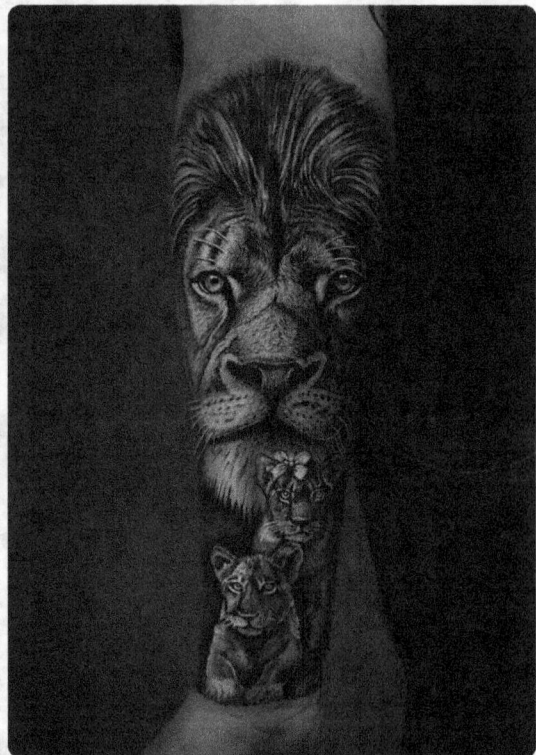
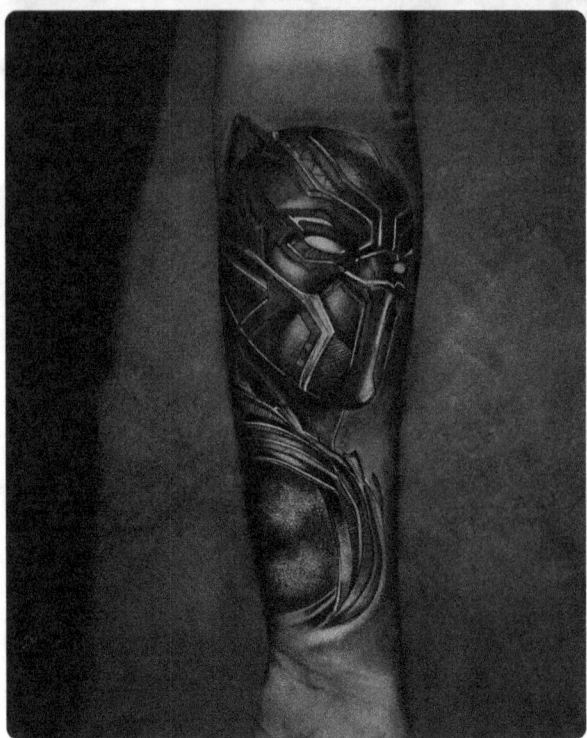
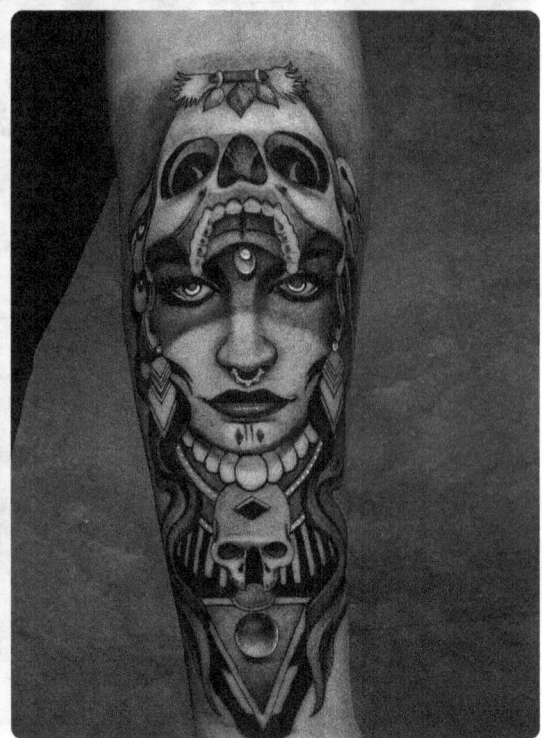

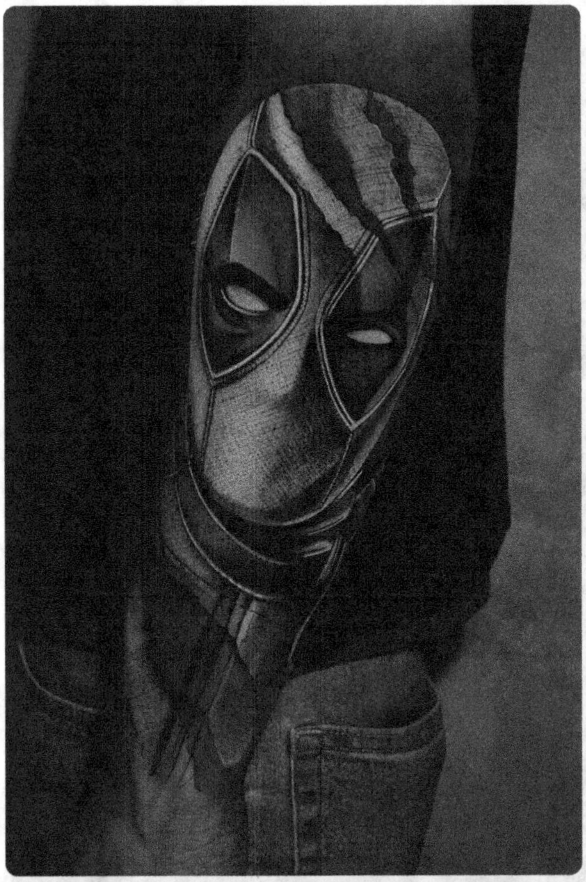

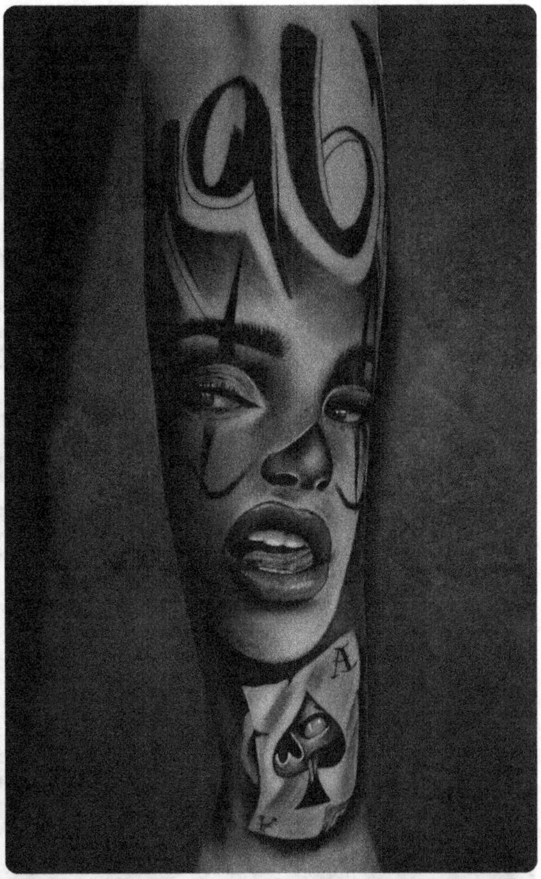

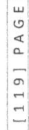

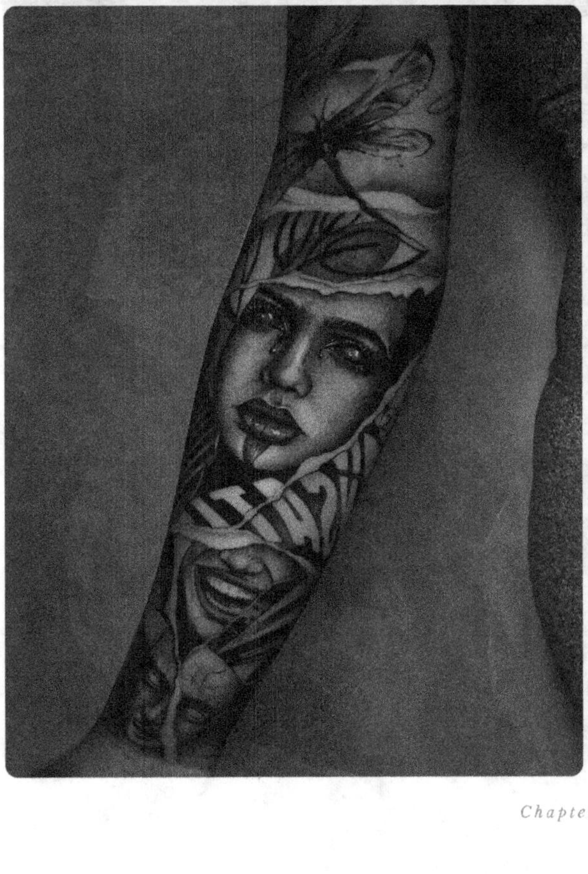

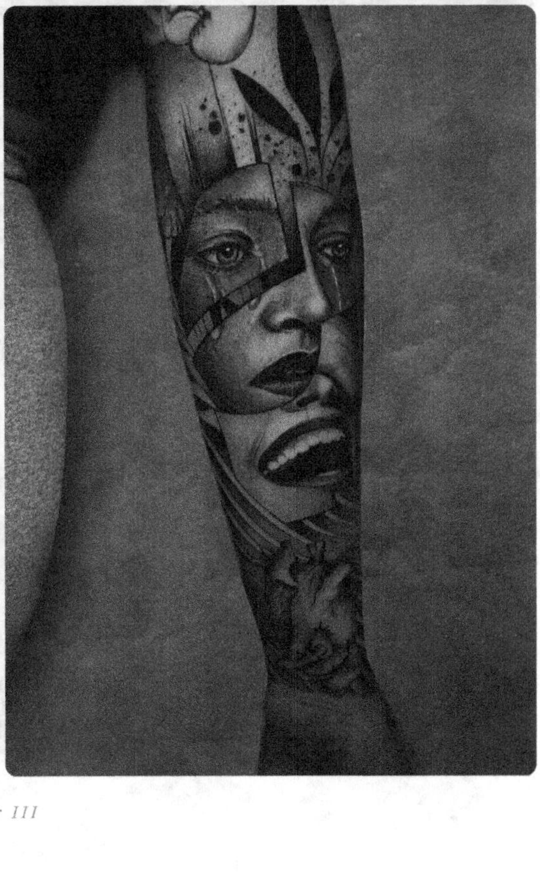

Chapter III

SHOGUN

OZTATTOOSHOP | @SHOGUN.T.T.T | FRANCE, MARSEILLE

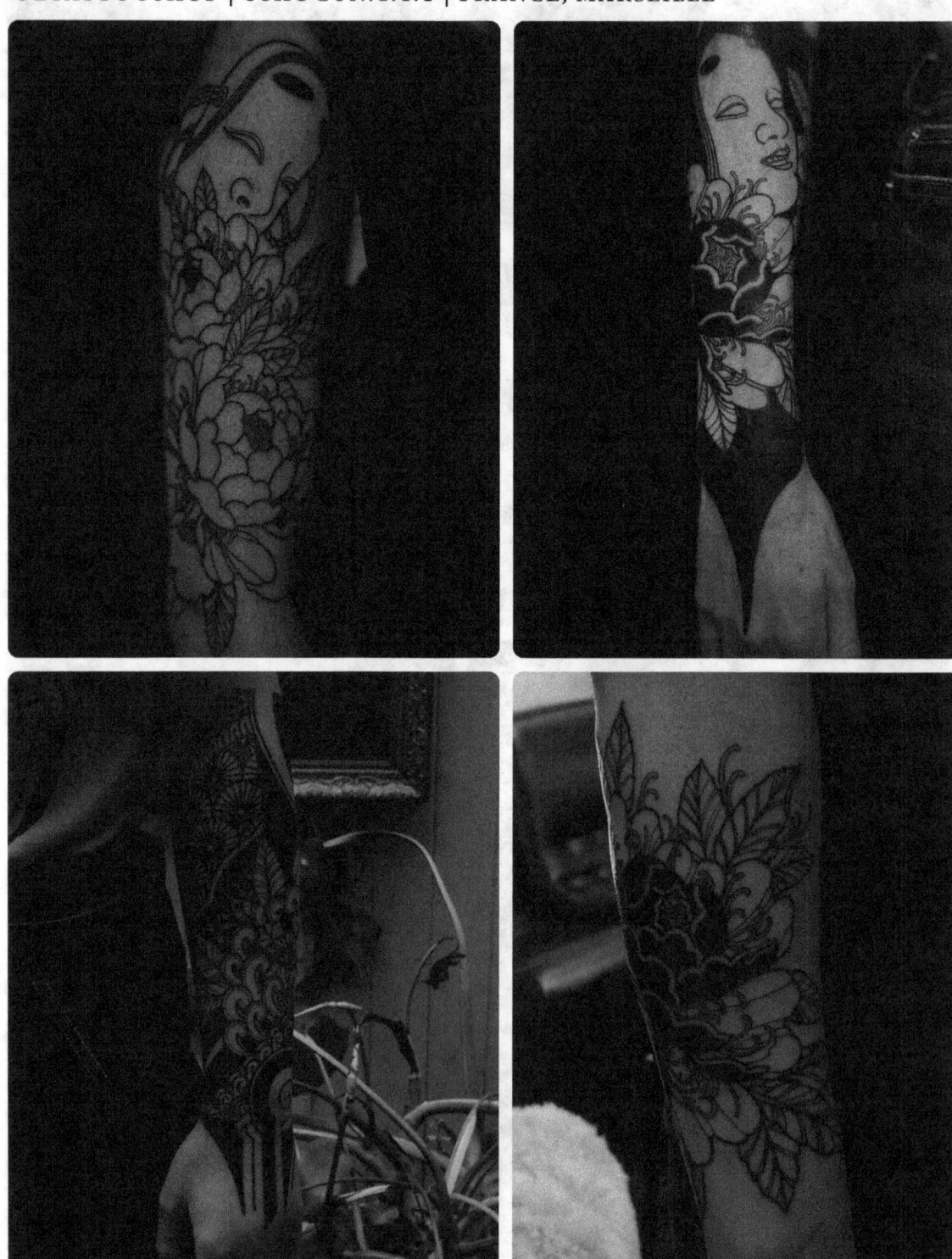

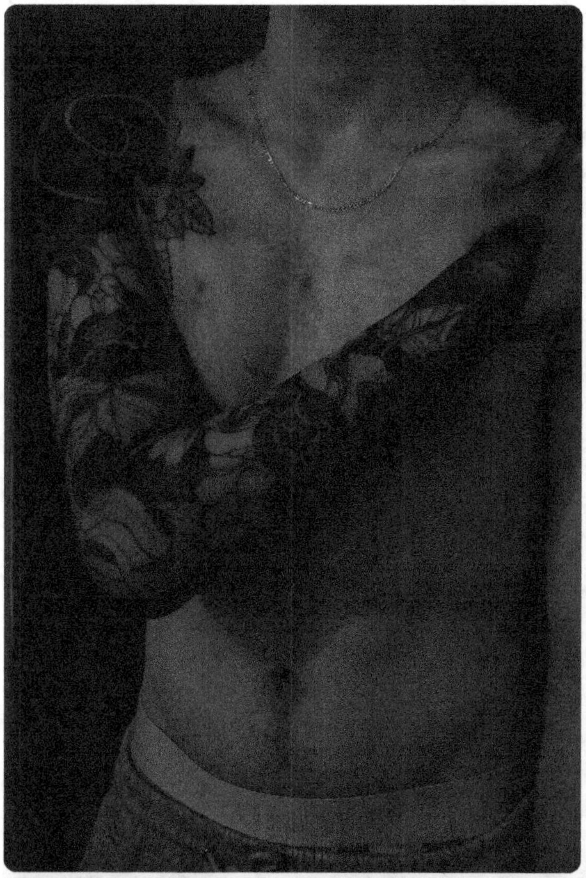

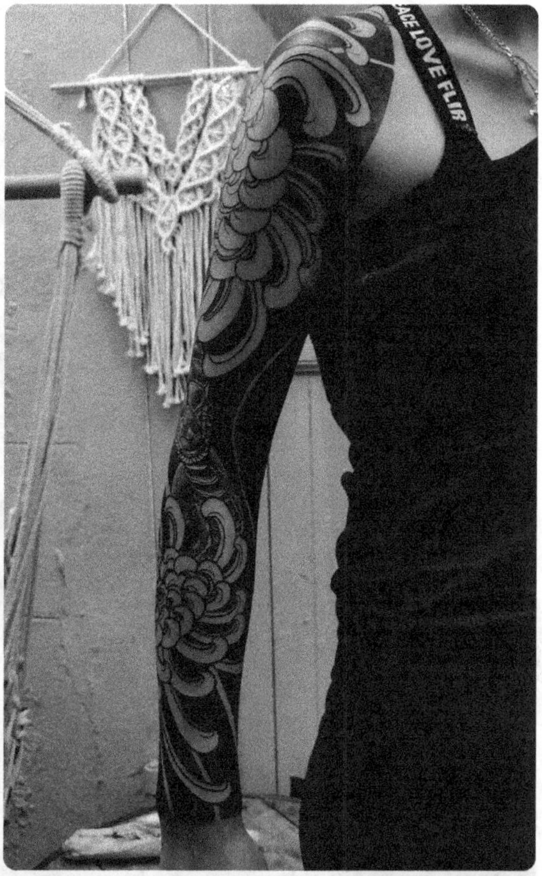

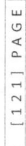

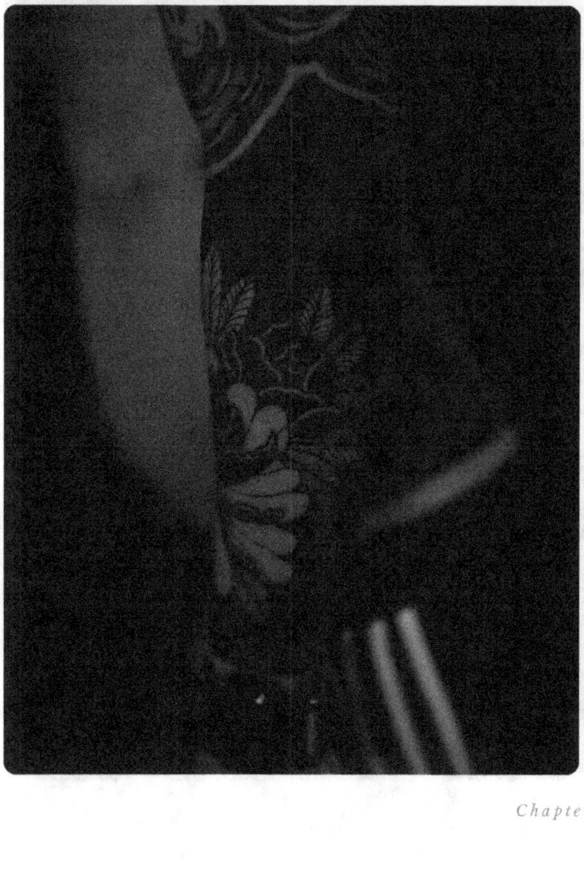

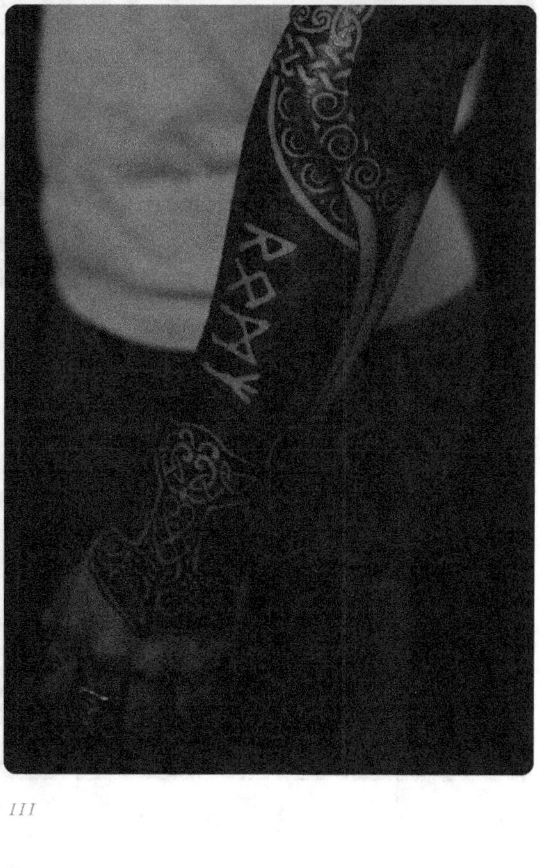

Chapter III

Global Tattoo Magazine

SIMBA INK TATTOO

@GIANPYTATTOOSTUDIO | @SIMBAINKTATTOO | ITALY, MILAN

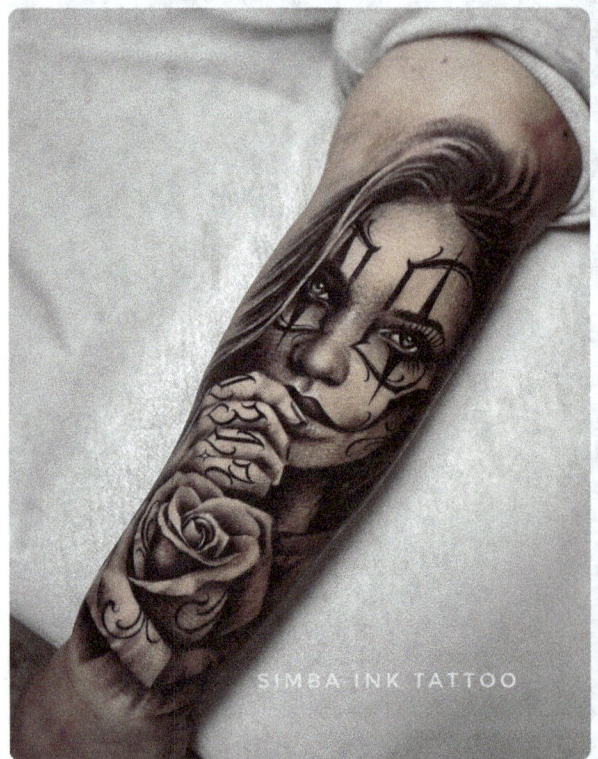

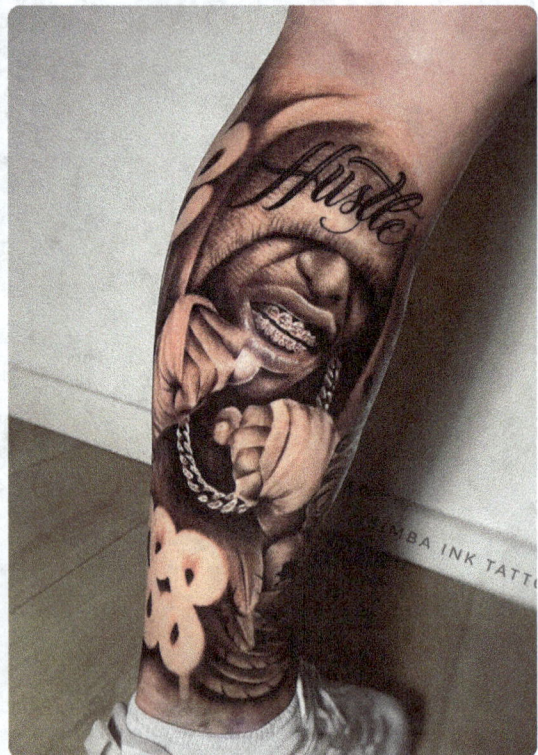

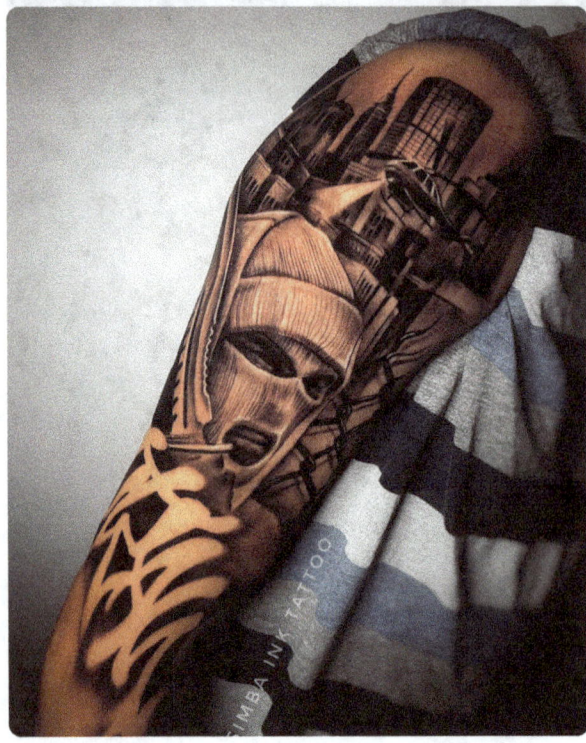

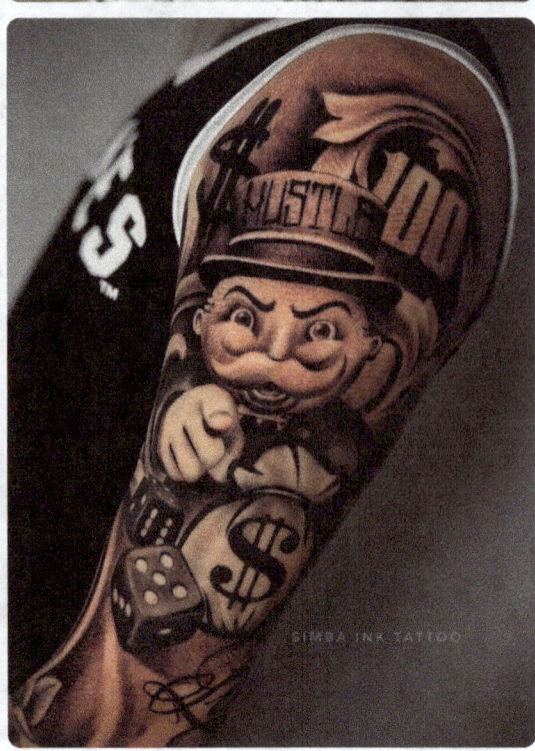

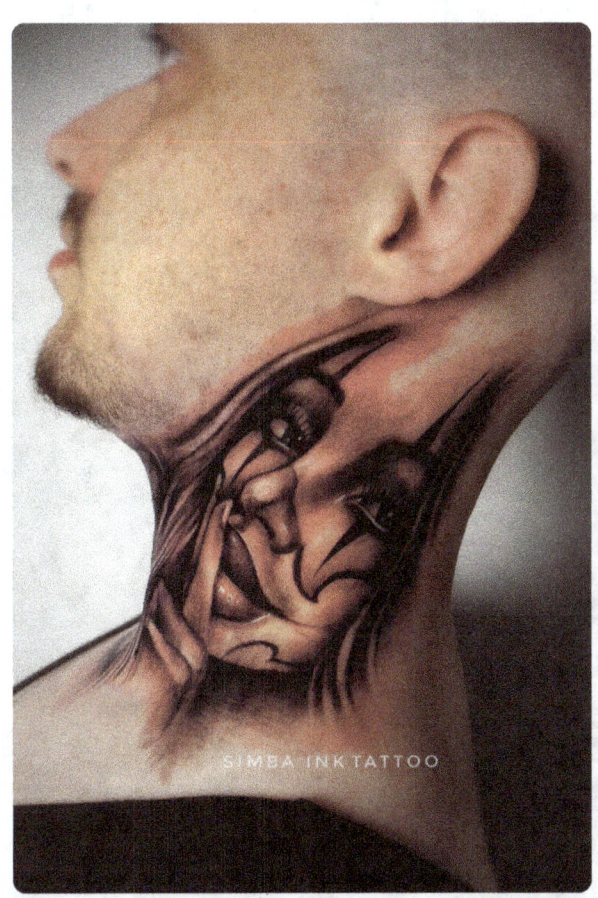

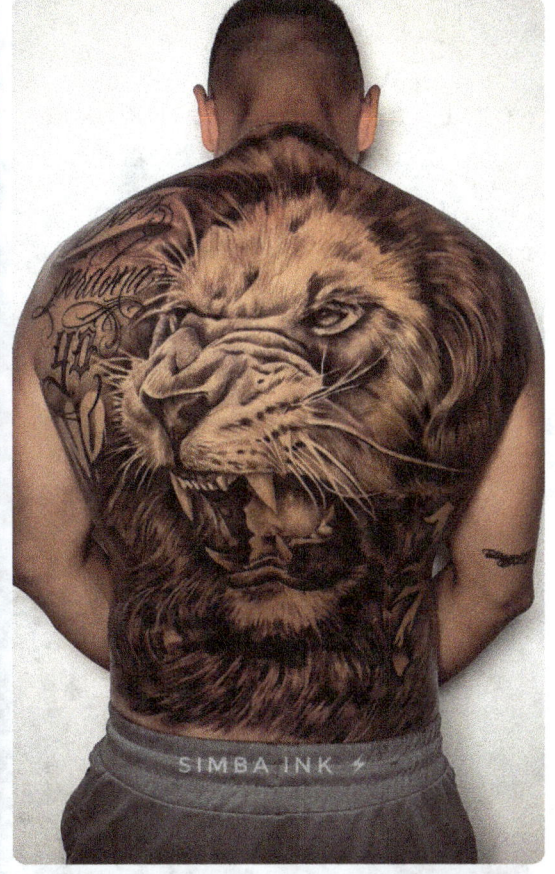

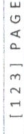

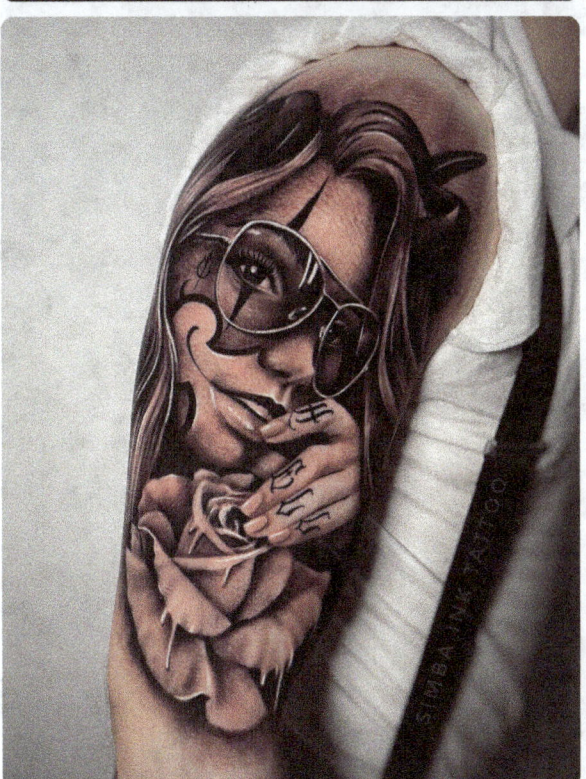

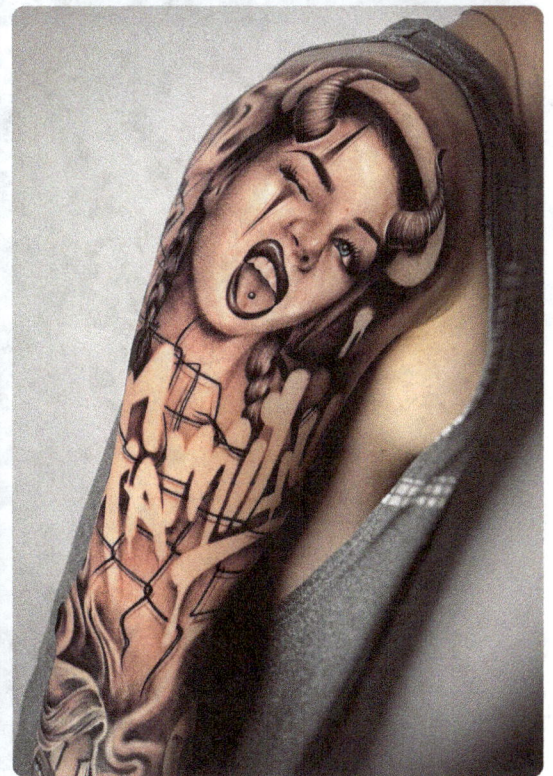

Chapter III

TESTA

NOBLE ART | FB: TESTTAINK | @TESTA.INK | NEW YORK , USA

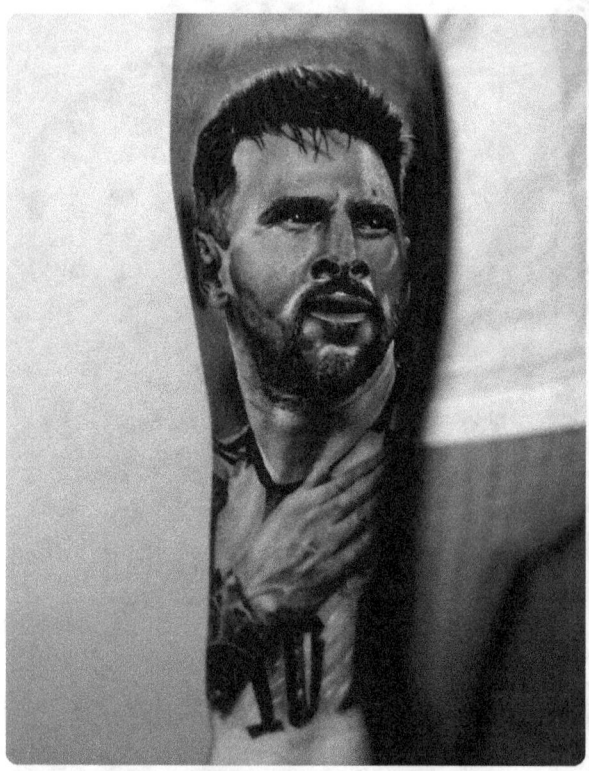

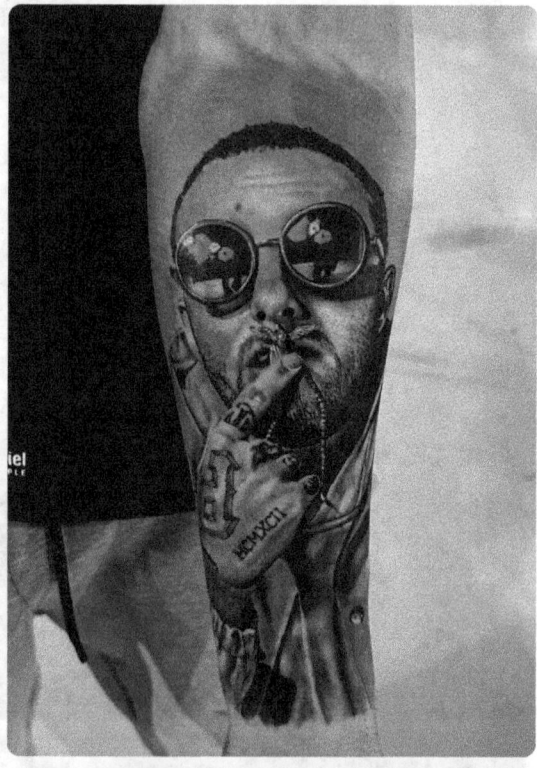

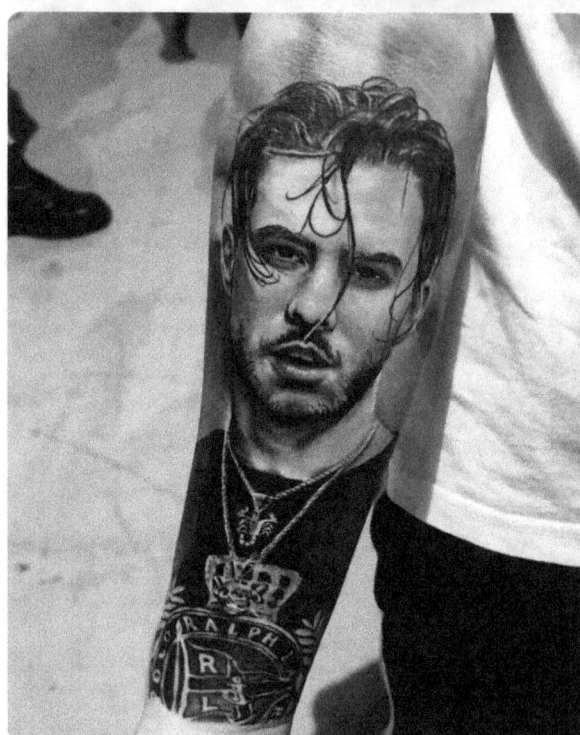

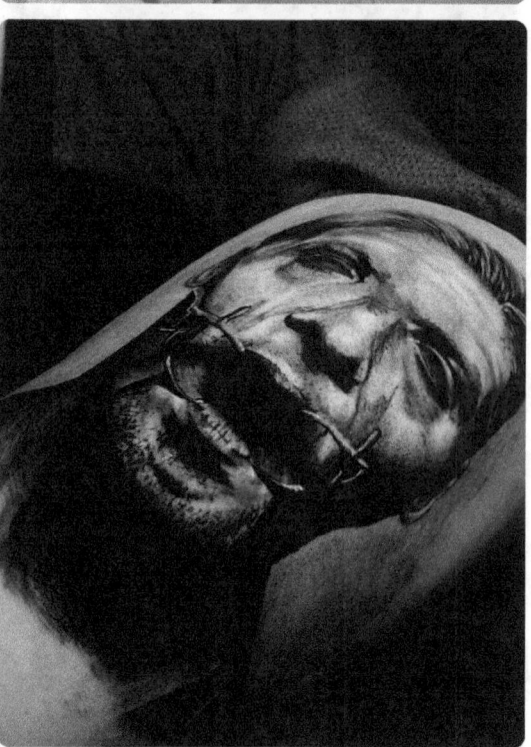

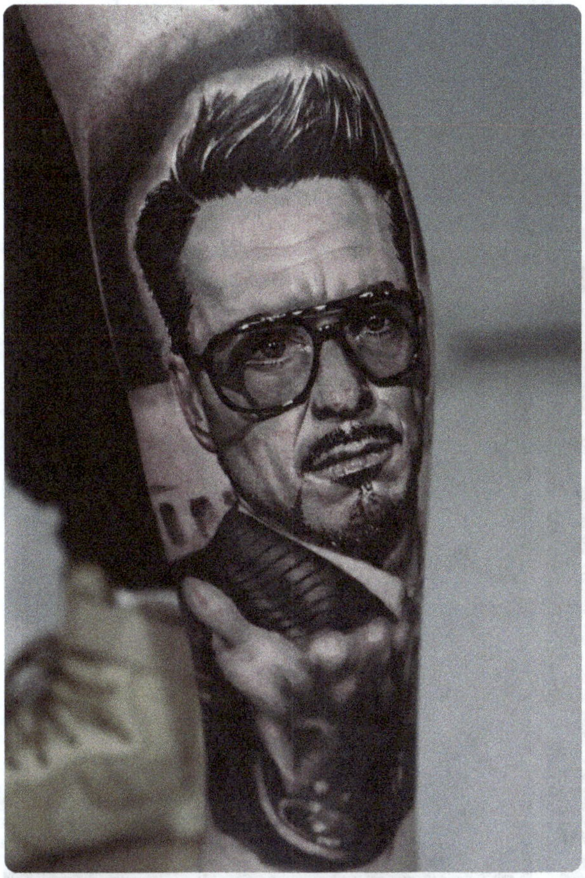

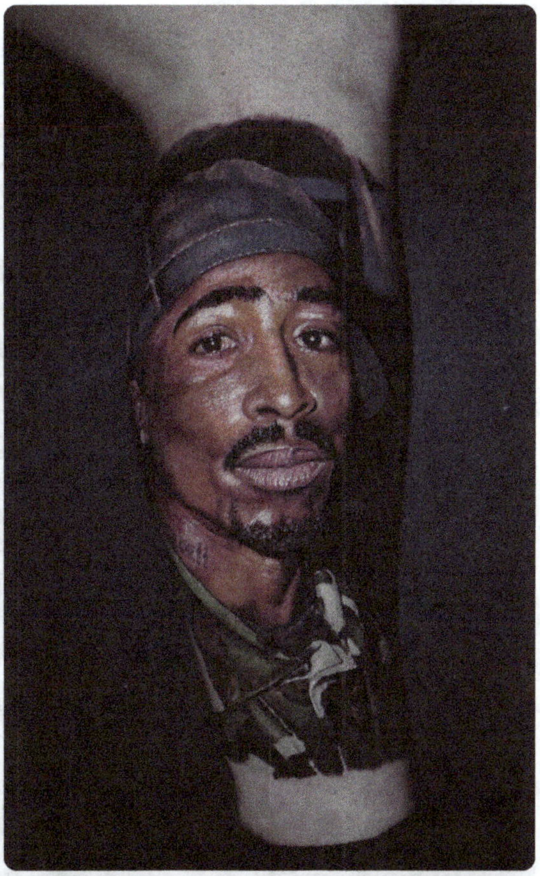

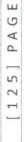

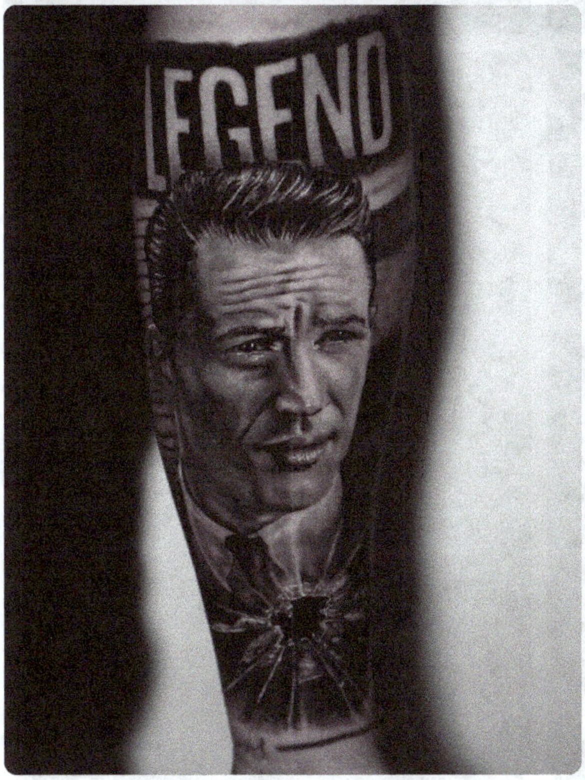

Chapter III

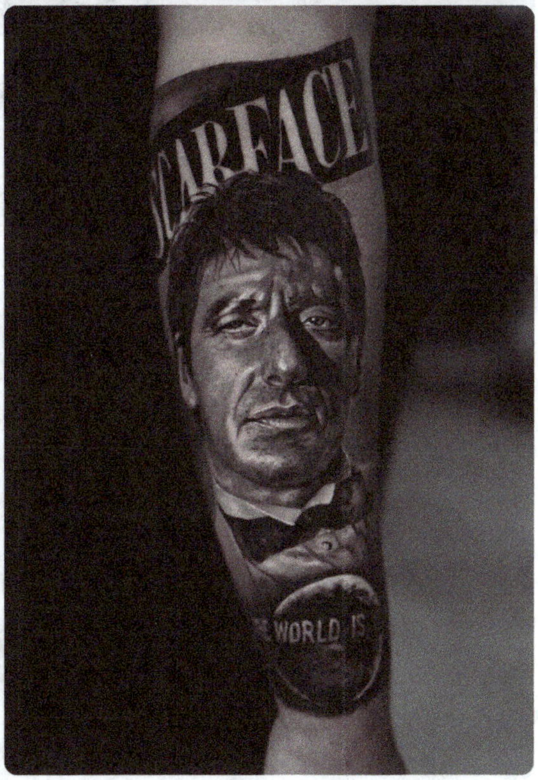

Global Tattoo Magazine

VIKTOR HÍR

FB: VIKTOR.HIR | @VIKTOR.HIR | SLOVAKIA, KOLÁROVO

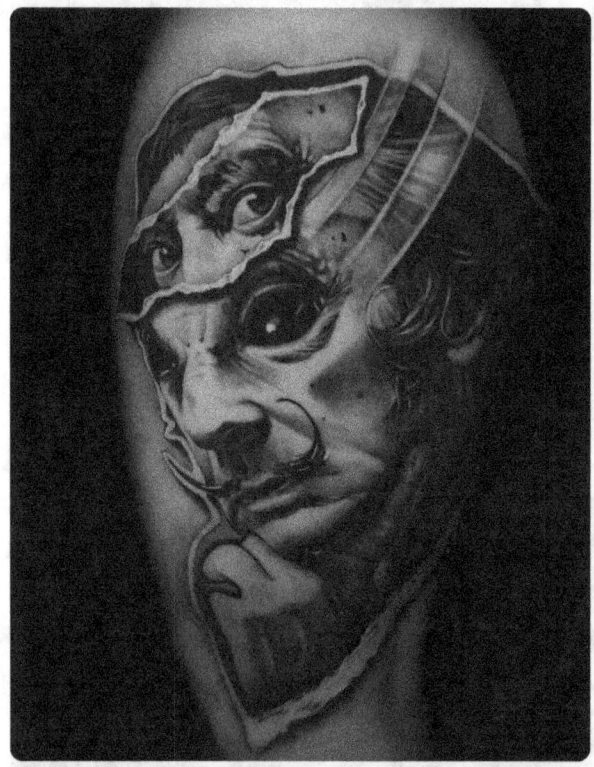
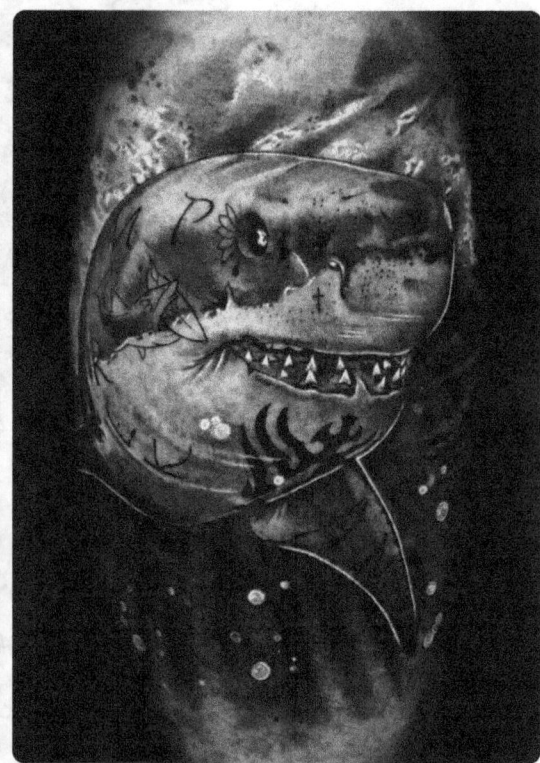
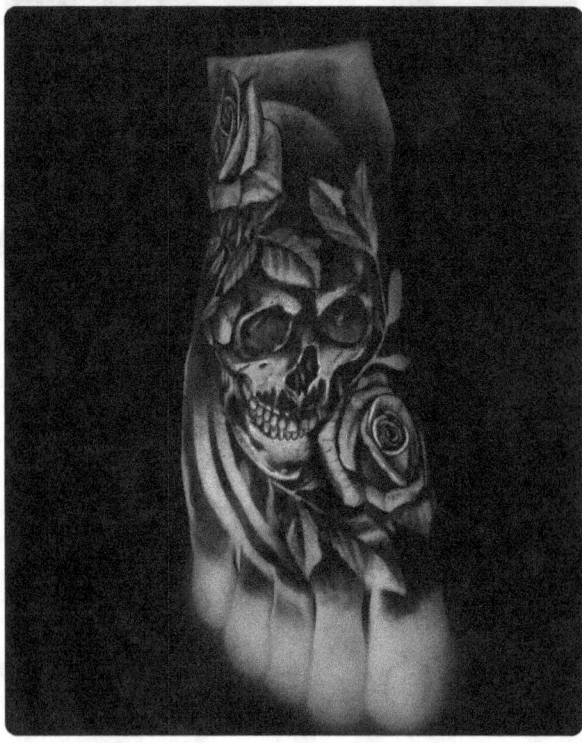
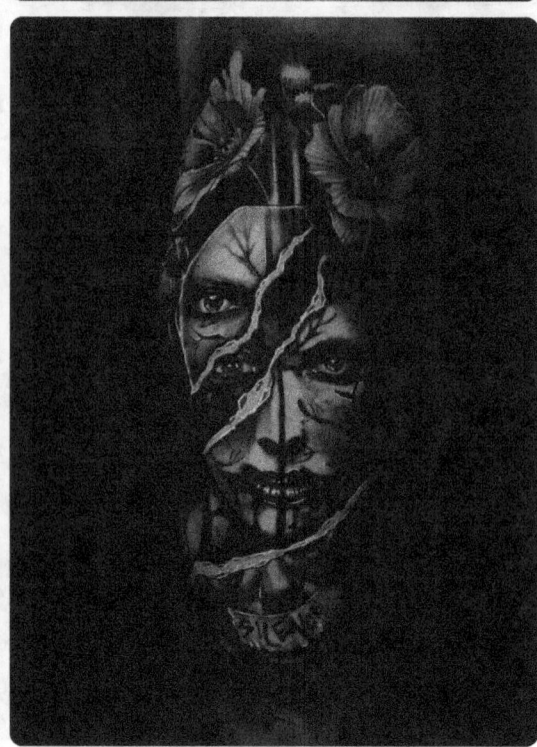

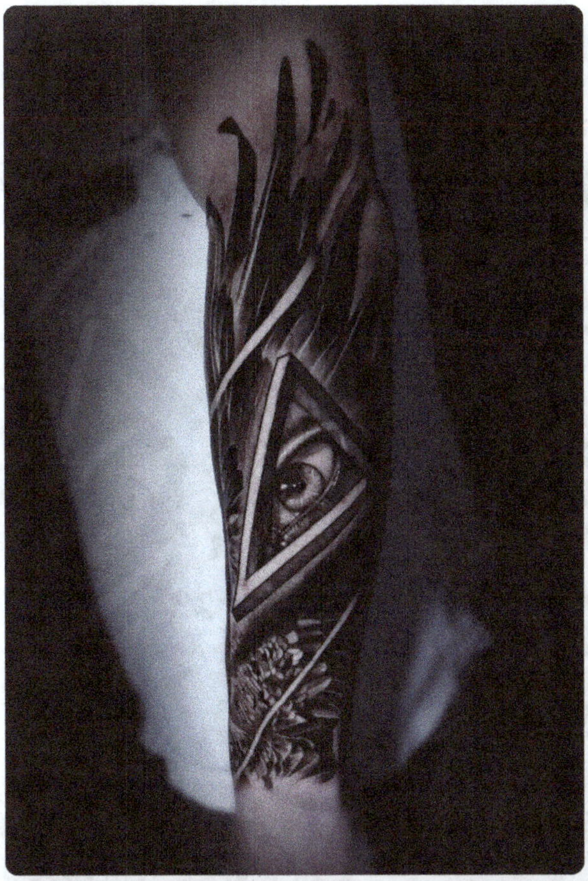

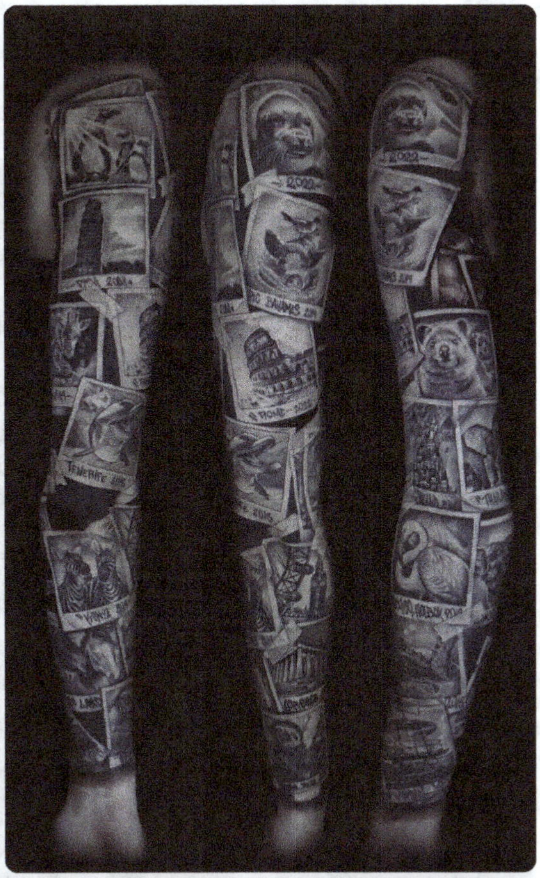

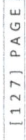

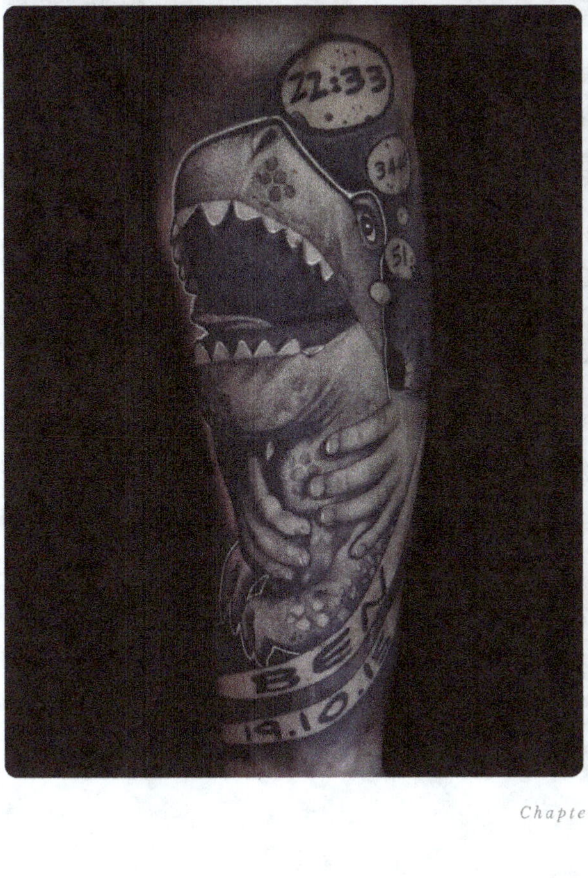

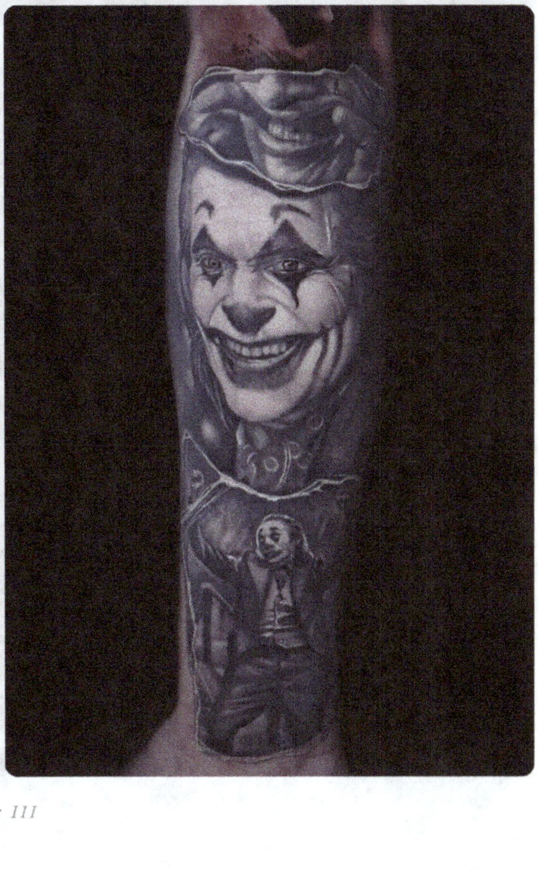

Global Tattoo Magazine

VITTORIO MARTINI

TATTOO | @TATTOOJOEY_VITO | NETHERLANDS, EINDHOVEN

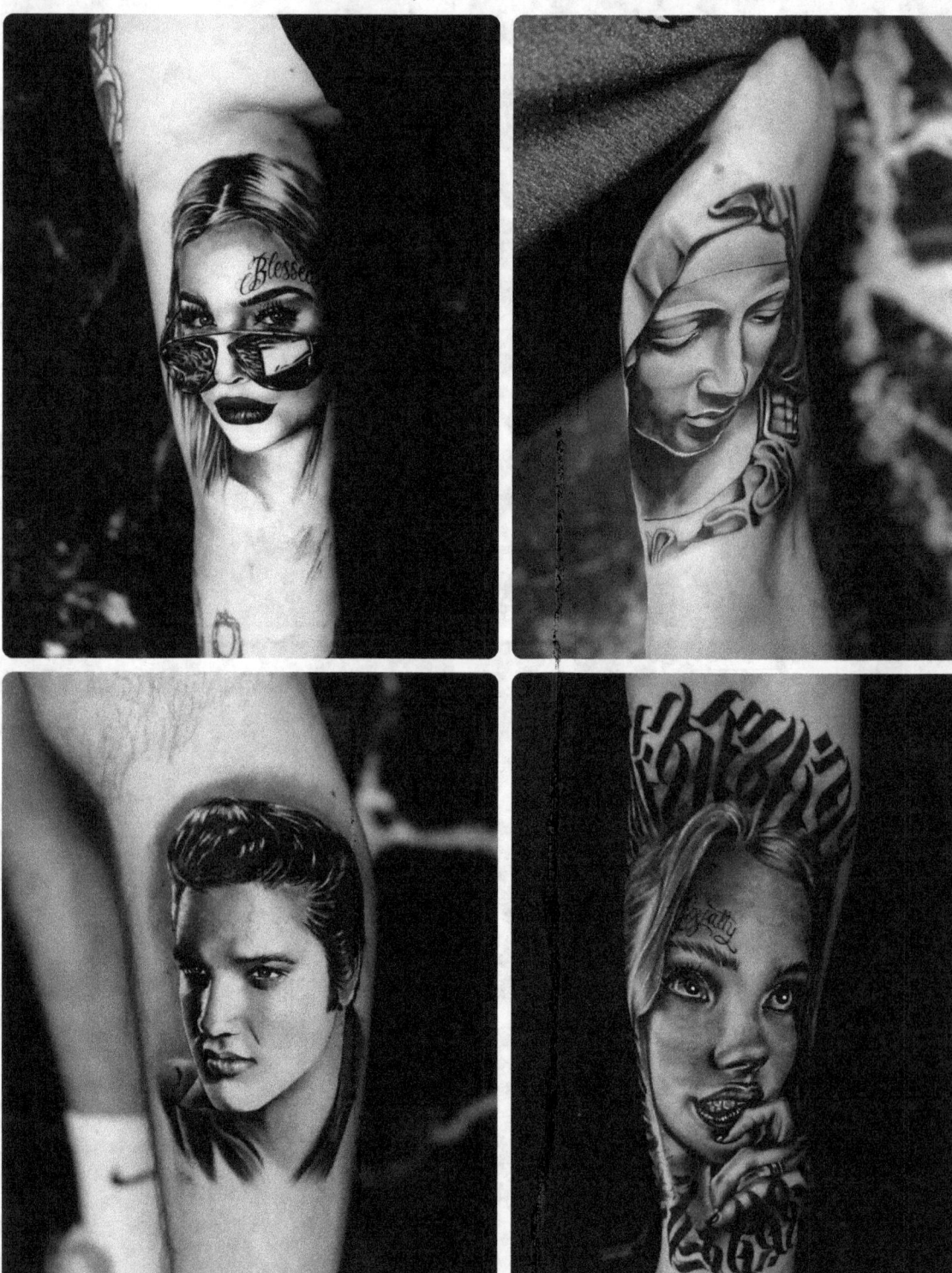

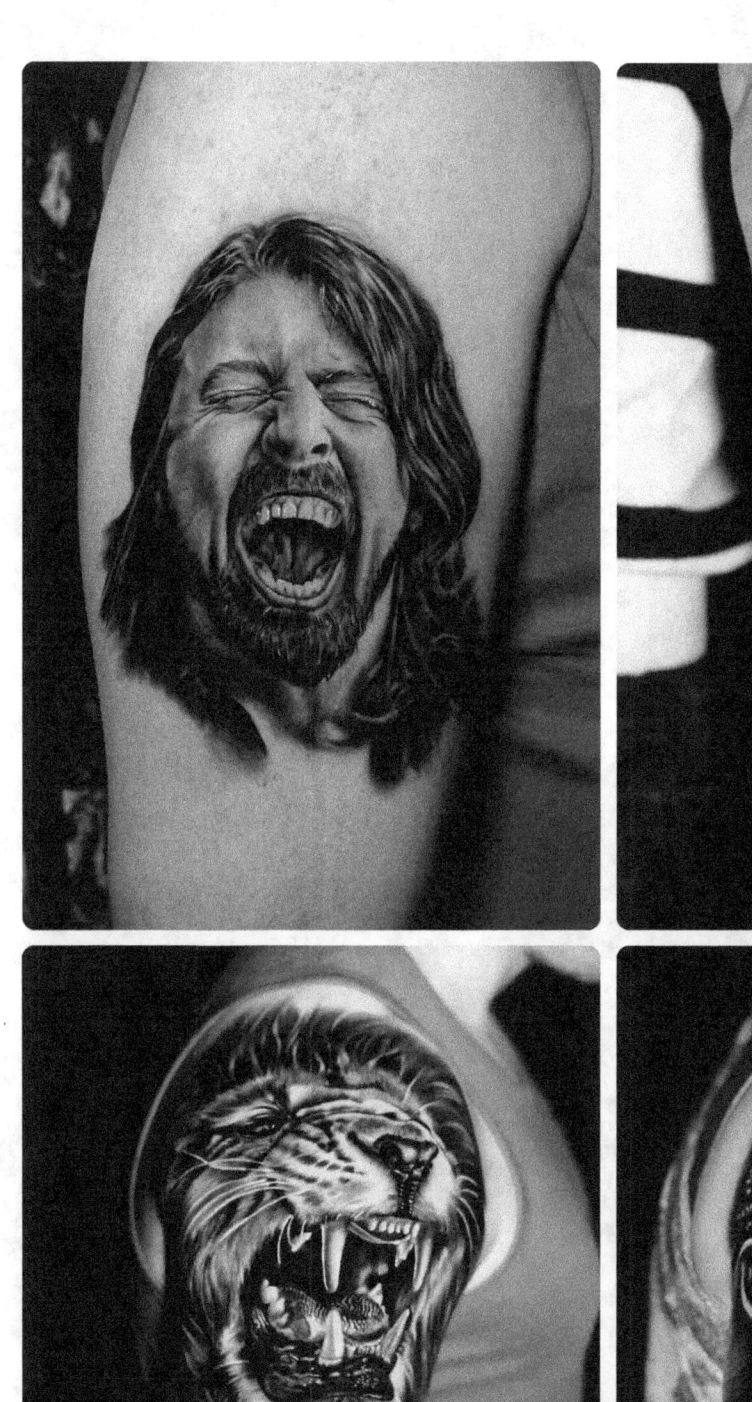
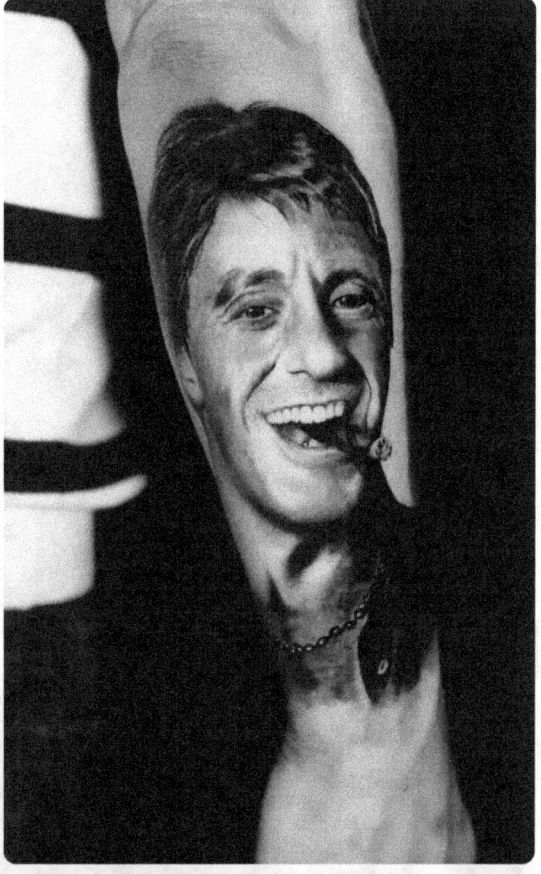
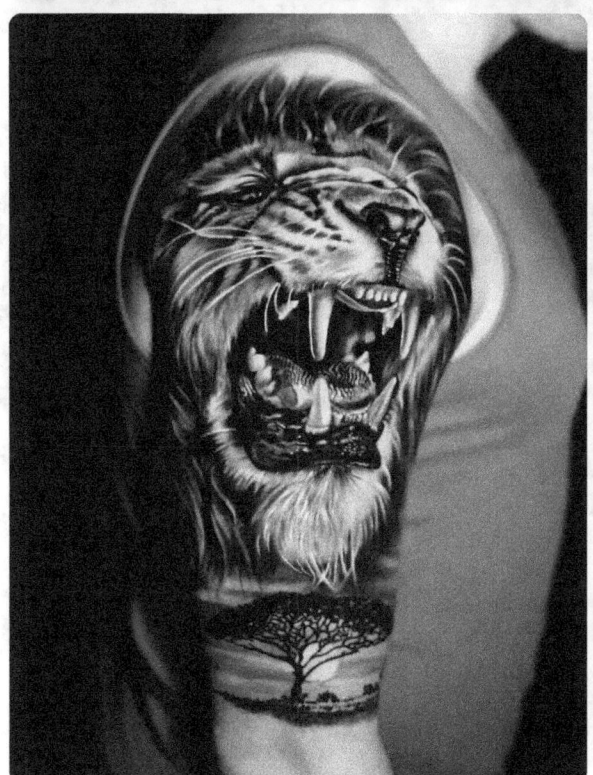
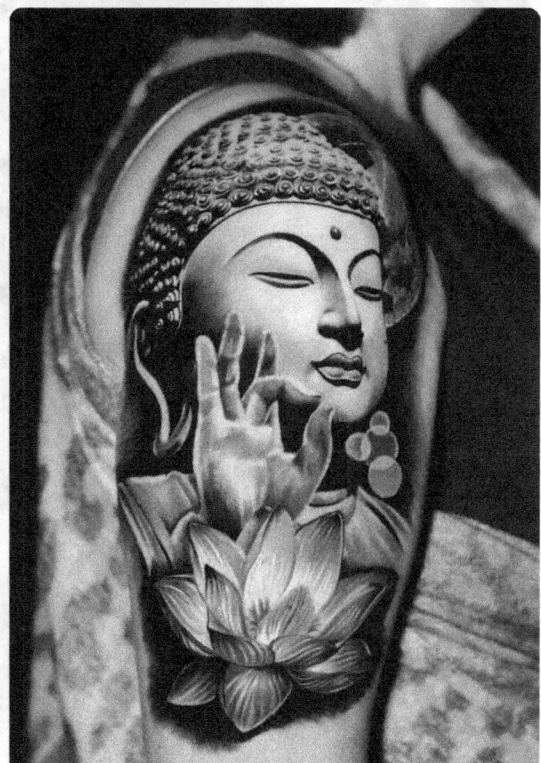

Chapter III

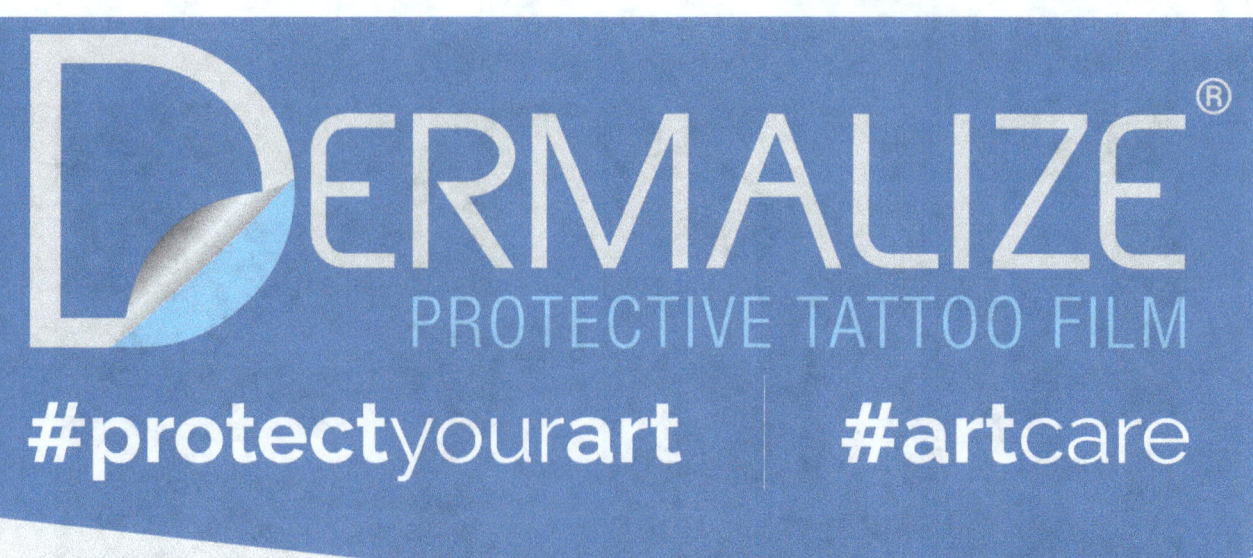
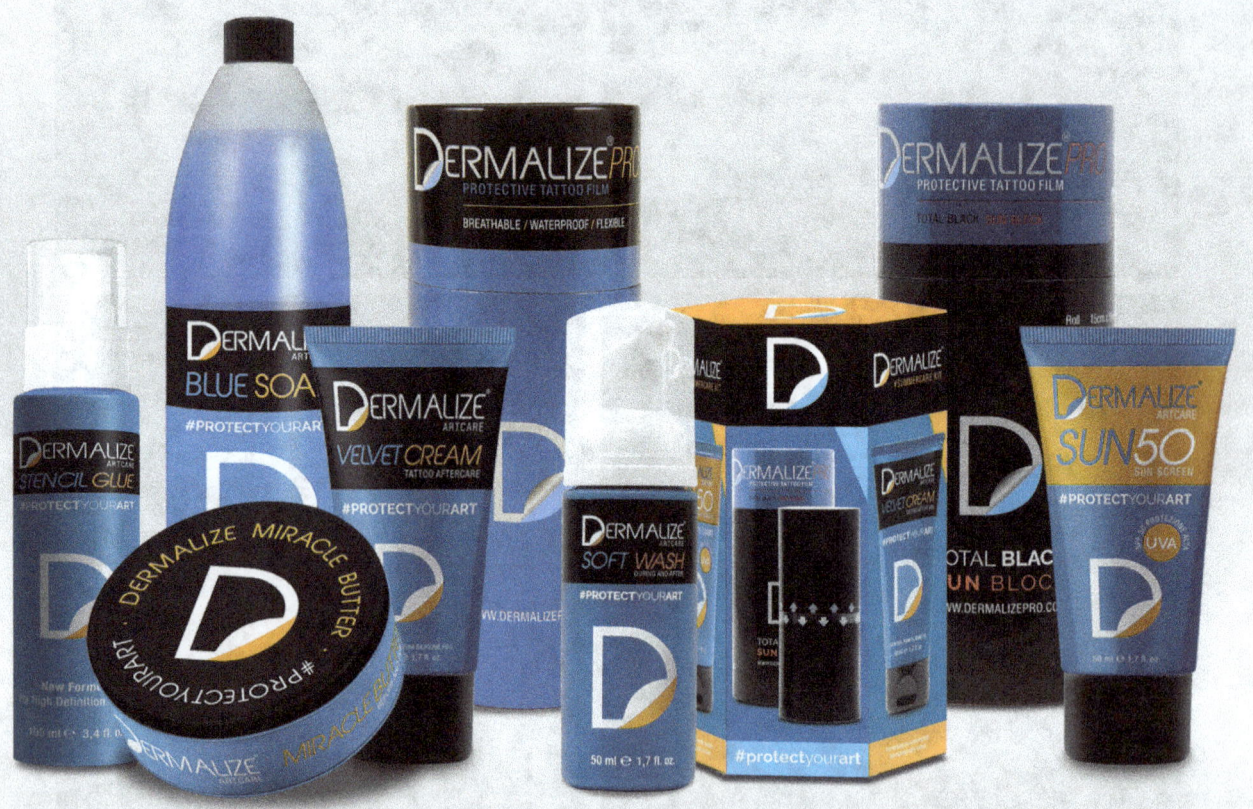
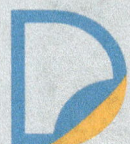

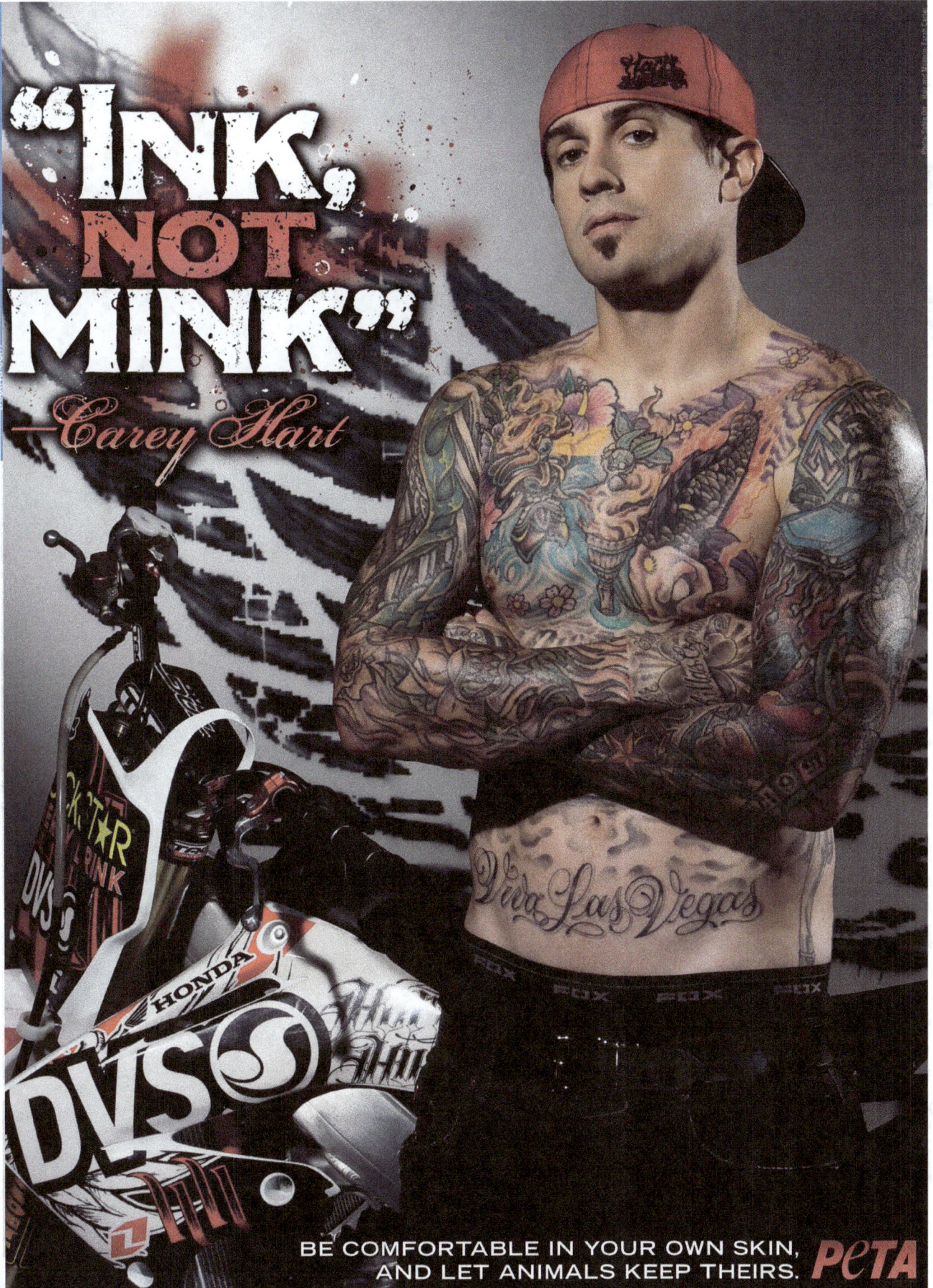

"INK, NOT MINK"
—Carey Hart

BE COMFORTABLE IN YOUR OWN SKIN, **PETA**
AND LET ANIMALS KEEP THEIRS.

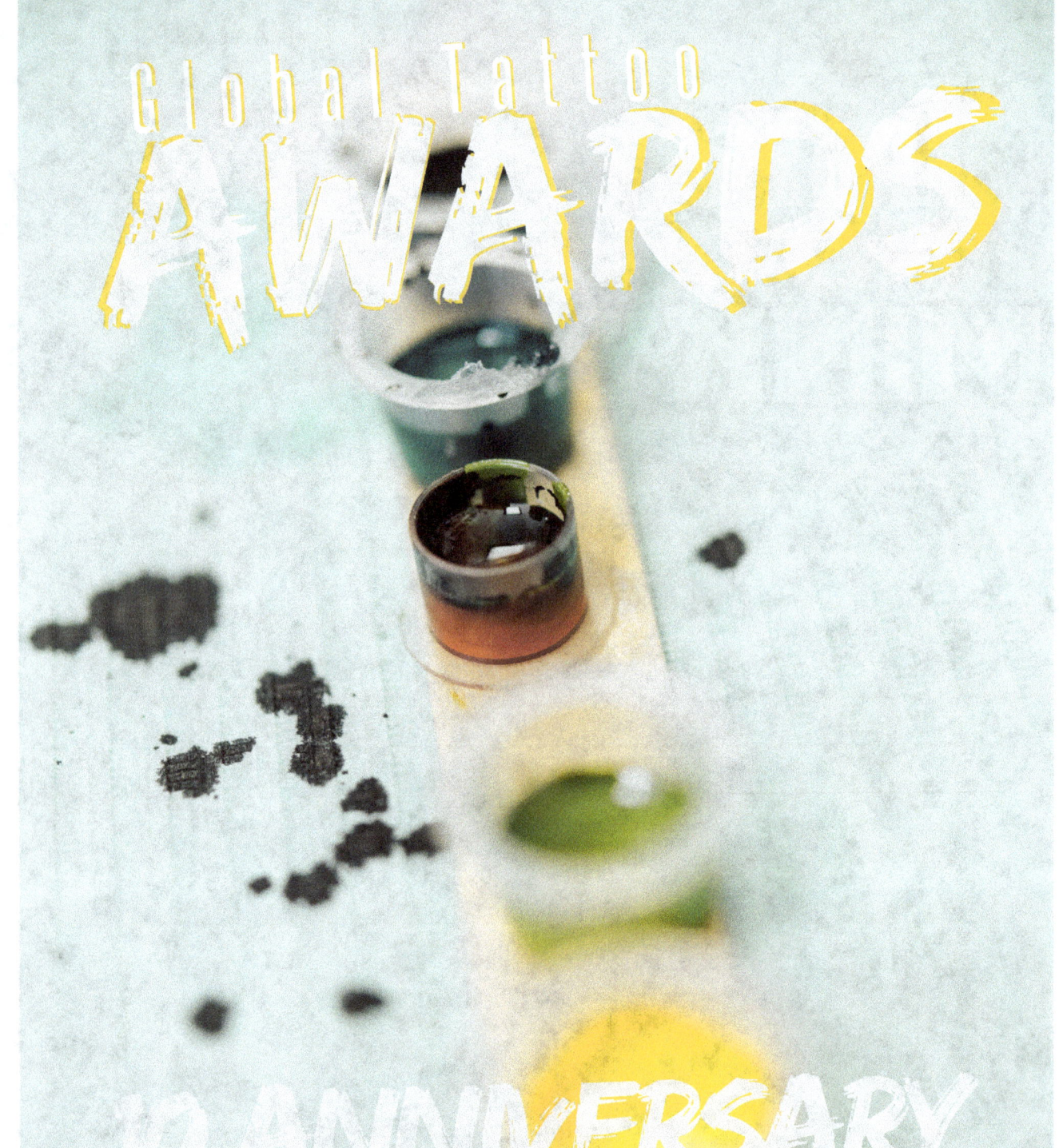

Global Tattoo
AWARDS

10 ANNIVERSARY

COMING SOON